The Middle East in International Relations
Power, Politics and Ideology

The international relations of the Middle East have long been dominated by uncertainty and conflict. External intervention, interstate war, political upheaval and interethnic violence are compounded by the vagaries of oil prices and the claims of military, nationalist and religious movements. The purpose of this book is to set this region and its conflicts in context, providing on the one hand a historical introduction to its character and problems, and on the other a reasoned analysis of its politics. In an engagement with both the study of the Middle East and the theoretical analysis of international relations, the author, who is one of the best known and most authoritative scholars writing on the region today, offers a compelling and original interpretation. Written in a clear, accessible and interactive style, the book is designed for students, policymakers and the general reader.

FRED HALLIDAY is Professor of International Relations at the London School of Economics. His publications include *Nation and Religion in the Middle East* (2000), *Two Hours that Shook the World* (2001) and *100 Myths about the Middle East* (2005).

The Contemporary Middle East 4

Series editor: Eugene L. Rogan

Books published in **The Contemporary Middle East** series address the major political, economic and social debates facing the region today. Each title comprises a survey of the available literature against the background of the author's own critical interpretation which is designed to challenge and encourage independent analysis. While the focus of the series is the Middle East and North Africa, books are presented as aspects of a rounded treatment, which cut across disciplinary and geographic boundaries. They are intended to initiate debate in the classroom, and to foster understanding amongst professionals and policy makers.

The Middle East in
International Relations
Power, Politics and Ideology

Fred Halliday
London School of Economics and Political Science

CAMBRIDGE
UNIVERSITY PRESS

CAMBRIDGE UNIVERSITY PRESS
Cambridge, New York, Melbourne, Madrid, Cape Town, Singapore, São Paulo

Cambridge University Press
40 West 20th Street, New York, NY 10011–4211, USA
www.cambridge.org
Information on this title:www.cambridge.org/9780521592406

First published 2005
Reprinted 2005

Printed in the United States of America

A catalogue record for this book is available from the British Library.

Library of Congress Cataloguing in Publication Data
Halliday, Fred.
The Middle East in International Relations / Fred Halliday.
p.   cm. - (The contemporary Middle East ; 4)
Includes bibliographical references and index.
ISBN 0-521-59240-2 — ISBN 0-521-59741-2 (pbk.)
1. Middle East – Foreign relations.   2. Middle East — Politics and
government — 20th century.   I. Title.   II. Series.
DS63.18.H354   2005
320.956'09'045 — dc22   2004052643

ISBN-13   978-0-521-59240-6 hardback
ISBN-10   0-521-59240-2 hardback

ISBN-13   978-0-521-59741-8 paperback
ISBN-10   0-521-59741-2 paperback

Contents

Part IV   Conclusion

Maps

Tables

Acknowledgements

Any introduction of this kind must hint at, but cannot do justice to, the influence and friendship of those who have over the years (in my case, for forty) sought to encourage, correct and inform the author. Three constituencies of people have been particularly important for me. In the first place, friends and comrades from the region itself. Secondly those, be they academics, journalists or general writers, who, while often of different, sometimes very different, orientation to the author, were my teachers and who served to inspire, and contest with me, the study of the region. I may not have accepted, or now accept, their conclusions, but I certainly have remembered their questions. Finally, and in an ongoing community of critique, interaction, theoretical debate and the rushed but treasured, exchange of political jokes from the region, the specialists and academics with whom I have worked over the years. This third category includes MERIP in Washington, the Gulf Committee and the Middle East Study Group in London, many colleagues in British and other western, including Russian, universities, and journalists, from the region and without. A special word of praise and thanks too to LSE's neighbours at Bush House in the Aldwych, London, for my colleagues of the BBC World Service in English, and the Arabic, Turkish and Persian services. They have been objects of entrapment and vilification by those with power, and universally admired and respected throughout the region: these, not the spokesmen of governments, the *munafiqin* of east and west, and the pedlars of supposedly holy texts and ancient entitlements, nor, in academe, the traders of epistemological trickery and cargo cults, are the real heroes of the dialogue of peoples, of civilisations, and indeed of the construction of a saner, more informed and more peaceful, world.

   In all cases it would be odd, a disappointment indeed, if there had been complete agreement between us, but without interaction with these colleagues no insight would ever have been achieved. I have been privileged to know them, now over four decades, and to discuss the shared interests that we face. Against all of this background, I claim little originality, but rather partnership in an ongoing, and internationalist, endeavour. I stand, in the best sense of intellectual and academic continuity, on the shoulders of these people, as well as amidst a never-ending milieu of information, disputation and good humour.

In regard to the second group, those under whom I studied, I would mention, in particular, those whom I would call, in the old and valid phrase, not eroded by post-modernity or epistemological fashion, or the transnational banalities of globalisation, my teachers. Those whom I knew personally, at Oxford, at SOAS, and in the broader Middle East and social science communities of the 1960s and 1970s: Hamza Alavi, Tony Allan, Terry Byers, Donal Cruise O'Brien, Ernest Gellner, Thomas Hodgkin, P. J. Holt, Albert Hourani, Nikki Keddie, Abbas Kelidar, Anne Lambton, Bernard Lewis, Robert Mabro, Roger Owen, Edith Penrose, Maxime Rodinson, Teodor Shanin, P. J. Vatikiotis, Bill Warren. They were people at once wise and of their times, cosmopolitan, concerned and, where they judged appropriate, awkward in their views and judgements. Despite all differences of opinion, they are respected and read in the Middle East as much as in the west. Successor generations in universities, the media and policy fields would do well to learn from their scholarship, not least their linguistic abilities, and from their independence of mind. Here a time-honoured saying is especially relevant: they do not make people like that any more.

In writing a book of this kind there are also many contemporary colleagues and friends to whom I owe appreciation and gratitude. To the readers of the manuscript in whole or in part – Louise Fawcett, George Lawson, Roger Owen, Eugene Rogan, David Styan – I express warm thanks for their criticism and careful reading. Eugene Rogan, of St Antony's College Oxford, and Marigold Acland, of CUP, were the ideal commissioning editors, patient but insistent. In production, Alison Powell and Carol Fellingham Webb were the most supportive and efficacious of allies. At LSE, my colleagues the late Philip Windsor, one of the most economical and wisest of observers, and Katerina Dalacoura, who brings to the teaching of our students at LSE the political acumen for which her people have been known for more than two thousand years, and a sensibility for the variant idioms, conceits and cultures of the Mediterranean. To the veterans of IR 419, now 'The International Relations of the Middle East', *quondam* 'The Middle East and the Great Powers', drawn from east and west, from diasporas emigrant and homeward-looking, and onto whom, in future years, the responsibility of understanding this region will pass, I express my thanks for their stimulation, questions, reading suggestions and, not least, pertinent regional anecdotes. My Departmental Convenors, Michael Yahuda and Margot

Light, were of special assistance, at once, as befits their station, exigent and permissive, while Jennifer Chapa was, as ever, supportive and astute in helping with the preparation of the manuscript, and resilient in the face of multiple versions and drafts.

Among those others who have, over the years, enriched my understanding of the international relations of the region I would, in particular, mention: Ervand Abrahamian, Ayhan Aktar, Abdullah al-Ashtal, Shlomo Avineri, Mohammad Ayoob, Nazih Ayubi, Hanna Batatu, Jahangir Behrooz, Azmi Bishara, Mehdi Boroujerdi, Musa Budeiri, Stan Cohen, Victor Philip Dahdaleh, Khalid al-Dakhil, Mohamed-Reza Djalali, Abdulnabi al-Ekry, Anne Enayat, Hamid Enayat, Louise Fawcett, Abdel-Aziz al-Filali, Fawaz Gerges, Mai Ghoussoub, Said Hammami, Roger Hardy, Khalid Hariri, Mohammad Salman Hassan, Rosemary Hollis, Stephen Howe, Faleh Jabar, Omar al-Jawi, Deniz Kandiyoti, Rifaat Kandiyoti, Ibrahim Karawan, Mostafa Karkouti, Ahmad al-Khatib, Gilles Kepel, Joseph Kostiner, Robert Mabro, Kanan Makiya, David Menashri, Ali Mohammadi, Ghanim al-Najjar, Vitali Naumkin, Tim Niblock, Gerd Nonnemann, Jim Paul, James Piscatori, Ruhallah Ramazani, Johannes Reissner, Barbara Allen Roberson, Barry Rubin, Muhammad Rumaihi, Malise Ruthven, Farian Sabahi, Abdulaziz Sager, Hazem Saghie, Abdullah Yousef Sahar, Rosemary Said, Yezid Sayigh, Yousif Sayigh, Israel Shahak, Sharon Shalev, Udo Steinbach, Joe Stork, Yasir Suleiman, Charles Tripp, Daphna Varzi, Alexei Vassiliev, Giorgio Vercellin, Shelagh Weir, Tony Zahlan, Sami Zubaida.

In particular, the members of two communities that have their origins in the early 1970s, if not before – the Middle East Study Group in London and *MERIP Reports* in Washington – have, over more than three decades, provided a stimulating personal and intellectual context for discussion of the region. In all of these years, and in the writing of these pages, my family, Maxine and Alex, were of indispensable support, not least in visiting some of these countries with me and in following, in moments of quiet as of high and painful drama, the events unfolding in the Middle East itself, let alone in debating the relevance, or lack thereof, of broader issues of social theory and historical analysis to the events of this region in modern times.

A special word of thanks is also due to my research students at LSE since 1983. Over more than twenty years they have been a source of stimulation, challenge, sometimes of quite a spirited kind, and intellectual confirmation: if Socratic questioning of the assumed is a major part of the learning process, there are times, more often than one is professionally enjoined to admit, when one wonders who is the teacher and who the taught. I could write a paragraph of thanks to each.

The past four decades were years of high hopes, and bitter moments, of revolution, counter-revolution, war and political violence. The Middle East specialists of my generation lived, and argued, through these times. It is now for others to take this analysis, and some of theoretical perspective and 'complex solidarity', into the times to come: the least one can say is that, on the basis of the information we have, and the most basic historic sense, the next decades will be at least as momentous, and intellectually challenging, as those now past. The advice of the late Maxime Rodinson, *al-murshid al-akbar*, 'the greatest guide', quoted by way of conclusion to this book, at the end of chapter 10, should serve us all.

Introduction: world politics, the Middle East and the complexities of area studies

'History', said Stephen, 'is a nightmare from which I am trying to escape.'
James Joyce, Ulysses

The end of the twentieth century and the onset of the twenty-first have not been kind to students of International Relations, let alone to those of the Middle East. For decades prior to the 1990s it was the claim of political scientists, and of their separate but cognate colleagues in International Relations, that they could, within some broad framework of modernisation – capitalist, socialist or other 'third' way – and of a changing world system, i.e. what has now, since the early 1990s, been termed 'globalisation', analyse and to some degree anticipate the development of societies.

History had, however, not lost the knack of surprising and in the last decades of the twentieth century was to demonstrate that its cunning, famously noted by Hegel, was far from dead. The Tunisian sociologist Professor Freij Stambouli once explained to me, as he was driving with characteristic ebullience around his home town of Monastir, then the residence of the former President Habib Bouguiba, that three events in recent times had discredited the claims to knowledge of social science with regard to the Middle East and more generally: the outbreak of the Lebanese civil war in 1975, in a society hitherto noted for being the most tolerant and prosperous in the region; the Iranian revolution and the fall of the Shah in 1978–9, a political rather than armed revolt which toppled a regime that had immense political and economic power, an army of 400,000 men, the latest western military equipment, and the unanimous backing of Washington, London, Paris, Moscow and Beijing alike; and in 1989–91 the fall of the Berlin Wall and the collapse of Soviet communism and its east European empire, an event that few, except some lucky eccentrics, had ever anticipated, and which brought to an end the last of the four great conflicts – European colonial rivalry (1798–1914), World Wars I (1914–18) and II (1939–45) and then the Cold War (1946–91) – that had marked world politics, and the Middle East, in the previous two centuries. In words with similar import, the Israeli academic and former general Yehoshafat Harkabi had observed that with the fall of the Berlin Wall in November 1989 we had seen the end of two ideologies: in the east Marxism-Leninism and in the west Political Science.[1]

This critique of social science in general, and of area studies and its associated expertise in particular, may have delighted the sceptic, and those whose view of social science was confined to the arid stratospheres of a narrowly conceived methodology, but it was itself seriously flawed. In particular, it set an immediate trap: faced with the charge of having been blind to the future, the western specialist, or the commentator from the region itself, might have been tempted to reply that, after all, they did *not* get things so wrong. Indeed, for many in the field of Middle Eastern studies, for whom explanations were made in terms of 'Islam' – this seen as a continuous and all-pervasive social and political entity, or in terms of the new guiding principle of the age, 'Culture' – there was no need to be modest. Surely, their general assumptions and predictions had held.

From this perspective, and whatever else may have changed in central Europe, or the whirling markets of East Asia, the Middle East region remained broadly as it was. Its state–state relations were, as ever, in turmoil. Religious discourse prevailed. It was up to the outside world to understand this region through such a cultural perspective. The bearded representatives of these religions, 'bearers' of an apparently invariant ideological instance, remained in full voice. Every self-serving selection of phrase of Tanakh, *sunna* and Holy Book was ready on the tongue, to be backed by the odd knife, bullet and whip if need be. And, of course, so the argument went, as any person with a mite of historical perspective, and who was not seduced by the idiocies of modern political *theory*, domestic or international, could see, the region remained in the grip of basic transgenerational processes, 'Rules of the Game' no less, or their equivalents.[2] These submerged but ascertainable verities, equal in longevity, as is implied in the word 'Rules', to, say, chess or polo, were invisible to mere social scientists, or those with a misguided sense of social or historical change, but they could be divined by a subtler mind, freed of modernist hubris.

One supposed route to such special knowledge of the Middle East lay through language. That reasonable competence in the language of a

[1] As retailed by my late LSE colleague, Philip Windsor.
[2] For a classic, methodologically quite unabashed, statement of this approach see L. Carl Brown, *International Politics and the Middle East: Old Rules, Dangerous Game*, London: I. B. Tauris, 1984. Brown argues both for the *distinctiveness* of Middle Eastern politics, and for their *transhistorical continuity*, from the eastern question of the nineteenth century through to the present day. On both these, central, points his arguments are diametrically opposite to those underlying this study: let the reader decide which provides the more persuasive theoretical and explanatory approach!

country or region that is studied is essential is an obvious, if now too often ignored, basis for any social science research, or broader human or current policy engagement. Language is also certainly one of the central ways in which history and culture are reflected, in contemporary life and ideas, and is, at the same time, a major form of human interaction. In it are inscribed past and present.

However, the philosophy of language that pervades much of the study of the Middle East asserts something more. Here language becomes not just the necessary but the sufficient condition for comprehending politics and society. This curious but pervasive idea is evident, for example, in the word 'Arabist', a term which implied that someone who knew Arabic could, by that very means, 'know' or intuit the social and political character of the country (the same was true of the terms, albeit less used, 'Persianist', 'Turkist', even 'Hebrewist' and no doubt finer gradations – all the way to Himyaritic, Canaanite and Nabatean). Now, if 'Arabist' just means someone who has studied Arabic and is somewhat familiar with the history or contemporary politics of the Arab world it is a reasonable term. However, the word, much used of anyone with a serious interest in the Middle East who knows, for example, the difference between Iran and the Arabs, or Sunni and Shi'a, is, in epistemological and socio-linguistic terms, ridiculous, as are the debate and set of counter-arguments marshalled against it. The claim that knowledge of the Arabic language is equivalent to knowledge of a society rests, as a moment of attention to the general rules of the philosophy of science will show, on three absurd premises: first, that knowledge of a language as such gives knowledge of the country, and adequate understanding of its politics, or even, as residents of the Middle East as much as outsiders claim, some insight into the 'mind' of the Arab/Iraqi/Lebanese/Kurd or whoever; secondly, that indeed there is such a thing as a single 'Arab' language when it comes to spoken culture and vocabulary or grammar, something assumed by nationalists, and by many teachers of the language, but a linguistic sleight of hand achieved by calling all the, in reality, *different* languages spoken in the Arab world by the same name, 'Arabic';[3] and thirdly, that there

[3] Yasir Suleiman, ed., *Language and Society in the Middle East and North Africa: Studies in Variation and Identity*, London: Curzon, 1999; Yasir Suleiman, *The Politics of Arabic*, London: Curzon, 2003; Fred Halliday, 'Words and States: Language and Politics in the Middle East', chapter 4, *100 Myths about the Middle East* (London: Saqi, 2007). Similar claims as to the oneness of two idioms, nationalist in aspiration and sentiment, but invalid by any independent linguistic or philological standards, are made with regard to the unity of the, at least, three distinct Kurdish languages, and that of ancient Hebrew, *ivrit tanakhit*, and the modern, reformulated (*not revived*) and contemporary language of Israel. By contrast, nationalists in other contexts confect differences of *language* when only differences of *dialect*, if that, operate – most notably Persian/Dari (Afghanistan)/Tajik, and Serbian/Croatian/Bosniac.

is in some sense an Arab 'essence' to be known, that one can, in any significant way, and beyond some obvious shared historical reference points way back in time, for example, the death of the Prophet in AD 632, or the fall of the Ummayad empire in 750, find a history that is common to the *Arabs* as a whole, rather than to distinct regions, and, in contemporary terms, to the very different distinct Arab states (twenty-two in the Arab League in 2000).

Language is, therefore, certainly part of the study of any society; it helps to constitute power, identity and hierarchy as well as encode history. Yet language is only a necessary, but not sufficient, condition for understanding a country. To grasp its relation to the rest of social reality you need to have a historical and international context, and have studied some of the history, politics and sociology of a country. Indeed, you need to do this to understand the vocabulary and the resonances of history, and of power, in the language itself (the meanings of words such as, for example, 'state', 'nation', 'heritage', 'tradition', 'community', modular modern code words, but with somewhat different registers in every country).

The key to this problem of how to analyse the Middle East, or, indeed, anywhere else, is not, therefore, to swap insights, predictions and claims of deep-structural characteristics, or to argue that 'Islam' is an overarching explanatory category, or to overstate the explanatory powers of language. It is rather to question the very premises on which the argument about the 'failure' of Middle Eastern social science rests, namely, first, that is the job of social science to predict, and secondly, that the region, or any other part of the world, can be comprehended through taking an entity called 'culture', or some version of religious belief, or some linguistic 'essence', as a general explanatory factor, an independent variable.

First of all, prediction: assessing the future is a necessary part of life – psychologically, to make sense of one's everyday existence, plans and, as was dramatically highlighted world-wide after 11 September 2001, one's vital, everyday, sense of security. Some view of the future is also a necessary part of any organised social life – be it having a family, pursuing an education, running a business, a political party or an intelligence system. It provides, even if through a set of supremely unfalsifiable but enduring human thought systems, such as ancient vatic prophesy, the interpretation of dreams or astrology, a way that many people, including in the modern world, make sense of their lives.

However, even in natural science prediction is not as precise as is assumed: the most quantitatively confident predictive branch of social science is that of demography, a factor of immense importance for the coming decades in the Middle East. Yet even the demographers, if pressed off the record, admit that, while the mortality rates can be anticipated over three-quarters of a century, with birth rates there is only reasonable certainty over twenty-five years, in effect a generation. For its part, meteorology, let alone seismology, can make only vague predictions, quite insufficient, if you own a house in Turkey, Iran, Egypt or, for that matter, California, to calculate the risks of living or working there. As for evolutionary biology, we cannot know, nor indeed would we probably want to, what humans will look like in two or three million years.[4]

Far away from the natural sciences, in the necessarily uncertain world of human affairs and politics, the Middle East has given many examples of how even the most precise, or as they like to claim 'hard', social sciences are not really that capable. The most obvious area is that of oil prices. Nothing makes a fool so quickly of an economist, a minister of finance, a speculator or an economic forecaster than the unexpected reversals, or resistances, of oil prices – predictions of world price spikes being followed by crashes and depression, gloomy (or, if a consumer, cheerful) vistas of low prices for a generation being followed by sudden shortages, suddenly discovered but hitherto invisible 'bottlenecks' (this last a great cop-out of the falsified visionary).

As for quantified data in general, these are sometimes oversold. Quantification is essential for social science, and the latter has, quite rightly, aspired to measurement, and mathematical abstraction, since its inception in the nineteenth century. But there are limits to what quantification can address, even given proper data. Major comparative issues, such as

---

[4] In all of this I am much influenced by the classics of the philosophy of science and of social science that I studied as a student: Rom Harré, *The Philosophies of Science: an Introductory Survey*, Oxford: Oxford University Press, 1972; Alan Ryan, *The Philosophy of the Social Sciences*, London: Macmillan, 1970; W. G. Runciman, *Social Science and Political Theory*, Cambridge: Cambridge University Press, 1965; E. H. Carr, *What is History?*, Harmondsworth: Penguin, 1962; later, A. F. Chalmers, *What is This Thing Called Science?*, second edition, Milton Keynes: Open University Press, 1982; Eric Hobsbawm, *On History*, London: Weidenfeld & Nicolson, 1997. These inject respect for the study of method. Much has been made of epistemological 'breakthroughs', even 'revolutions', in International Relations, Middle East studies and so forth in recent decades, of all of which I am sceptical, *not* because I am sceptical of theory in general, or of the need to be literate in issues in the philosophy of social science, but for the *opposite* reason, namely that it is necessary to do this work well, to read what others who specialise in the field have already written and not to rush about reinventing the wheel. Core guidance on the appropriate relation of method and social science is found in: Thomas Kuhn, *The Structure of Scientific Revolutions*, London: University of Chicago Press, 1961; C. Wright Mills, *The Sociological Imagination*, London: Oxford University Press, 1959; Ernest Gellner, *Postmodernism, Reason and Religion*, London: Routledge, 1992. For judicious reflection on IR theory and history see Thomas W. Smith, *History and International Relations*, London: Routledge, 1999. In one sentence, echoing Gellner, *Postmodernism*: those who, quite properly, want to do philosophy of social science should go and work in a philosophy department.

the causes of war, the rise of nationalism, the durability of states, the bases of co-operation, the consequences of terrorism, the preconditions of democracy, do not lend themselves to precise quantification. There are also, even in areas of apparent precision, large areas of guesswork and inference, all of which is compounded, in the case of an area like the Middle East, by the simple unreliability of data on even those broad public issues where it is possible elsewhere – population, foreign reserves, oil income, state expenditure, income inequality.[5] The most apparently secure Middle Eastern statistic of all is the daily oil output of producer states – 3.2 million barrels per day or whatever. Yet there are at least four rival sources for such figures, none of which has adequate authority.

The simple rebuttal of our critics is therefore not to claim some dubious if seemingly precise social science foresight. It is rather to question the very claim that social science should, in some vain and misplaced attempt, try to imitate natural science. Such a rebuttal can also assert, with an open agenda that should keep us all busy with the Middle East or anywhere else, that the task of social science, IR included, is something else, and richer, namely to *explain*, in as persuasive a manner as possible, what has occurred and to identify what constitute significant contemporary trends. This explanatory function, rather than grabbing at superficially sage but, on closer examination, banal platitudes about a reified 'Islam', the specificities of the 'region', and the atavistic and irremediable ways of its inhabitants, is the appropriate touchstone for social science work on the Middle East. It is this explanation that this book, and the major social science works of regional study, seek to address.

It is not the future of the Middle East, but its past, that, with this in mind, poses the greatest challenge. It was, perhaps, little surprise in the face of the region's events of the past century, that the confidence of social science might appear somewhat shaky. Everyone can remember one or two, probably more, occasions on which the region's politics, all of it indeed, had been 'transformed' for ever by some new event, be this a disaster, war or revolution. This could be some sudden burst of embracing and oneiric posturing in front of the cameras, and of potential donors, or some breakthrough in the political and ideological systems: in recent times, 1991, the liberation (for such, for all its limitations, it was) of Kuwait from Iraq; 1993, the Oslo peace accords between the Arabs and the Israelis, and the Rabin–Arafat handshake on the White House lawn; 11 September 2001, with the attack on the World Trade Center in New York; and 2003, the start of a new 'democratic' epoch following the occupation of Iraq in the March–May war: these were,

[5] For an incisive critique of apparent numerical precision even in OECD countries see Harry Gelber, *Sovereignty through Interdependence*, London: Kluwer, 1997, chapter 11, 'Appendix: Control by Numbers?'

at the time of writing the book, the most obvious candidates for such watershed moments. Those with a longer memory, even one that was shaped as was mine in the 1960s, could add to this list: June 1967, the Arab–Israeli war that apparently turned the Middle East upside down; the 1973 October war and quadrupling of oil prices; 1979, the Iranian revolution, and the rise of radical Islam. The list could, however, be stretched further back. The 1908 Young Turk revolution was arguably the greatest turning point in the modern history of the Middle East.[6] It was this event which set off political and military conflict in the Balkan wars (1912–13) and led, through the events in Sarajevo in June 1914, to World War I, then on to redrawing of the map of the modern Middle East in 1918–26 – through British and French colonial demarcation, on the one hand, and, in the Peninsula, the rise of the modern Yemeni and Saudi states, the first independent Arab countries in modern times, on the other. Other transitional periods were 1945–9, with the British and French withdrawal in formal terms from the region, and the emergence of Israel, against Arab opposition; the Suez crisis of 1956; and the Iraqi and related Jordanian and Lebanese crises of 1958.[7]

The critic could have replied that indeed these events did not lead to a brave, peaceful and democratic Middle East. The events of 1908

---

[6] It can be argued that, in terms of both historic impact *and* the laying down of an agenda, a set of major and still unresolved political and social questions for the whole region, the Turkish revolution of 1908–23 was *the* most important upheaval in modern Middle Eastern history. These questions included the relation between modern European scientific and secular ideas and religion; the role of the armed forces in politics; the construction of a modern state in a multi-ethnic society; the role of women in social and economic life; the modernisation of language; the resolution of state territory and nationalist aspiration; the modernisation of education; and, not least, the definition and flourishing of a supposedly 'national', but in glorious and ever-changing reality cosmopolitan, cuisine. All subsequent Middle Eastern revolutions have given their answers to the questions raised, but none has resolved them. If future relations between the Middle East/the Islamic world and the west are to be based on a solid foundation, then the fate of the still ongoing Turkish experience may be not just influential, but decisive. The particular international/diplomatic focus of this process, Turkey's possible accession to the European Union, is but the visible part of a much broader political, economic *and* cultural interaction. Significantly, the regional revolution that most resembled the Turkish in its resolute secular modernism, and its impatience to catch up with a 'western' model, was that of the People's Democratic Party in Afghanistan, 1978–92; it was this one which, of course, led to the most ferocious backlash, a reaction in both senses of the word, not to be forgotten, that the 'west' energetically supported. On this last point see Fred Halliday, *Two Hours that Shook the World*, London: Saqi, 2001.

[7] On 1958 see Roger Owen and Roger Louis, eds., *1958*, London: I. B. Tauris, 2002. David M. Lesch, *1979: the Year that Shaped the Modern Middle East*, Boulder, CO: Westview Press, 2001, signals three events of that year as constitutive – the Iranian revolution of February, the Egyptian–Israeli peace treaty of March and the Soviet invasion of Afghanistan in December – to which he could have added the inter-Yemeni war of February and the decisive intra-Ba'th purge by Saddam Hussein in Iraq in July. His overall category 'annualisation' could have been strengthened by examination of the concept 'conjuncture', used in both Marxist and *Annales* writings.

were followed by nationalist conflict between Turk, Arab, Armenian and Kurd, and the bloody wars of the Balkans – this was why the year was, arguably, the decisive step in the onset of the century of wars and revolutions. The new state map of 1918–26 did endure, but within it older affiliations, transnational tribal and family links on the one hand, and new radical forces such as nationalism, fundamentalist Islam and mass protest on the other, were on the march. As ever, though, the professors were not so quick to join the unemployment queue. Some proclaimed, in a fine burst of transhistorical equanimity, or perhaps complacence, that all this showed that nothing had really changed and that world politics, the Middle East and the affairs of men could only be understood in terms of some timeless maxims: the balance of power (of which there was precious little sight in the post-1991 world), the struggle for dominance, the rise and fall of empires, the clash of civilisations, the anarchy of states, even, a threadbare and fatuous generalisation if it were not so dangerous, the conflict between Islam and Christendom/the west.

The partisans of 'historic' turning points could, therefore, find almost one moment a decade into which they could project their hopes and forecasts; but, for as many such 'turning points' as the former divined, there were the protagonists of reserve, be they world-historical and pessimistic believers in the folly of human progress and modernity, or the equally ferocious and unmovable tribes of regional identity, specificity and, a great favourite, 'faultlines' (a complete and always tautological historical fancy that has become, sadly, one of the dominant global-analytic tropes of late twentieth-century international analysis, *à la* Samuel Huntington, Robert Kaplan and their clan). Thus, for every 'turning point' there came, inexorably it seemed, a historic reverse, or reassertion of timeless verities. This was perhaps never more so than in the aftermath of the Iranian revolution in 1979 when, as social theorists and radical Muslims alike proclaimed a new epoch of Shi'ite revolution and Islamic transnationalism, the regrouped exponent of 'Islam' as an explanatory category and of the 'Muslim mindset' came back to sweep all analytic challenges before them. These were replete with sage references to the Battle of Qadissiya, the fates of the Shi'ite founders Ali and Hussein, the allegedly never-ending wars of Ottomans and Safavis. This ahistorical outburst was all filtered through the eternal but unique etymologically determined ideations through which 'Muslims', supposedly identifiable political and social (sometimes even economic!) actors, engaged, or rather failed to engage, with the modern world.[8] As if Muslims are not allowed to change.

[8] Much was made after 1979, by writers who knew little of Iran, of the 'radical' nature of Shi'ism, ignoring the fact that like all sects and religions Shi'ism allowed of multiple readings and that, in Iran as in Iraq, many clergy were political quietists.

Into all these regional battles rode the outriders or vanguards of other broader, global and/or epistemological campaigns – Islam and Christendom, arid and agrarian societies, nomads and settlers, 'Civilisations' locked in the timeless circularity of 'Challenge and Response' (another transhistorical catchall), Semites and, well, Semites again (each of whom claimed they could not hate or kill the other because they were all descendants of the same son of Noah), of course Semites and Aryans, in the Peninsula, the sons of Adnan and the sons of Qahtan. More recently, we have had a long list of set-piece debates: 'traditional' versus 'modern' society, elite versus mass politics, men with holy texts versus those on horseback, socialists versus monarchists, socialists (Nasserists) versus socialists (Ba'thists), each pitted against various forms of Marxist (particularly the subjects of my Ph.D., the South Yemenis, who at least coined the world historically unique slogans 'Workers and Peasants, Fishermen and Nomads, Unite!' and 'Arm the Women!'), *munafiqin* versus *molhidin*, *shu'ubis* versus *taghutis*, Mu'awiya and Yazid against Zoroastrian Magi, crowns versus turbans, and, far from least in the lists of recurrent conflicts, rulers and ruled, rich and poor, landlords and peasants, women and patriarchs, even, in an idiom now seemingly more dated that the hegemonic phrases of seventh-century Mecca and Medina, workers and peasants. Finally, and never to be silenced, certainly not when short of historic detail, textual precision or linguistic capacity, the most dominant, entrenched and, in my view, misconceived and diversionary regional epistemological combat of all, that of 'Orientalists' versus their critics.[9]

Others were, however, waiting in the wings not to rethink area studies but to try, once again, to bury it. This disdain for regional expertise was an enterprise in which many had engaged over the previous decades, in Europe these tending to be historians or cultural essentialists, in the USA quantifiers, behaviourists, methodological obsessives without due concern for epistemological or historiographic content. The latter wanted to reduce social science to the teaching of a banal, but authoritarian, set of methodologies, and to ignore the very real, and lived, differences between the OECD rich and the increasingly rancorous rest of the world. These foes of area studies, purveyors of vapid taxonomies and inflated quantification, took the stalling of the analytic and area studies

[9] On this last, see my '"Orientalism" and its Critics', chapter 7 of *Islam and the Myth of Confrontation*, London: I. B. Tauris, 1996, based on a 1993 BRSMES Lecture at SOAS. The debate on this issue, for all its 'anti-imperialism', was *on both sides* dominated by an introspective US academic narcissism. Far superior to the normally cited combatants is the work of Maxime Rodinson, unabashed 'Orientalist' *and* 'Marxist', *Europe and the Mystique of Islam*, London: University of Washington Press, 1991; original French edition 1980.

specialists of the 1980s and 1990s as an excuse to escalate their promotion of some particular, arguably more 'scientific', theoretical approach: rational choice theory, constructivism, longitudinal surveys of things that the more sceptical doubted could ever be measured in the first place (for example, the how and when of one community of peoples trying to massacre the others), the various tribes of post-modernism. The latter, *ansar*, or loyal followers, of discourse, but negligent of the real components of power, were, despite their supposedly ironic and multivalent orientation, vying for supremacy in this field.

Such were, from the vantage point of the western academy but also much of the Middle Eastern discussion, some of the dominant intellectual trends of the last part of the twentieth century.[10] The Middle East was far from being the only region of study where this malaise of methodology and over-specialism was to hit, but there were certainly reasons, even avoiding what I term 'regional narcissism' (the belief that the whole world spends all its time plotting and worrying about the Middle East, and that everything that happens in the region is somehow dissimilar to that which takes place elsewhere, and is singularly evil or angelic as a result), to feel that the history of the late twentieth century had in some way set upon the Middle East with particular vengeance. There were three main reasons for this. The first was to do with the predominant role of the issue of security. Security, of states and in particular of rulers, and coercion, or the plausible threat thereof, lies at the core of all political and international orders. In the modern Middle East, however, as in the Latin America of the 1970s and 1980s, or East Asia during the Cold War, this predominance of security, internal and/or external, has been greater, and more visible, than in the developed world, where a 'democratic peace', idealised but nonetheless real, has prevailed.

In the decade from the late 1980s to the end of the 1990s, moreover, a number of what were termed in the idiom of the time 'regional conflicts' were brought, through some mixture of exhaustion, arm-twisting and abandonment by the participants of their maximal goals, to conclusions, even if imperfect ones[11]: this was true of the wars of southern Africa (Mozambique, South Africa itself, Angola, Namibia), of Central America (El Salvador, Nicaragua, Guatemala) and of East Asia (Cambodia, East Timor). In the Middle East the record of these last two decades of the

[10] Much has, rightly, been made of the need to create a 'non-western' approach to social science in general, and IR in particular. But as the book and journal literature to date shows, this has *not* materialised.
[11] Fred Halliday, 'Peace Processes in the 1990s: a Mixed Record', in Michael Cox, Adrian Guelke and Fiona Stephen, eds., *A Farewell to Arms? From 'Long War' to Long Peace in Northern Ireland*, Manchester: Manchester University Press, 2000.

twentieth century was less positive: the Iran–Iraq war did end in 1988, with an estimated million dead, but it was not followed by any reduction of tensions between Iran and Iraq, which remained deeply suspicious of each other, even as 'dual containment' seemed to push them together in the 1990s. Iraq itself, precisely because it had not prevailed over Iran in war or subsequent peace, decided instead to occupy Kuwait. It lost Kuwait but, after more than a decade of confrontation following its expulsion from that country, it was so at odds with major western states that the latter decided, in 2003, to invade. For its part, the Arab–Israeli dispute, after some optimism in 1993–4 in regard to both PLO–Israeli and Syrian–Israeli relations, relapsed into new, and seemingly more intractable, violence. The leaders of all parties involved resorted to demagogy and militaristic posturing that ill served the interests of their own people, let alone of any other party involved. As these long-burning fires continued among the Arabs, a new axis of regional tension was created, with the establishment of a military alliance between Turkey and Israel from 1996 onwards, coupled with Turkish intimations that it might reduce the supply of water to Syria and Iraq (through the Tigris and the Euphrates).

The second reason for pessimism about the Middle East in the 1990s concerned the economies of the region. This related to several factors: the resilient control of states, and associated elites, republican as much as monarchical, over income from oil and foreign investments alike; and the growing contrast between the slow process of change, and the inexorable rise in population and the demand for employment associated with this. It was not so much a matter in the Middle East of managing a revolution of *rising* expectations, but of handling a widespread *decline* in hopes for the future across oil-producing and non-oil-producing states alike.

The third occasion for concern about the region was that of the ideological atmosphere increasingly prevalent in the Middle East from the late 1970s onwards, and reinforced across the 1990s. This atmosphere was one of often stifling nativist self-delusion, phrased in terms of religion, tradition, 'authenticity', that inhibited open discussion and rational solutions in many countries by the inhabitants themselves, rewarding the retrogressive and the particularist. This atmosphere cast the very real, and long-standing, inequalities of power between the developed and Middle Eastern states not, as was previously the case, in terms of identifiable economic, social and military indices, as a result of the expansion of the capitalist world market, but in protean cultural terms, as part of some supposedly enduring 'faultline' between 'Islam' and the 'west'. All three of these latter terms, so apparently reasonable as they sounded, were on closer examination historical myths, ignoring both the enormous variations of power and idea within each bloc, and the many shared values and interests between them. Far from recognising or expressing real cultural differences, they instead promoted an instrumental, selected when not invented, definition of culture that led to further rancour, suspicion and conflict.[12]

All of this was reflected in the academic climate of the west. The 1980s and 1990s were a time of methodological and theoretical academic free-for-all, something in general to be welcomed, but which led not, as it could have, to a creative implementation of rival, theoretically founded, research agendas, or to a clarification of issues of philosophy of social science or epistemology, important in their own right as they were, but rather to a progressive attenuation of substantive research on these societies, and to an unresolved, circular debate on methodological issues, what the anthropologist Clifford Geertz has termed 'epistemological hypochondria'.[13] This general intellectual climate was, however, reinforced in regard to the Middle East by the specific debates already mentioned about the study of this region, in particular, first, the debate on 'culture' and 'difference' and, secondly, the debate on 'Orientalism'. Neither yielded much epistemological progress of any general help to social science. Rather, they diverted large numbers of teachers, researchers and students, at times it seemed a whole generation who had to jump through these hoops before saying anything substantive about the 300 million people living, fighting and dying in the region, before their analytic feet touched the ground. I have written elsewhere on these debates, questioning, against much academic opinion on both sides of the Atlantic, and in the Middle East, the scholarly claims, and originality of these battling factions.[14]

There is not much that any single book can do to redress these problems, in their general social science and theoretical contexts, or in regard to the study of the Middle East in particular. The limits of reason, and of substantive coverage, are implicit in the work of writing about any region, or indeed country. Such selectivity is not, therefore, something accidental, or casual, a result of the failure to include one country, movement or politician. Rather it is inscribed in the very task of social science itself which, with states and nations, as with individuals, does not deny some variation and singularity. It argues, rather, that it is shared human characteristics, a product *both* of common, anthropological nature, for example, fear, love, respect, shame, *and* of shared historical epoch and

[12] *Khamsin*, ed., *Forbidden Agendas: Intolerance and Defiance in the Middle East*, London: Saqi, 1984, and Richard Tapper and Sami Zubaida, eds., *A Taste of Thyme: Culinary Cultures of the Middle East*, London: I. B. Tauris, 1994; second edition, 2000.
[13] Ernest Gellner, *Reason and Religion*, London: Routledge, 1992.
[14] Halliday, ' "Orientalism" and its Critics'.

world system, that produce commonalities. These in large measure, and sadly for all individuals or nations which think they are unique, show how much they have in common. This commonality, a deep denial of the uniqueness of which modern nationalism makes such a fuss, can be argued about peoples, culture, religion, states and social movements. It is strikingly evident in the modular requirements which modernity, global in its intrusion and its stipulations, dictates. Anyone who has ever looked at a collection of the world's national anthems, supposedly the expressions of each people's unique history and culture, will know what to find: they are all, pretty well, the same, and as banal as each other.

It is against this background, of contestation both conjunctural and regional, that this book is offered to the reader. Its aim is to provide an introduction to the politics and, in particular, international relations of the Middle East, both through offering a history organised around particular explanatory themes and through examining a set of analytic issues in the politics of the region. Such an endeavour presents particular challenges. Some of these challenges are conceptual. Engaging with any region, be it the Middle East, East Asia or western Europe, in terms of the general analytic and theoretical categories of the academic discipline International Relations is always difficult: in a positive, creative way, such an engagement challenges both regional studies and IR theory alike. Suffice it to put down here my overall argument: whatever the difficulties of applying a body of theory to a particular set of cases, the central concerns of International Relations involve issues that are certainly of relevance to the Middle East and of relevance in explaining its international politics. These issues include the relation of particular states, and regions, to global structures of power; the pattern of relations between regional states; the causes of war and of co-operation; the impact of domestic factors on the foreign policy of states; the role of transnational or 'non-state' forces in international relations; and the place of ideologies and belief in relations between states and societies. This is far from being the full agenda of International Relations, but it does provide a set of issues, analytic and comparative, with which to approach this region.

Some difficulties are, however, more specific to this region. One of the particular approaches of International Relations is the analysis of how foreign policy is formed, and the combination of domestic, historical and external factors that shape foreign policy. This involves getting away from the simple assumption that foreign policy is 'made' by a one-dimensional unit, a state or government. In this region, however, and quite apart from the lack of evidence on the actual process of foreign policy formation, this may appear to be a forlorn venture: 'How can you write a whole book about the foreign policy of Middle Eastern states?', one sympathetic Arab friend asked me: 'There is only one sentence: all decisions are taken by the ruler.' Other, equally sympathetic but concerned, observers point to the difficulty in this region of separating analysis from opinion, of the weight, convergent in many cases, of external preconception, and endogenous, regional myth. Western writers have purveyed one set of confusions about the region, not least the downplaying of regional factors and concerns. Yet these writers are often well matched by those from within the Middle East who assure you that, as discussed above, all can be explained in terms of some simplification – be it some claim about the timeless character of particular ethnic or religious groups, the role of 'Islam', or the machinations of imperialism, and other, flexible and recycled, conspiracy theories. The idea that the Middle East is somehow different from the rest of the world is as prevalent within the region as without.

Above all, of course, the apparently unending dramatic character of the region, beset by inter-state and inter-ethnic conflict, and apparently unmarked by the progress of democratic politics and market economics prevailing elsewhere in the world, must give pause. The Middle East is a region that has for much of the past century been afflicted by war and upheaval, and which shows little sign of overcoming this pattern. External intervention, inter-state war, money, oil, religion, economic paralysis and a surfeit of passion seem to beset it. It is for these reasons a region that challenges any observer, be they seeking to understand and predict it from outside, or inhabitants of the area themselves. Yet analytic reflection may serve not only the better to understand the region but also to recognise the impact on it of global context. It is in the very history of subordination to external influences and ongoing inequality of power vis-à-vis the developed countries that the modern Middle East has to be understood; this history has also defined the ways in which it is similar to the rest of the third world. When seen in the context of the states of early modern Europe, the Middle Eastern state of the 2000s is, rather typical – brutal, kleptocratic, competitive, insecure. This context, international and historic, must above all qualify how far the region, whatever its own inhabitants and external observers repeatedly aver, can be understood as distinct.[15]

Some challenges are, however, more immediate. Analysis of the region is, quite properly, shaped by the drama and insistence of international events themselves. On the afternoon of 11 September 2001, as I was

[15] Stephen Humphreys, *Between Memory and Desire: the Middle East in a Troubled Age*, Los Angeles: University of California Press, 1999, chapter 4, 'The Shaping of Foreign Policy: the Myth of the Middle East Madman', is one excellent example of how to counter regional stereotyping in regard to foreign policy.

working on chapter 8 of this book, suitably perhaps the one on 'transnational movements', a telephone call informed me of the events then taking place in New York and Washington. To say that such a moment, affecting as it does the Middle East itself, but equally relations between the Middle East and the rest of the world, has *no* implications for the broader analysis of the region would be absurd. To argue that it somehow changes *everything*, that the history, state structures, ideologies, domestic politics of the region prior to this event were absolutely transformed, would be equally so. It is this kind of immediatist seduction, ignorant of historical precedent and structural restriction alike, that has allowed for some of the most preposterous claims of the post-Cold War world – the End of History, the Clash of Civilisations, the New World Order, the Democratic Peace, not to mention Global Jihad, to name but some. The challenge posed by any such crisis is both to recognise what has changed and, at the same time, to explore that from the past which continues to be relevant. The events of 11 September 2001, to take that example, did provoke dramatic developments in Afghanistan, Palestine and later in regard to Iraq. They did stimulate deep feelings of antagonism in the USA towards the Islamic world and against the USA in the Middle East and beyond. They constituted a moment at which the politics of the Middle East and those of the west were dramatically conjoined: apart from the consequences, this was the first time in five hundred years of European and American interaction with the non-European world that the latter had hit back at the territory of the dominant states. It did not, however, sweep away the political, economic and social structures of the region. There were, moreover, quite a few states in the Middle East, as well as the Horn of Africa and Central Asia, who sought to take advantage of the crisis to make sure that things did *not* change.

Engagement with such an event is all the more necessary for two other reasons, both relating to history. One is to do with our core job, to *explain* the causes of an event like that of 11 September 2001. Explanation serves not only to uncover the causes of the present but to set the past in a different light, emancipating it from retrospective myth, and to reassess that which is significant and that which is less so. The other reason why discussion of history is important in the aftermath of dramatic events is to make sense of claims by the very participants in these events about historical cause. Here history is often used by the latter not to explain but to provide supposed legitimation and inevitability to the present. The very claim that a conflict, in this case between 'Islam' and the 'west', whatever is meant by either of such terms, has been going on for eight, or eighty, years, or indeed that contemporary conflict is really an expression of historic cultural 'faultlines', serves such confusionist purposes. So do claims about the age-old conflict of Persians and Arabs, or Jews and Palestinians, or Middle Eastern and European peoples. Nothing is inevitably transmitted from one generation to another, and much that is supposedly of ancient, historic derivation is recently invented. Any claim about continuity is, at least, in need of justification. It imposes on us all the requirement of historical precision.[16]

This challenge, of relating analytic and historical analysis to contemporary events, is not, indeed, new. In my own case, 11 September 2001 was but the latest, if arguably the most dramatic and globally resonant, in a long series of such dramatic intersections, of regional drama and analytic reflection, of the conflicts of that region with intellectual and academic concern, that have marked the years of my study of the Middle East. My undergraduate examinations began on the morning of Monday 5 June 1967: I can well remember coming out onto the street at 12.30 to see the newspaper headlines announcing the start of the Six Day War between Israel and the Arab states. I have had occasion to visit, and discuss international issues in, many countries of the region, in Iraq and Iran, Israel and Palestine, Turkey, Egypt and Libya, Tunisia and Morocco, Yemen, Oman, Kuwait, Saudi Arabia and in the country where I did my Ph.D., South Yemen. Such encounters are not a substitute for, but they greatly enrich and stimulate, academic analysis.

It is the direct engagement with these countries, their policy-makers, academics and critics, their popular aspirations and myths, as well as engagement with the academic literature, that informs this book. In all these countries I found my preconceptions, about international relations and the region, challenged, and my knowledge enriched. I have encountered great hospitality and patience, a deep sense of the historical and ongoing impact on the region of external powers, and global inequality generally, not a little rhetoric, and widespread and often passionate criticism of the role of western states. More disturbingly, however, I have noted a recurrent, self-reproducing suspicion of each other by the elites of every country, this last of serious import for the future of inner-state and transnational relations in the region.

In sum, it is worth restating general principles, guidelines for a broad approach that are prior to, and go well beyond, even as they are pertinent to, the Middle East. I retain, more than ever amidst inter-ethnic conflict and talk of 'civilisational clashes', a commitment to going beyond simplifications about the region, whether generated from within or without, and a belief in the ability of rational categories at once to explain and to

[16] I have gone into greater detail on this question in *Islam and the Myth of Confrontation* and *Nation and Religion in the Middle East*, London: Saqi, 2000. See below, chapter 7.

enrich the discussion of its politics. My concluding chapter is one attempt to use reason, in the form of comparative judgement, for such purposes. Analysis, discussion, rational explanation, above all education, will not solve all the problems of the region. Yet they can certainly help to promote understanding among the peoples of the Middle East and, where this is also so lacking, amongst those from outside the region concerned with understanding the Middle East. In this sense, the academic aspirations that lie at the core of this book can, hopefully, serve some broader, public, purposes.

Part I

Concepts, regions and states

1 International Relations theory and the Middle East

Analysing the IR of the Middle East: five approaches

Theories are like mushrooms: they can be classified into three categories – 'edible', 'poisonous' and 'indifferent'. The criteria for good or sound theory are evident enough: it should be conceptually clear and rigorous, historically aware, able to yield substantive analysis and research agenda, and, where appropriate, able to engage with ethical issues. Theory is a necessary part of all human understanding, from the numbers of mathematics or divisions into colours we use in everyday life to the abstractions of Hegel, or of the sociologist Talcott Parsons. This is not the issue. The issue, not least in an academic and policy climate where institutional interests, epistemological fashion and sheer competitive ambition all hold sway, is as with mushrooms to discern and hold to the difference between good, bad and harmless theory. Some is edible, some is indifferent, but some is definitely poisonous. Of all of this the study of the Middle East is far from being irrelevant.[1]

As noted, International Relations theory, any more than any other branch of social science, is not about prediction, though like all human activities it may speculate, nor is it about the assertion of timeless, if sometimes nice, banalities about state behaviour. It is a discipline concerned with explanation, of historical events and processes, and with the examination, in theoretical and comparative vein, of the concepts underlying our understanding of global affairs. It is based on a set of concepts that help to explain and understand relations between states and societies. IR is conventionally divided into 'analytic' theory, sets of concepts designed to explain how international relations work, and 'normative' theory, concepts about norms, and ethical issues within the international sphere.

---

[1] I have gone further into this in *Rethinking International Relations*, London: Macmillan, 1994, where among other things I express reservations about the 'post-modern' turn (pp. 37–46); and 'The Future of International Relations. Fears and Hopes', in Steve Smith, Ken Booth and Marysia Zalewski, *International Theory: Positivism and Beyond*, Cambridge: Cambridge University Press, 1996.

While ethical issues, for example, with regard to war, and the claims of national and religious 'community', receive some attention, discussion of IR theory here is largely confined to the first, 'analytic', category: it is concerned with how states relate to each other, how their foreign policy is formed, and the role of global structures and social movements in the international realm and in the Middle East region. Such an approach throws up a two-sided challenge: on one side, that of how far concepts and insights ('unscientific' as they may be) from IR can illuminate our understanding of the Middle East; on the other, that of seeing how far the example of the Middle East can convey the scope of theories and categories within IR. IR theory has to meet the terms of any social science, those of conceptual precision, theoretical range and historical sensibility. But the opposite also applies: one can indeed ask of any theory of international relations what it can contribute to the study of a region: in this case of the Middle East, if it cannot help to explain the region, it cannot fly as an IR theory of general scope.[2] The impact of such a two-sided challenge is that of showing how the study of the Middle East itself can be enriched and changed by the categories of International Relations. Not just IR theory but assumptions about the states, societies, ideologies of the region – many of them, it has to be said, espoused by more local nationalist and other social movements – may be altered by an IR analysis.

Social theory, like religion, is marked by paradigmatic pluralism, and pluralism sometimes creative, sometimes sterile. The field of International Relations in general has been dominated over recent decades by a set of debates concerning analytic frameworks.[3] These debates have, in varying degree, affected the study of the Middle East and have produced a body of literature that seeks to explain, through the application of theory or at least broad analytic framework, the practice of Middle East states. History itself is not enough. The following study itself seeks to give an account of the region's international history, but to combine this with, and subject the history to, a set of analytic questions derived from the contemporary discussions in International Relations. The conceptual argument of this book, for an approach based on an international and historical

---

[2] See four examples of IR theory applied creatively to, and tested by, the region: Adeed Dawisha, *Egypt in the Arab World: the Elements of Foreign Policy*, London: Macmillan, 1976; Ken Matthews, *The Gulf Conflict and International Relations*, London: Routledge, 1993; Fawaz Gerges, *The Superpowers and the Middle East: Regional and International Politics 1955–1967*, Boulder, CO: Westview Press, 1994; and Bassam Tibi, *Conflict and War in the Middle East, 1967–91: From Interstate War to New Security*, second edition, London: Macmillan, 1998.

[3] For one overview see John Baylis and Steve Smith, eds., *The Globalization of World Politics: an Introduction to International Relations*, Oxford: Oxford University Press, 2001, Part II, 'Theories of World Politics'.

sociology, is one answer to this challenge. It is an approach I have tried to develop elsewhere, and which draws on the work of many others within the field of International Relations.[4] It cannot explain everything; the hope is that it does what any social theory worth its salt should do: generate one, open, research agenda.[5] This approach is, however, far from being the only possible way of analysing the International Relations of the Middle East as the following summary overview of writing on the region will demonstrate.

For the sake of argument, and at the risk of simplification, it is possible to divide this IR literature on the Middle East into five broad categories.

Historical analysis

The first relevant body of literature on the IR of the Middle East is one that is predominantly narrative, that is, the history of a specific country's foreign policy with a focus on diplomatic and state activity, within a stipulated period. Some historical work is also regional in approach (cumulative or strategic, but not comparative).[6] More specific work on Turkey, Iran, the Arab–Israeli dispute, the Iran–Iraq war and the Kuwait war has all been carried out in this vein.[7]

History, suitably processed, can go a long way. It is certainly possible to dispense with theory, to tell the story of the international relations of a region in predominantly historical, narrative terms: there are excellent examples of this in regard to the Middle East as a whole, as there are in regard to specific countries. Too easily dismissed by those of a more 'scientific', but often more arid, approach, such historical work is not only the basis on which any other, more theoretical or comparative, work may be based, but is also often more insightful than that of supposedly more

---

[4] *Rethinking International Relations*; *Revolution and World Politics*, London: Macmillan, 1999, *Islam and the Myth of Confrontation*, London: I. B. Tauris, 1996.

[5] Those who have written comparative books on the IR of other regions of the third world have addressed and in varying ways resolved these questions: their works have been a constant point of reference for me in this regard. Christopher Clapham, *Africa and the International System: the Politics of State Survival*, Cambridge: Cambridge University Press, 1996; Michael Yahuda, *The International Politics of the Asia-Pacific, 1945–1995*, London: Routledge, 1996; Peter Calvert, *The International Politics of Latin America*, Manchester: Manchester University Press, 1994.

[6] Malcom Yapp, *The Near East since the First World War*, London: Longmans, 1991; George Lenczowski, *The Middle East in World Affairs*, Fourth edition, Ithaca: Cornell University Press, 1980. For general overviews see William Cleveland, *A History of the Modern Middle East*, Boulder, CO: Westview Press, 2000, and Reinhard Schulze, *A Modern History of the Islamic World*, London: I. B. Tauris, 2000.

[7] Shahram Chubin and Sepehr Zabih, *The Foreign Relations of Iran*, London: University of California Press, 1974; William Hale, *Turkish Foreign Policy 1774–2000*, London: Frank Cass, 2000.

rigorous accounts. So too may be cognate approaches, biography and
literature. A life of Atatürk or an Iranian ex-guerrilla, or the novels of the
Egyptian writer Naguib Mahfouz, can, and do, give a greater knowledge
of these societies than the claimants of IR theory: but not about IR itself
selectively chosen. The converse argument also applies: unless there is
sufficient historical, and/or documentary, material available on a topic
it cannot be dealt with by *any* theory, or none: the making of foreign
policy in Iraq, 1968–2003, and the formation of Saudi policy towards the
Muslim world since the shock of the Yemeni revolution of 1962 are most
certainly interesting and significant topics, but they cannot be written
about intelligently as there is simply not enough documentation, or free
interview access to sources, to do the work. History is not the answer: it
is a necessary basis and gate-keeper.

There are, however, some limitations to the narrative approach. First,
there is always a tendency, when giving the history of a country, as nation
or diplomatic actor, to *overstate* the degree of continuity over time, assum-
ing that the 'past' explains the present. Thus Egypt, or Iran, is analysed
in terms of continuities to which historians, and analysts of culture, are
particularly drawn. 'Understanding' from without, often an indulgence
of local fashion or whim, and nationalist historiography from within,
reinforce this all too common trap. Secondly, a predominantly narrative history makes more difficult something that is the task of all social
science – comparison. As the founders of sociology Durkheim and Comte
insisted, it is comparison that displaces claims of national, or individual,
uniqueness. It not only avoids drawing out what the theoretical implications of such a study may be, but may also overstate the degree to which
that country is distinct from others, regionally or on a global scale, let
alone the impact of international factors on these supposedly bounded
societies. The most important question left open, however, is not *whether*
history but *which* history. Statesmen and diplomats have no monopoly
here. The options range from accounts of wars and diplomacy to those
of social change, the international political system and the long-term
incorporation of the region into the world economy. Certainly a historical perspective is essential to any analysis of the region, *both* to explain
the formation of the Middle East *and* to emancipate discussion from the
shackles of a manipulated past. It cannot in itself, however, resolve the
theoretical issues such history poses.[8]

---

[8] A notable example of this is the work of L. Carl Brown, *International Politics and the Middle
East: Old Rules, Dangerous Game*, London: I. B. Tauris, 1984, which, pp. 16–18, lays out a
set of seven 'rules' which it is claimed have applied to the region since the early nineteenth
century. These are either generic to politics the world over or based on questionable
assumptions of historic continuity. A more popular version, blissfully insouciant of its
prejudices, theoretically innocent, historically ramshackle, but intermittently perceptive

The most enduring paradigm: realism, systems and states

The second, 'realist', body of literature addresses a theoretical debate concerning the role of systems and states. The theoretical underpinning of much discussion of systems and states is what in International Relations theory is termed 'realism', an approach which focuses on security and the maximisation of power. Realism treats states as unitary actors seeking to maximise their advantages within a competitive, or 'anarchical', system, pursuing power politics. This work may look at the foreign policies of individual states, or at the ways in which states form alliances on the basis of perceived threats and opportunities.[9] It understands states as monoliths, politically and legally.

The limitations of realism have, however, been widely discussed in the International Relations literature: a neglect of ideology and belief systems, a minimisation of factors internal to states and societies, inadequate attention to economics, and, of special importance for the misrepresentation of the Middle East, a view of inter-state relations as marked by timeless, recurrent, patterns.[10] Defenders of realism might argue that, while it may not provide an adequate account of relations between developed states – with the more open and co-operative societies of the post-1945 developed world, other forms of, power have emerged – it does offer an accurate account of the international relations of Middle Eastern states. Realism may, therefore, have its limitations when applied to relations between developed, democratic states that trust and trade with each other; however, faced with authoritarian states, which do not trust each other, and where war is ever-present, a concern with power and security may appear paramount. This would be a qualified defence. Yet critics could reply that it is *above all* in parts of the world where states, and societies, have long been subordinated to structures of global power that the limits of realism, above all an emphasis on the unitary state, are most evident. Realism, it can be argued, is *less*, not *more*, relevant the further you move from the developed, OECD states.

This concern with states, seen in either realist or sociological terms, also underpins discussion of how far Middle Eastern states themselves control their own international relations. Much of the earlier literature on

and entertaining, is Saïd Aburish, *Brutal Friendship: the West and the Arab Elite*, London: Victor Gollancz, 1993.
[9] Two strong examples of realist analysis are Stephen Walt, *The Origins of Alliances*, Ithaca: Cornell University Press, 1987 and Raymond Hinnebusch and Anoushiravan Ehteshami, eds., *The Foreign Policies of Middle East States*, London: Lynne Rienner, 2002, where the overall framework proposed is based on a modified, 'neo-realist', approach.
[10] For a classic critique of realism see Justin Rosenberg, *The Empire of Civil Society*, London: Verso, 1994.

the international relations of the Middle East focused, if only implicitly, on the systemic, that is, global and strategic side of the argument: it saw the region in terms of international context, be this the nineteenth-century balance of power and Ottoman decline, colonialism, World Wars I and II or the Cold War.

This systemic approach is a perspective implicit in much international *history* but may be explicit in International Relations *theory*.[11] It is just as evidently the premise on which works analysing the policy of one or other external power towards the region – the UK, USA, Russia, France – are based. This literature engages with the relationship as one between states, assessing the relative importance of what are termed 'systemic' and 'sub-systemic' factors: in so doing it adjudicates between external influences, broadly those of the global or international system, and intra-regional relations. If the former encompasses imperial and great power rivalries of the nineteenth and twentieth centuries, world wars, and Cold War, the latter would give primacy to such issues as the conflict between Arabs and Israelis, the competitive rivalry of Arab states themselves, and relations between Iran, Turkey and the Arabs as a whole.

There are, therefore, at least two 'realist' perspectives, the systemic or global and the regional. The difficulty is to produce an analysis which, with due attention to these two dimensions of foreign relations, and with a sensitivity that defies the ahistorical complacency of realism to shifts over time and place, combines global and regional.[12] Even within the regional, or sub-systemic, there are, however, possibilities for difference of emphasis. The foreign policy of a significant regional state, such as Syria, Iraq, Iran, Saudi Arabia or Egypt, may be seen primarily in terms of the Middle East region as a whole, and of the regional mosaic of inter-locking conflicts.[13] The 'Greater West Asian Crisis' discussed in chapter 5 is one example of this. Foreign policy may also be analysed in terms of the more specific sub-region, of which there are four in the Arab world:

[11] Lenczowski, *The Middle East in World Affairs*, is one example from history. See also the Bibliography. The classic IR statements are Hans Morgenthau, *Politics Among Nations*, New York: Knopf, 1948, and Kenneth Waltz, *Theory of International Politics*, New York: Random House, 1979. For an upgraded, 'neo-realist' account that takes international economic factors into account, see Stephen Krasner, *Structural Conflict: the Third World against Global Liberalism*, Berkeley: University of California Press, 1985.

[12] For subtle analyses that combine both dimensions see Gerges, *The Superpowers and the Middle East*, and Tibi, *Conflict and War in the Middle East*. For general discussion see Yezid Sayigh and Avi Shlaim, eds., *The Cold War and the Middle East*, Oxford: Clarendon Press, 1997. For a sceptical view of the literature see Fawaz Gerges, 'The Study of Middle East International Relations: a Critique', *British Journal of Middle Eastern Studies*, vol. 18, no. 2, 1991.

[13] The work of Anoushiravan Ehteshami and Raymond Hinnebusch has paid special attention to the role of *regional* context in shaping foreign policy. See their *Syria and Iran: Middle Powers in a Penetrated Regional System*, London: Routledge, 1997.

the Mashreq, or East; Egypt and the Sudan; the Arabian Peninsula; and north-east Africa respectively. Typically the larger state may present its politics in broader, regional, if not global, terms, for example, with regard to the Cold War, or, in the 1960s, the 'Non-Aligned Movement', while the smaller state that is the object of greater power intervention may see things in rather more specific terms. If you are in Lebanon, Kuwait or Yemen, the regional, let alone the global, seems rather far away, compared with the looming power of your neighbours Syria, Iraq and Saudi Arabia respectively. Thus realism, seemingly the hegemonic paradigm, the one to which all academics and practitioners adhere, or the one within which they tend to seek refuge in time of trouble, contains both more conceptual weakness, and more analytic uncertainty, than at first appears.

How 'decisions' are ready made: foreign policy analysis

So far the focus has been on states understood in realist terms, as monoliths that try to maximise power. Yet if it is certainly possible to write accounts of Middle Eastern international relations in terms of the conceptual frameworks derived from this general conventional, realist study of international relations, it is also possible to write about the region from the perspective of what is termed 'foreign policy analysis', the examination of how foreign policy is formed, in particular, of one that does not take for granted either the unity or the autonomy vis-à-vis the external world of the policy-making state.[14] FPA, which emerged in the 1960s, rests on a body of literature that, while aware of the importance of states and systems, seeks to go beyond the category of state.[15] FPA questions how far analysis should focus on the conventional, 'realist', core of international relations, namely states, and how far differences within the state and other factors, be they economic or transnational, should come into play. Here 'Egypt', 'Israel', 'Iran' are not political or legal boxes, or coherent actors, but themselves the objects of diverse, often conflicting, forces within and without.

The most comprehensive comparative survey of Middle Eastern foreign policies yet produced (2002), edited by Hinnebusch and Ehteshami, takes FPA and realist concerns and shows how external context *and*

---

[14] Bahgat Korany and Ali E. Hillal Dessouki, *The Foreign Policies of Arab States: the Challenge of Change*, Boulder, CO: Westview Press, 1984; Dawisha, *Egypt in the Arab World*.

[15] For one early classic introduction to foreign policy analysis see Lloyd Jensen, *Explaining Foreign Policy*, Englewood Cliffs, NJ: Prentice Hall, 1982. A robust recent statement of the claims of FPA is Christopher Hill, *The Changing Politics of Foreign Policy*, London: Palgrave, 2003.

internal factors shape outcomes.[16] Prior to this the most ambitious comparison of the Arab world, *The Foreign Policies of Arab States*, edited by Korany and Dessouki (1984), had taken four components of foreign policy as analytic starting points: domestic environment, foreign policy orientation, decision-making process, foreign policy behaviour.[17] In both these comparative cases, and in similar case studies, it was precisely not the unitary state actor but the wider set of concerns that explained foreign policy. The unitary state was, in this way, replaced by a diversity of forces within a shifting complexity of contexts within and without. One of the main insights of foreign policy analysis has been in regard to the role of different institutions within the state, or bureaucracy, in shaping policy, be this in crises or over a longer period. To what degree this model applies to authoritarian states is debatable: evidence from the USSR, or Nazi Germany, suggests it does to a considerable degree. This bureaucratic politics model involves, however, a level of information on the internal functioning of states that is, Turkey and Israel apart, not available in the region.

A realist account of the modern international relations of the Middle East can do much to illuminate strategy. In some issues, such as oil policies of producer and consumer countries which are controlled at both ends of the process by states, it remains resiliently relevant.[18] Yet a focus on states alone, in the Middle East as elsewhere, runs the risk of ignoring other formative processes, to which foreign policy analysis and historical sociology, cognate but distinct approaches, draw attention. For example, the structure of the world economy, and changing patterns of demand and investment within it, are only partly explicable in statist terms as variants of a balance of power. Hence the emphasis of foreign policy analysis on the 'external environment', regional and global, political, economic, and, very significant where Middle East states are concerned, ideological. Equally, relations between states of the region, involving migration, remittances and private capital flows, often with a political purpose, are not controlled by states. Moreover, in politics, whether international or regional, the state may be less influential than is conventionally claimed: nationalist movements, religious fundamentalism, movements of social protest may try to enlist the support of other states but are not controllable

[16] Hinnebusch and Ehteshami, *The Foreign Policies of Middle Eastern States*.

[17] Thus (see note 5) Peter Calvert on Latin America and Michael Yahuda on the Asia-Pacific have taken very much a realist approach, while Christopher Clapham on Africa has given greater attention to economic and transnational factors.

[18] Although it is now more than four decades after the founding of OPEC in 1960, and there is a wealth of books on oil companies and state plans, we have no informed study of what actually happens at OPEC meetings or in the subtle but never visible interaction of Saudi/OPEC oil policy-makers and the US Department of Energy.

by them. Values and images, not least the rival theatres of public display between rulers, are also important.

The instability of much analysis of the region stems from the fact that it wanders from assessing an all-powerful state to unease about whether, in such radically contrasted countries as Saudi Arabia and Iran, it makes sense to talk of a 'state' at all. Political polemic may also distort analysis of this issue of the state's role in *both* directions. Thus the role of states may be exaggerated. It is conventional in the Middle East as elsewhere to *claim* that apparently autonomous forces are controlled by states, be these imperialist, communist or otherwise interventionist. This goes for Arab nationalism, Zionism, Kurdish guerrillas, Islamic fundamentalism in whichever country it operates, 'terrorism' – all have, at one time or another, been charged with being controlled by states. Since the 1990s it has become common for states and *salafis* (literally, 'the ancestral ones', that is those who wish to return to traditional teaching) to assert that human rights groups, liberal newspapers and aspirant (usually very aspirant) NGOs are tools of western 'cultural' aggression and conspiratorial globalisation. It may, however, be that such control is almost always overstated, as is the role of western powers in the coups, uprisings and revolutions of modern history. These events could not have occurred without considerable internal support. On the other hand, all that appears, or claims, to be 'non-state' may not in fact be so, as supposedly independent bodies turn out on closer inspection to be run by states or members of ruling families. In the Middle East, as in authoritarian former Soviet republics, not all that calls itself 'non-governmental' lives up to this name.

Here the insights of foreign policy analysis in regard to domestic context come into their own. FPA study of the Middle East may examine the impact of different political factions within a state (e.g. Turkey, Israel, Bahrain, Syria), that of ethnic and religious communities and social classes on making foreign policy, as well as that of personal, tribal and bureaucratic factions. In relatively open societies, such as Israel or Turkey, or Iran of the post-revolutionary period, it is clear that a variety of institutions, pressures and points of view contribute to the formulation of foreign policy, when not contributing to preventing anything decisive or coherent emerging at all. In more secretive, but factionalised, states, particularly those where through oil revenues the boundaries between state and private, or family, interest are more than normally blurred, it is often hard to say where the state, as originator of foreign policy, ends and private initiative begins: Saudi Arabia is an obvious case – where the boundary lies between the policy of Saudi ministries and the initiative of individual princes and businessmen is difficult to assess. 'Domestic context' or 'environment', in the language of FPA, is always far more than the internal functioning of the state.

In what certainly is a paradox for those of a liberal persuasion, foreign policy may also, in authoritarian states, be affected by public opinion: Saddam Hussein calculated when he invaded Kuwait in 1990 that even those Iraqis who opposed him on other issues would in all probability support him in this matter, against the widely despised Kuwaitis, and the al-Sabah family. Whatever realistic Arab elites may have wanted to do with regard to recognition of Israel and development of relations with it since the 1970s was constrained by the hostility of public opinion to the Jewish state: this is certainly true of Syria, Egypt and Yemen. On the other hand, when the Turkish state began to develop its relations with Israel in the 1990s, it knew that it could count on widespread anti-Arab sentiment within Turkish society, on the grounds that 'they betrayed us in World War I' and so forth.

So far so good: FPA takes us, therefore, away from the realist model of the unitary state. It provides a more complex, subtle, explanatory system *and* research agenda. Its problem is, however, that it abandons the concept of the state altogether, dissolving the primacy of this coercive and administrative institution into a labyrinth of contingency and, often, will-o'-the-wisp 'decisions'.[19]

The force of ideas: ideologies, perceptions and norms

Central to the fourth major approach to international relations is the issue of ideology is: this addresses the question of the *values* and of the *perceptions* of those involved in making foreign policy. This is a pervasive question in the study of international relations, indeed in all social science. Social scientists have, over more than a century, been denying the 'autonomy' or independent impact of ideas, not seeing them as primary, determinant or independent variables. The Middle East might not be the best place to start a sedate discussion of this issue, but it is most certainly central to any analysis of it. It pertains to the impact of ideas and belief, and the balance between 'explanation' in terms of objective, what are claimed as 'real' criteria and entities, and 'understanding', in terms of the perceptions of actors within the states concerned.

This debate evokes categories such as 'idealism', 'constructivism', even 'Orientalism'. There are, however, different variants of an approach that

---

[19] The concept 'decision' may appear to have an analytic solidity like 'price' and 'vote' in economics and politics respectively. But once analysis cames near to it this clarity dissolves all too easily, except in a few, dramatic but atypical, moments.

looks at ideas and values. A concern with the role of ideas, and in particular of political ideologies, has long been present in analysis of the Middle East and its international relations. Here ideas and values were, however, understood in relation to interests, of those states, social movements and, some time long ago, classes who articulated them, rather than as autonomous cultural entities.[20] Recent trends in general social science, backed up by dissatisfaction in the study of the Middle East with the approaches of external, imperial or 'hegemonic', writers, have led by a different route to a much greater attention to perception, to images most importantly and to what those from the countries and region concerned have to say. Moreover, from the early 1990s on, and on a global scale, a number of writers emphasised the importance of cultural difference in shaping relations between states and societies. Samuel Huntington was, in the 1990s, but the most prominent, if not the most judicious or learned, of these.[21] All of this is pertinent to the Middle East: indeed, in the context of simplistic claims about the Muslim world, cultural explanations seemed to take the Middle East as being *the* exemplar of this approach. Those in the region who presented their relations with the outside world as a conflict between 'Islam' and the 'west', of whom there were more and more, also did so. With the fall of realism, Marxism, rationalism and, it seemed, all else, 'culture', never defined very clearly, and, in any case one of the most difficult social concepts to define, became the fetish of the age, an apparently all-explanatory source from which all else could be deduced.

Two forms of this ideology-based approach to IR are particularly evident in the study of the Middle East. One is that which stresses differences of regional, and cultural, perspective in analysing the Middle East itself. This contrasts 'northern' or 'hegemonic' literature, with its stress on order and conformity, with one that argues from the perspective of those with

---

[20] Malcolm Kerr, *The Arab Cold War*, third edition, Oxford: Oxford University Press, 1971; Mark Katz, *Revolutions and Revolutionary Waves*, London: Macmillan, 1997; and Fred Halliday, *Revolution and Foreign Policy*, Cambridge: Cambridge University Press, 1990. All three of us make a case, in my view a strong one, for the importance of ideology and ideological rivalry, but *not* for 'inter-Arab' norms.

[21] Famously Samuel Huntington in his *The Clash of Civilizations and the Remaking of World Order*, New York: Simon and Schuster, 1996, pp. 254–65. Among his most infamous sayings was 'Islam has bloody borders', a statement which left entirely out of the question the issue of who shared responsibility for this blood, in, say, Bosnia, Kosovo, Chechnya, Palestine, Kashmir, Sudan to name but some places. A tide of Islamist writing makes the same case, all repeating itself. The general literature on culture and IR addresses a major and intellectually legitimate issue, as for example in *the Annales* school of writing and Bertrand Badie, *Culture et politique*, Paris: Economica, 1986. For one other assessment see Fred Halliday, 'Culture and International Relations: a New Reductivism', in Michi Ebata and Beverly Neufeld, *Confronting the Political in International Relations*, London: Macmillan, 2000.

subordinate positions.[22] This latter 'anti-hegemonic' approach stresses that we need not just to look at differences of social and political composition, or interest (e.g. in regard to trade or oil), but also to know how Middle Eastern states, and their peoples, regard international relations, not least to explain why they make the choices they do. Too often external analysis ignores not just history and context, the roots of protest and the perspective of regional actors: how else, for example, to explain the widespread, if not entirely universal, sense in the Arab world that Saddam Hussein, murderer as he was, was, after his arrest in 2003, *ramz al-'arab,* 'the model of the Arabs'. This approach is reinforced by a more general, methodologically distinct position within social science: this stresses perception and values themselves – what is termed *constructivism.*[23] Constructivism argues, in particular, that state behaviour, in the international domain, is based on cultures in the sense of shared ideas, norms and experiences. The supposedly 'real' categories of states, economies and interests need to be analysed in terms of their meaning for social actors. Otherwise it would, for example, be rather hard to see why states remain part of organisations, the Commonwealth or, in this case, the Arab League, which offer little to their members in terms of either strategic or economic interest.

The long-established concern with values and ideology is, properly, part of any sociological approach; one cannot explain any society, political system or international relationship without it. This was easily forgotten by the too eagerly 'scientific' theories of the twentieth century, be they realism or Marxism. Yet an ideational approach, be it that of the 'non-hegemonic' or that of constructivism, raises certain difficulties. First of all, in regard to the 'west'/Middle East dichotomy, it would be a mistake to swap an external, imposed set of categories for one based on a simple acceptance or 'understanding': for the vantage point of the regional actor may contain its own illusions, its own distortions of history and of text, its own warped animosities towards other peoples in the region. Nor is such discourse, what political leaders or representatives of opposed groups say, necessarily an index of motive in the Middle East or anywhere else, let alone a guide to historical accuracy. If realism ignores values and ideas, constructivism and its outriders run the risk of ignoring interests and

---

[22] For an influential general work on western perception of the Middle East see Edward Said, *Orientalism,* New York: Pantheon Books, 1978. For my own assessment of the debate see *Islam and the Myth of Confrontation,* chapter 7, 'Orientalism and its Critics'.

[23] Michael Barnett, *Dialogues in Arab Politics: Negotiations in Regional Order,* New York: Columbia University Press, 1998; chapter 1 gives the case for such an approach. See also Marc Lynch, *State Interests and Public Spheres: the International Politics of Jordan's Identity,* New York: Columbia University Press, 1999.

material factors, let alone old-fashioned deception and self-delusion. We do need to know what leaders, peoples and experts from the region say; but if our aim is to explain the course of events, and critically evaluate different accounts of these events, the arguments of leaders and rebels, as much as those of external observers and powers, need to meet criteria of plausible explanation and of accuracy. Iraq, for example, claimed that when it invaded Kuwait in 1990 it had acted upon the invitation of a popular uprising within that country. Other states justify their actions by saying that they are 'defending' Islam or in the name of what is, arbitrarily, perceived as the one 'true' Islam. Such claims need to be registered, but treated with caution. The 'non-western', the 'subaltern', the 'non-hegemonic' also need to be held to rational, and empirical, account. They too can mislead, lie, fabricate and, as the record of the Middle East shows too well, kill, especially those whose discourse is contradictory to theirs.

Realism, with its emphasis on states and interests, presents one, enduring alternative to any analysis based on ideas and values. Marxist analysis of the Middle East has, for its part, an equally sustained questioning of the claims of rulers, and ruled, with regard to ideas and values.[24] Argument by rulers and ruled alike in terms of 'Islam' get short shrift from class analysis, which instead sees hypocrisy, false consciousness, not least material interest. The problems with the cultural and ideational are, however, most evident in some recent writing on the region by writers from the Middle East; here is to be found a creative, if counter-intuitive, reversal of theoretical positions, one too little noted in western academic discussion with its methodologically introverted obsession with 'Orientalism'. At the moment when writers in the west have turned to a more sympathetic analysis of Middle Eastern values and discourses, that is in the 1980s and 1990s, many in the region went in the opposite direction, questioning the claims of indigenous ideologies and the essentialist and nativist presuppositions involved, and identifying the authoritarian, and sometimes murderous, projects served by such ideas. Thus constructivism and the critique of 'Orientalism' meet their nemesis not in a revitalised realism or class analysis, but in an excoriating critique of ideology and its claims from writers within the region itself. In the Arab world Sadik al-'Azm, Fouad Ajami, Hisham Sharabi and Aziz al-Azmeh, in Iran Ervand Abrahamian, Reza Afshari and Daryush Shayegan provide an antidote to any simple acceptance of proclaimed norms.[25] Those not entirely persuaded by these critiques by Middle Eastern social scientists might do worse than

[24] Simon Bromley, *Rethinking Middle East Politics*, Cambridge: Polity Press, 1994.
[25] Hisham Sharabi, *Neopatriarchy: a Theory of Distorted Change in Arab Society*, Oxford: Oxford University Press, 1988; Sadik Jalal al-'Azm, 'Orientalism and Orientalism in Reverse', *Khamsin*, no. 8, 1981; Fouad Ajami, *The Arab Predicament: Arab Political*

look at what the novelists and press of the region, no fools with regard to official bombast, have to say.[26]

There is one further difficulty with any 'ideas-based' approach. For the 'anti-hegemonic' and the 'subaltern' may in the end pose as many problems, of disentangling the ideological from the real, as do the hegemonic and the 'Orientalist'. This often starts from a false premise, of there being *distinct* 'non-western' voices to which the 'west' should, or should not, listen. Leaving aside the fact that there may be many 'non-western' voices, the question needs to be posed as to what 'non-western' consists of. What is critical of the west may not be 'non-western' at all. It is often mistaken to assume that a *difference of position within the international system* is necessarily equated with a *difference of cultural perspective*. Those who are disenfranchised may demand, above all else, equality with those who are more powerful, but this is based on a claim to equality, not on culture. Many third world countries that protest against the west do so not in the name of different values, but in the name of universal values which, they argue, are wrongly applied: equality of nations, the right to compensation for historic plunder or wrongs, self-determination of peoples, non-interference in the affairs of other states. In particular, the Arab, and Muslim, critique of western policy on Palestine is based not on different values, but on the argument that the Palestinians, like other peoples, are entitled to a state of their own, as in Bosnia, Chechnya or Kashmir. This was, of course, the core Zionist claim about the Jews – Israel as equal, not Israel as different. To take another example, Iranian, like Chinese, opposition to western criticism of their human rights claims that these criticisms are an interference in their internal affairs, and not based on other cultures or values.[27]

Some of the best scholarship on the Middle East, and in particular on the interpretations and realities of 'Islam', addresses this issue of ideology. Maxime Rodinson's *Islam and Capitalism*, Aziz al-Azmeh's *Muslim Kingship*, Ervand Abrahamian's *Khomeinism*, Sami Zubaida's *Islamic Law*, Maliv Ruthven's *A Fury for God*, Faleh Jabar's *The Shi'ite Movement in Iraq* all engage not with 'Islam', the subaltern or 'non-western voices', but with the realities and contingencies of text, culture and power. A similar

Thought and Practice since 1967, Cambridge: Cambridge University Press, 1981; and *The Dream Palace of the Arabs: a Generation's Odyssey*, New York: Pantheon Books, 1998; Daryush Shayegan, *Cultural Schizophrenia: Islamic Societies Confronting the West*, London: Saqi, 1992.

[26] To give four examples: Naguib Mahfuz on Egypt, Abd al-Rahman Munif and Hanan al-Shaykh on Saudi Arabia, and the poet Ahmad Fuad Najam on Arab nationalism.

[27] I have argued this at length in *Islam and the Myth of Confrontation*, chapter 5, to little avail, it must be said. See also Ervand Abrahamian, *Khomeinism: Essays on the Islamic Republic*, London: I. B. Tauris, 1993.

approach, critical *and* universalist, can be seen, sometimes, in politics. An example of such a critical use of universal principles was evident in a speech on Iranian foreign policy given by Dr Said Kamal Kharrazi, the Iranian foreign minister, in January 2000 to the Royal Institute of International Affairs in London[28]. The speech was formulated, it does not need stressing, in terms of the political priorities of the then mainly reformist Iranian government (*not*, a separate conservative institution, the unelected leaders of the state). Kharrazi began by appearing to give support to those, such as Samuel Huntington, or post-modern theorists, or Islamists, who see the world as governed by culture. 'The fundamental and challenging question relates to the cultural foundation on which this new world order will rest,' he said. But what he then went on to say was of a quite different import. The world, he said, was divided into two cultures, one of 'exclusion', and one of 'inclusion'. The culture of exclusion was marked by centralisation, authoritarianism and the evasion of law, discrimination and injustice, accumulation of wealth and militarism. That of inclusion was marked by cultural pluralism and diversity, democracy, freedom and participation, justice, tolerance, collective security. 'The culture of inclusion', he said, 'is the culture of free-minded, justice-seeking and peaceful persons. The new world order must be based on the culture of inclusion so that our world will manage to pass through the remaining traces of the culture of obscurantism and move towards the culture of a new enlightenment, and put our global house in order on the basis of the rule of law and equity.' Here, what might have been expected to be a speech rejecting a shared, global set of values became one that contained a critique of the global political and economic system, on the basis of universal values critically applied. It was not an academic or irrelevant reading, but nor was it casual; it met head on the question of 'culture' in international relations and did so in order to make a political argument, one addressed not only to the RIIA audience, but also to an audience, itself very fragmented, at home. This is, and always was and will be, what invocation of norms in IR is primarily about – political calculation.

Historical and international sociology

Such, then, are four of the major established approaches to the international relations of the Middle East. The fifth approach is that of historical and international sociology: like realism it gives prominence to the 'state', even while its conception of the state is a very different one. Equally it shares common ground with foreign policy analysis in looking at domestic

---

[28] Text from Islamic Republic News Agency, London.

context, but retains a concept of the state as a distinct institutional category, not the sum of myriad decisions. In this theory, analysis of foreign policy is often a matter not so much of reducing or qualifying the role of the state as of seeing the state as an actor which, through its influence on society, creates the context for the formation of foreign policy and which establishes and implements that policy. Through an analysis of domestic factors, elements that are often presented as separate, or timeless, features of Middle Eastern politics, be they nationalism or religious fundamentalism, may turn out to be much more closely formed and transformed by their association with the state. Just as a more flexible and specific view of history has made historical analysis more effective, a more specific view of the state may, thereby, lead to a recognition of its greater influence.

It is in such a vein that this book takes as its starting point the approach that is broadly derivative of historical sociology, and of the stronger insights of Marxism, and, by extension, of the international dimensions, at once of history as of contemporary politics and society, that historical sociology addresses. This perspective looks at the core components of a political and social order, the state, ideology and society, and focuses specifically on how institutions, be they of political or social/religious power, are established and maintained. It seeks to locate them within the historical and international contexts in which they originated, and in terms of a set of questions about how, at any one time, they are created and maintained. There is no space here for the ahistorical verities of realism, or the timeless invocation of 'Islam' or the 'Arab mind'.

The starting point for a historical perception of the state is two central, enduring categories: *modernity* and *force*. The state as an institution of coercion, administration and extraction has existed for millennia. But the contemporary state is only in a superficial sense a continuation of these earlier institutions. Rather, in Europe and the Middle East, it is a creature of modernity, of the economic and social changes associated with the transformation of the world since around 1780 and of the new inter-state system created as part of the process. The origin of these states, and historically their primary activity, has, for all claims of religious or popular legitimacy, been violence. All states, whether endogenously generated, forged through inter-state competition, as in the case of western Europe, or created from outside, owe their origin and central reproduction to force. This is more overtly so in the Middle East, where it is not easily forgotten, but was also the case for Europe in the five centuries since 1500, some of that extreme violence being not so long ago.[29]

[29] For two classic discussions, Anthony Giddens, *The Nation State and Violence*, Cambridge: Cambridge University Press, 1985; Charles Tilly, ed., *The Formation of National States in Europe*, Princeton: Princeton University Press, 1975.

In general, historical sociology has made a significant contribution to the study of international relations, above all in regard to how to analyse the state: here as already noted the state is seen not as a unitary entity, as it is in realist IR thinking, but, more specifically, *as an institution of coercion and appropriation* which operates on two levels, the internal state–society dimension and the external state–state dimension. If states, however administered and legitimated, are central to the analysis of the region and of IR generally, then historical sociology provides a more elaborate means of analysing their operations.[30] Most importantly Middle Eastern states were established in modern times. Historical sociology is also relevant to the range of other issues that dominate the study of the Middle East – conflict and its causes, the role of ideology and religion, transnational actors and movements, the role of domestic change within society. Historical sociology encompasses, but in an arguably more systematic manner, those issue which the theories identified above address, be they systemic approaches, foreign policy analysis or constructivism. Thus the 'system' is not, as realism claims, a timeless world of interstate anarchy but a result of the expansion of modern capitalism: Hobbes would have to understand global markets, and the small arms trade, to restate his theory. In this theory foreign policy is a product not just of personal and bureaucratic process within the state but of the interests, and clashes, of state and class alike. Ideology and norms are central, not as the constitutive domain of politics, but rather as part of the process of legitimation and coercion.

Two obvious questions to historical sociology follow from its emphasis on the state. One concerns the ways in which, in its argument for the centrality of the state, it differs from IR realism. The definition of the term 'state' is very different in each of the two theories, as are the questions posed with regard to domestic politics and transnational linkage. The other obvious question concerns the relation of historical sociology to Marxism. In some respects, there is a shared theoretical approach

[30] The work of Michael Mann, John Hall and Theda Skocpol is particularly pertinent in this regard. See Theda Skocpol, ed., *Vision and Method in Historical Sociology*, Cambridge: Cambridge University Press, 1984, and Stephen Hobden and John Hobson, eds., *For an International Sociology*, Cambridge: Cambridge University Press, 2002, for an overview of this subject, and my own 'State and Society in International Relations' in *Rethinking*. A considerable body of work on the Middle East has, in recent years, examined the region in terms of these concepts: Anouar Abdel-Malek, Kurt Steinhaus, Roger Owen, Nazi Ayubi, Halim Barakat, Simon Bromley on states; Ervand Abrahamian, Aziz al-Azmeh, Sami Zubaida on ideology; Hanna Batatu, Joel Beinin, Mazyar Behrooz, Zachary Lockman on social movements. In regard to international relations, the challenge is to apply these insights, from international relations and Middle East studies alike, to the history of the region, to its states and ideologies and to the particular combination of political, security and socio-economic forces that constitute the Middle East as a whole.

between the broad views of history, class and global process: a focus on historical formation, an analysis of the socio-economic context, an examination of the relation of states to social forces, and in particular of the role of social forces in opposition to states are all common. However, in several other respects they diverge: historical sociology allows examination of, but does not prejudge, the relation between states and ideologies, and between states and social classes; it concedes more autonomy than nearly all Marxism to the role of political conflict, and war; above all, and unlike Marxism, it does not reach a foregone conclusion about the direction of historical change and hold some ideal outcome before its readers and followers in the name of which the present, and its real if limited possibilities, can be judged.

If historical sociology can, therefore, provide a theoretical framework for understanding the Middle East, any such comparative project, based on a broad theory of power and change, has its problems. One is the risk of excess generalisation, the question of how far it is possible to talk in aggregate terms about such a wide variety of states and societies. Similar questions arise in regard to other regions, but on some indices the problem is greater in regard to the Middle East. To combine Israel with Iraq or Syria or Iran, to talk of large, low-income, Arab countries such as Egypt or Sudan in the same sentence as Kuwait or Qatar, to compare Turkey with Jordan may on some levels be preposterous. However, on more rigorous examination, many of the differences, of history, location, natural endowment, politics, within most Middle Eastern (Israel excepted) states are, arguably, less than those between the countries of Africa, Latin America or East Asia. The most striking anomaly may, of course, be Israel, but here too some proportion and aggregation may be in order: the basic categories of historical sociology – state, ideology, modernity of 'nation', instrumentality and fragmentation of religion, not to mention race, class and gender, and all the implication of these for IR – most certainly do apply. The very 'Middle Easternisation' of Israel since the 1950s has its own impact, as does, for all Israel's democratic character, the fact that four of its prime ministers began their careers not just as soldiers (as did Rabin) but as politically authorised killers (Begin, Shamir, Barak, Sharon).

In addition to these shared characteristics, all Middle Eastern states are subject to a common external context, and for two reasons: first, by dint of their shared historical and contemporary encounter with the international system, one that continues to affect them after the end of colonialism and Cold War, two global processes that each left a powerful legacy, and which has been followed by globalisation; secondly, because as a result of their very interaction with each other they come to share common concerns, to participate in the same conflicts and, in certain respects, to share characteristics. The politics of the Arab world in particular, whatever nat- ural or historical differences, are intertwined, not least because of sim- ilarities produced through the influence of example, through personal influence and through money, as well as the shaping of the expectations of elites and a common political language. Turkey, Iran, Israel have been drawn into this regional system. To take even the most remote state, Afghanistan, central to the events of 11 September 2001 and to the broader West Asian crisis associated with it, was long quite separate from the region but has, since the late 1970s, been increasingly interwoven with it: the Afghan wars of the 1970s and 1980s were fuelled by the Arab world, and then, from the 1990s onwards, came back to haunt it.

Beyond strategic interaction, there are two obvious examples of, in par- ticular, the shared *political culture* of the region. First, in political systems and forms of legitimation: in the inter-war period it became conventional for Arab states to have kings, so numerous monarchies were created. In the 1950s radical military regimes were in vogue. From the late 1970s greater invocation of Islamic symbols was noted. In the 1990s it was com- mon for republican presidents to prepare their sons to take over: where Iraq led, Syria, Yemen, Egypt, Libya followed suit. The Taliban's leader Mullah Omar took the Islamic monarchical title, also used in Morocco, 'Commander of the Faithful', *Amir al-mu'minin*. A second example is that of a regional norm, or absence of norm. This is the slight respect for the principle of non-interference, what may be termed the 'low salience of sovereignty', or, in more direct terms, the repeated interference and intervention of Middle Eastern states in each other's internal affairs. This is a regional trait of which Israel, with its role in Lebanon, and Turkey, with its interventions into northern Iraq, are by no means innocent. The spread from Saudi Arabia of conservative Islamic thought, from the 1960s onwards, with varying degrees of 'state' involvement, is another strong and disquieting index of the spread of regional norms.

This is, of course, an area that historical sociology has to 'reclaim'. Recognition of this shared culture is not a matter of ascribing Middle Eastern political behaviour to some timeless 'Islamic' or 'Arab' mind or to unseen but all-effective 'rules of the game', dreamed up in academic seminars, terrorism institutes in Washington or Tel Aviv, or the bar of St George's Hotel in Beirut. It is rather a matter of how, under modern political and social conditions, states, elites, whole political systems come to operate in broadly similar ways, in other words, how they are moulded by modernity and regional context alike. A parallel process has taken place in, for example, Latin America and in western Europe: national particularities remain but the areas of convergence are in many ways greater, whether in the spread of democratisation or the size of personal namecards. Historical sociology, with its emphasis on the formation and reshaping of ideas, is well suited to analysing such processes, and recapturing political culture from purveyors of essentialism, and gossip.

There are certainly other candidates in terms of which the foreign policy of a particular country can be explained: the international military and economic systems for some, the workings of transnational forces, social, ideological, economic, for others. Some would see the state in the context of the workings of longer-term factors, geography or religion. In the Middle East as elsewhere (e.g. political culture in the UK) the *longue durée* can be long indeed. Above all, 'history' can be invoked as explanation. It is certainly important to look at history, and for two reasons above all: history is necessary to explain why countries act as they do, and, equally, to provide a basis for analysing how states, and their opponents, claim to use, select and falsify history to justify what they do. The historical formation of the Middle Eastern state is an essential part of any understanding of the international relations of the region: hence the three chapters on history which follow, in Part II. Some, academics and journalists alike, dismiss the very resort to the state as an abstraction, preferring instead to focus on the decisions of the ruler. Yet as both historical sociology and foreign policy analysis can demonstrate, the decisions, and capabilities, of rulers are to a considerable extent formed by the history and context within which they operate. There has to be a critical take on history, both as explanation and as pretext, domestic and international. This was true in the face of nineteenth-century colonial abstractions about the 'Arabs', the 'Orient', the 'Levant' and the Muslim 'mind', various generalisations that have lasted long into modern times. Never was this take on history more pertinent than in the face of claims about cultural confrontation that came to the fore in the 1990s, in 'east' as well as in 'west'. What follows is one attempt, in historical and theoretical terms, to establish such an analytic space, the empirical record, a broad social science framework and a concern, a 'complex solidarity', with the fate of the peoples of the region.

2 The making of foreign policy: states and societies

One trap we must avoid is seeing older forms of political organisation and action as direct re-enactments of their forbears. Tribe and tribal loyalty in the twentieth-century Middle East are qualitatively different from their seventeenth- or eighteenth-century antecedents. So too are sects, ethnic groups, families, and coteries. What has changed momentously is the degree of state and market penetration into all sectors of Middle Eastern society. Just as economic subsistence is a thing of the past, so too is political isolation.

Alan Richards and John Waterbury, *A Political Economy of the Middle East*, second edition, London: Westview Press, 1988

Starting with the state

'The politics of the countries of the Middle East and North Africa bear testimony not to the enfeeblement or the crisis of the state, but rather to its resilience as a form of organization and as an imaginative field.'[1] Thus writes Dr Charles Tripp, one of the most learned and astute of contemporary political sociologists writing on the region. The central institution for understanding politics, and hence international relations, is, it has been argued, the state. This is the institution that administers and coerces the peoples and territories over which it rules and over which it claims supreme authority, sovereignty. Politics are first and foremost not about oppositions, but about the state's ability to control challenges from within and without, and to meet the expectations of its peoples, including, in modern times, that of representing the wishes of the people, if only in the field of standing up to the outside world. In pursuit of these goals, states use relations with society, and other states, to strengthen their position. Where states are challenged by opposition these latter are movements that do not reject the state as such: rather they aspire, in the name of what they see as their legitimate rejection of one particular state, to

---

[1] Charles Tripp, 'States, Elites and the "Management of Change"', in Hassan Hakimian and Ziba Moshaver, eds., *The State and Global Change: the Political Economy of Transition in the Middle East and North Africa*, London: Curzon Press, 2000, p. 227.

seize power for themselves. Secular revolutionaries and Islamist radicals may challenge existing states, but they are committed to establishing their own, coercive, alternatives.[2] The revolutions of the twentieth century – Turkey 1908, Russia 1917, China 1949, Ethiopia 1974, Iran 1979 – all overthrew one state, and system of legitimacy, to create another stronger and more interventionist alternative.

States are not 100 per cent free in pursuing policy, but they characteristically exercise considerable independence, or autonomy, in what they do and this gives them room for manoeuvre with regard both to the societies over which they rule and to other states.[3] This state 'autonomy' lies at the heart of the conduct of foreign policy and includes, against arguments that would 'reduce' it to being an expression of some determinant internal factor – despotism, class, a particular ethnic factor – a policy-making role. International relations is also a classic arena for such autonomy: it is less under the control of domestic faction than internal politics, and it is justified by the promotion of a supreme 'national interest', security. Seen in this light, of autonomy, not full freedom or abject determinism, the international relations of the contemporary Middle East are, therefore, in considerable measure a reflection of the character of the regional states themselves, of their responses to global powers and structural processes, and of their real, if restricted, room for manoeuvre within the international context.

That autonomy is, however, limited, by both internal and external forces: states and leaders cannot do whatever they want in foreign policy. Mistakes – for example, Reza Shah in 1941, Nasser in 1967, Saddam in 1990 – lead to the state paying high costs. This poses a particular problem for the analysis of external relations: on the one hand, a concept of state autonomy draws attention to the ways in which states can act independently of their own society and of each other, especially in international politics, for example, by launching war, forming unpublicised alliances; on the other, the analysis of foreign policy indicates ways in which, for all the appearance of state and leadership independence, their choices are

---

[2] Tripp, 'States, Elites', pp. 216–19; Sami Zubaida, *Islam, the People and the State*, London: Routledge, 1993, chapter 2, 'The Quest for the Islamic State: Islamic Fundamentalism in Egypt and Iran'; Fred Halliday, *Nation and Religion in the Middle East*, London: Saqi, 2000, chapter 7, 'Fundamentalism and the State: Iran and Tunisia'.

[3] The historical sociologist Theda Skocpol, following Weber, and keeping Marx at arm's length, classically defined the state as 'a set of administrative, policing and military organizations headed, and more or less well coordinated, by an executive authority': *States and Social Revolutions*, Cambridge: Cambridge University Press, 1979, p. 29. The argument that follows develops this approach but takes more heed of social movements *and* of ideas. For a cognate comparative study see Joel Migdal, *Strong Societies and Weak States: State–Society Relations and State Capabilities in the Third World*, Princeton: Princeton University Press, 1988.

framed by the domestic and international contexts. In theoretical terms, this involves the partial reconciliation of two distinct analytic approaches, those of historical sociology and of foreign policy analysis. In practice, the challenge in analysing the international relations of the Middle East is to combine an awareness of that margin of independence, or autonomy, indeed insistence on it in the face of all theories of total foreign control of events, with a study of the factors that do constrain and shape a state's foreign policy.

The place to start is with *historicisation*, that is, how this particular state came into existence, as distinct from early states, and the context, socio-economic and international, in which it is located and reproduced. The state as it exists today in the Middle East is a product of modernity, of the impact on the region of, first, external pressure, that of western military powers and of the expanding capitalist market (from around 1600), then of colonial rule (mainly 1882–1945) and, most recently, of global economic and political change (especially 1989 and after).[4] Yet, while the contemporary state *is* a recent creation, this importance of the state in general is not recent: it reflects the centrality, over decades and centuries, of political and coercive institutions in the region. Pre-modern states existed in the Middle East long before the impact of the modern world. They were far weaker, less extractive and less intrusive than modern states, but states they were nonetheless. Indeed some of the most ancient states of which we have knowledge, going back thousands of years, were to be found here: Sumer in Mesopotamia or Iraq, the ancient kingdoms of Persia and Egypt, the states of ancient Yemen (Saba, Himyar), the Davidic state in Jerusalem, the city-states of Phoenicia (Tyre, Carthage), to name but some.[5] In the fourteen centuries following the emergence of the Islamic religion, there emerged three major empires (Ummayad, Abbasid, Ottoman), and many smaller and more transitory parallel or dissident states (e.g. Fatimid in Egypt, Rassulid in Yemen, Safavi in Iran).

---

[4] For discussion of the different meanings of 'state' in regard to the Middle East see Roger Owen, 'The Middle Eastern State: Repositioning not Retreat?', in Hakimian and Moshaver, *The State and Global Change*, chapter 10. For discussion of the formation and modern character of the Middle Eastern state see in particular Zubaida, *Islam, The People and the State*, chapter 6, 'The Nation State in the Middle East'; Simon Bromley, *Rethinking Middle East Politics: State Formation and Development*, Cambridge: Polity Press, 1994; Nazih Ayubi, *Over-stating the Arab States: Politics and Society in the Middle East*, London: I. B. Tauris, 1995; Roger Owen, *State, Power and Politics in the Making of the Modern Middle East*, second edition, London: Routledge, 2001.

[5] On this early state, in a fine study devoid of normative or culturalist reductions or explanations, see Michael Mann, *The Sources of Social Power, vol. I: A History of Power from the Beginning to AD 1760*, Cambridge: Cambridge University Press, 1986. Ideology is important for Mann, but this is ideology as an instrument of the state, not as an autonomous explanatory factor.

This is a rich field for any historically comparative, and substantive, theory of the state.

Side by side with the history of these states, as institutional entities, there emerged a normative theory of politics, a body of religious and political theory relating to how the state should and should not behave, and not least its relation to Islamic text and tradition. Much of this is subsumed in the term 'the Islamic theory of the state' – a sound category provided it is clear, as its proponents usually are not, that this is about ideal not real. This normative literature is also not about *one* model: every proponent claims sole interpretation but text and history show otherwise. It allows of *many* readings, and *different forms of state*. The fact that the claim that Islam does not permit a distinction between religious and secular powers is belied by history is one example.[6] For example, while all states claimed legitimacy in Islamic terms, most were named after their different ruling families. In practice, moreover, and as against a unitary theory of, for example, the Caliphate or the *velayat-i faqih*, these states also exhibited a clear distinction between those with religious authority and those with executive power. For instance, the Ottoman Sultan directed politics, while the *Seyh-ul islam* was responsible for religion. In Saudi Arabia the Al Saud had temporal, executive and military authority, the ulema and Al Shaikh, the family who are descendants of the Wahhab, religious authority. This institutional and normative part does not explain the modern state, but it is in many ways pertinent to discussion of it.

Modern states and all kinds of nationalism like to confuse the issue; they make much of this legacy of the pre-modern state, in their symbols, terms of legitimation, national histories and so forth: many Middle Eastern states seek to present themselves as the inheritors of an earlier, pre-Islamic state tradition. Equally opposition movements invoke the pre-modern past to justify contemporary political programmes. This involves, in particular, ideals of 'Islamic government' derived from the time of the Prophet Muhammad and of the legitimate ruler or Caliph (from the Arabic *khalif*, literally 'successor' to the Prophet). As explanatory, as distinct from legitimating, factors, these pre-modern models are, however, limited. What is decisive for understanding the modern Middle Eastern state is the way in which, through internal formation and external interaction alike – the latter including war but also imitation – these modern states have over the past century alone been created. Such states

---

[6] For general discussion see Marshall Hodgson, *The Venture of Islam, vol. III: The Gunpowder Empires and Modern Times*, London: University of Chicago Press, 1974; for a lucid engagement with one case see Abdulmalik Abdullah al-Hinai, 'State Formation in Oman 1861–1970' Ph.D. thesis, London School of Economics, Department of International Relations, 1999.

differ fundamentally from pre-modern ones in the range and extent of their power: their control of territory, economy, society and culture, including religion, is far greater than that of their predecessors.

The reason that these states may torture and kill more often than their predecessors did is because they face new challenges. At the same time, they have to operate in a world of other states, which are themselves modern and often more powerful than they are. The external world began to have impact on the pre-modern states of the Middle East in the late eighteenth century. World War I marked the decisive break point; in the case of a few countries, there was some continuity with anterior states after 1918, in administration and definition of territory and people. This was true of Turkey and Iran, and of four Arab states – Yemen, Oman, Egypt, Morocco. However, even here the character and legitimation of the state in question were almost completely altered by the upheavals of modern times. The Young Turk and the Kemalist transformation of Turkey from 1908 to the 1920s, the Pahlavi and, even more so, the Islamic revolutionary changes in Iran, from 1921 and 1979 respectively, the Yemeni revolution of 1962, the changes in Oman after 1970, created new, contemporary, states. The states of Egypt and Morocco were radically reconfigured by the impact with Europe and, later, colonialism. Elsewhere in the Arab world, externally imposed colonial rule on the one hand and access to various forms of rent (oil money, foreign aid, remittances) on the other produced a set of new institutions, states that ruled over their more recently delineated territories and peoples. Kleptocracy, i.e. rule through theft, as opposed to just autocracy, requires there to be a great deal more to steal. It is not cultural or dynastic legacies but this modern formation, and the links of this formation to external structures of military, economic and political power, that explain the character of contemporary Middle Eastern states. If the Caliph, the Mahdi or Sultan Suleiman the Magnificent returned to power today, he would still need to join the UN, the World Trade Organisation (WTO) and the World Bank, build international airports and hospitals, and present himself as a representative of some, albeit dimly discerned, 'people'. He would also most certainly claim to be environmentally friendly, combat terrorism and welcome the growth of 'civil society'.

Autonomy and context

As indicated in chapter 1, taking the state as the core concept for the Middle East, as for international relations generally, involves some broad analytic assumptions. The historical sociological approach involves a particular concept of the state itself. We use the word 'state' in two senses:

what can be termed a 'national-territorial' one, and an organisational or institutional one – the first, that of country, an Egypt, Israel or Kuwait, and the second, that of ruling institutions, the government, ministries and administration.[7] The former usage is convenient in some contexts, and as a legitimate, everyday and legal, abstraction. But it presents each country as an undifferentiated unit, like a block of colour on the map; it does not allow us to look inside that block, to distinguish the institutions of rule from those of society, let alone to evaluate either how 'autonomous' or how determined the behaviour of that state is. Since much of the activity of states is involved with trying to manage society and other states, the firm, unitary, national-territorial concept of the state has a real, but limited, explanatory power.

By contrast, the second, institutional concept of the state allows us to examine how power is distributed, as between institutions of government or society, what the relative balance of social forces inside a country is, how public opinion comes into the picture, and, not least, how different factions or power centres inside the state affect policy. There are many ways of trying to explain the foreign policy of a state, in terms of natural endowment, class structure, religion or history, but to understand any of these we need to look inside the country itself, at this state–society relationship. Certainly 'autonomy' can be overstated, analytically careless and an excuse for irresponsibility, but the power is there. Such an analytic approach still leaves open the *degree* to which any state, even the most coercive or powerful, can act independently of its own society as well as of other states; but, to reiterate the central argument, it does identify the state as a separate entity within both domestic and international contexts, as distinct from the country as a whole, or the mesh of 'global' but, as far as states are concerned, undifferentiated processes.

The institutional concept of the state also provides a way of grappling with two of the most recurrent problems used to analyse Middle Eastern states: explanations in terms of culture, and those in terms of external determination. Put more succinctly, these refer to explanations in terms of 'Islam' or other perennial cultural forms, the 'Arab', 'Bedouin', 'Iraqi' mind, and of 'imperialism', or 'global arrogance', its equivalent. To take the first: what was around 1900 a common form of explanation for state behaviour by reference to culture has in recent times, especially with the Iranian revolution of 1979, become prevalent again. The states of the Middle East are once again often described in a range of particularistic terms: as 'Arab', or 'Islamic', or 'Jewish', 'Iranian' or 'Turkish'. By this

---

[7] Fred Halliday, *Rethinking International Relations*, London: Macmillan, 1994, chapter 4, especially pp. 78–84.

is meant, in the first place, an explanation of their structure within, and behaviour without, in terms of enduring cultural categories. Such terms must certainly have some relevance, in regard to discourses of legitimation, and forms of solidarity with others, but *not* as substantive explanations of state structure or general policy. What cultural categories can tell us a great deal about is how states legitimate themselves, and appeal to their own subjects. Thus states, in addition to ruling and engaging with each other, also seek to justify their rule over their subjects, and to cast a favourable light on their relations, of co-operation and conflict, with others. *Legitimation* is therefore a major preoccupation of states in regard to foreign relations, be it in the terms used to justify foreign policy, or the ways in which a certain idea of the nation, its history and its rulers, is inculcated in schools, or in the rhetoric used by leaders in speeches. A cold, clear and modernist eye on the provenance and questionable 'authenticity' of this vocabulary is also in order. Turn the coin and the opposite, *delegitimation*, of domestic enemies and external forces alike, is also a major activity of states.

It is, however, important to distinguish these cultural or religious terms, as forms of *self-image*, from cultures as forms of *explanation*. Two of the Arab monarchies, those of Jordan and of Morocco, claim descent from the Bani Hashim, the tribe of the Prophet, but how far this explains the way they rule, and the particular mechanisms by which the external world has supported them in modern times, is debatable.[8] The Saudi monarch enjoys the title *khadim al-haramain*, 'Servant of the Two Holy Places', a title earlier adopted by the Ottoman Sultans; but the timing of this re-adoption by the Saudi state had less to do with the revival of tradition than with rivalry with the monarchy in Jordan, themselves descendants of the former custodians of Mecca and Medina – the title was only adopted by King Fahd, in 1986. The Islamic Republic of Iran claims to be implementing a model of government based on the record of the Prophet in the seventh century; but its institutions, and the society and economy over which it rules, are very much ones of modern times, and so too, although they do not admit it, is their *theory* of Islamic government, the *velayat-i faqih*, or 'Vice-Regency' of the *Faqih*, the religious authority. Arab nationalist states – Egypt, Syria, Iraq, Libya among others – legitimate themselves by asserting that they defend the interests of the 'Arab nation', in addition to those of their particular peoples. Syria's claim to be *qalb nabid al-'uruba*, the 'Beating Heart of Arabism', is most certainly *not* an explanatory statement. The Israeli state claims to be the

[8] Halliday, *Nation and Religion in the Middle East*, chapter 5, 'The Fates of Monarchy in the Middle East'.

inheritor of the Davidic kingdom of three millennia earlier, as well as to be sovereign over a territory given to its people by divine authority; this is fine, modular, atavistic stuff, but it tells us nothing about how the Israeli state was created in 1948.

Foreign policy is, certainly, not only an activity which states have to justify, not least because of the costs involved, but also one that serves, or should serve, to justify the state to its own population. Some writers go so far as to see this domestic legitimation, or befuddling of their own society, as the *main* function of foreign policy in the Arab world.[9] Whether or not this is so, the perception and self-image of states are an important part of the overall explanation of how states conduct relations with each other. Their impact, independent of interests and institutions within the state, must, however, remain an open question. It is thus open, indeed highly questionable, as to whether such cultural categories can tell us very much about how states actually work, about the ways in which bureaucracies are formed, how rent is disbursed, the role of the military, about public opinion, let alone who gets which contracts. Monarchs may justify themselves by historical and religious title, but this does not tell us much about how the states they control operate in the contemporary world; this has rather more to do with jobs, ministries, money, guns, intermarriage, control of the media, external allies.

The institutional concept of the state also allows of a more measured analysis of the second issue mentioned, the impact on states of the external environment. The external *may* constrain, or impel, states in their foreign policy, but this is *not necessarily* so. All states have, by dint of their institutional autonomy, some options. For example, in the late 1990s the small Gulf Emirate of Qatar, with an adult population of 100,000, began to pursue an active, if eclectic, foreign policy, hosting US bases and allowing a discrete Israeli embassy, while promoting Arab nationalism and Islamist influence in its media and society. The institutional concept of the state therefore allows analysis of the latter's place within the international system of power and resources. In regard to this system, realists emphasise the strategic, military context, political economists the global economic framework. Historical sociology recognises the importance of these factors, but it addresses analysis above all to the interests, options and policy formulation of the state itself. It also has a comparable, but distinct, conception of the international context. Here it is not so much inter-state competition and power politics that are important, as the workings of global structures, of which these are but one, but only one, dimension.

[9] Adeed Dawisha, 'Arab Regimes: Legitimacy and Foreign Policy', chapter 11 in Giacomo Luciani, ed., *The Arab State*, London: Routledge, 1990 .

Historical sociology also emphasises the fact that states, and their critics, can overstate their uniqueness. This is what I have termed 'regional narcissism'. For all the talk of a special, unique region, the states of the Middle East bear comparison with others in similar positions within the international system, in Asia, Latin America and Africa.[10] Like these states they share a *historical* formation as a result of centuries of external domination and colonial rule. In the particular case of the Middle East, and for all the invocation of a pre-modern past, the distribution of territory between states and the very names they have are one determined by the aftermath of World War I, as distinct from East Asia and Africa (late nineteenth century). When Iraq occupied Kuwait in 1990 it claimed that the latter was an artificial creation; but so too was Iraq, and all other regional states except Yemen, Egypt, Iran and Turkey. This historical formation applies equally to the *character of state institutions* themselves: in all these states without exception, the institutional structure is a product of the engagement with the west, the impact of military and economic power alike, not timeless or geographical generalities. The bureaucracies, the military structures, the system of appropriating and distributing income are all expressions of this interaction.

The Middle Eastern state is therefore in large measure a product of the colonial period, hence its 'post-colonial' character, in the formative, if not generic, sense of having state institutions, armed forces and a culture shaped by the colonial period. This predominance of external factors is true even of those states, such as Israel or Iraq, which have, since independence, sought to reject the colonial past: the legal system of the former, the military structure, indeed the very military uniforms of the latter, bear a British stamp. Even where colonialism never prevailed, in Turkey, Saudi Arabia, Yemen, and not least Afghanistan, the influence of external factors, in terms of the consequences of competition with other states, education, models of government and administration, has been persistent over time. In all colonial states the language itself betrays a colonial legacy: *garaj* in Lebanon and Syria, *warsha* (i.e. 'workshop') and *girat* (car 'gears'), not to mention *barmil* ('barrel' of oil, a contraction of Burmah Oil) in Yemen and the Gulf, *fiamaferi* (matches) and *semafori* (traffic lights) in Libya. All of these states, too, bear traces of earlier, Ottoman linguistic and gastronomic influences. This external pressure has affected Turkey since the early nineteenth century.

At the same time Middle Eastern states are located in a position within the international system of *structural weakness* or, as chapter 10 suggests, 'differential integration': these states, with the partial exceptions of Israel

---

[10] See Migdal, *Strong Societies and Weak States*, and below, chapter 10.

and Turkey, rule over, at most, developing economies, with relatively weak exports, low levels of income, and a high degree of dependence on external markets. True, OPEC, a coalition of oil-producing states with some non-Middle Eastern members, has sometimes been able to determine oil prices, but only within a context set by the world economy. These characteristics of structural weakness are shared with many other economies in the developing world. In some ways, most notably the availability of large amounts of rent from oil exports, some Middle Eastern states are better placed, because of this capital, although unearned income is a social curse in all societies; in other respects, such as in the degree of education, let alone re-education, of the labour force, agricultural self-sufficiency and the enabling as opposed to despotic role of the state, they are in a less advantaged position. This structural context, whether understood in realist strategic terms, or in terms of international political economy, or in the perceptions of historical sociology on how global dependency distorts state form, therefore acts to constrain but also to shape what these states can do. Autonomous the state may be, of domestic classes and concerns, but this is an autonomy circumscribed by history on the one hand and by the constraints of a pervasive and asymmetric international system on the other.

Leadership model: the ruler decides

The directing body within any state is constitutionally or formally the government, in effect the chief political officials and the immediate group around them. In democratic societies there are supposed to be checks by the legislature, regular and effective decisions, and public scrutiny, through the press and independent investigation, on what governments do. It is, however, notorious that in the field of foreign policy, above all in that pertaining to security and defence issues, even democratic governments have enjoyed a large measure of latitude vis-à-vis political and social contracts, with the institutions responsible, ministries of defence and intelligence services, having their own considerable unaccountabilities. Any study of the USA, Britain or France would bear this out.[11] Foreign policy is, par excellence, the domain of state autonomy and within that of the autonomy of the security apparatus.

The implications of this even for countries in the Middle East that have a degree of democratic politics, notably Turkey and Israel, is that

---

[11] Such that in the standard liberal critique of US government since 1945 it is referred to as a 'national security state', foreign entanglement explaining domestic authoritarianism. The fact that *all* states have such a dimension is inconvenient here.

in foreign and security policy political leaders also, as we shall see later, have a large degree of freedom. This is all the greater because, in both countries, security threats – in the case of Turkey, from neighbouring states, Syria, Iraq and Greece, and from the Kurdish revolt, and, in the case of Israel, from Palestinians and the Arab world – have been enduring.[12] Where societies are not democratic, or where discussion is seriously curtailed, with clear 'red lines' beyond which public discussion cannot go – and this comprises most of the Middle East – such leeway for the conduct of foreign policy by states is apparently greater. Hence the belief, widespread in the Middle East, that it is the top government, and in effect the leaders themselves, designated as *al-kibar* ('the big ones'), *le pouvoir* (in Algeria, 'the power') and similar terms, who determine external relations. It is, however, one of the paradoxes of the region that the belief that the leadership alone decides coexists, in uneasy tension, with the idea, equally widespread, that external powers control these societies, and their foreign policy. Both simplifications, myths of modern political times, serve to disable, in effect paralyse, the rest of the population.

The examples of this autonomy in the making of foreign policy are many. Under the three main presidents who ruled Egypt after the 1952 revolution, Nasser (1954–70), Sadat (1970–81) and Mubarak (1981–), Egyptian foreign policy was marked by a number of major decisions – in regard to relations with other Arab states, in regard to Israel, in regard to shifting allegiances as between the west and the USSR. No analysis of how these policies, and related decisions, were made can avoid the conclusion that it was the Egyptian president, and his close advisers, who took and implemented the decisions. In some cases, such as the decision to launch the war of October 1973, these decisions were taken in conditions of the highest secrecy. In Iraq a similar process of concentration of power has been evident, before and after the revolution of 1958: the Iraqi challenges to Kuwait, in 1961 and in 1990, and the decision to go to war with Iran, in 1980, were the product of secret decision-making at the top, preceded, and followed to be sure, by moulding of public opinion through the media and popular mobilisation.[13] In post-revolutionary countries, such as Egypt (after 1952) or Iraq (after 1958), a formal participation of the people has been part of the 'mobilisation' process; but such processes

[12] That both countries came out of military struggle – one based on the regular army in Turkey's case (1920–3) and one based on irregular warfare in Israel's (1946–9) but then continued by the army of the new state, the IDF – has only confirmed this.
[13] On Egypt, Ali Hillal Dessouki, chapter 5 in Baghat Korany and Ali E. Hillal Dessouki, eds., *The Foreign Policies of Arab States: the Challenge of Change*, Boulder, CO: Westview Press, 1984; on Iraq, see the very perceptive, if necessarily intuitive, Mohammad-Mahmoud Mohamedou, *Iraq and the Second Gulf War: State Building and Regime Security*, San Francisco: Austin and Winfield, 1998.

are controlled, when not manipulated, by the state. In the conservative monarchy of Saudi Arabia there was until very recently no such pretence of consultation; however, even here the ruling elite, reinforced by claims of Islamic legitimacy that were upgraded in the 1980s and by a compliant media, has sought to keep public opinion on its side, but has taken decisions as it sees fit, even as it has parcelled out foreign policy to different factions, in the case of Saudi Arabia to princely quasi-states, and their own institutional, budgetary, legitimating and security apparatuses.

It is debatable how far, in other Middle Eastern countries, where the state has not been able, at least for some periods, to exercise a monopoly over public discussion of foreign and domestic relations, the situation has been different. In the case of revolutionary Iran, there is certainly an argument to be made that, in the first months after the revolution, from February 1979 onwards, foreign relations were not controlled by any one part of the state. This was precisely because the state itself was so fragmented – the 'Lord of a Thousand Sheriffs' as an exasperated and soon to be dismissed Premier Mehdi Bazargan was to say. One of the factors leading to the inflaming of Iran's relations with Arab states such as Iraq and Bahrain in 1979 and 1980 was that individuals and factions outside the state were calling for the overthrow of these regimes and encouraging dissidents within them.[14] It is hard to argue that the Iranian 'state' as such got into a situation of confrontation with Iraq in the months after the fall of the Shah.[15] Responsibility for the actual launch of regular hostilities on 22 September 1980 lies with Baghdad, but the causes of the war lie in irresponsible, and inflammatory, actions and words by both sides in the preceding months.

[14] On this period see Mohammad-Mahmoud Mohamedou note 13 above and Gregory Gause, 'Iraq's Decision to Go to War, 1980 and 1990', *Middle East Journal*, vol. 56, no.1, 2002. If there was *one* moment when the Iran–Iraq war became inevitable, when Iraqi strategy moved from angry, but episodic clashes to a decision to launch an actual war on the IRI, it was April 1980, following an attempted assassination of Deputy Premier Tariq Aziz on 1 April by an Iranian agent, Samir Nur Ghalam, while he was visiting the Mustansariyah University in Baghdad. The following night Saddam went to the university to deliver his response: 'It is not our tradition to make smears, but we tell you by God, by God, by God, in the name of every particle of earth in Iraq that the pure blood that was shed in Mustansariyah University was not shed in vain . . . The Arab nations will triumph everywhere, so that the banner of the Arab revolution will fly aloft everywhere, and so that the banner of revolution will be raised high in Iraq . . .' BBC *Summary of World Broadcasts* ME/6388/A 3–4, 11 April 1980. The author was in Baghdad at the time, lecturing at the College of Law and Politics, later the Saddam Hussein College of Law and Politics. He had had an appointment to see Tariq Aziz later on 1 April. The meeting was abruptly cancelled without reason. Only later did the truth emerge.

[15] On conditions inside Iran at that time see Shaul Bakhash, *The Reign of the Ayatollahs*, London: I. B. Tauris, 1985; on the political backdrop to the Iran–Iraq war, R. K. Ramazani, *Revolutionary Iran: Challenge and Response in the Middle East*, second edition, London: The Johns Hopkins University Press, 1988, chapter 4.

Perhaps the most spectacular case of an initiative with immense foreign policy implications that was *not* initiated at all or at first controlled by the state was the seizure of the American embassy in Tehran in November 1979 by a group calling itself 'Students Supporting the Imam's Line', *daneshjuan piramun-i khatt-i imam*. This was a spontaneous act by a wild political faction; yet within hours of this occurring, the state, and in particular Ayatollah Khomeini, had moved to assert authority over this group and to derive benefit from it. The seizure of the American embassy was, indeed, a turning point, not only in Iran's external relations, but in its domestic politics as well. This event, and the crises which followed it, led to the consolidation of power by the Iranian revolutionary regime and the elimination of its rivals. When it came to war with Iraq in 1980, a formal national security statute had already come into being. In subsequent years, and amidst all the clamour and public discussion of political issues across the Iranian spectrum, Iran's external relations have remained very much the prerogative of the ruling elite: the conduct of the war with Iraq, from 1980 to 1988, the resistance to opening relations with the USA or Israel, the management of oil prices, the very difficult restraint in 1998 when Iranian diplomats were killed in Afghanistan and public opinion wanted action, have been the preserve of the ruling Islamic elite, even as the press and parliament have sought to exercise influence over them.

In other countries, such as Turkey and Israel, a comparatively more sedate, complex, but nonetheless striking picture of leadership control is evident. In Turkey, security matters, and that includes foreign policy, have remained the preserve of the military elite: thus the decisions to invade Cyprus in 1974 and to launch incursions into northern Iraq in pursuit of Kurdish guerrillas during the 1980s and 1990s were taken by the military.[16] A striking counter-example, but one that reinforces the picture of elite control of the foreign policy making process, is that of the decision taken by Ankara in 1990 to support the western and Arab coalition against Iraq, following the invasion of Kuwait. Prior to the Iraqi invasion, Turkey had had reasonable, if distrustful, relations with Baghdad and benefited from trade and transit fees from the Kirkuk–Yumurtalik pipeline. After 2 August 1990 sentiment within the Turkish military and political elites was strongly against western sanctions, let alone military action, on Iraq. Yet the civilian president, Turgut Ozal, took the decision to impose economic sanctions on Iraq, cutting the pipeline. Later he gave support to the military actions taken by the allies of Kuwait: in a move that was of considerable strategic assistance to the USA and its allies, Turkey

[16] Gareth Jenkins, *Context and Circumstance: the Turkish Military and Politics*, London: International Institute for Strategic Studies (hereafter IISS), 2001, pp. 72–82.

allowed US and British planes to use Turkish air bases, and, in a supportive action, moved an estimated 100,000 troops to the Iraqi frontier. What Turkey did not do, and what Ozal apparently wanted it to, was to participate directly in the war and open a second, northern, front against Iraq. What was significant about these decisions by the Turkish president was that the foreign and defence ministers, and the chief of general staff, resigned: they had not been told about the decision to close the pipeline prior to its announcement. It was the civilian president, backed by external support, who, to some degree, prevailed. He remained limited in what he could do, but on this occasion the president showed considerable autonomy exercised with panache.[17]

In the case of Israel, controls certainly do prevail, in the form of a lively when not disputatious press, a parliament, the Knesset, and, in the long run most importantly, periodic elections. Yet the record here too identifies a large measure of manoeuvre open to the prime minister and his closest political and security advisers. This has been true ever since 1948. Certain issues are out of limits to the otherwise uncontrolled press (notably nuclear policy), but the key control has come through the secrecy, generally accepted, of security policy formulation. Israeli prime ministers have traditionally operated with a high degree of freedom in foreign affairs. In the 1950s David Ben Gurion developed a foreign and defence policy without hindrance from society and indeed sought to forge a 'nation in arms'; in the 1990s the contrasted policies of Rabin, Netanyahu and Barak also exhibited a high degree of independence, if one, ultimately, subject to the control of elections, and, of course, to the flexibility of their Arab interlocutors.[18]

Domestic context

The picture of a leader, or small secretive elite, making foreign policy decisions, therefore, not only is widely held in the Middle East but also has a significant truth about it. Were it the full truth it would weaken, if not completely destroy, any argument as to the centrality of the *state*, since even in the smallest of countries the state is something more than the individual ruler and his advisers. However, the leadership model, if

---

[17] William Hale, *Turkish Foreign Policy 1774–2000*, London: Frank Cass, 2000, pp. 218–28; Nicole and Hugh Pope, *Turkey Unveiled: Atatürk and After*, London: John Murray, 1997, pp. 218–27.

[18] Clive Jones, 'The Foreign Policy of Israel', in Raymond Hinnebusch and Anoushiravan Ehteshami, eds., *The Foreign Policies of Middle East States*, London: Lynne Rienner, 2002; Michael Brecher, *The Foreign Policy System of Israel: Setting, Images, Process*, London: Oxford University Press, 1972; Mark Heller, *Continuity and Change in Israeli Security Policy*, London: IISS, 2000.

such it be, is, in the Middle East as much as elsewhere, a simplification. People may believe that the leader and his advisers take all decisions. Indeed, the leaders themselves may enthusiastically foster such an image, even as they are aware, often to a paranoid degree, of how public opinion disturbs them. However, such latitude does not exist in politics, any more than in economics or social behaviour. In the case of foreign policy there are several, indeed five, main reasons why this is a simplification. Leaders decide, but within major constraints: to these we can now turn.

Bureaucratic interests

As already suggested, the state is more than the leader himself: institutional and other interests within that state, civilian and military, have their own interests which they make known, overtly or not, and of which, even in the most cowed of administrations, the ruler has to take note. The efforts made by many Middle Eastern states to satisfy the material and social aspirations of the military elite are an indication of this. The reluctance of these states, during the 1990s, to privatise their economies illustrates how deep resistance to this from within the state sector has been.[19]

There are certain aspects of state structure which are particularly relevant to the shaping of foreign policy. Most obviously, states contain institutions, foreign ministries, intelligence services and military apparatuses, with a direct interest in foreign policy. Rulers preside over a bureaucracy with its own concerns, of which the maintenance of budgetary support and employment is a primary goal, as is differential representation of ethnic, tribal and regional groups. The very administrative structures of states are shaped by concerns where economic factors are subordinated to political concerns, of *political* economy: the history of the Middle Eastern state in modern times has, indeed, to a considerable extent been that of expanding employment in the state sector for political reasons and increasing the state's role in the economy to manage society under the guise of 'development'. Political economy is also likely to be as important a factor in foreign policy as is any direct ideological view on relations with other states: even when they were at war, Iran and Iraq held similar views on oil prices within OPEC and sat together at its ministerial meetings; radical Syria has long had an alliance with conservative Saudi Arabia, because of the financial support it received from Riyadh, this latter in

[19] Hakimian and Moshaver, *The State and Global Change*; Clement M. Henry and Robert Springborg, *Globalization and the Politics of Development in the Middle East*, Cambridge: Cambridge University Press, 2001.

part to boost Damascus against Baghdad.[20] It is not pre-ordained how far those with an interest may push for a forward, or more restrained, policy: in Syria or Egypt the military may benefit from higher budgetary appropriations, but fear war itself, while in Iran the Islamic Guards or Pasdaran pushed for a continuation of the war against Iraq in 1982 (successfully) and for an invasion of Afghanistan in 1998 (unsuccessfully). What is clear is that no ruler can pursue an active foreign policy without in some measure ensuring the consent, initial and ongoing, of those within the state concerned with implementing it.

In some cases a connection of policy and interest is more obvious. The military elite of Egypt clearly stood to benefit from the confrontation with the outside world in the 1950s. This led, amongst other things, to the nationalisation of foreign-owned businesses in Egypt and to their takeover, as administrators but also benefactors, by the 'new class', *al-tabaqa al-jadida*, drawn from the military elite.[21] The Syrian occupation of Lebanon was of direct benefit to the Syrian military who used their contact with the free market of Lebanon to promote their trading interests inside Syria. A similar prospect was, mistakenly, held out to the Iraqi army when they were sent into Kuwait in August 1990. Syria, like Iraq and Yemen, long had trading enterprises run by the military, with titles like *al-mu'assasa al-askaria al-iqtisadia* (the Military Economic Organisation). The enthusiasm of the northern Yemeni army for unity with the south, in 1990, and for the incorporation of the latter in the Seventy Days War of 1994, was to a degree based on hope of gain: access to oil revenues, shipping fees and international donor funds on the former occasion, seizure of property and (ex-colonial) villas in Aden on the latter.

Public opinion

Against simple theories of totalitarianism or tyranny, in all societies, even the most dictatorial, public opinion matters; it may not be allowed to express a positive preference, but it does set limits beyond which the ruler cannot go. Yet to introduce public opinion as a formative influence on foreign policy may appear far-fetched. Even in democratic countries, the majority of the population have little knowledge of, or interest in,

---

[20] On the interaction of formal and informal factors in Riyadh–Damascus relations see the very perceptive study by Sonoko Sunayama, 'Syria and Saudi Arabia 1978–1990 – a Study of the Role of Shared identities in Alliance Making', Ph.D. thesis, London School of Economics, 2004.

[21] John Waterbury, *The Egypt of Nasser and Sadat: the Political Economy of Two Regimes*, Princeton: Princeton University Press, 1983. For an early critique of the class character of the Egyptian state, Anouar Abdel-Malik, *Egypt, Military Society*, New York: Random House, 1968.

external affairs. Issues of foreign policy, and even more so of security, are kept out of public debate by the state. Yet public opinion has played, and continues to play, a powerful part in the politics of the Middle East, in authoritarian as well as more open societies. This is above all because of the origins and character of regional states themselves and their links to western power. Insecurity is inherent in their very character. Moreover, the modern history of the Middle East has seen extensive and recurrent popular mobilisation and involvement in politics, against colonial rule, and, intermittently, against dictatorial rulers: the rise of Arab nationalism, before and after World War II, and through the 1960s and 1970s involved appeals by rulers, and states, to a public enthusiastic about the national causes. The decline of a unitary pan-Arab nationalism since the 1970s has not removed public concern, be it over Palestine, or Iraq, or in regard to issues particular to each Arab state. In a country like Egypt, public opinion is also concerned, as much after colonialism and the Cold War as during it, about the degree of external, particularly American, influence over the state. It has been equally sensitive to the ways in which external pressure from, say, the International Monetary Fund (IMF) may lead to a reduction in state subsidies and public employment. In the Arab world the bearers of this power have changed, from secular nationalism and communism in the 1940s–1970s to various strands of religious movements, but the critique and popular sentiments are the same.

In the non-Arab parts of the Middle East public opinion can be equally important. Within Israel, political leaders and parties have, by dint of the parliamentary and electoral system – a prisoner of the percentages of a rigid proportional representation – to win and sustain public support, at least through the chicanery of Knesset factions. In Turkey, where elections, rather more circumscribed than in Israel, are also held, public opinion on such issues as Cyprus, the Aegean, the Kurds and the Armenian question is vibrant and influential. In Iran disaffection with the Shah's ties to the USA and to Israel played a certain part in his loss of prestige and power in the 1970s. Public opinion is, therefore, a function of the very formation of modern Middle Eastern politics and states, of the importance of nationalism and state economic policy in the legitimation and re-legitimation of states, and in the need rulers, and states, feel to avoid confrontations with their subjects.

This concern, to reiterate the point, operates in non-democratic countries as well as in democratic ones. Two further examples may illustrate this: Egypt's relations with Israel after 1967 and Iraq's invasion of Kuwait in 1990. In neither case are we dealing with open, or democratic, states: yet in both cases public opinion was an influential factor in what states could do. Immediately after the 1967 war President Nasser announced that he would not negotiate with Israel; in 1973 his successor, Anwar Sadat, launched the October war: the purpose of this 1973 war was not to defeat Israel but to restore that degree of Arab, and particularly Egyptian, prestige which *would* enable Egypt to negotiate with Israel. Though he was losing ground militarily, Sadat gained that political margin, for negotiation, from the war and proceeded to negotiate a peace with Israel that culminated in the 1979 Camp David accords. The accords themselves were apparently accepted by the majority of Egyptian, but not of Arab, opinion; but even Egyptian opinion was not prepared to go further and engage in full economic or people-to-people relations with Israel. The assassination of Sadat in 1981 produced, therefore, little public emotion in Egypt: his strategic legacy, while it endured, was not respected. A 'cold peace', sustained by both states but limited in effect, followed. Despite the interest of the state itself in improving relations with Israel, and despite sustained encouragement from the west, particularly the USA, to do so, it was public opinion within Egypt, itself reinforced by a more widespread hostility to the peace accords with Israel in the Arab world as a whole, that limited what the Egyptian state could do.[22] In the 1990s, the slogan *dud al-tatbia* 'Against Normalisation', not always as clear as it seemed, became a rallying cry in the Arab world.

As suggested earlier, the role of public sentiment in Iraq's invasion of Kuwait in 1990 was, in a contrary vein, equally significant. Iraq had fought its eight-year war with Iran from 1980 to 1988 in part to eliminate any threat which the Iranian revolution posed to the Iraqi state, in part to promote itself as the champion of Arab nationalism as a whole; yet the war had ended, in August 1988, without a defeat of Iran, and at immense financial, human and administrative cost to Iraq. Here the two-sided character of the state, as institution of rule and of vulnerability to domestic and external pressure, was evident: the twin goals, of reinforcing the state at home and promoting it abroad, had not been achieved by Baghdad's war. The Iraqi population was well aware of this, and was also concerned about the failure of the negotiations that followed the August 1988 ceasefire to secure the release of Iraqi prisoners of war held by Iran. Iraq had also borrowed heavily from its Arab neighbours, Kuwait and Saudi Arabia, to pay for the war, an estimated $40 billion. It was this impasse, one that weakened the legitimacy and economic capacity of the Iraqi state after the ceasefire, that formed the background to the decision to invade Kuwait. That decision to invade was, however, also one that resonated with public opinion: the view that Kuwait was part of

---

[22] See Mohamed Heikal, *Autumn of Fury*, London: Deutsch, 1983, for an evocation of dissatisfaction within Egypt leading up to the death of Sadat.

Iraq, a Nineteenth Province, illegitimately 'amputated' by the west, was almost universally held within Iraq. Wider Arab public opinion held to the view that the Arab Gulf states had enjoyed disproportionate wealth: if the Sheikhs and Amirs were challenged, and even occupied, this would be to the benefit of the Arab world as a whole. Regional factors also came into play. This was also a time of renewed Arab indignation about the Palestinian question, following the outbreak of the *intifadha* in 1987, and the inability of the Arab world to act. The Iraqi state had, therefore, strong reasons in terms of its own public opinion, frustrated as it was by the war with Iran and its consequences, and in terms of Arab sentiment as a whole at that very time, for launching the attack on Kuwait.[23]

State capacity

The broader domestic environment of any state provides a third, ever-present, context for foreign policy. Indeed not only states, in the sense of rulers and governments, but public opinion too, are constrained and shaped by this environment: in regard to both of the former, it is possible, if not frequent, for aspiration to outrun capability, for aspirations to arise which are simply beyond the reach of the state concerned. Arab nationalist states in the 1960s, and the Iranian state in the 1980s, paid a price in allowing rhetorical, and strategic, ambition to outstrip national capability. Revolutionary states, from the Algeria of Ben Bella (1962–5) to the People's Democratic Republic of Yemen (PDRY) (1969–82 especially), exhibited such rhetorical overreach, one that, as in Cuba, their long-suffering populations did not usually share. Here ideology, 'norm' and so forth *did* matter, and led, at high cost, to public disillusion with socialism. As an example: a conversation in Aden in 1970 with a taxi-driver as we passed the offices of the revolutionary 'fronts' represented in the Maala district: 'Why do we have to go on poking our noses into the business of all the Gulf States and annoying them so much?'

The range of options open to any Middle Eastern ruler, or state, is not, therefore, limitless: every state is limited by its economic capacity, and shaped by its economic needs, and by a range of other contextual or environmental factors, of which natural endowment, population, geographic location are the most evident. Geography in the narrower sense, of natural endowment, climate, position, is something that is often adduced

---

[23] On general background see Lawrence Freedman and Efraim Karsh, *The Gulf Conflict 1990–1991: Diplomacy and War in the New World Order*, London: Faber and Faber, 1993, chapter 2, 'Saddam's Crisis'. On conditions inside Iraq see the very perceptive account by Said Aburish, *Saddam Hussein: the Politics of Revenge*, London: Bloomsbury 2000, chapter 10, 'The Friend–Foe Game', esp. pp. 259–62.

as an overall explanation for states and state behaviour; the oldest explanation for the despotic character of Middle Eastern states is that this reflects the need for authoritarian, centralised governments in arid society, where control of water gave power to the state – what was termed 'Asiatic despotism'. There are, however, several problems with this apparent fit between geography and state, the first being the much abused history itself: close examination of the classic case, Pharaonic Egypt, shows that while for part of the time the Nile valley was ruled by a centralised state, for much of the time it was not. When the record, as divined from rapid invocation of the Pharaonic past, is examined, there seems to be no automatic linkage between geography and state form here. To extend the model to encompass countries such as Iran, or Iraq, and to cover centuries, if not millennia, is unwarranted, another version of ahistorical 'history'.

What is warranted is examination, in the light of the modern state, of the role of agricultural and industrial potential, of demographic patterns and of the impact of these on the state. For Arab oil-producing countries of the Gulf, the reliance on rent from oil affects not only the character of the state, and much of the economy, but also the external alliances and security policy they pursue. For Egypt the need for substantial food aid from the USA, at over $4 billion a year, is an important limit on how far it can substantially alter its foreign policy – faced with conflicts of dependence and nationalist sentiment, it too easily lapses into a sort of ill-tempered submissiveness, interrupted by ineffectual bursts of indignation and waving of an 'Arab' stand. When geography intersects with strategic vulnerability it is of direct importance: Israel's concern at its lack of strategic depth, Iraq's with its limited access to the sea, are cases in point.

The broader question this analysis of geography and economy raises about domestic context is of how far the foreign policy of Middle Eastern, or any other, states is in effect *determined* by the political economy of that society – note, not the economy but the *political* economy. In the sense of immediate, short-term economic benefit this may not be the case; there are many examples in modern Middle Eastern politics where the contrary, a policy that is economically catastrophic, has been pursued. The costs to Iran of its foreign policy after 1979 (leading to embargoes and a freeze on credit and investment), Arab refusal over many decades to settle with Israel, the partial support by Yemen of Iraq in the 1990 crisis, and Iraqi resistance to sanctions in the years after that crisis, are all cases where foreign policy *cannot* be read as following simply from economic calculation. Where the connection is sometimes more flexibly found is in the long-term structural impact of political economy, in the ways in which the state, located both as the controller of the domestic economy and of the distribution of wealth, and as the mediator between domestic society and international market, seeks to balance and derive benefit from these two arenas of activity; oil revenues, and more recently World Bank and other foreign aid and rent, are means to this end.

The external relations of states are, moreover, affected by the composition of the population they rule over. As noted, this is most obviously the case in regard to the armed forces, who much of the time act not as guardians of security against external attack but as an instrument for allocating resources within the country. The social composition of a country is also evident in the role that a diverse ethnic and religious composition may play in shaping that country's relation with the outside world. No state in the Middle East is entirely homogeneous in religious and linguistic terms; in each case this can affect its external relations. Within Israel, and despite the promotion of a single Israeli-Jewish identity and polity, differences in origin, and hence political culture, have affected both domestic and foreign policy. The erosion of the power of the Labour bloc, which ruled after 1948 and was mainly composed of European Jews, reflected the rise of an opposition drawing its influence from the Oriental Jewish population. The influx of up to one million immigrants from the former Soviet Union in the 1990s also contributed to a strengthening of Labour's opponents. All were more hostile to Arabs, more careless of Israel's long-term strategic weakness and less willing to make or hold to compromise than the Labour-dominated bloc, with long-term consequences, yet to be seen or, as yet, recognised, ones that may, inexorably, place in question the survival of the Jewish state.

Many Arab states are also affected by this internal diversity. Thus in Iraq, where a predominantly Sunni Arab elite, drawn from the Sunni quarter of the population, ruled for most of modern history, there was strong incentive for this elite to strengthen its identification with *Arab* nationalism; this is in order precisely to compensate for the importance of the Kurdish and Shi'ite Arab components in the society and to offset the influence, to the east, of Iran. In Lebanon, the country has been riven by the lack of stable political balance between its Christian and Muslim populations, one exacerbated by the entry of the Palestinians in the early 1970s, *all* of which factions, for all their protestations of nationalist devotion, have sought, indeed invited, external intervention. In Jordan, the state, a Hashemite elite installed by Britain in the 1920s, and in particular the monarch, have had to sustain policies that appeal to both the Jordanian and Palestinian elements in society, and give them a sense of incorporation into government employment. In Turkey, which has (although long hidden by Kemalist monolithism) strong communities drawn from former inhabitants of both the Balkans and the northern Caucasus, the state had during the wars of the 1990s to express its concern about developments in these areas, while for reasons of national security seeking to prevent too active an official Turkish commitment. The great success and maturity of Turkish policy in the 1990s vis-à-vis Bosnia, Kosovo, Nagorno-Karabakh, Chechnya and more, was that it did *not* become significantly involved, overtly *or* covertly, even when this left the initiative to other, often Saudi-backed, tendencies.

Norms

If, so far, discussion has concerned objective or, to use a good old word, 'real' constraints on state activity, it is equally important to bring into the picture that which is subjective, the values, ideals, norms which states, and their peoples, may have. As will be discussed at greater length in chapter 7, three strands of ideology have most certainly contributed to the formation of Middle Eastern politics and international relations: nationalism, revolution, Islamism. The first served for most of the twentieth century as the dominant force, amongst Arabs, Turks, Israelis and Iranians. Despite affirmation of a single identity, there was never *one* nationalism, one clear ideology, within each people, but rather a variety of interpretations along religious/secular, liberal/revolutionary lines of division. This did not detract from the impact of nationalism but served, rather, to promote greater competitive claims by each tendency. In the case of Arab states, the assertion of a common Arab nationhood, and of a solidarity in the face of western and Israeli hostility, provided the basis for decades of formal inter-Arab co-operation, after the founding of the Arab League in 1945. Revolutionary ideas were promoted in part by radical Arab and Iranian nationalists, in part by communist movements, but also by Islamists. Radical Arab nationalists in Egypt, Syria, Iraq, Libya and elsewhere called for the removal not only of imperialist controls but also of the local rulers, 'agents' no less, who supported them: in other words, their Arab nationalist foreign policy promoted social revolution.

It was indeed dispute over such ideas, between ideologically rivalrous Nasserist and Ba'thist factions, that characterised Middle Eastern politics in the 1960s. The greatest claim for 'constructivism' can be made not in regard to the suffocatory platitudes of Arab summits and stilted 'exchanges' of views, but in the words and consequent deeds of radical regimes of the 1960s and 1970s. In the case of South Yemen, a radical regime ruling there from 1967 to 1990 called for social revolution throughout the Arabian Peninsula and backed this up by providing, at immense economic cost to itself, military and diplomatic support to those in neighbouring states pursuing this end.[24] The most dramatic of all examples of revolutionary ideology was that of the Islamic Republic of Iran which, from 1979, called for the uprising of 'oppressed' *mustaz'afin* Muslims throughout the Middle East and beyond and did all it could to further this end: 'In Islam there are no frontiers,' it was announced. Whilst Iran's export of revolution, *suduri-i inqilab*, was often stronger on rhetoric than on substance, it was an *official* policy and in three countries at least – Afghanistan, Iraq and Lebanon – it involved substantial and sustained military support for opposition groups. In the last of these three cases this was with some success through Hizbullah. Islam and Islamism have therefore themselves, whether in radical or more conservative form, provided the basis for formulating and pursuing foreign policy by many states – not, as pious followers and their western sympathisers predicted, because of a genuine belief system, but because this system can be used selectively to endorse state action.

Here, therefore, there may also, as suggested in chapter 1, be a place to recognise the *limits* of ideas, and ideologies, or at least of analysis that takes them as independent forces: for ideology makes claims that may, or may not, be true, and may express aspirations, for example, for a pre-Islamic state or world-wide Islamic revolt, that may not be reached. In the realm of domestic politics, leaders claim to have the support of their people and to represent a nation when they do not; the more unrepresentative they are, and the more they steal and oppress, the more they may be driven to make countervailing claims, about God, history, enemies, the 'nation'. There may well also be, as noted, a gap between claim and reality because of that rhetorical overreaching which is part of the international stance of all states. Some check on claim, some evaluation of ideology in terms of social and political reality, needs to be, and can be, made. Herein lies the critique of Arab nationalism and of Islamist ideology that emerged in the 1990s. At the same time, a distinction has to be made between the declared and implicit, but practical, goals of ideology, between what the state or movement in question claims to be doing and what it may be judged in reality to be doing. In inter-Arab relations all that is *shaqiq*, 'brotherly', may turn out not to be. Some of the more savage Arab political jokes are told by Arab leaders and diplomats about *each other*.

Ideology is important, therefore, yet it cannot be taken at face value. In the case of inter-Arab politics, which are organised in the Arab League, claims of solidarity, with other states and with Palestine, may amount to

---

[24] Fred Halliday, *Revolution and Foreign Policy: the Case of South Yemen, 1967–1987*, Cambridge: Cambridge University Press, 1990; Vitali Naumkin, *Red Wolves of Yemen*, Reading: The Oleander Press, 2004.

far less than initially appears, if this contribution is evaluated in terms of financial, diplomatic or military support. Moreover, claims of solidarity with Palestine may serve, not so much to assist the Palestinians, as to present the state in question as a superior defender of the Arab interest than rivals: the logic may lie as much in, say, Egyptian rivalry with Syria and Iraq, or in Iraqi attempts to discredit other Arab states as traitors of the cause, as in any coherent policy of support for Palestine. A striking example, of which the author was a close observer, concerned the initiative taken by some PLO officials in western Europe after 1973 to open dialogue in public with members of the Knesset; in 1978–81, on the orders of Saddam, then keen to undercut Egypt as champion of the Arab 'cause', they were assassinated one by one in their capital of accreditation.[25] A similar scepticism can be applied to the issue of Arab unity, *al-wahda*. That Arab nationalist opinion and many Arab states promoted unity, from the 1940s onwards, is indisputable. Egypt presented itself as the champion of unity in the 1950s, being joined by Syria and Iraq as rivals in the 1960s, whilst, with Egypt's separate peace with Israel in 1979, it was Iraq's turn to cast itself as the *qala'a*, the citadel, of the Arab nation. For its part, and to some degree in reaction to the Egyptian variant of radical Arab nationalism, Saudi Arabia came from the mid-1960s to promote a coalition of Islamic states, and to finance and encourage Islamic opposition groups in a range of states. All of this was presented, on left and right, by republics and monarchies, as a product of ideological commitment, backed by domestic public opinion. Yet, as ever, *raison d'état*, Arab/Persian *maslahat*, watched contentedly from the wings.

However, as with proclamations of Arab solidarity, so with similar statements of unity, other interpretations suggest themselves in regard to *wahda*. In the first place, unity serves as a means of asserting a claim, not of fraternity but of hegemony, over the other state, and, potentially, its people, resources and territory. The slogan of 'unity', by denying the validity of frontiers between societies and presenting these as the creation of colonialist division and partition, subverts any concept of sovereignty and indeed self-determination of the separate peoples. In overriding the principle of non-interference in the internal affairs of other states, 'unity' legitimates working to weaken or overthrow that other state. As for the many forms of public displays of common purpose – conferences, joint communiqués, telegrams despatched, visits of ministers and heads of state, theoretically earnest exchanges of view on ornate sofas and so forth – these allow of an understanding in terms of state calculation as much as in terms of shared inter-Arab norms: leaders of poor states visit the oil producers to get money, conferences are held so that the more influential

---

[25] Patrick Seale, *Abu Nidal: a Gun for Hire*, London: Hutchinson, 1992, pp. 162–6.

states can recruit the others to their agenda and undermine their rivals, leaders of potentially rival states meet and embrace to prevent the other from supporting opposition *within* each state. In the Gulf, at least, all are driven to outdo the other in some evanescent form of competition – state mosques one day, international airports the second, corniches the third, private universities the fourth. Unity can therefore have, in international relations theoretical terms, a liberal or realist significance. Egyptian nationalist calls for unity were seen by many other Arabs as a campaign for Egyptian control of other states: union with Syria in 1958 was followed by the revolt of Syria against Egyptian rule in 1961. The Egyptian role in Yemen (1962–7) was a success but most Yemenis resented it. The Iraqi campaign for union with other Arab states had an equally practical import, as Kuwait found out in August 1990.

Similar concerns may be expressed about the uses, and abuses, of Islamic identity and solidarity in the Middle East, and beyond. 'Islam' became a significant factor in the foreign relations of Middle Eastern states when Saudi Arabia sought to promote opposition to Egyptian nationalism in 1965 and set up *al Rabita al-alimiya al-islamiya* (World Islamic League). It is striking how, despite the disbursal of large amounts of money, this Islamic 'petro-dollar' policy had, when other more concrete political interests came to the fore, limited effects. Saudi financial support for Egypt's break with the USSR in 1974–6 was substantial, but did not prevent President Sadat from deciding, in 1977, to visit Israel and from signing what Arab nationalist opinion called a 'capitulationist' peace with Israel in 1979. Many of the Islamist groups financed by Saudi Arabia in the 1980s proceeded, during the crisis following the Iraqi invasion of Kuwait in 1990, to support Iraq. Kuwait, similarly, had disbursed large amounts of money from the 1960s onwards to help poorer Arab states, yet in August 1990 the largest recipients – Sudan, Yemen, Jordan, as well as the Palestinians – all supported Iraq.[26]

The Iranian revolution of 1979 did, like all revolutions, denounce the division of societies into different nations and states, and sought to spread a radical cross-border, transnational message; but it is questionable here too how far Islamist radical internationalism went beyond the interests of Iran as a state. Iran was widely perceived, especially after it began its war with Iraq in 1980, as being a threat to other Muslim states. In addition, it was itself always careful to restrict its appeals for Islamic solidarity to cases where this was consonant with its interests; on other issues, where Islamic solidarity might have been expected to be evident – Nagorno-Karabakh, Chechnya, Kashmir, Sinjiang – Iran was largely

---

[26] James Piscatori, ed., *Islamic Fundamentalism and the Gulf Crisis*, Chicago: The Fundamentalism Project, American Academy of Arts and Sciences, 1991.

silent: state interest, a desire not to stimulate ethnic turmoil within Iran, and the wish to maintain relations with the non-Muslim states concerned – Armenia, Russia, India, China – prevailed. In sum, all that sounds normative is not ideological, about political belief. Actions, and interests, define words. If the ideological and the discursive are important, and need to be analysed and understood, this needs to be offset by an assessment of how other, less evident and more realist, concerns operate in determining state behaviour. Ideology is *a* factor in foreign policy, but as an *instrument* of state, as much as it is an independent limit on what the state does.

External context

Since state autonomy is two-sided, directed at society within and other states without, states may, as we have seen, derive *advantage* from this. In both dimensions this two-way context provides a *limit* on what states can do. It may also force them to act in unintended or unanticipated ways. In short, the ruler may wish, or dream, of full freedom of manoeuvre in the external realm; the reality is very different. And, of course, for many in the Middle East this is taken for granted: the policies of individual states are to all intents and purposes determined by external context, when not determined by external control. Ancient agendas, ever adaptable it would seem, live on. This latter is understood either as the conduct of other, usually menacing, regional states or as the control, overt and covert, exerted by prominent external powers, particularly the USA. Yet this is not just disjointed public culture. Analytic studies of Middle Eastern foreign policy take this as essential, be this in 'systems' or 'Cold War' terms.[27]

Both arguments, popular and academic, involve, therefore, a cogent assertion of the supposed link, mediated through the state, between external context and internal political and social system. Those who emphasise the regional system argue that, far from Middle Eastern conflicts being the *product* of the domestic, authoritarian, militarised and nationalist systems in each country, the opposite applies: it is the endurance of conflict and military rivalry *between* regional states that shapes the domestic system, and which, through a process of rivalry and spiralling insecurity, determines the foreign policy of the states in question. Those who emphasise the wider, international context make the same claim but on a global, extra-regional basis: here it is the Cold War, the world capitalist system or the global security structure, more recently the process termed

[27] Korany and Dessouki, *The Foreign Policies of Arab States*; Hinnebusch and Ehteshami, *The Foreign Policies of Middle Eastern States*, chapters 1–3.

'globalisation', which determines the character, including the foreign policies, of these states; either they are unable to act, by dint of being caught in a global structure of inequality and direction, or they are, through mechanisms overt and not so overt, controlled by external powers and their 'arrangements'. At its simplest this latter argument amounts to a theory of determinant external control, at times to a conspiracy theory. The two arguments, regional and international, are not, however, necessarily alternatives: one of the means by which, it is argued, external powers control Middle Eastern states, and their foreign policies, is precisely through regional allies, who are themselves the clients of the great powers. Thus, at various times, Israel, Iran, Saudi Arabia, Jordan were seen as clients of the west, while Iraq, Syria, Egypt, South Yemen were seen as clients of the Soviet bloc.

Realism and sceptical analysis may suggest a different conclusion, but to assert, as it is certainly the case, that within the Middle East itself it is almost universally believed that this external, regional and international, context determines foreign, indeed *all*, policy is important, in so far as an 'understanding' of the region is concerned. Israel blames enduring confrontation with the Arab states for the militarisation of its society, as does Turkey, confronting the Arabs, Russia and Greece; in both cases the claim is reinforced by stating that these external powers not only involve the state in an arms race and the threat of military confrontation, but support rebellious communities – Palestinians and Kurds respectively – within their own borders. The Arab world for its part justifies much of its foreign policy, and many of its internal difficulties, as a response to the threat posed by Israel and the generalised insecurity it maintains.

Such arguments may be overstated in so far as they are apologetic; they can by so doing justify the continuation of intolerant or authoritarian rule that is motivated by internal concerns. There is, however, an important element of truth in such claims: foreign policy, any foreign policy, is a process of interaction. This is the very meaning of the term 'system' as in 'international system', that is, of interaction whether it is in arms procurement, trade policy, the establishment and development of international organisations as with the UN or the Arab League. No state, whatever its internal character or wishes, can ignore what its neighbours and global interlocutors are doing. This is so especially if these neighbours make claims on territory, and appeal to citizens of the other state to revolt, let alone question the legitimacy of the other state's existence on the grounds that it is an imperialist or colonialist creation. The two most obvious forms of such regional system interaction in the Middle East are the arms races provoked by both the long-running Arab–Israeli and Gulf conflicts, and the coalition, rivalrous but concerted, of oil-producing states in regard to

oil prices and production arrangements with international energy companies. These classic forms of systemic determination of foreign policy
through competitive interaction have, more recently, been compounded
by concern at another form of regional context that no state can ignore,
that relating to the environment and shared issues pertaining to water.[28]
Here there is a great deal of (nationalist and self-serving) alarm and fake
compliance with international norms and laws, but in reality less is done.

This interaction of states is the most obvious, and long-established,
form in which regional context determines foreign policy. Yet in one
important sense such arguments about system do not go far enough,
for they miss what is another, equally important form of regional, and
global, determination: as historical sociology has argued and as has been
described above, external influences shape not only the foreign policies of
states, but, to a considerable degree, their *internal* character as well, and in
two ways. First, the very need for external confrontation, or collaboration,
affects the character of the state in regard to levels of military expenditure, deployment of investment on a regional basis, structuring of the
educational system. Beyond this institutionally formative consequence
of external interaction there is, moreover, something equally important
but longer term – what has been termed 'emulative linkage', the process
of imitation and competition in the fields of political system and social
policy. In the case of radical regimes, all had to have the forms of such
political systems, with ruling parties, central committees, mass organisations of workers, peasants, women, youth, five-year plans. At the same
time the press and media, and indeed the very language of politics, are
shaped by the regional context. In the 1920s Kemalist Turkey adopted
such a modular set of republican terms; in the 1950s and 1960s it was the
turn of the Arab states. In the case of Arab radical regimes, this may be
explicable in terms of a shared, proclaimed commitment to modernity.
Yet such competitive mimesis is also evident amongst more moderate,
and conservative, regimes. Thus examination of the origins of monarchy
in the Arab world show that the institution of 'king', *malik*, as opposed
to longer-established systems of authority such as Amir, Sultan or Imam,
was very much a product of the post-1918 world. The latest in a long
line of rulers turned monarchs was the Amir of Bahrain who, in 2001,
proclaimed himself King.

In the 1980s and 1990s this process of emulative homogenisation and
imitation was evident across a range of activities, from competition in
the Gulf states for prestige projects such as international airports, state
mosques and new universities, to the adoption by all regional states of

[28] See chapter 9.

bodies concerned with the environment. In the case of the more developed world, Europe or North America, such processes of homogenisation, for example, through the European Union, WTO and myriad other
international and private sector bodies, are evident, and part of a more
liberal interdependence. Even in areas like the Middle East, without such
co-operation or open internal regimes, interaction produces, therefore,
not only the shared interaction of the system, but an internal convergence and imitation as well. That this imitation is motivated as much
by the desire to compete as it is by any convergence of policy does not
diminish its importance.

   Popular allegations of control by external powers raise the same, equally
complex questions. Mention has already been made of the degree to
which, in the Middle East, the actions of all states are often perceived at
popular level in terms of 'links' to external powers, east and west in the
Cold War, the USA in the years following 1991. That conspiracy theory
is common, indeed pervasive, in accounts of Middle Eastern politics is
indisputable: almost no account of political change, be it the removal
of a minister of government or a coup d'état or revolution, is complete
without its conspiratorial element. External forces, with apparently all-
powerful planning capabilities, are invoked to explain what happens; no
local actor, let alone the chance of political events themselves, is permitted to intervene, to interrupt this tide of western manipulation and,
it seems, ever-successful scheming. Imperialism never makes a mistake.
Freemasonry, Zionism, MI6 and CIA are easily brought into the picture. The Iranian revolution was a product of British machinations; all
the demonstrators in Tehran in 1979 were Afghans. Saddam Hussein
invaded Kuwait in 1990 as part of an American conspiracy, and the USA
kept him in power thereafter. The Internet, and globalisation, are but the
latest chapters in this plan, one of whose aims is to undermine the Arabic
language. Every event fits a pre-ordained plot. Every people is the victim
of a worldwide and tireless enmity. The events of 11 September 2001
were, of course, the work of just such a plot, by Zionists, Serbs, the CIA,
or whatever.

   That this external influence should be seen as so powerful is, however,
hardly surprising. This is for a historical reason, the fact that *the* most
influential force affecting the Middle East over the past two centuries has
indeed been that of a more developed, prosperous and aggressive external world. Conspiracy theory generalises from a more limited set of *real*
conspiracies. Later chapters will examine in more detail the development,
intention and impact of external powers. Such influence can be seen as
acting at several levels: direct pressure or intervention by an external
power, sanctions and embargoes, long-run influences of dependence and

policy co-ordination, the very calculation by regional states and rulers as to how best to win the support of their great power allies. But the overall reality of this influence, and at times control and conspiracy, is not a myth: it is the dominant fact of the Middle East over two centuries, and more.

Here too, however, what appears as a distinctive regional trope needs some corrective context. Conspiracy theory may be the highest form of regional narcissism, but it is also, for the same reasons as are other forms of exaggerated particularism, flawed. With peoples as with individuals, a paranoid world view is disabling, and irrefutable; but it also reflects something real that happened in the past. The British *did* oust the nationalist Egyptian premier Ali Mahir in 1942. The CIA *were* behind coups in Syria in 1949. The overthrow of the Iranian prime minister Mosadeq in 1953 *was* the result of a conspiracy, between the CIA, MI6 and Iranian collaborators. The Tripartite Aggression by Israel, Britain and France against Egypt in 1956 *was* a conspiracy. On the other hand, conspiracy thinking is no preserve of the Middle East: the recent history of the Balkans, India and China shows plenty of evidence of conspiracy theory, as do the politics of the USA, or, in regard to the European Union, the UK.

Finally, recognition of this formative external influence must, however, be matched by two contrary considerations. First, there is a general need to question the degree to which Middle Eastern explanation in terms of such external control is, on closer examination, justified. The use of terms like 'clients', 'proxy', let alone 'agent' overstates the relationship. Secondly, there is a need for an examination of how, in particular cases, such influence actually worked. For some, perhaps many, in the Middle East the second part of this exercise is itself questionable, more evidence of a resistance to the obvious, historically enduring, western control of the region. Many cases of direct influence by external powers can be given: the most obvious are those coups d'état in which the US or British intelligence services played a role – Syria in 1949, Iran in 1953, Oman in 1970. Longer-run processes of state formation, including the training of military and civilian elites and the development of administrative structures, also reflect such externally dominant relations. Here we need to return to the international, colonial and post-colonial, formation of states. It is this, not some invisible, timeless, ever-scheming 'west', that has left a legacy of influence and contacts.

Yet within the undoubted, continuous context of external influence at all levels, from the strategic to the technological and entertainment, the significant autonomy of regional actors has always to be recognised. Thus during the Cold War none of the Arab allies of the USSR, not even the less powerful – guerrillas such as the PLO in Palestine or the Popular Front for the Liberation of Oman – accepted Soviet policy in full. The pro-Soviet Arab states – Egypt, Syria, Libya, Iraq, PDRY – all proclaimed policies and took initiatives that went against Moscow's wishes. In the two most spectacular cases of disagreement with Moscow, involving Egyptian initiatives vis-à-vis Israel, actions leading up to the 1967 and 1973 wars were taken without recourse to, let alone compliance with, Soviet policy. On the pro-western side, the two countries supposedly most linked to the USA were Saudi Arabia and Israel; yet they were unable in any overt way to resolve their own differences, and each took its foreign policy decisions with a considerable measure of autonomy, pleading, not least, the strength of domestic public opinion. Saudi Arabian refusal, despite US advice and over decades, to recognise Israel or liberalise at home, and the protracted Israeli refusal to respond to US wishes in regard to the West Bank and Gaza were indications that, for all that the external provides a context and constraint, it was not determinant. When it came to the more diffuse, but sensitive and important, areas of social and economic change, or response to the Internet or trade liberalisation policies, the limits of external influence were equally evident. The most important 'western' sense about the Middle East, in 1900, 1950 or 2000, was not of power, but of powerlessness, in the face of ideas, social forces and, not least, states over which they had, and could never have, significant control.

Back to the state

This chapter began by exploring the ways in which the institutional concept of the state, as developed within historical sociology, can be applied to an understanding of the Middle East. The case made here with regard to the state and international relations is not only that this can serve as the central analytic concept, but that through the state it becomes possible to assess the role of other formative factors such as economic ideas and social forces, and to analyse particular countries and specific events in a creative, comparative, but not straitjacketed, manner. The institutional concept of the state also provides a means of assessing the claims, central to all discussion of the region, made about the role of leaders, culture and external powers in shaping foreign policy.

The chapters that follow seek to take further the initial remarks made in this chapter. They aim to illustrate how, with due regard to the differences between societies and states, it is possible to provide a broad overview of the politics and international relations of the Middle East. The approach to this more detailed analysis must be first through history, with regard both to formation, to explain how we got to the Middle East as it is, and the *modern* Middle East, and also to assess those arguments, some theoretical, many partisan and conspiratorial, which beset the explanation of the region by misusing history, in detail and as general reductive framework. Here too the state is a central organising theme, but one which must be balanced by an awareness of that which constrains it: the global structure of power on the one hand, the impact of ever-changing non-state, social forces on the other.

Part II

History

3 The modern Middle East: state formation and world war

Perhaps no process has affected, through manifold and intricate mediate causes, the life of Iraqis more enduringly than the gradual tying up of their country in the course of the nineteenth and present centuries to a world market anchored on big industry and their involvement in the web forces or the consequences of forces unleashed by the Industrial Revolution. To this process is related, in one way or another, a series of large facts: among others, the advance in Iraq of England's power and capital, the turning to Europe's advantage of the system of Capitulations, the appearance of steam-propelled transports, the incipient imitation of modern techniques, the English conquest, the dismemberment of the Ottoman Empire and the severance of Iraq's northern Arab provinces from their natural trading regions in Syria, the setting up of a dependent monarchy with a new standing army and a new administrative machine, the exploitation of Iraq's oil resources, and the diffusion of elements of European culture.

> The Old Social Classes and the Revolutionary Movements of Iraq: a Study of Iraq's Old Landed and Commercial Classes and of its Communists, Ba'thists, and Free Officers[1]

The Middle East and the formation of Europe

For all its upheavals, the Middle East is a region of stable state entities. Its boundaries and constituent states have been relatively constant in modern times, far more so than, for example, twentieth-century Europe or East Asia. At the dawn of the twenty-first century the Middle East and North Africa comprised a world of nearly 400 million people, divided into twenty-one states (see Table 1 in the appendix). The majority of these states, eighteen in all, were Arab, while three others were, respectively, Turkish, Iranian and Israeli. On its frontiers were other countries, historically and strategically separate, but linked by culture, belief and trade. In the late twentieth century these countries had been brought

---

[1] Hanna Batatu, *The Old Social Classes and the Revolutionary Movements of Iraq: a Study of Iraq's Old Landed and Commercial Classes and of its Communists, Ba'thists, and Free Officers*, Princeton: Princeton University Press, 1978.

closer to the Middle East by the international effects of their own political conflicts: the Balkans, Transcaucasia, Central Asia, Afghanistan, India, Pakistan, the Horn of Africa.

Beyond diplomacy, such 'transnational' factors as migration, trade, tribe, arms, linguistic affinity, religious sect, all played their part, as some had done for centuries. The Middle East map had therefore, for all the conflicts of the region, been a relatively constant one since the end of World War I. There were exceptions to this record of continuity. Israel had been created in 1948 out of part of the British mandated territory of Palestine. Its status remained contested by much of the Arab world, a *kian* (entity), *musta'mar* (colony) or *'amil* (agent). For its part, Israel had not, after five decades of conflict, yielded to the demand for the creation of a Palestinian state in some of the same area, resorting to ludicrous ancient quotations, recycled tribal bigotry from 700 BC, or denial of the Palestinians' nationhood on arguments that applied equally to itself. Another more recent change to the map was in the Arabian Peninsula, where the two Yemeni states, North and South, separate since the early eighteenth century, had merged in 1990 into one state. But the greatest challenge to the post-1918 state system, the long-held Arab aspiration to a broader unity, had not been achieved. The reason is very simple: not that the Arabs are not a nation, but that separate states, once created, have little intention of surrendering their power. The most spectacular attempts to achieve *wahda* were, first, by negotiation, between Egypt and Syria in 1958–61, and, secondly, by force, in the Iraqi occupation of Kuwait in 1990–1. Both failed. Out of World War I a relatively resilient system of states had, therefore, been forged, which, for all the conflicts between and within Middle Eastern states, had endured for much of the twentieth century. Even if, improbably, the upheavals of the early twenty-first century were to destroy this system of states, it had, nonetheless, continued for close on a century.

The map of Middle Eastern states at 2000, indeed the very category of a region called 'the Middle East', is a product of two processes, the first long term, and the second modern: the evolution over centuries and millennia of the states and culture of the region, and the impact on the area, and in particular on the Ottoman empire, of the nineteenth- and early twentieth-century European economic and political system.[2] 'Arabia', the term now applied to the Peninsula (in Arabic *jazira*, literally 'island'), is over two thousand years old, having been used by the Greeks and Romans, and pre-dating by centuries the emergence of the Arabic language itself in the

[2] Bernard Lewis, *The Middle East: 2000 Years of History from the Rise of Christianity to the Present Day*, London: Weidenfeld and Nicolson, 1995.

fourth century AD. The modern Middle East, in shape and name, has in large measure been formed much more recently and by external pressures: the very term was invented in the early twentieth century (1902) as a function of imperial strategy.[3] Yet these external pressures of modern times have interacted with cultures, Christian and Islamic, indigenous peoples and, in some cases, states that long pre-dated the rise of European power. Modern states superimpose on, but do not eliminate, earlier divisions: that in western Libya, around Tripoli, food is based on couscous, whereas in the east, separated by hundreds of miles of desert, it is based on rice, is a *longue dureé* fact if ever there was one. Indeed for much of the history of the past millennia it has been in what is today called 'the Middle East' that some of the world's most effective and enduring states, and empires, have existed: Egypt can claim to have been a distinct state, with numerous interruptions for fragmentation and external rule, for seven millennia, and there have been distinct states in Iran and Yemen for three millennia, in Oman and Morocco for one. Of the four states in the world that can claim continuity over three millennia – China, Persia, Egypt, Yemen – three are in the Middle East. However, continuity of name is no guarantor of continuity of state; for example, the term *'iraq* existed in medieval times, but it denoted, not a state but an area, divided into Arab and *'ajami* parts, that covers what are today parts of Iraq and Iran.[4]

The interaction with the Middle East played a part in the creation of Europe itself. The legacy of this encounter has itself became a theme in the ideologies of European and Middle Eastern politics. This legacy can be used for diverse purposes – to profess a tendentious amity, or to claim that there has been a timeless antagonism.[5] In an age when there is much discussion of the role of the 'other' in constituting identity, it is worth examining this claim in the light of European–Middle East relations.[6] Some of this discussion overstates the function of the 'other' in the formation of societies and states, as if 'Europe' was constituted by interaction with the Muslim world or, more generically, with 'Islam'. This is not the case: for most European countries it was conflict with other Europeans, not 'Islam', that was most formative. The modern identities of the major western European powers – Britain, France, Germany – were formed in conflict with each other and through endogenous state

---

[3] Roger Adelson, *London and the Invention of the Middle East*, New Haven: Yale University Press, 1994, p. 22.

[4] See the entry, 'Iraq' in *The Encyclopaedia of Islam*, Leiden: E. J. Brill, 1960–.

[5] As in Samuel Huntington, *The Clash of Civilisations and the Remaking of World Order*, New York: Simon and Schuster, 1996.

[6] For comparison, Iver B. Neuman, *Russia and the Idea of Europe: a Study in Identity and International Relations*, London and New York: Routledge, 1996.

and economic growth. If there is a non-European world that has been important, it is first and foremost North America, in two world wars and in subsequent cultural, and political, incorporation. There was a major formative encounter with what is today the Middle East in the period *prior to* the rise of Islam, namely the conflict between classical Greece and Persia. The starting point of the history of Europe can be found in the Persian–Greek battles of Marathon (490 BC), Thermopylae (480 BC) and Salamis (480 BC), moments later canonised for state purpose even, in some cinematic versions where Thermopylae is cast as a battle between (Greek) freedom and (Persian) despotism, as prefiguring the west's battles in the Cold War. But this was followed by the conversion of much of Europe to a religion originating in the Middle East, Christianity, and the integration into the Muslim world of Andalucia and, later, the Balkans.

The pattern of external challenge, and cultural definition, was to recur with the rise of the Islamic states, in the seventh century AD. The Arab occupation of the Iberian Peninsula from the eighth to the fifteenth centuries, the continuous conflicts between Arab navies and European powers in the Mediterranean thereafter and, from the fifteenth century, the advances of the Ottoman empire through Turkey and then the Balkans, form an important part of the history of the continent. Yet while conflict there was, there was also much exchange and diplomatic alliance. Throughout the nineteenth century, as the diplomatic corps assembled for their annual audience with the Sultan, he would start the proceedings by declaring: 'And where is the representative of my great friend, the King of Poland?' Across the millennia and above all in that great marketplace of cultural interaction, fine music and good food that is the Mediterranean era, the Europe/Middle East contrast soon dissolved.[7] Nor has Islam as a religion been something external *to* Europe: Islam has been *in* Europe, in the Iberian Peninsula and in the Balkans, as well as in much of European Russia and Poland, throughout medieval and modern history.[8] The Middle East has not, therefore, been a distant, or passive, participant in the history of Europe, but neither has it been a constant 'enemy' against which Europe has defined itself.

Confrontation with Europe, 1600–2000

From the seventh century 'Islam' had the advantage, culturally as well as strategically, for almost a millennium, but a major reversal of Islamic

---

[7] For discussions at once evocative and elegiac see P. J. Vatikiotis, *The Middle East, from the End of Empire to the End of the Cold War*, London: Routledge, 1997.

[8] David Abulafia, ed., *The Mediterranean in History*, London: Thomas and Hudson, 2003.

influence came in the fifteenth century, with the Christian *reconquista* of Spain. This led to a standoff in the western Mediterranean, one facilitated by the displacement of Spanish expansion onto the Americas. The rise of modern Europe as an economic and strategic power after 1600 did not so much create this Muslim–European link anew, as it did for the Americas, Africa and Asia, as reverse the flow of influence in a context already marked by interaction. The dominant pattern of the modern period, that is since the seventeenth century, has been for non-Muslim Europe to prevail, over Muslim Europe on the one hand, and over the non-European Muslim world on the other; this has been true in the political and cultural fields as it has been in the economic and the strategic. The period of reversal in this relation lay therefore between 1492, the expulsion of the Jews and Christians from Spain, and 1683, when, after two or three centuries of advance, the Turks were turned back from the gates of Vienna.

This reversal was never wholly a Mediterranean affair. A few decades after Vienna, another European power in the north-east, Russia, began to push the Ottoman and Persian empires further into retreat. Russia advanced along the north coast of the Black Sea and then both into the Caucasus and Iran, to the east, and down the west side of the Black Sea: 1768–74 saw the first Russo-Turkish War; 1787–92 the second. In the treaties of Gulistan of 1813 and Turkmanchai of 1828, Iran ceded its Transcaucasian provinces, Armenia, Georgia and Azerbaijan, to Russia. In the late nineteenth century this Russian advance was reinforced by the emergence of nationalist movements amongst the Christian peoples of Turkey's European empire – in Greece, Serbia, Bulgaria, Romania. It was in the conflicts of the Balkans that World War I found its immediate cause; but this conflict was not an Ottoman–European one, but rather one between an assassin driven by Serbian nationalism and the Austrian state, represented by Archduke Franz Ferdinand. This 'intra-Christian' tension, as it was, provided the spark to war, when the archduke was shot in Sarajevo in July 1914: not much sign of the 'Clash of Civilisations', the supposed motor of history, here.

As Russia advanced southwards around the Black Sea, a parallel process of European encroachment was taking place, somewhat more slowly, on the southern coast of the Mediterranean, and in the countries around the Persian Gulf. The most dramatic western European incursion into the Ottoman empire was Napoleon's expedition to Egypt in 1798: although the French left in 1801, turned back by Egyptian and British pressure alike, Napoleon's occupation encouraged two processes, of indigenous autonomy, later Egyptian independence, from Istanbul, and of European competition for the spoils of the Ottoman empire. These set the pattern for the nineteenth century. The Congress of Berlin in 1878 brought independence to Romania and Bulgaria, while France acquired Tunisia, Britain Cyprus, and Austria control over Bosnia.

This protracted Ottoman retreat was to be the prelude to the most dramatic, and formative, period of state formation in the modern history of the region. By 1914 Turkey had lost nearly all of its empire in Europe, whilst in North Africa the British held Egypt and Cyprus, the French Tunisia, Algeria and Morocco, and the Italians Libya. Russia was established in the northern Black Sea, Caucasus and Transcaucasian regions, whilst in the Arabian Peninsula Britain had established a ring of client states, from Kuwait at the top of the Gulf to Aden in the south-west, the better to protect its strategic interests. This external encroachment intersected, however, with the continued formal independence, in law and in practice, of some Middle Eastern states. In the nineteenth century there persisted a continued autonomy, or room for manoeuvre, of regional states in relation to external powers. Conventional wisdom may long have held that the Ottoman empire and other regional forces, a semi-independent Egypt or a fully independent Iran, were passive actors in the international arena, but this is a simplification. The Ottomans were able to pursue an active policy of alignment with different European powers – fighting, for example, with Britain and France against Russia in the Crimean War of 1853–5, and with Germany and Austria against Britain, France and Russia in World War I.[9] Egypt was in effect independent from the time of the French withdrawal in 1801, and under Muhammad Ali and his son Ibrahim pursued an autonomous policy in the Levant and the Red Sea. But rising debts and external pressure limited its scope, and it succumbed to an Anglo-French condominium, in effect a British takeover, in 1882.

It was in this context, of Ottoman retreat and inter-European rivalry, that the modern concept of the 'Middle East' was born. Hitherto other, more specific, terms had been used – the 'Near East' referred to those Arab areas that bordered the eastern Mediterranean, the 'Levant' to the same, 'Asia Minor' to the Turkish land mass that divided the Arab world from Russia. 'Araby' was a half-political, half-literary term, sometimes denoting the Peninsula, sometimes the Arab East as a whole, sometimes an imaginary zone of Amirs, harems and tents. Coined by the American Admiral Mahan in 1902, the term 'Middle East' reflected a new awareness of the unity not only of the Ottoman domains, but of those wider areas, former Ottoman provinces, Arabia and Iran which lay between

[9] For a cogent rebuttal of conventional 'Sick Man of Europe' analysis see Inari Rautsi, 'The Eastern Question Revisited: Case Studies in Ottoman Balance of Power', Ph.D. dissertation, Faculty of Social Sciences, University of Helsinki, 1993.

Europe and India and the Far East: the 'Middle' distinguished it from these areas.[10] 'Middle East' became indeed the term used in the languages of the region itself – *al-sharq al-awsat* in Arabic, *khavar miane* in Persian, *haMizrach haTichon* in Hebrew, *ortadogu* in Turkish. Yet despite its apparently general acceptance, this was not a term universally used in the west, where some foreign ministries still continued to use 'Near East' to distinguish these countries from Arabia and Iran. Only after 1945 did the term 'Middle East' acquire general international currency. In Russia the western sense of the term was never adopted: there the distinction was between *srednii vostok*, or 'Central East', that is, those countries which bordered Russia and later the USSR – Turkey, Iran, Afghanistan – and *blizhnii vostok* or Near East, in effect the Arab world.

It was World War I which ended the long dismemberment of the Ottoman empire and which founded the modern state system that was to endure more or less thereafter.[11] This transformation took place in three ways. First, the Ottoman empire, already weakened by the pre-1914 wars in Yemen (the Vietnam of the Ottomans) and the Balkans, succumbed to military pressure, of Russia in the east, and Britain and its Arab allies in the south. Some of the bloodiest battles of World War I were fought on the Turkish–Russian front. In the Arab regions from which Turkey was expelled, the British and the French defined a set of new territorial entities which later became states: Lebanon, Syria, Iraq, Transjordan and Palestine. Secondly, out of the Turkish areas of the Ottoman empire a new, Turkish, state was created. Turkey itself was initially subject to severe external controls, formalised in the Treaty of Sèvres of 1920; this, amongst other provisions, allowed for the possibility of a separate Kurdish state in eastern Turkey, ceded areas in the west to Greece and placed the straits under international control. But a nationalist movement, led by Mustafa Kemal Pasha, rejected this settlement and, in a series of successful campaigns, reasserted Turkish independence; in 1923 a new agreement, the Treaty of Lausanne, defined the boundaries and independence of the new Turkish state. Thirdly, in another area vacated by Turkey, the western parts of the Arabian Peninsula, a power vacuum was created. In the rebellious province of Yemen, where Turkey had in effect recognised the autonomy of the local ruler, the Imam, in the Treaty of Da'an in 1911, an independent state emerged in 1918. Elsewhere, a new aspirant to power, the coalition of tribes led by the Saudi family, arose in Central Arabia and, in a series of campaigns, conquered four-fifths of the

---

[10] Adelson, *London and the Invention of the Middle East*.
[11] For a general introduction see Malcom Yapp, *The Near East since the First World War*, London: Longman, 1991.

Peninsula. In 1926 they proclaimed a new state, the Kingdom of Hijaz, and in 1932 the Kingdom of Saudi Arabia, named by regional convention after its ruling family. Thus while Turkey and Iran, non-Arab powers, emerged from World War I as independent and, once the new military rulers had settled in, unified states, the Arab world was fragmented: the latter lay, with the exception of the then impoverished Peninsula states of Yemen and Saudi Arabia, under colonial rule.

Colonialism and independence

In analysis of the politics, internal and international, of a region subjected to foreign domination, it is evidently tempting to ascribe everything to external forces. Much of the debate on modern Middle Eastern history is taken up with these external pressures, with, for example, the effects of the contradictory promises made during World War I by Britain and France. Yet external, imperial policy can only explain so much, just as it is limited in accounting for the coups and wars of the post-1945 period. The challenge for the writer is to establish an account in which all three layers of international relations – the policies of external powers, the development of relations between regional states, and the evolution of transnational and internal forces – are accorded proportionate recognition. As elsewhere, narrative is never a given. Middle Eastern facts there most certainly are, but there is and can be no single Middle Eastern history. Discussion of the period after 1918 involves, as ever, analytic choice; the choice is about *how* international forces operated: how far it is factors external to the region, how far it is regional states, and how far it is other processes, internal and transnational, that determined the course of events.

Compared with centuries of domination in Latin America and South Asia, the period of formal European colonialism in the Middle East was short-lived[12]: the former Ottoman territories appropriated after World War I were given independence within a decade or two – Iraq in 1932, Egypt in 1936, Syria and Lebanon in 1943 and 1946, Jordan in 1946. In Palestine the British announced in 1947 that they had abandoned the attempt to reconcile Jews and Arabs and in May 1948, in an act of extraordinary culpability, one that had consequences for many decades

---

[12] Elizabeth Monroe, *Britain's Moment in the Middle East 1914–1971*, London: Methuen, 1971; Michael Cohen and Martin Kolinsky, eds., *Demise of the British Empire in the Middle East: Britain's Response to Nationalist Movements 1943–55*, London: Cass, 1998; Malcolm Yapp, 'Suez Was Not the Turning Point', *Times Literary Supplement*, 10 July 1999. Yapp writes of Britain's 'speedy and unexpected departure': 'kicked out, bowed out and ran out'.

thereafter, at least, departed entirely.[13] Elsewhere, the impact of formal European rule was limited: the British protectorates in Arabia, with the exception of the colony of Aden port, were held for strategic reasons without great transformation of internal economic and social life. Iran was never formally subjugated to European rule: Britain and Russia delimited spheres of influence in 1907, and in 1919 the British tried to impose a protectorate, only to face nationalist as well as international opposition.

Although the colonial period was a matter of decades only, it nonetheless had a significant impact on politics and society, building as it did on centuries of informal influence. The external powers, long held at bay by the Ottoman empire and by their own inter-imperial rivalries, now came to play a determinant role in the central Middle East. Commitments made in World War I, which some Arabs saw as promising an independent, united Arab state, were not realised: the Arab world was now fragmented *and* subject to external rule. Yet it was in this period that the state system, in the sense of the coercive and administrative apparatuses, and the delimitation of geographic entities that they ruled, was established. Much of the later pattern of state behaviour, internally and externally, has its roots in this post-1918 period. Beyond its delineation of states, their names, capitals and boundaries, the period after 1918 was, therefore, one which also saw the creation of new administrative, and military, structures, and in which new patterns of international relations developed. States in both the juridical *and* historical-sociological sense derive from this period. Britain, in addition to its pre-1914 domains in Egypt, Cyprus and the Arabian coastline, now had two core strategic interests in the region: one was the traditional interest, of the Middle East as a component of imperial communications and strategic deployment, linking the Mediterranean to India and East Asia; the other, increasingly, was oil.

Prior to World War I oil exploration had been limited to Iran and what was later to be northern Iraq, then part of the Ottoman empire; but with the transfer of the British navy from coal to oil in 1914, and the growing world market interest in oil, the availability of oil in the Gulf, especially Iran, and the security of its transport came to have increasing importance. For its part, France now possessed in Syria and Lebanon states that it could add to its already substantial presence in North Africa, and which confirmed its status as a Mediterranean power. A third European power, Italy, which had increasing Mediterranean ambitions phrased in

---

[13] In regard to Malcolm Yapp's pithy summary of the end of British rule in the Arab world (note 12), there is no doubt as to the verdict here.

terms of a revival of the Roman empire, invaded Libya in 1911 and in the 1920s began large-scale colonial settlement. In the 1930s Italy sought to win support amongst Arab nationalists, and enhanced its overall strategic position by the occupation of Ethiopia in 1935. *Africana Italiana* now seemed to be secure.[14] All of these strategic advances were, of course, accompanied by grand, when not grotesque, ideologies of imperial vision and destiny on the part of each colonial power: the English as one of the 'lost tribes of Israel', the French as agents of civilisation, the Italians as inheritors of the Roman empire.[15] The Germans, excluded for the moment, had Goethe's *West-östlicher Divan* (1819)[16] and, briefly, the Afrika Korps of World War II.

The two outside powers that were later to dominate the politics of the Middle East were, at this stage, still on the margins. The USSR, formed in 1922 out of the Bolshevik revolution and inheritor of much of the Tsarist empire, retained a common frontier with the non-Arab Middle East, Turkey and Iran. In the immediate aftermath of World War I, as revolution and civil war in Russia intersected with upheaval in Middle Eastern states, it appeared that the Bolshevik revolution would spread in the region; thus Bolshevik forces briefly supported a Soviet republic in the Gilan province of northern Iran, while Moscow initially gave backing to radical forces inside Turkey. In September 1920, at the Congress of the Peoples of the East, held in the Baku Opera House, where at one point over-enthusiastic delegates forced the speaker to flee the stage in panic as they fired their rifles into the air, Soviet leaders, some of them Jewish, called for *jihad* against imperialism. But by 1921 this had come to an end: the pro-Soviet forces in Iran and Turkey had been defeated, and the USSR now sought to make peace with the new nationalist regimes along its southern frontier – Turkey, Iran and Afghanistan. The sealing of the frontier between the USSR and its neighbouring states in effect cut the Middle East and the Soviet Union off from direct contact with each other; this was a situation which was to endure, with some exceptions

---

[14] For a well-told and revealing account of the life of one Italian aristocrat who worked in Libya and Ethiopia before and during World War II see Sebastian O'Kelly, *Amedeo: the True Story of an Italian's War in Abyssinia*, London: Harper Collins, 2002.

[15] Virtually every European state claimed to have some special or mediating relationship with the region on the basis of connections past, present or imagined. The Greek claim to be the *yefira* or 'bridge' between Europe and the Middle East, or some part of it, is replicated across the continent; only the Dutch, who studiously avoided the region by sailing round Africa, and who, as a result of World War II, have a particular affinity with Israel, have forsworn such a self-serving mission.

[16] A collection of poems in twelve books (named *Singer, Hafiz, Love, Timur, Suleika*, etc.). In it the then love of Goethe's life, Marianne von Willemer, is cast as Suleika, inspired by the 1812 translation into German of Hafez's *Diwan*.

in World War II, until the end of the 1980s.[17] For its part, the USA
had almost no historic interest or interests in the Middle East, beyond
the work of its missionaries and certain isolated episodes: clashes with
'Barbary pirates' from Tripoli in what later became Libya, in 1801–5,
the opening of relations with Oman in 1833, and Theodore Roosevelt's
pressure on Morocco to rescue an American kidnapped there in 1904.[18]
After World War I, the USA had, under President Wilson, played a role in
the establishment of the League of Nations and hence in the trusteeship
system under which Britain and France took control of the former Arab
territories of the Ottoman empire. At one point an American Trusteeship
of parts of Anatolia was contemplated. However, Atatürk put a stop to
that. In effect the USA had, prior to World War II, no significant military
or political interests in the region.

The development of the Middle East after 1918 was not, however, just
a matter of external impact: here we return to the analytic balance of
external and internal factors. Within the strategic context shaped by this
international domination, the states of the region continued to play some
autonomous role, even when not fully independent; this autonomy was
evident both in relation to each other and in their development of foreign
policy stances that strengthened their position with their domestic public
opinion. It was these inter-state relations of the post-1918 period that
were in part to lay the bases for the regional politics of the post-1945
period. In the Arabian Peninsula, Saudi Arabia had established itself as
an independent kingdom in 1926, but, while forced to keep out of the
Syrian desert by the French and British control of the new Syria and Iraq
respectively, had also annexed two-thirds of the territory belonging to
Kuwait (Treaty of 'Uqair, 1921) and then took three provinces of Yemen
(Treaty of Ta'if, 1934); constrained by British power established on the
periphery of the Peninsula, and recipients of a small subsidy to ensure
good behaviour in World War I, the Saudi state was in no significant way
thereafter subject to British control. For its part Turkey made no preten-
sions of being beholden to external powers and from 1923 conducted an
independent foreign policy, maintaining neutrality in the growing conflicts of Europe and in the initial phases of World War II. Iran under Reza
Khan, who crowned himself Shah in 1925, also came to assert itself more

---

[17] On the early foreign policy of the USSR see E. H. Carr, *The Bolshevik Revolution*,
Harmondsworth: Penguin, 1973, vol. III. See also the outstanding study by Dr Ayla Gol,
'The Place of Foreign Policy in the Transition to Modernity: Turkish Policy towards the
South Caucasus, 1918–1921', Ph.D. thesis, London School of Economics, 2000.
[18] The 'Barbary' incident is commemorated in the words of the battle song of the US
Marines, 'From the Halls of Montezuma, To the Shores of Tripoli'. Oman was the first
Arab state to have diplomatic relations with Washington (1833).

forcefully, challenging Britain over the royalties of the Anglo-Persian Oil Company in 1933. The fact that the British force in Iran helped Raza Khan to come to power in March 1921 meant little in later years. During the 1930s, and in an attempt to offset the influence of Russia and Britain, the two powers that had dominated it, Iran developed a closer relationship with Germany, long favoured as a country *without* imperial designs on it. It also took a step, albeit a small one, to formalise co-operation with other states, in the Saadabad Pact signed with Iraq and Turkey in 1937.

Of the Arab states initially under British control, Iraq was the most assertive, in seeking, especially after independence in 1932, to influence the affairs of the 'Fertile Crescent', that is, Syria, Lebanon and Palestine. Egypt sought to reassert its historic claim to Sudan, based on the 'unity' of the Nile valley. However, over these inter-state relations hung, to an increasing degree, the Palestine issue. During World War I, in the Balfour Declaration of 1917, Britain had declared its support for a 'Jewish national home' in Palestine. As the years passed, and as relations between Arabs and Jews worsened in Palestine, all the major Arab states came to play, or seek to play, a more important role in that affair, and to form a united front against the consolidation of a Jewish political community in Palestine. By the end of World War II, the basis of an inter-Arab politics had been laid: a League of Arab States was established in March 1945, with British encouragement, in the hope that it would be dominated by Egypt. In the UN negotiations over Palestine in 1947 the Arab states sought collectively to resist pressure for partition. When it came to inter-state war in 1948–9 with Israel, Egypt, Syria, Jordan and Iraq were all directly involved in the conflict. In this way, through the incremental advent of independence, increasing contact with each other *and* confrontation with an enemy, an inter-Arab politics had been formed. Much of what the Arab states sought to do – overcome post-colonial fragmentation, resist the creation of Israel – failed. Yet this did not diminish the significance of these inter-Arab relations, or the pan-Arab feelings which were created over modern times and which persisted, and persist, despite the divisions, calculations *and* rivalries of states. It was easy to say Arab nationalism had later failed. But nationalism is partly a matter of sentiment and a shared sense of collective grievance; neither in August 1900 nor in the aftermath of March–April 2003 would it be said that these feelings had disappeared.

State formation and social change

In retrospect, however, these relations between states, external and regional, in the 1918–39 period may have been less important for later history than what was taking place *within* states. It was not only in the great power politics, nor in the growing inter-state relations of the region, but in the less visible, but potentially equally significant, domain of the formation of states and societies that the post-1918 period was to prove so important for later events. In large measure, the political, social and international formation of the region took place in this period. It was through this *internal* process of change that the social, ideological, and hence political dimensions of the modern Middle East were so decisively shaped.

Four processes in particular merit attention. One was the creation of modern state institutions. Defining a Middle Eastern map in the years immediately after 1918 provided the set of empty boxes or shells within which these states could, and did, develop as institutions of power and appropriation, with aspirations both internal and external. These were institutions of administration and coercion, run by colonial and then nationalist powers, that imposed more effective control on the territories they came to rule. They provided employment for growing numbers of people, and came to direct society – economic development, education – according to the wishes of the rulers. Of no little importance for the later politics of these countries, the inter-war years saw the development of armed forces; these were the first institutions in these societies to be attuned to modern values and, with their now distinct social and economic interests, increasingly became aspirants to political power and to the status of defenders of the nation.[19]

Secondly, these states embarked, as part of their attempt to assert control and in order to forge more effective and malleable political communities, on the forging of a national identity. Part of this involved the assertion and maintenance of claims with regard to other states, based on what were viewed as historic rights, or on denunciation of the partitions and divisions imposed by colonialism. Egypt claimed Sudan, Syria, Lebanon, Iraq, Kuwait, Saudi Arabia the rest of the Peninsula. Yemenis, citing al-Hamdani, the medieval geographer, said that Yemen ran from Mecca (or Ta'if) to Muscat. Education was a central means for the promotion of these new identities, and rested upon the creation of a national history, drawing where available on both Islamic and pre-Islamic elements; while each state sought to assert its own individual identity and historic validity, each also made a claim to be part of wider communities – Pharaonic (Egypt), Sabaean and Himyaritic (Yemen),[20] Sumerian and

---

[19] On Iraq see Charles Tripp, *A History of Iraq*, Cambridge: Cambridge University Press, 2001; on Egypt, P. J. Vatikiotis, *Nasser and his Generation*, London: Croom Helm, 1978.

[20] Though the nuances of the Phoenician, or Punic (Arabic *buniqi*), varied: in Lebanon a Christian community used it to ward off association with (Arab) nationalism, in Malta it served to proclaim the island was not Arab at all, in Tunisia and Libya it was part of just an earlier step towards a composite Arab Muslim identity.

Mesopotamian (Iraq), Phoenician (Lebanon, Libya, Tunisia), but also Islamic, Arab in some cases, Iranian and Aryan in the case of Iran, ancient Hittite, Anatolian and modern Europe in the case of Turkey. Zionism engaged in a similar promotion of a modern nationalism, while drawing on both selected and invented elements of the biblical past. School textbooks, public statues, presidents' speeches, even cookbooks, were moulded to meet this need. That these ideologies were new, multi-layered and instrumental, and were subject to considerable dispute within their respective countries, did not detract from their impact at the time or their influence on later events. On this, more will be said in chapter 7.

Thirdly, these states embarked, or thought they had embarked, on a process of cultural and ideological change, closely linked to the consoli-dation of their own power; this state-directed change in society promoted a certain form of secularisation. Secularisation, a term not often well defined (Arabic *almaniya*, Turkish *laiklik*, Persian *sekularizm*), reflected a commitment to the values of the modern world, as exemplified in Europe; but in the modernisation of Middle Eastern states, secularism was not part, as it had been in areas of Europe, of a process of building tolerance between communities or of creating a civic and legal space independent of the state. *Secularisation was, above all, a policy intended to strengthen states*: it was a reflection of the desire of these states to reduce, or break, the power of an alternative centre of power, the *ulema* in the Arab world, the *mullahs* in Iran, the *hocas* in Turkey, who had hitherto exercised such influence on education, land and law, and to forge a new ideology of control over society.[21] The most dramatic instance of this secularisation was the abolition by Atatürk, in 1924, of the institution of the Caliphate, up to then the formal source of Islamic authority and direct descendant of the Prophet's authority, as well as of the Ministry of *shari'ah* and the *shari'ah* (Turkish *Çeriet*) courts.[22]

All of these three processes – state formation, nationalism, secularisa-tion – were changes brought about from above and in response to external pressures; of equal import was the fourth process, what was happening below. The final years of the Ottoman empire and, even more so, the years following the imposition of the post-1918 settlement saw the emergence, in a range of countries, of popular movements, combining social with eco-nomic demands. Prior to World War I there had been major upheavals in Iran (the Constitutional Revolution of 1906–8), Turkey (the Young Turk

[21] Nikki Keddie, 'Secularism and the State: Towards Clarity and Global Comparison', *New Left Review*, no. 226, November–December 1997.
[22] Bernard Lewis, *The Emergence of Modern Turkey*, Oxford: Oxford University Press, 1961, pp. 256–60.

revolt of 1908 and its aftermath) and Egypt (1907). Armenian nationalism and those of the Balkans had become more assertive, and violent. In
the years after 1918 there were local and nationalist uprisings in Egypt
(1919), Iraq (1920), Syria (1925) and Palestine (1936), as well as in
Morocco (1926). The Kurds of Turkey, Iraq and Iran also rose in revolt
against military ruler and colonial power alike. These created a context
in which both colonial rulers and incumbent states faced challenges from
below, to which they replied with a combination of coercion and co-
optation. These revolts contested external domination and, in the case of
Palestine, immigration; they also challenged incumbent social and political elites, some only just installed, who were seen as tied to the colonial
powers.

Inevitably, too, the process of secularisation, promoted by states and
social change alike, was to produce a counter-reaction, one that was,
decades later, to emerge in the form of an Islamist, or fundamentalist, politics that throughout the region challenged the power of secular
states.[23] The most powerful of these groups, the Muslim Brotherhood,
was founded in Egypt in 1928, in reaction to the secularising trends in
the Arab world and Turkey. In Turkey and Iran the bases of later Islamist
movements were also formed at this time: the electoral victory of the
Democratic Party in Turkey in 1950, the June 1963 uprising in Iran and
all that followed were part of the rejection of a secularisation driven by
states. The later emergence of religious movements across the region
invoking Islam therefore grew out of the state's extension of control in
this formative period: the ideological roots of 11 September 2001 lay, as
its exponents like al-Qa'ida themselves proclaimed, in the 1920s.

In sum, the rise of nationalisms, the disruptions of World War I, the
very formation of the new state system and resistance to secularisation had
produced a context in which more widespread social and political movements could, and did, emerge. The stage was set, by this combination of
external and internal processes, for a more dramatic and radical phase
of Middle Eastern politics; that much of this drama and radicalisation

[23] The term 'fundamentalist' was originally coined in the 1920s to refer to Christians who
insisted on a literal reading of the Bible, in regard to the issue of creation. It has come more
generally to be applied to all those who, within their specific religion, seek to combine a
return to the sacred texts with the promotion of a political movement justified in terms
of those texts. There are problems with the application of the term to other religions –
Islam, Judaism, Hinduism, Buddhism – but not so as necessarily to invalidate its use.
The term 'Islamist', preferred by some, is used in this book interchangeably with Islamic
fundamentalist. 'Muslim' or 'Islamic', by contrast, refer only to the profession of a religious belief or culture, not to the aspiration to a particular politics. For more clarification
see Nikki Keddie, 'The Islamist Movement in Tunisia', *Maghreb Review*, vol. 11, no. 1,
1986, pp. 26–39.

was promoted from outside did not contradict the fact that the forces unleashed had been formed *within* these states and societies.

The impact of colonialism

Beyond its impact on states, economies and societies, colonialism had one further consequence – its important impact on the ideology and sentiment of peoples in the region.[24] In North Africa, European colonisation involving large-scale settlement and agrarian change generated major armed resistance in Algeria and Libya, and powerful mass nationalisms in Morocco and Tunisia. Yet of the core countries of the Middle East, and leaving out the dramatic and exceptional case of Palestine, only the society and economy of Egypt were, on broad socio-economic indicators, transformed fundamentally by, and subjected to the extended rule of, European power. In effect, from the late 1860s, when the rural economy was transformed by the development of cotton, until the military coup of 1952 and the later resolution of the control of the Suez Canal, Egypt experienced a form of domination comparable in its economic and social effects to that which had been imposed on Latin America, India or South-East Asia in the colonial era. Hundreds of thousands of European immigrants settled in the towns and cities. The rural economy was oriented to exports designed to meet the needs of industrial Europe. The political system was pervaded by external influence. The key strategic points – ports and the canal – were under direct foreign control.[25]

   Yet this appearance of a relatively superficial and transitory colonialism in the Middle East as a whole belies a deeper impact of the European colonial powers in the late nineteenth and early twentieth centuries. In the first place, the economic, social and intellectual impact of Europe had long pre-dated, and was far wider than, that of formal colonial control. From the late eighteenth century onwards rulers, intellectuals and soldiers in the region had been concerned to compete with, and learn from, that which was taking place in Europe. The formal colonial experience therefore compounded a much more sustained European hegemony. Some of this response by rulers was designed to strengthen states – the Ottoman empire, Iran, Egypt – *against* European power; some was designed to reconcile what could be learnt from Europe, as in the field of science, with the claims and values of a reformed Islam. As elsewhere in the world,

[24] Alejandro Colás, *International Civil Society: Social Movements in World Politics*, Cambridge: Polity Press, 2001.
[25] Roger Owen, *The Middle East in the World Economy 1800–1914*, London: I. B. Tauris, 1993, chapters 5 and 9.

the contact with, and partial imitation of, European hegemony provided the form, the language, the very goals of resistance and rejection –
'independence', development, political mobilisation.[26] The contrast
between newspaper titles of 1900 and 2000 is often striking – the former proposing change and modernity, the latter some return to tradition. Secondly, the extended form of European control over the region,
ranging from direct military intervention and colonial rule, to commercial, financial and cultural, not to mention religious, influence, produced
in the region a strong sense of resentment at this external power. Two
factors are worthy of special note: the breaking of promises made to
some Arabs in World War I, and the behind-the-scenes manipulation of
governments and rulers.[27] Later nationalisms and religious movements
combining Islamic with nationalist themes drew on this experience of
domination, one that was resented as much, arguably even more, because
it was as often indirect as direct. From the 1990s, globalisation', later,
a free-fire zone for wild claims about exploitation, 'cultural aggression',
conspiracies and so forth, was a gift to such opponents of the 'west'.
Thirdly, the post-1918 formation itself contained within it the seeds of
later rejection and contestation: the events that followed World War I, as
western powers sought to impose their rule in the Arab world, but also in
Turkey (the Treaty of Sèvres, 1920) and Iran (the attempted 1919 imposition of a protectorate, the 1941 invasion), provided a historical reserve
of rejection that was to fuel nationalism in these countries for the rest of
the century.

For the Arabs two issues above all, arising from the promises of World
War I, were predominant: partition, or *taqsim*, the division of the Arab
world into separate states where nationalism has posited a single people;
and the settlement of large numbers of European Jews in Palestine. These
two themes, partition and Zionism, formed the tinder of much nationalist
resentment, to which were later added in plentiful supply other sources
of protest – western control of the Arab world's oil revenues, support
for conservative rules such as in Saudi Arabia, the retention of military
strongholds in Suez and Aden, and support for post-1945 Israel. For the
Iranians the sense of indirect western control was reinforced by the reality, substantive enough even if less than the Iranians supposed, of covert
intervention: many believed Reza Khan had come to power with British

[26] Albert Hourani, *A History of the Arab Peoples*, London: Faber and Faber, 1991, Part IV,
'The Age of European Empires'; Reinhard Schulze, *A Modern History of the Islamic
World*, London: I. B. Tauris, 2000, Part I, 'Islamic Culture and Colonial Modernism
1900–1920'; Lewis, *The Middle East*, chapter 17, 'New Ideas'.

[27] George Antonius, *The Arab Awakening: the Story of the Arab National Movement*, first
published 1938; reprinted New York: Capricorn, 1965.

help in 1921, a not entirely inaccurate supposition, but of limited sub-sequent import. External manipulation was most spectacularly evident in the 1941 Anglo-Russian invasion and in the case of the military coup organised in 1953 by the American and British secret services. As for Iraq, no one can comprehend the depth of nationalist feeling there in the 1980s and 1990s, without taking into account resentment at the suppression of the Rashid Ali rising of 1941 and the illegal British reoccupation of the country that followed (*inter alia*, a major ideological element in the nationalist upbringing of one Saddam Hussein, born 1937).

This history of external intervention, and continued external attempts to influence the states of the region, not least during World War II, entailed that the mere fact of formal independence did not remove, or substantially diminish, the sense of external control pervasive in the region. For many Arabs, the persistence through the 1950s, 1970s and beyond of western support for Israel, and for conservative and profligate oil-producing Arabian monarchies, was an index of continued and malevolent external domination. In regard to the latter, the process known neutrally in western literature as 'recycling' (of petrodollar income and funds) was just another form of theft, reappropriating with one hand, as investment in western markets, what had just been given, in higher oil revenues. The wars and insecurity of the region, stimulated when not directly perpetrated by Israel, were just a means of discouraging any investment of oil revenues, or multinational foreign direct investment (FDI), in the region and peoples themselves. For Iranians, the view of the world as hostile and conspiring lasted beyond the reign of the Shah through the years of the Islamic Republic. In Turkey in the late 1990s, in a country strong in economic and military terms, government officials would lean across their desks in Ankara and lecture western visitors who raised the Kurdish question about the 'Sèvres Syndrome', the tendency, as understood in Turkey, of western governments to divide, weaken or interfere in the affairs of Turkey and its neighbours.[28]

All of this sense of domination, at both popular and elite levels, was, of course, overlain by a reality, that of economic imbalance, great and growing, between the region and the west; far from diminishing, this continued to increase throughout the twentieth century, as it had through the eighteenth and nineteenth. In overall terms, the fundamental international relation, one that underlay and gave meaning to the military or political systems, was the gap in economic, scientific and military power between the Middle Eastern states and peoples and those of Europe and other developed countries. In sum, nationalism and a sense of powerlessness

[28] Author's research visit, Foreign Ministry, Ankara, April 1998.

were not autonomous ideational constructs, part of some free-floating, immovable and to the west impenetrable political culture. It was very tangible external hegemony, whether direct or indirect, that from the recomposition of state power after 1918 to the rollercoaster of globalisation underlay the pervasive political culture of domination.

World War II and its consequences

In its promotion of 'the', or perhaps, rather, 'an' Arab revolt,[29] in its impact on the Arabian Peninsula and Iran, and, above all, in bringing about the final end of the Ottoman empire, World War I laid the foundations of the modern Middle East. Yet World War II, if a degree less dramatic in its direct impact on the region and in its mid-term consequences, had nonetheless a major transformative role. In contrast to the case in World War I, the central areas of the Middle East were not directly involved in combat: only North Africa, where Italian and German forces on the one hand and Allied forces on the other fought between 1939 and 1943, was a direct theatre of war. Even there, the participation of local military and political forces was minimal. In Iran the British and Russian occupation begun in August 1941 ended in 1946. Soviet support for autonomous regions in Azerbaijan and Kurdistan was unsuccessful. In contrast to World War I, and with the exception of the partition of Palestine between Jewish and Arab forces in the immediate aftermath of World War II, the political map of the region remained as it had been before.

Yet this comparative insulation of the Middle East from the global, anti-Axis campaign contrasted with other, dramatic changes in the international and internal politics of the region during the early 1940s. In the first place, World War II hastened, as it did elsewhere, the end of the British and French imperial regimes, their 'moments', in the Middle East. During the war itself British rule had been challenged and those challenges suppressed: in the nationalist military revolt in Iraq in 1941, led by Rashid Ali Gaylani, and in resistance from the Egyptian government in 1940 and 1942. But although British power and its military presence in Egypt and elsewhere increased during the war, for strategic reasons, this marked a penultimate flare-up before a final demoralised withdrawal, rather than a re-establishment of enduring colonial power.

---

[29] Symbolically important in some later nationalist accounts as this may have been, the role of the Hashemite forces under Amir Feisal in the overthrow of the Ottoman empire in the Arab east was minimal. The maximum number of ill-trained and ill-equipped 'Arab' forces was 3,000, in contrast to a British-officered and profesionally trained and equipped imperial force of 250,000. Up to 300,000 Arabs fought with the Turks.

For some, Britain remained in its Arabian colonies, and France in North Africa. There was also the unresolved question of British control of the Suez Canal Zone in Egypt, from which London did not withdraw until 1954. Yet while formal independence had preceded it, the real independence of the major Arab states was definitely hastened by the world war, by an attendant rise of nationalism in the Arab world, and by the first stirrings of a global anti-colonial climate to which a new assertive USSR would contribute.

One Arab country that was, however, considerably affected by World War II was Egypt: the crisis of the monarchy, and the rise of communist, nationalist and Islamist movements dates from this period. Iraq too lived through nationalist upheaval following the events of 1941; as noted, these were to influence, and harden, later generations, including that of Saddam Hussein.[30] This British disengagement was nowhere more evident than in its most controversial Middle Eastern territory, Palestine. In the late 1930s British policy had oscillated between favouring partition into Jewish and Arab zones, in the Peel Commission Report of 1937, and envisaging an independent Palestine with an Arab majority within ten years, in the White Paper of 1939. The shift to the latter position had been motivated by the desire to prevent Germany and Italy from mobilising Arab opinion against Britain and its allies in World War II. By the end of the war, however, the balance had shifted dramatically the other way: belated knowledge of the fate of the Jewish population in Nazi-occupied Europe, with six million dead, the greater engagement of the USA *and* the USSR on the side of Zionism, the outbreak of a Jewish guerrilla campaign against British forces in 1946, and Britain's general weariness with empire following an exhausting global war, all led in 1947 to the British announcing that they would withdraw from Palestine without making arrangements for a successor political settlement.

As a consequence, conflict between Jews and Arabs within Palestine began in 1947 and Arab armies intervened after British forces left in May 1948. Jewish forces gradually prevailed over their Arab opponents, and the territory of Palestine was thereby divided: Israel took part of the territory, Jordan took the West Bank and part of Jerusalem, Egypt the Gaza Strip. Up to a million of the 1.4 million Arab Palestinians of Mandate Palestine became refugees.[31] For the Middle East, the Palestine war was, perhaps, the most dramatic consequence of World War II, the

---

[30] Said Aburish, *Saddam Hussein*, London: Bloomsbury, 2001, p. 32.
[31] Christopher Sykes, *Crossroads to Israel*, London: Collins, 1965; Naomi Shepherd, *Ploughing Sand: British Rule in Palestine 1917–1948*, London: John Murray, 1999; Eugene Rogan and Avi Shlaim, eds., *The War for Palestine*, Cambridge: Cambridge University Press, 2001.

one case where, as a result of processes both international and regional, a redrawing of the Middle Eastern map occurred. Yet in the longer run even the extent of this territorial redrawing remained open: in negotiations on the settlement envisaged fifty years later, in the Oslo Accords of 1993, the Israelis and Palestinians were arguing, and later still fighting, over the partition of the very same territory that had been covered by Mandate Palestine. An unhappy couple they were, destructive and self-destructive in turn, but they fought within a house, a territorial box, delineated by the UK and France decades earlier, after World War I.

World War II had, however, other significant consequences for the region.[32] For Turkey it marked the end of the Kemalist policy of neutrality, as Ankara, sensing the victory of the Allies over Germany, and concerned about the demands of a now emboldened Russia, belatedly joined the anti-German alliance in February 1945 and then sought a closer relationship with the west. For Iran World War II had very different consequences. In its attempt to offset Russian and British influence by building ties to Germany, Iran had finally overreached itself: following the German invasion of Russia in June 1941, with a possible German advance on the oilfields of the Caucasus, Britain and Russia ordered Iran to expel German advisers. When this had not occurred, they occupied the country in late August. The ruling monarch, Reza Shah, was exiled, his young son Mohammad Reza Pahlavi II installed. This occupation ushered in a period of economic tension and political upheaval, one in which rival political forces challenged the monarchy as well as each other.[33] As in Egypt and Iraq, nationalism, socialism and Islamism all bred among intellectuals, aspiring politicians and, to some degree, the people in this new atmosphere.

These changes within the Middle East during and after World War II also involved a shift in the balance of external powers in the region. If hitherto Britain and France had been the dominant external powers, and were to retain influence into the 1960s and even 1970s, their place as external hegemon was gradually being taken by the USA. Four trends in particular helped the USA come to play this role: first, the establishment during and after World War II of police and military links with some states, initially Iran and then Turkey; secondly, a rising US interest in what was now the major economic prize in the region, oil; thirdly, the growth, slowly formed if decisive at first and later much more comprehensive, of an especially close relationship between the USA and Israel; fourthly,

---

[32] Barry Rubin, *The Great Powers in the Middle East, 1941–1947*, London: Frank Cass, 1981.
[33] Louise Fawcett, *Iran and the Cold War: the Azerbaijan Crisis of 1946*, Cambridge: Cambridge University Press, 1992.

a strategic concern with the newly influential, and potentially 'forward', USSR. These processes combined were to lay the basis for what was to become the pattern of international relations in the Middle East during the next great phase of global politics that lasted from the late 1940s through to the late 1980s, the Cold War.

As much in establishing the state system as in the creation of other, intra-regional conflicts and aspirations that were to feed into the Cold War, the period from 1918 to 1948, from the end of the Ottoman empire to the emergence of the state of Israel, thus laid the foundations for later developments. This influence was as evident in the internal dimensions of state, society and economy as it was in inter-state relations as such. From the late 1940s onwards the Cold War was conducted within a global, strategic, ideological and economic context, and it was determined, as far as the Middle East was concerned, from outside. Yet neither east nor west ever found it easy to influence their allies, Arab, Israeli, Turkish or Iranian. The impact of that Cold War was, to a considerable extent, shaped by the states and societies that were already established in the region.

4   The Cold War: global conflict, regional upheavals

Global confrontation, asymmetric interests

The intersection of great power and regional states on one hand, with that of states and social movements on the other, was, therefore, to be dramatically reaffirmed in the Cold War. The Cold War, which lasted from the late 1940s to the end of the 1980s, was a multi-layered competition: while it most evidently did involve wars and military competition between east and west, directly and in support of allies in the Middle East, it also involved more than a mainly military contest, a rivalry for political loyalties and for economic advantage.[1] Yet it is not enough to list this diversity. No international context presents as much analytic challenge as do these four decades of Cold War: here dramatic military crises, protracted inter-state negotiations and upheavals within states, the events of politics itself, were interwoven with a set of less visible, but in the longer run decisive processes, of social, economic and ideological change. The challenge to any analysis of the Cold War is to do justice to both dimensions, relating events and conflicts of the Cold War at the state level to underlying historical and sociological dynamics.

The inter-relationship of these different dimensions was not one of straightforward confrontation between the two blocs as it was in Europe. Rather the Cold War in the Middle East was beset by strategic crosscurrents. The United States, for example, had political and strategic interests in Israel, but its main economic interests, in oil, were in the Arabian Peninsula.[2] Even that interest in oil was not so much one of direct dependency of American firms importing oil to the USA itself, as it was financial and political, in terms of the advantage given over other developed allies that were so reliant on Gulf imports. For its part, the

---

[1] Richard Crockatt, *The Fifty Years War: the United States and the Soviet Union in World Politics, 1941–1991*, London: Routledge, 1995; Yezid Sayigh and Avi Shlaim eds., *The Cold War and the Middle East*, Oxford: Clarendon Press, 1997.

[2] Simon Bromley, *American Hegemony and World Oil*, Cambridge: Polity Press, 1991; Daniel Yergin, *The Prize: the Epic Quest for Oil, Money and Power*, London: Simon and Schuster, 1993.

Soviet Union established strategic alliances with Arab nationalist regimes, such as Egypt and Iraq, even as the latter suppressed communist parties. The two major powers in the Cold War also had very different geographic interests in the region: the USSR, which bordered the Middle East, was most concerned about the emergence of strategic and other challenges along its southern border, and therefore concentrated particularly on its non-Arab neighbours – Turkey, Iran, Afghanistan – what it termed the 'Central East'; the USA was more concerned with Israel and the Arab world. The USSR, the largest oil producer in the world at 12 mbd in the 1970s, had no direct interest in Middle Eastern oil, except in so far as it benefited from OPEC price rises, while the USA, and the western economies as a whole, came increasingly to rely on it for oil supplies, trade and investment funds, a reappropriation of oil rent masked as 'recycling'. The European colonial powers, Britain and France, sought to manage a transition from colonial to post-colonial influence, in ways that were not always consistent with US aims. For its part China had for decades maintained a rhetorical and remote stance on the Middle East that only matured into a strategic and commercial engagement in the 1990s.[3] Much as it postured on Middle Eastern issues, above all to discredit the Russians, China had no significant impact on any regional country or issue; indeed, for most of the period upto the 1990s at the earliest, the modern history of the Middle East could be written without any reference to it.

The Cold War involved a reciprocal relationship between the international 'system' as a whole and the 'sub-system' or region, of global rivalry on the one hand, and regional manoeuvre and initiative on the other. In the region, this marked a significant shift: in contrast to the two world wars, which involved, in large measure, the imposition on to the Middle East of a wider conflict, the Cold War involved to a much greater extent than the high colonial epoch, 1918–45, the *interaction* of global *with* regional forces. Thus, while the Cold War had a major impact upon the states and societies of the Middle East, to a considerable degree the states and social movements of the region also pursued individual policies. They had their own impact upon the global confrontation: states such as Israel, Turkey, Egypt, Iran were themselves actors in the Cold War, as were region-wide social movements of communist, nationalist and, later, Islamist character. The Middle East was therefore, in several important

[3] Yitzhak Schichor, *The Middle East in China's Foreign Policy, 1949–1971*, Cambridge: Cambridge University Press, 1979; Hashim Behbehani, *China's Foreign Policy in the Arab World, 1955–1978*, London: KPI, 1978; Lillian Craig Harris, *China Considers the Middle East*, London: I. B. Tauris, 1993; Fred Halliday, 'China and the Middle East: an Enigmatic Involvement', *Arab Affairs* (London), no. 12, autumn 1990.

respects, dominated by the Cold War, but this was as much because local states and social movements sought to take advantage of it for their own ends as because it was a passive object of external strategic rivalries.

Phases of the Cold War

The evolution of the Cold War in the Middle East can be seen, in terms of this interconnection of global and regional, as having fallen into four broad historical periods: 1946–55, 1955–74, 1974–85 and 1985–91. Thus the dynamic of Middle Eastern events, while certainly autonomous of the world conflict that was the Cold War, was necessarily interconnected with it. In the first period, from the latter part of the 1940s through to the middle of the 1950s, Soviet–western rivalry was concentrated largely in the non-Arab 'northern tier' of countries bordering the USSR itself, namely Turkey and Iran. In this phase of the global contest, the USSR possessed neither the will nor the capacity to challenge the west in the Arab world itself. This was to change dramatically in the second phase, which lasted from 1955 to 1974: now the USSR established itself as the major ally of a number of radical Arab nationalist regimes, the most important of which was Egypt, but also including Iraq, Syria, later Libya, and South Yemen. In this period Arab nationalism, in alliance with Moscow, posed a challenge to western domination in the region; regional wars, not only those between the Arabs and Israel, but also in Algeria (1954–62) and Yemen (1962–70), were conducted in east–west terms, the forces of the 'Arab revolution' being pitted against the allies of the west.

It was in this second phase of Cold War that the west appeared to be losing ground in the Arab world, especially in the aftermath of Suez in 1956 and the 1967 Arab–Israeli war. Yet while it was apparently retreating in the Arab world, the west was at the same time apparently consolidating in the non-Arab states in the late 1950s and early 1960s: Turkey was, for the moment, a secure member of NATO, Iran was developing its power under the Shah, and, most importantly, the USA consolidated its strategic relationship with Israel, which had been shakier at the start. This second period was to give way, in the first part of the 1970s, to what became known as the 'Second Cold War', one of tension comparable to the tensions of 1947–53; this phase was one in which the Middle East came to be a scene of continuous east–west manoeuvring and an important part of the Soviet–American rivalry for strategic positions in the third world. While the USSR was expelled from Egypt in stages, between 1972 and 1976, Moscow retained its position in other Arab states, notably Syria, Iraq and South Yemen. Its relations with Libya continued, but were always relatively tense, as the Russians found Qaddafi an unreliable ally.[4] By contrast, the USA gained ground in the Arab world in the 1970s, but it had increasing difficulties with its NATO ally Turkey, after the Turkish invasion of Cyprus in 1974. It was to suffer its greatest reverse in the region in 1979, with the triumph of the Islamic revolution in Iran. The overall sense of regional rivalry was further exacerbated by the war in Afghanistan, a country on the borders of the Middle East but now increasingly interlocked with it, via Iran and Saudi Arabia. A pro-Soviet coup in April 1978 was followed by the entry of Soviet forces at the end of 1979. This led to a protracted war in Afghanistan in which the USA, supported by Pakistan, Israel, Egypt and Saudi Arabia, sought to wear down the Red Army. Over the coming two decades Afghanistan, a state hitherto remote to western and Middle Eastern concerns alike, was to be drawn more and more into the regional play of forces,[5] and to become the fulcrum of a broader global struggle, in effect the late twentieth-century equivalent of the Spanish Civil War (1936–9).[6]

A fourth stage of Cold War opened in 1985, with the election of Mikhail Gorbachev to leadership of the USSR; in what he termed 'new thinking', Gorbachev set out to break the mould of Cold War rivalry. He worked to find common ground with the west even as he encouraged settlement of regional disputes that east and west had hitherto exploited for their own benefit. The fruits of Gorbachev's initiatives, combined with shifts in policy by regional states, were evident in the latter part of the 1980s in at least four domains: the Iran–Iraq war ended in August 1988; in November of the same year, the PLO declared itself willing to recognise Israel; in February 1989 the last Soviet forces left Afghanistan; in May 1990 the two Yemens, a pro-western North and a pro-Soviet South, merged to form a single state, with a transitional period that ended in 1994. It can indeed be argued that the Cold War had ended earlier in the Middle East, earlier indeed than in any other region of the world; for if by 'Cold War' is understood the domination of inter-state relations by US–Soviet rivalry, then this ceased to be the *dominant* line of division in 1980, with the outbreak of the Iran–Iraq war. Cautiously from 1980, and more overtly as Iran appeared to gain the initiative in the war from 1982, both east

[4] At one point in the early stage of their relationship a Libyan paper ran a banner headline in large red letters – *rusia, daula isti' maria*, 'Russia, Imperialist Country'.

[5] On the general background and on the relation of domestic change to external context see Barnett Rubin, *The Fragmentation of Afghanistan: State Formation and Collapse in the International System*, New Haven; Yale University Press, 1995; on diplomacy following the Soviet intervention, see Diego Cordovez and Selig Harrison, *Out of Afghanistan: the Inside Story of the Soviet Withdrawal*, Oxford: Oxford University Press, 1995; Fred Halliday, *Rethinking International Relations*, London: Macmillan, 1994.

[6] See Fred Halliday, *Two Hours that Shook the World*, London: Saqi, 2001.

and west supported Iraq against Iran. This was made all the easier by the USSR's abandonment of its hitherto active internationalist policy in the region, a reflection at once of exhaustion at popular level, calculation of advantage vis-à-vis the west by the leadership as a whole, and Gorbachev's own evident disinterest in the third world and its problems. By the time of the dissolution of the USSR in December 1991 the Middle East had already, therefore, to a quite considerable degree, been freed from the intersection of strategic rivalry with local conflict. The region had come to be overtly dominated by that autonomous inter-state rivalry that had always partly shaped and underlain the Cold War.[7]

Iran

Against this schematic outline of the Cold War in the Middle East, it is possible to look in more detail at the way specific states were affected by the conflict. The Middle Eastern states where the Cold War first took effect were Iran and Turkey. Of all the countries in the Middle East, Iran was the one most affected by World War II: the occupation by Soviet and British forces that lasted from 1941 to 1945 unleashed strong political and social forces within the country. Iran, not Europe, then became, in effect, the place where the first chapter of the Cold War was written. While British forces withdrew from the country at the end of the war, British influence remained strong, in the politics of Tehran and the oil fields of the south. The USSR did not immediately withdraw its forces from the north and made demands for rights to oil exploration in the north comparable to those of the British in the south. At the same time it encouraged regional allies in Azerbaijan and Kurdistan to set up autonomous – not, as is frequently claimed, independent – republics. The Azerbaijan issue led to a major diplomatic confrontation in March 1946 between the USSR, on the one hand, and the Iranians and their western allies, on the other. A combination of western pressure and skilful Iranian diplomacy led, in the end, to a Soviet withdrawal in May; the autonomous republics were overrun by the Shah's forces in December 1946. Subsequently, an agreement on oil originally offered by the Iranians to the Soviet Union was revoked.[8]

Yet while Iran was now officially in the pro-American camp, its unstable domestic politics threatened to undermine the Shah's commitment to the

---

[7] Robert O. Freedman, *Soviet Policy toward Israel under Gorbachev*, New York: Praeger, 1999.

[8] Louise Fawcett, *Iran and the Cold War: the Azerbaijan Crisis of 1946*, Cambridge: Cambridge University Press, 1992; Ervand Abrahamian, *Iran Between Two Revolutions*, Princeton: Princeton University Press, 1982, *passim*, esp. chapter 8.

west. The Shah's position was challenged both by the nationalist forces of the National Front, led by Mohammad Mosadeq, and by the pro-Soviet Tudeh (literally 'masses') party, communist in effect if not name, founded in 1941, which organised the first, and to date, only modern popular party seen in Iranian history. In 1951 Mosadeq became prime minister and proceeded to nationalise the British-owned oil fields of the Anglo-Iranian Oil Company, the precursor of BP. While the Tudeh initially failed to support Mosadeq, seeing him as a US servant (*noukar-i amrika*) being used against the British, western states came increasingly to see the prime minister as a threat to their interests, in both economic (oil) and strategic (Cold War) terms. An international boycott of Iran's oil produced widespread hardship in the country. A failure by Iran to reach a compromise with the oil company and the British, and a shift in Washington from Democratic to Republican presidents in January 1953, led to a hardening of western attitudes: in August 1953, British and US secret agents, with a range of Iranian collaborators, staged a coup in Tehran which ousted Mosadeq and installed the Shah as undisputed ruler.[9] The coup date, 19 August 1953, in the Persian calendar 28 Mordad, acquired iconic status in Iranian political discourse. For the Shah it became a date to celebrate as a national holiday; for his opponents it was a day of betrayal.

August 1953 was a decisive moment in Iranian politics and in Iran's relation to the Cold War. It settled for a generation the instability that had begun with the invasion of 1941. The opposition bloc of nationalist and communist forces was destroyed, and power came increasingly to be held by the Shah. In 1953 a strategic and internal security relationship was consolidated between Iran and the USA that was to last until the revolution of 1979. The coup also led to a reorganisation of Iran's oil industry, with US firms now acquiring a 40 per cent share of total output, in a new consortium (technically the nationalisation of 1951 was not reversed). For close on a decade Iran remained very much a military dictatorship aligned with the west against the USSR; but from the early 1960s onwards this began to change.

---

[9] On the western role in the 1953 coup see Mark Gasiorowksi, *US Foreign Policy and the Shah: Building a Client State in Iran*, Ithaca: Cornell University Press, 1991; James Goode, *The United States and Iran: In the Shadow of Musaddiq*, London: Macmillan, 1997; Stephen Kinzer, *All the Shah's Men: an American Coup and the Roots of Middle East Terror*, Hoboken, NJ: John Wiley, 2003. On US–Iranian relations in general, see James Bill, *The Eagle and the Lion: the Tragedy of American–Iranian Relations*, London: Yale University Press, 1988, and Barry Rubin, *Paved with Good Intentions: Iran and the American Experience*, Oxford: Oxford University Press, 1980. But one note of caution: focus on external 'hands', without due regard to internal forces and political misjudgement by those ousted, can be misleading, cf. also Chile 1973. Mosadeq mismanaged his own following and missed opportunities to obtain a reasonable compromise settlement on oil.

First, in parallel with the removal of American missiles from Turkey in 1963, there was an improvement in Iran's relations with the USSR: as was to be the case with Turkey, the USSR became a significant trading and investment partner. Moscow desired stability on its southern frontier, and this is what the Shah, like King Zahir Shah of Afghanistan, offered. For its part, Iran became more preoccupied by the challenge not from the north but from the west and the south. To the west the Iraqi revolution of 1958, in which the Hashemite monarchy was overthrown, alarmed the Shah, as did, on the eastern front, the fall of the monarchy in Afghanistan in 1973. The British withdrawal from the Gulf, begun in Kuwait in 1961 and effected in the other smaller lower Gulf states a decade later, led the Shah to project Iran as the new dominant power in that region. Social upheaval to west and east, therefore, as much as the strategic manoeuvring of the Cold War, altered Iran's international perspective. By the 1970s Iran's strategic orientation was southwards, not to the north. In the 1970s, in line with this vision, the Shah took a number of military initiatives: from 1969 to 1975 Iran fought a low-level but persistent border war with Iraq, in effect the first 'Gulf war'. This war was only ended with the Algiers Agreement of 1975 in which the land and water frontiers of the two states were settled, and a pledge of mutual non-interference provided. This confrontation presaged interventionist action elsewhere. In 1971, on the eve of the British withdrawal, Iranian forces occupied three Arab islands, Abu Musa and the Greater and Lesser Tunbs, belonging to the United Arab Emirates. In 1973 Iran sent several thousand counter-insurgency troops to the southern Omani province of Dhofar to fight revolutionary guerrillas active there. To the south-east it provided support to counter-insurgency campaigns by Pakistan against rebels in Baluchistan.

The policies of the Iranian state were, however, vulnerable, not to defeat abroad but to a growing strain in state–society relations within. At the same time as the above-mentioned shifts occurred in Iran's external relations, there was set in train another internal process, one also shaped by exogenous processes, that was to have dramatic international consequences. Iran was, historically, a country little affected by the world economy. It had endured military occupation in world wars, but not colonialism. This transformation, and its explosive consequences, were to come later than elsewhere, via the impact on Iranian society of a state increasingly endowed with oil revenues. In the early 1960s the regime, concerned about social unrest in the absence of reform, and encouraged by the USA which feared Soviet exploitation of unrest in Cold War competition, as it did in America, began to undertake pre-emptive reform – what came to be termed 'the White Revolution'. This comprised a set of reforms including state-led industrialisation, land reform, a literacy programme and the promotion of women's place in public life. This set of modernising changes from above served to strengthen the power of the state, but was made possible, first gradually and then dramatically, by the rise in Iran's oil revenues in the 1960s and 1970s. Opposition to these reforms came primarily not from the opponents of the 1940s and 1950s, secular forces who shared the Shah's vision of modernisation while doubting his intentions and effectiveness, but from clerical forces to whom the Shah was a threat, both as powerful monarch and as ally of the USA. Here, as discussed in chapter 3, the impact of secularisation, initiated in the 1920s as an instrument of state transformation of society, was to become more intense, and fateful. An uprising in June 1963 brought to the fore a hitherto unknown and politically quiescent clergyman, Imam Ruhallah Khomeini. In October 1964, following his objections to an agreement concerning the legal status of American servicemen in Iran, he was sent into exile, first in Turkey and then in Iraq.[10]

The Iranian state, impelled by external strategic and financial processes alike, had thereby set the context for its own overthrow. A decade and a half later the twin conditions of internal revolt established in the early 1960s were to combine in the Islamic revolution. The very changes brought about by the Shah's modernisation programmes, and the tensions they generated, laid the social basis for a mass movement of opposition. It was the political vacuum created by the suppression of the left-wing and nationalist movements, and the uprising of June 1963, which made Ayatollah Khomeini the leader of this movement. Opposition began to emerge into the open in early 1978. The regime retaliated. The result in the latter part of 1978 was a growing opposition mobilisation on the streets. This brought out millions of people in demands for a republic and for independence, and led to the departure of the Shah on 15 January 1979. Two weeks later, on 1 February 1979, Khomeini returned from exile and, in March, proclaimed the Islamic Republic of Iran. The very processes set in train to lock Iran into the Cold War alliance system, and to secure the Iranian state, had therefore generated revolt. The increasingly autonomous *foreign policy* role of Iran with regard to the Cold War was undermined by the explosive impact of that strategic rivalry on Iran's *internal* social and political order.[11] Significantly, and a fact never adequately explained, the 400,000 strong armed

[10] Baqer Moin, *Khomeini, Life of the Ayatollah*, London: I. B. Tauris, 1999; Nikki Keddie, *Roots of Revolution: an Interpretive History of Modern Iran*, New Haven: Yale University Press, 1981.

[11] Hossein Bashiriyeh, *The State and Revolution in Iran 1962–1982*, London: Croom Helm, 1984; Shaul Bakhash, *The Reign of the Ayatollahs*, London: I. B. Tauris, 1985.

forces failed to contest the revolution and, in a space of a few weeks, fell apart.

The evolution of Iranian foreign, and domestic, politics in the Cold War period exemplifies the manifold ways in which the global conflict of the Cold War, combined with the impact of the world economy, *did* shape events within particular countries, but also illustrates the limits on this process. The course of events in Iran from 1945 to 1953 was decisively influenced by the onset of Cold War, by the policies of Britain, the USA and the USSR. It was, however, shaped by the ways in which internal Iranian forces, pro-Soviet, pro-western and neutral, sought to manoeuvre in this context. The coup of 1953 had not one, but several, preconditions: an offensive strategy by Washington and London on the one hand, but also a passive abstention by the USSR *and* a divided, ineffective, pro-Mosadeq coalition within. The consolidation of 1953–63 followed Cold War pressures. Yet, after that, the course of events began to be more autonomous of global confrontation: on the one hand, the Iranian state itself came to play a more independent role, vis-à-vis the USSR and the Persian Gulf, whilst within the country the very changes brought about in part to prevent a revolutionary upheaval were themselves, combined with the injection of large oil revenues, to lay the basis for the revolutionary challenge from Khomeini and his supporters. Sharpening state–society relations, and the contradictory impact on these relations of the international context, thereby produced the explosion.

The outcome of this escalatory process was the revolution of 1979; here Khomeini, playing on Iranian nationalism as on Islamic hostility to Soviet and western influence alike, took up the policy of Mosadeq, 'negative balance', *mizan-i manfi*, and propounded the slogan 'Neither East nor West', *na gharb, na sharq*.[12] While both the USSR and the USA *feared* that the Islamic Republic would align with the other, Iran in fact continued to pursue an independent path, denouncing the 'Great Satan', *sheitun-i bozorg*, America, and the 'Little Satan', *sheitun-i kuchik*, the USSR, and encouraging revolt by Muslims against both sides. By the end of 1979 Iran was in conflict with *both* Satans, enraging the USA by its detention of diplomats in Tehran and antagonising the USSR by opposing its intervention in Afghanistan. Soviet commentators long continued to hope that the Iranian revolution would align with the anti-western bloc, that 'the mullahs will come to their senses'.[13] This was not to be.[14]

[12] Nikki Keddie and Mark Gasiorowski, eds., *Neither East nor West: Iran, the Soviet Union, and the United States*, London: Yale University Press, 1990.
[13] For background see Aryeh Yodfat, *The Soviet Union and Revolutionary Iran*, London: Croom Helm, 1984.
[14] R. K. Ramazani, *Revolutionary Iran: Challenge and Response in the Middle East*, Baltimore: The Johns Hopkins University Press, 1988. Years later, in a quite candid discussion with

The most dramatic challenge to the Islamic revolutionary regime came, however, not from either Satan, Great or Small, but from Iraq which in September 1980 launched an all-out invasion; this was to lead to eight years of war. Yet this war, by far the greatest and most costly conflict seen in the Middle East in modern times, and one of the longest inter-state wars of the twentieth century,[15] fitted into no easy Cold War pattern. Nor indeed did Iran's overall foreign policy during the 1980s as a whole conform to the global pattern: Iran continued to oppose western influence in Saudi Arabia and in the Arab world at large, yet it also opposed the Soviet forces in Afghanistan as it called for greater freedom for Muslim citizens of the USSR. In 1989, as the crisis in the USSR developed, Khomeini in a symbolic repudiation sent a message to Soviet leader Gorbachev encouraging him to embrace Islam. This was not to occur, but, as the USSR collapsed, the end of the Cold War revealed a large new strategic panorama, replete with opportunities and perils for Iran, in the former Transcaucasian and Central Asian republics.

Turkey

The other Middle Eastern country most immediately affected by the onset of the Cold War was Turkey. Atatürk's death in 1938 had been followed by a cautious shift of Turkey's international alignment away from neutrality and towards an alliance with the west. This reflected two calculations by Turkey's leaders: on the one hand, they wanted to develop alliances with the Allies that would be economically advantageous; on the other, they anticipated that Turkey's historic rival, Russia, would emerge from World War II in more powerful and threatening mood, demanding from Turkey the kinds of strategic and other concessions it was imposing in eastern Europe. This latter anxiety was to prove accurate: in 1945 the USSR proposed revisions of the territorial agreement concerning the eastern frontier, and a revision of the 1936 Treaty of Montreux governing the passage of shipping through the Dardanelles, the straits linking the Black Sea to the Mediterranean. It was also reported by the Turks

the author about twenty years of radical diplomacy and rhetorical self-delusion, a senior Iranian official was to list the three great mistakes of the post-1979 period: the detention of the US hostages, 1979–81; the pursuance of the war with Iraq after July 1982, when a favourable deal was in the offing; and the failure to bail out the Kabul regime. For comparative context, of rhetorical excess by revolutionary states, see Fred Halliday, *Revolution and World Politics*, London: Macmillan, 1999.

[15] This war began in September 1980 and ended in August 1988. The Sino-Japanese war lasted from July 1937 to August 1945, two months longer.

that the USSR was demanding a base on the straits.[16] In response to this confrontation with Russia, Turkey appealed to the west for help and in 1947 the country was included in the new US policy for the region, the Truman Doctrine. In 1950 Ankara despatched forces to fight with the UN in the Korean war. In 1952, remote as it was from the North Atlantic, Turkey became a member of NATO. Fourteen years after the death of Atatürk, the country's international alignment had, therefore, radically altered. This external shift was, however, both facilitated and challenged by the process of political *and* social change within Turkey. After initial control by the Kemalist state, the Turkish economy and society began to allow greater room for a private sector, Thus, in a manner contrasted to that of Iran, it was the change of society in reaction to Atatürk's statism that was to bring the country *closer* to the west. Yet over the ensuing decades the opposition to this realignment with the west, from Islamist right and very secular left, was to pose major problems to the Turkish state.

This realignment of the country's international position did not resolve many of the issues it faced in the subsequent decades of the Cold War. First of all, although Turkey maintained membership of NATO and sought to associate itself with the rising tide of European integration, its own internal politics were markedly different from those of most other members of the alliance. In 1950 a relatively free election brought to power the opposition Democratic Party (DP). This represented those social and political forces who resisted the Kemalist state and its official party, the Republican People's Party (RPP), and who had been able to gain ground during the relative liberalisation of the 1940s. In 1960, however, the army overthrew the DP, executed its leader, Adnan Menderes, and reimposed the RPP. When a successor to the DP, the Justice Party, was elected, it too was ousted in 1971; a further coup occurred in 1980, against a background of economic crisis and violent opposition from right and left. In 1984 the Turkish state was challenged from another quarter, that of a guerrilla uprising in the Kurdish regions led by the PKK, Partiya Karkeran Kurdistan, or Kurdish Workers' Party. The PKK, arising out of the radical student milieu of the 1970s, espoused a 'Marxist-Leninist' ideology and sought to establish a separate Kurdish state.

---

[16] This is widely asserted in the secondary literature, but the only source cited is the then Turkish ambassador in Moscow, Selim Sarper; to my knowledge, there was no public statement to this effect at the time by the USSR nor any other documentary confirmation. See William Hale, *Turkish Foreign Policy 1774–2000*, London: Frank Cass, 2000, pp. 111–12.

This domestic turbulence was only indirectly related to the Cold War. Turkey had a significant communist tradition, but was not a country, as were Iran and some Arab states, in which an organised pro-Soviet mass movement had existed. But the political instability in the country, combined with continued human rights abuses, was to lead, from the 1970s onwards, to considerable criticism in western Europe. This inhibited that full integration of Turkey with the west to which the Kemalist leadership had from the 1940s onwards aspired. The west had in the main remained silent about human rights abuses during the early phase of the Cold War, but as the subject came to occupy a more prominent place in western criticism of the USSR, so the same criteria were, intermittently, put to critical use against members of the NATO alliance itself. The Cold War, therefore, had a contradictory impact on Turkey and on state–society relations: it both led it into a closer alignment with the USA and other western states and created a context in which external criticism of its domestic policies became more insistent.

The tensions generated by these state–society conflicts were compounded by the conflicts between Turkey's global, pro-western policies and its policy on regional conflict. The second major difficulty in the country's Cold War alignment therefore revolved around the relationship with Greece. Initially both faced a common challenge in the USSR: while the challenge to Turkey was territorial, on the east, to Greece it was internal, in the form of the civil war between monarchist and communist forces that raged from 1945 to 1949. Relations between Turkey and Greece had, however, been bitter in the past: Greek nationalism was partly defined in terms of the early nineteenth-century revolt against Ottoman rule, and in the early decades of the twentieth century there had been wars and hostility between the two states, ended by an agreement between Atatürk and Greek leader Venizelos in 1930.

The issue that reactivated conflict was the island of Cyprus off the southern Turkish coast, occupied by the British since 1878. In 1960 its population totalled half a million, of whom 80 per cent were Greek, 20 per cent Turkish. A rising Greek Cypriot nationalism was dominated by a demand for union, or *enosis*, with Greece, something Turkey resisted, countering with a call for partition. Tripartite negotiations between Turkey, Greece and Britain produced an agreement in 1960 for the independence of Cyprus and guarantees for both communities, but also for the right of external intervention in the event of a community being threatened. This was not long in coming. In 1963 worsening relations between the two communities produced the first, limited, Turkish intervention. In 1974, however, following a coup in Nicosia by Greek Cypriot forces backed by the then right-wing junta in Athens, Turkey staged a full-scale invasion: up to 40 per cent of the island was occupied, and all Greeks expelled from the Turkish sector, with Turks fleeing the Greeks.[17]

Greece and Turkey never went to war over Cyprus: restraint based on rational calculations of self-interest, and external, especially US, diplomatic pressure, ensured that this did not occur. But the Cyprus issue, beyond the human suffering it caused, led to a degree of tension in Turkey's relations with the west. The first phase of this came in 1964 when US President Johnson wrote to the Turks warning them against using in Cyprus military equipment they had received through NATO. In 1974 a more dramatic break occurred as the USA cut all military assistance to Turkey and the Turks closed US access to the numerous air bases that country had in Turkey. Only in 1978 was a new understanding between the two countries reached. Later developments were, however, to reconfirm Turkey's importance: the Iranian revolution of 1979 underlined Turkey's strategic utility to the USA; the Iraqi invasion of Kuwait strengthened this further. The dissolution of the USSR in 1991 was to make Turkey a significant actor in the new Turkic republics, and in the geopolitics of Caspian oil and gas. In the flux of post-communist Transcaucasia and the Black Sea, and amidst the upheaval of West Asia, Ankara was Washington's indispensable ally, less truculent than Saudi Arabia, more useful, far more so, than Israel.

The difficulties Turkey encountered during the 1970s and 1980s with the USA, and with growing human rights concerns in western Europe, were accompanied by modifications in Ankara's relations with both the USSR and the Arab world. After the confrontations of 1945–7 the USSR came to accept the status quo with Turkey. Soviet leader Nikita Khrushchev even apologised for Moscow's mishandling of relations with Ankara after World War II. As relations with the USA worsened, Soviet diplomacy concentrated on first stabilising relations with Turkey and then seeking to win it away from NATO; to the irritation of its allies in the third world, and especially to that of the largest pro-Soviet communist party in Europe, the Cypriot AKEL, the USSR backed Turkey's, not Greece's, position on Cyprus. When the breach between Turkey and the USA came in 1974, there was speculation in Moscow that this could form the basis for Turkey leaving NATO altogether. Throughout the Cold War and as part of the attempt to encourage 'national

---

[17] The author, then on holiday on the island, witnessed the course of events, from the fascist coup on Monday to the Turkish parachute drop over Nicosia on Saturday morning. Years later I attended a lecture by Turkish premier Bulent Ecevit in London. My question began: 'Mr Ecevit. You once interrupted my breakfast . . .'

democratic' forces in Turkey, Moscow also developed economic relations with the country. Although a member of NATO, Turkey was,
paradoxically, the largest recipient of Soviet economic aid in the non-
communist world.

In the end, these Soviet enticements came to nothing. The generals
were no more susceptible to Moscow's charm than were the mullahs
in Qom. Yet Turkey's relation to NATO was never put to the ultimate
test; it was sometimes said, quietly, in western circles that, in the event
of an imminent third world war confrontation between NATO and the
USSR, Turkey would have left the alliance the day before hostilities broke
out. Here, in contrast to Iran, strategic defection was anticipated. Yet in
the end, the reverse happened: Turkish state–society tensions, and its
conflictual regional policies, did *not* destroy the pro-western alignment
that had been established in the aftermath of World War II.

The Arab–Israeli dispute

If after 1945 Iran and Turkey became early allies of the west, only to
achieve a relative stabilisation of their relations with the USSR from the
1960s onwards, the opposite was in many ways to be the case further
south, in the Arab world and Israel. In these countries the first decade
after the end of World War II was dominated by two trends: on the one
hand, decolonisation, as Britain and France withdraw from the positions
they had acquired after 1918, even as they sought to preserve forms of
influence and military presence; on the other hand, increasing involvement in the Cold War as the Arab world, the Jewish community in
Palestine, and then, from 1948, the state of Israel involved the great
powers in the escalating conflict over Palestine.

The French were quick to cede independence to Syria and Lebanon as
they had promised during World War II, but took far longer before they
agreed to leave their colonies to the west – Tunisia, Morocco and Algeria.
If the British were to remain for another three decades in parts of the
Arabian Peninsula, they withdrew after World War II, as we have seen,
from their former Arab colonies elsewhere in the Middle East: Egypt,
Iraq (these two formally independent already) and Sudan (granted independence in 1956). In the first two they sought, to the anger of local
nationalists, to preserve military and strategic assets, while the independence of the third was marked by a growing conflict over Egyptian claims
to the lands and waters of Sudan, to the south. The most controversial
of all withdrawals, however, was that from Palestine: the British tried
initially to continue the balancing act of the pre-war years, but this now
proved impossible. Zionist forces emerged stronger from World War II

and enjoyed much greater sympathy; they were now more determined than ever on an independent, internationally recognised, Jewish state. The Arab world, including most of the Palestinian leadership, refused to accept it. In 1947 the British decided to pull out without a resolution, and in 1948, following a UN resolution on partition into two states, war broke out between Arab and Jewish forces. The local Palestinians were joined by forces from Egypt, Jordan and Syria. In the end the Jewish forces prevailed and Palestine was partitioned, not between Jews and Palestinians, but between a new Israeli state, proclaimed by Ben-Gurion in the municipal museum in Tel Aviv on 14 May 1948, and the forces of Hashemite Jordan who occupied much of the West Bank and East Jerusalem.[18]

The events of 1947–9 in Palestine were to dominate much of the international relations of the Middle East for the next half a century at least: for much of the outside world the 'Middle East' conflict was mistakenly seen as identical to the Arab–Israeli one. It was not possible to write the history of the rise of Arab nationalism across the region, or chart the course of Arab politics in the 1950s and 1960s, without recognising the catalytic role of the Palestine question. Yet in two important respects the dominant perception of the Arab–Israeli dispute was deceptive. First, the conflict of the late 1940s was only indirectly related to the Cold War – in 1948 the USSR supported the establishment of Israel and armed it. It was only in subsequent decades that the lines of division in the Arab–Israeli conflict came to fall along Cold War lines. The close relationship between Washington and Israel was formed during the Johnson administration, after 1963. Secondly, while the Palestine issue sent shock waves through the Arab world for decades, and did much to promote a more radical Arab nationalism and sense of Arab identity, the Arab–Israeli conflict itself was only of limited relevance in explaining the broader course of events within Arab states, or the development of relations between them. The Palestine question was central to, but far from being the sole determinant of, the broader pattern of Middle East politics in the decades that ensued.

The immediate results of the first Arab–Israeli war were felt in the states bordering Palestine itself. In Syria a constitutional parliamentary

[18] Amidst an ocean of sources for general background see Walter Laqueur and Barry Rubin, eds., *The Israeli–Arab Reader: a Documentary History of the Middle East Conflict*, Harmondsworth: Penguin, 1995; Kirsten Schulze, *The Arab–Israeli Conflict*, London: Longman, 1999; Ahron Bregman and Jihan al-Tahri, *The Fifty Years War: Israel and the Arabs*, Harmondsworth: Penguin, 1998; Avi Shlaim, *The Iron Wall: Israel and the Arab World*, London: I. B. Tauris, 1999. The literature on the Arab–Israeli question in English alone is, perhaps, second in volume only to that on the 'Irish question'.

system installed by the French was abolished in 1949, setting a pattern of military rule in Syria that was to outlast the Cold War. In Egypt, World War II had created a political climate similar in some ways to that in Iran, with movements of a secular or religious kind challenging the monarch and western influence. In this country, however, the monarchy proved unable to contain the tide of popular anger that followed the defeat by Israel. The British presence in Egypt was another destabilising factor: it was even more overtly provocative than in Iran, taking the form of control of a zone along the Suez Canal and ownership, along with France, of the Suez Canal itself. Amidst rising social and nationalist upheaval and intermittent *fedayin* raids against British positions, the Egyptian army seized power on 23 July 1952, exiled the king, and proclaimed a republic. It was the first time in more than two millennia, since the conquest of Egypt by Alexander the Great in 333 BC, that the country had been governed by Egyptian rulers.[19] The sons of *pashas* and *effendis* had been replaced by the sons of the *bilad* (countryside). In Nasser's case this went against him as his elite critics derided him as *ibn al-bustagi*, 'the son of the postman', a derision matched later in Iraq when the first republican president, Abdal-Karim Qasim, was mocked as the 'son of a railway worker'.

The revolution of 1952 was to unleash a process of radicalisation that profoundly affected Egypt as well as the Arab world. It brought the Cold War to the Arab world, or, perhaps more accurately, allowed the Cold War to come to the Arab world, aligning Arab states with one or other bloc in the Cold War itself, and dividing Arab states themselves along Cold War lines. It also provided a new ideological context for the rising tide of popular, if also conspiratorial, pressure (from *within* the state and from outside) on states. At first, the Egyptian revolution appeared *not* to fit the prevailing international divisions: the USA sought to advise and assist the Free Officers, to the point of providing former Nazi missile specialists for the Egyptian rocket programme, while the USSR saw the Egyptian revolutionaries, as they saw Mosadeq, as untrustworthy bourgeois nationalists.[20] Local Egyptian communists at first also saw Nasser as another fascist military ruler, his agrarian policy not a land 'reform' but a land 'distortion'. Yet by 1955 this had begun to change: as conflict

---

[19] For general background see John Waterbury, *The Egypt of Nasser and Sadat: the Political Economy of Two Regimes*, Princeton: Princeton University Press, 1983; P. J. Vatikiotis, *Nasser and his Generation*, London: Croom Helm, 1978.

[20] On covert US support for Nasser in his early years see Miles Copeland, *The Game of Nations: the Amorality of Power Politics*, London: Weidenfeld & Nicolson, 1969. Among other revelations was that the 'Cairo Tower', *burj al-qahira*, across the Nile from the Hilton, was built to use up some spare CIA cash.

between the Egyptians and the British was apparently resolved, by the final British withdrawal from the Canal Zone in 1954, new developments were exacerbating the relationship of Egypt to the west. Western support for a regional military alliance established in the Middle East in 1955, the Middle East Defence Organisation (MEDO), later the Baghdad Pact, was seen by many Arabs, and especially Egypt, as another form of colonialist intervention. At the same time relations between Egypt and Israel deteriorated, as a result both of guerrilla attacks on Israel backed by Egypt and Syria and of Israeli retaliation. In 1955 the Egyptians, seeking support in this confrontation, acquired arms from a Soviet ally, Czechoslovakia, while Israel itself had, from the early 1950s, enjoyed worsening relations with the USSR.

In 1956 matters came to a head: Egypt, whose military government was now under the leadership of Colonel Gamal Abdel Nasser, was not only challenging the new Baghdad Pact, but sought to acquire ownership of the Suez Canal, both as a symbol of national independence and as a source of revenue to finance its development programmes. Cairo also appealed to the west, particularly the USA, for assistance in building a new dam in Upper Egypt, at Aswan, to manage the floodwaters of the Nile. US refusal to finance the dam (to be precise, withdrawal of an earlier offer), coupled with the nationalisation of the Suez Canal, led to an international crisis: the USSR backed Egypt while the British and French, outraged at the Canal's nationalisation, sought to isolate Nasser.[21]

It was on 23 July that Nasser announced he had nationalised the Suez Canal. At this point global and regional politics became intertwined, but not along Cold War lines. Israel, led by the hawkish David Ben-Gurion, entered into secret negotiations with Britain and France to plan a secret attack on Egypt: Israel would launch the first assault, and the British and French, under the pretext of 'separating the combatants', would then occupy the Canal. The plan duly went ahead: Israel attacked on 29 October 1956; on 31 October the British and French intervened. The conspirators had, however, reckoned without the great powers, indeed without the Cold War – their 'autonomous' neo-colonial fantasies, agency of a kind, collided with the structures of world politics. The USSR threatened to retaliate against London and Paris, whilst the USA, deeply hostile to Nasser but alarmed at the Anglo-French reassertion of colonial power, called for a withdrawal. Within weeks the invading forces had withdrawn and the USA, through the Eisenhower Doctrine, sought to

---

[21] For one excellent account of Soviet policy see Karen Dawisha, *Soviet Foreign Policy towards Egypt*, London: Macmillan, 1979.

rally Arab opinion. The shape of Middle Eastern politics had, however, been altered irrevocably by the Suez crisis: the Arab–Israeli dispute had been integrated into the Cold War; the radical Arab states, and much of Arab opinion, enraged by Palestine, Suez and the war for independence that had broken out in Algeria in November 1954, came to sympathise with the Soviet Union.

The Suez crisis, therefore, finally brought the Cold War to the Arab Middle East: it set a pattern in the international relations of the Arab world that was to last for the following two decades. The crisis transformed Egypt and the reputation of its leader, Nasser. He became the undisputed figure head of Arab nationalism. An inter-state crisis thereby intersected with an unfolding of popular sentiment and of social movements in parts of the Arab world. Borne along by a tide of opinion in his own country and in the Arab world, Nasser pursued a programme of radical reform at home, constructing an 'Arab socialism' that sought to end centuries of colonial domination. Land reform, nationalisation of industry, mobilisation of the population into state-run political structures all followed. In ideology, Nasser was careful to distinguish himself from Soviet communism on two grounds: he rejected the latter's atheism and its belief in what he termed 'class strife'. Arab socialism was, he stated, based on Islam and the socialism he interpreted from *shrk*, the root of the Arabic word *ishtirakia*, as 'sharing' between different social groups. He saw Egypt as spearheading an Arab drive for unity, overcoming the divisions created by colonialism, and as leading an Arab, and broader, third world drive for independence from the west and colonialism, in both its formal and informal variants. At the same time, Nasser challenged traditional Arab rulers and, not least, proclaimed Egypt as the vanguard of the struggle to liberate Palestine.[22]

The period between the second and third Arab–Israeli wars, the Suez war of 1956 and the Six Day war of 1967, marked at once the high point of the global Cold War in the region and the heyday of Arab radical nationalism, as ideology and movement. The proclamation of Arab socialism in Egypt in 1961 was accompanied by radical developments elsewhere: in 1958 the monarchy in Iraq was overthrown by a military coup and popular revolt; in the same year Egypt and Syria came together to form a United Arab Republic; after 1956 the monarchy in Jordan seemed to be 'shaking' – or 'tottering', *motamalmil*, a favourite radical word of the time, only a shade short of their other term of dismissal 'they are dispersed'.

---

[22] Adeed Dawisha, *Egypt in the Arab World: the Elements of Foreign Policy*, New York: Wiley, 1976; Raymond Hinnebusch, 'The Foreign Policy of Egypt', in Raymond Hinnebusch and Anoushiravan Ehteshami, eds., *The Foreign Policies of Middle East States*, Boulder, CO: Lynne Rienner, 2002.

In 1962 Algeria finally won independence from France; and in September 1962 the Imamate in Yemen was in its turn ousted by a radical pro-Egyptian coup. At the same time Egypt sought to exert greater influence beyond the regional level: while in 1955 Nasser had identified with third world radicalism at the Afro-Asian Solidarity summit in Bandung, Indonesia, in 1961 he formed, with India and Yugoslavia, the core of a new Non-Aligned Movement that included Latin America as well.[23] These were not, however, mere results of a superimposed global conflict. Here it was social and political forces *within* the region, and social upheaval, not least in Egypt itself, *not* global conflict, that drove the Cold War forward.

Yet this tide of radicalism soon encountered major limits, from society within and the state system without. First, inside the Arab world itself, Egypt's drive for unity met opposition from states and distinct national sentiment: attempts in 1963 to form a new union, this time with Syria and Iraq, foundered in acrimony.[24] The revolution in Yemen led to a debilitating civil war in which royalist forces, backed by Saudi Arabia and Britain among others, challenged the new republic; meanwhile conservative states, notably Saudi Arabia, but also Iran and Morocco, began to organise against Egypt and its allies.[25] Within Egypt itself the dynamic of the socialist period soon began to ebb: the economy, now dominated by the state sector, proved corrupt and inefficient; the land reform benefited only a small number of already reasonably well-off peasants, leaving a mass of landless labourers. It did not take long, in these eventful years, for the dream of Arab liberation to fade. In 1961 the Syrians seceded from the United Arab Republic. A counter-revolutionary war that was to engulf the region, carrying away the soldiers of Yemen and ultimately overwhelming the beleaguered secularists of Kabul, had been set in motion. In 1965, as peasants in the Egyptian town of Khamshish staged the first popular revolt against the bureaucrats of Arab socialism, conservative opinion regrouped at the regional level, with the Saudis founding the Islamic World League (*Rabita al-Alim al-Islamiya*) with like-minded monarchs.

---

[23] Many commentators have subsequently confused the 1955 and 1961 conferences, wrongly using of Bandung the term 'Non-Aligned', a word that came into general use only in the 1960s. The Afro-Asian People's Solidarity Organisation, at Bandung, very much an Afro-Asian conference, included China and Israel, states later excluded from the Non-Aligned Movement but not with Latin America. The NAM, while ostensibly directed against western influence, also had a strong anti-Chinese component as well. All three founder members (India, Egypt and Yugoslavia) were in the early 1960s seriously at odds with China.

[24] On this period the classic study is Patrick Seale, *The Struggle for Syria*, Oxford: Oxford University Press, 1965.

[25] Malcom Kerr, *The Arab Cold War*, third edition, Oxford: Oxford University Press, 1971.

Arab public opinion in general now began to question the achievements of Nasser, to yearn not so much for modernity, but for *turath*, 'heritage'.

Into this situation of growing domestic unrest and inter-Arab dissension there then exploded a dramatic inter-state confrontation, the third Arab–Israeli war of June 1967: Nasser, overplaying his hand, decided to call for the removal of UN forces stationed on the border with Israel and to close to Israeli shipping the Straits of Tiran at the top of the Red Sea. The Israelis, eager to complete the task that had been thwarted in 1956, launched a surprise attack on the morning of 5 June 1967 and in a matter of hours destroyed the Egyptian air force. Israeli forces then advanced into Sinai and reached the Canal. Meanwhile Syria lost part of its territories along the Golan, whilst Jordan was forced to abandon Jerusalem and the West Bank. Israel was now in a stronger position than ever, and backed by western states and much of western public opinion. The political contours of the Middle East had been redrawn: in particular the Israeli–Arab 1967 boundaries set a pattern that was to last for decades. The Arab world, aligned with the USSR, was now humiliated and on the defensive. In an address to the people of Egypt, Nasser offered to resign as president, but the Egyptian people poured onto the streets and begged him to remain; he was to die three years later, weakened at home and abroad, in September 1970. The Arab world mourned him, but the achievements of the 'eternal leader' were to prove transitory. After his death little of Nasser's legacy at home or internationally was to survive, beyond nostalgia for a period of high hopes, and a rhetoric of unity and liberation that others, of a far more brutal stamp, were to misuse for their own, far more catastrophic, purposes.

Regional turning point: the consequences of 1967

In 1967 Israel apparently gained much of what it wanted, in the region and internationally. In the Middle East, the Arab world was divided and defeated, the Palestinians appeared on the run. In terms of the Cold War, Israel was now more than ever aligned with the west and enjoyed the almost unanimous backing of western public opinion. While the USSR broke off diplomatic relations with Israel when the war began, the USA, and US public opinion, endorsed Israeli action in this war to a degree far greater than in the two earlier Arab–Israeli conflicts. Henceforward American reservations about a strategic alliance with Israel, and about Israel's pursuit of nuclear weapons (initially with French assistance), were reduced; instead Israel came increasingly to be seen as an ally in the Cold War, against Soviet influence. Needless to say, Israel and its friend in Washington made sure the message was driven home. As a consequence, the fourth Arab–Israeli war, launched by Egypt in October 1973, was interpreted in Washington as part of a Soviet assault on western interests. The Israeli invasion of Lebanon in June 1982 was given at least tacit encouragement from a Reagan administration keen to 'go after' Soviet allies, in this case Syria and the PLO, in the third world.[26]

This strategic adjustment, the aligning of the Arab–Israeli dispute with the Cold War, was compounded by other developments in the 1970s and 1980s. One was the issue of Palestinian military action. In an argument that won some favour in Washington, the rise of Palestinian guerrilla resistance after 1967 was presented by Israel as a form of 'international terrorism', itself a product of Soviet hostility to the west. At the same time, in the early 1970s, criticism rose within the USA over the refusal of the USSR to permit the emigration of Soviet Jews. This appeared to cast Moscow not only as an opponent of Israel but as an enemy of Jewish people in general; in 1974 the US Congress passed the Jackson–Vanick Amendment, proposed in the immediate aftermath of the October 1973 war, which made the award by the USA of Most Favoured Nation trading status to the USSR dependent upon increased Jewish emigration. Thirdly, as had occurred in Turkey before 1950 and Egypt in the post-Suez period, domestic change facilitated foreign policy realignment: in this case Israeli society changed. The shift within Israel, from a largely statist economy run by the Labour Party with strict, if not utopian, social controls (jeans were banned in the 1950s) to a more open market-oriented one ruled by Likud, matured in the 1970s along with an increasing influence of religious parties; the Likud victory of 1977, expressing the demise of the socialist bloc around Labour, removed a further obstacle to US alignment with the Jewish state.[27] The trauma of 1967 was evident here too: in Israel too people turned to atavism and religion.

However, this sealing of Israel into the Cold War system after 1967 did not produce stability in the region. The alignment of Israel with the USA and the apparent Cold War support Israel received did not, in the longer run, resolve the political and strategic challenges it faced. The first problem was to its north. From 1975 Lebanon had been beset by civil war, a coalition of Arab nationalist, Muslim and Palestinian forces being aligned against a coalition led by Maronite Christians. In 1976, in order to offset the power of the nationalist-Muslim and Palestinian bloc, Syria had intervened in the conflict, committing one of the greatest single

[26] On the general misrepresentation of Moscow's policy see Fred Halliday, *Soviet Policy in the 'Arc of Crisis'*, Washington, DC: Institute of Policy Studies, 1981.
[27] Among a large literature, see especially Steven Spiegel, *The Other Arab–Israeli Dispute: Making America's Middle East Policy from Truman to Reagan*, Chicago: University of Chicago Press, 1985.

atrocities of post-1945 Middle East history, the slow death through dehy-
dration of thousands of Palestinians at the camp of Tel el-Zaatar. From
1978 onwards Israel too sought to play a role in Lebanon: it aimed to
destroy the PLO and establish a friendly state based on the Maronites,
goals it did not achieve. The invasion in 1982 failed to destroy its enemies, and it, too, was to perpetrate, through criminal indifference at least,
another act of world perfidy, the killings in the Palestinian camps of Sabra
and Chatila in 1984. Eighteen years after it invaded, in July 2000, Israel
was forced to abandon its presence in Lebanon.

At the same time, its peace with Egypt yielded little in the way of
broader normalisation with the Arab world. Most strikingly, the Palestinian issue refused to go away: two decades of guerrilla action outside
Israel, and to some extent within, were followed in 1987 by the outbreak
of the first *intifadha*, a sustained Palestinian resistance. This took the form
of demonstrations, strikes and political protests that could not easily be
defeated and placed the question of Palestinian rights firmly back on the
international agenda. The limits of state action, through Cold War alignment and military conquest, were evident. As in Vietnam and southern
Africa, the masses did *not* 'understand' the language of force. The ebbing
of the Cold War in the late 1980s was, therefore, accompanied by an
enduring social and political resistance and by growing recognition,
among some Israeli and Palestinian leaders, that compromise was necessary. Whether a lasting Israeli–Palestinian compromise was possible, and
would command sufficient support on both sides, remained to be seen,
not least because of the fecklessness of the international community and
the lack of serious engagement by the Arab/Muslim and Jewish worlds
alike.

In contrast to Israel's victory in that war, 1967 signalled the end of
Nasserism as a model for Egyptian, and Arab, revolution. While a crisis
of Nasserism was evident beforehand, in Egypt and in the Arab world,
that year marked the beginning of its end as the ideology of Arab unity
and of struggle against colonialism and Zionism. Slowly, while Nasser
was alive, and more rapidly under his successor Anwar al-Sadat, the
Egyptian economy was liberalised and a private sector, backed by capital
from Arab states and protected by a still predominant state, began to
develop. To a considerable extent Egypt itself withdrew from its drive for
Arab unity: its forces left Yemen in 1967,[28] and it made peace with the

[28] It is almost conventional to state that Egypt's intervention in Yemen was a failure; despite
what most Egyptians will say, it was not. The Republic that Egypt sought to defend
survived, and a compromise peace that preserved it was signed in 1970. The subsequent
state was, with Yemeni characteristics, a variant of the military nationalist structure that
Egypt embodied in the ideology of the ruling party, the 'General People's Congress', a
replica of milder 'Arab socialism'.

conservative Arab states such as Saudi Arabia and its allies, which, emboldened by the defeat of Arab radicalism, were to become all the more powerful after the fourfold rise of oil prices in 1971–3. Sadat, who was wont to evoke his origins in a village, fell back onto appeals to the 'sons of the Nile', not Nasser's Arab *umma*. Egypt itself was, however, able to restore a degree of honour in the face of Israel when, in October 1973, it launched a surprise attack on that country: the aim was not to destroy the Jewish state but to restore Egypt's political credibility, at home and internationally, and to force the outside world to push for a negotiation with Israel. This strategy came to fruition in 1977–9: Egyptian president Sadat visited Jerusalem in 1977 and in 1979 signed an accord at Camp David in the USA. In this, Egypt recognised Israel in return for a withdrawal of Israeli forces from Sinai. Peace between the two main protagonists, albeit a cold one, was achieved.[29] The settlement Egypt aimed for in the war of 1973 was sustained; although derided by many Arabs at the time, it outlived not only Sadat, who was assassinated in 1981, but also the Cold War itself.

Like their precursors in 1948 and 1956, the Arab–Israeli inter-state conflicts of 1967 and 1973 also intersected with other trends developing *within* the region and in Middle Eastern states themselves. Indeed, beyond its strategic consequences, the war of 1967 had marked a turning point in three other respects. First, in discrediting militant Arab nationalism, it also undermined the prestige within the Arab world of the main backer of that nationalism, the USSR. Once ties began to loosen, Egyptians, never quick to take responsibility for their own disasters, began to talk of the difficulties they had had with the Russians, at the official and personal level.[30] For the Russians this was a shock; it was said that if the Americans suffered from a 'Vietnam Syndrome', the Soviets had an 'Egypt Syndrome', an aversion to third world commitment born of this particular experience. While at first it appeared that Arab nationalists would turn to the even more militant rival of the Soviet Union, China, the main trend was in the opposite direction, towards an accommodation with the west and a rejection of socialism, in all its variants. Sadat himself played this carefully: the president turned against Soviet allies inside Egypt in 1971, what he termed 'the uprising of thieves' (*intifadha al-harami-ya*), and in 1972 he expelled Soviet advisers. However, he needed Soviet weapons for his planned secret assault upon Israel and only in 1976

[29] William Quandt, *Camp David: Peacemaking and Politics*, Washington, DC: Brookings Institution, 1986.
[30] For one graphic if partisan account see Mohamed Heikal, *The Sphinx and the Commissar: the Rise and Fall of Soviet Influence in the Middle East*, London: André Deutsch, 1978. For a Soviet retrospective, informed and quizzical, see Alexei Vassiliev, *Russian Policy in the Middle East: From Messianism to Pragmatism*, Reading: Ithaca Press, 1993.

did he complete the break by cancelling the Friendship Treaty between Egypt and the USSR, and by abrogating Soviet naval facilities. Henceforward, in accordance with his own principle that the Americans held '99 per cent of the cards', Sadat pursued his negotiation strategy uniquely through Washington.[31]

Some other Arab regimes retained closer links to the USSR: Syria remained until the end of the Cold War dependent on Soviet military and diplomatic support, the Libyan military regime that came to power in 1969 also developed military links, whilst in southern Arabia the PDRY became Moscow's closest ally in the Arab world, rejecting 'Arab socialism' in favour of its 'scientific' Soviet variety.[32] Iraq pursued a more complex game plan: while Iraqi regimes had, after 1958, developed better relations with Moscow and had clashed with the west, the radical nationalist Ba'thist regime that came to power in 1968 diversified its foreign alignments.[33] It built a close relationship with France, and drew on considerable western, including US and British, support during its war in the 1980s with Iran. In this way the two decades that began in 1955, in which the Arab world as a whole was drawn into the Cold War, gave way to a more fragmented, and fluid, regional picture. Even as Soviet influence remained in some Arab states, the impact of the Cold War as a formative global conflict receded. A number of 'Arab socialist' regimes used the Soviet model of ruling party and state-controlled economy to consolidate their rule, but this was in a modified form and reflected an instrumental coincidence, not any ideological affinity. Five-year plans and elaborate grades of party privilege (the latter a particular speciality of the Ba'th) were part of the self-image of elites across the twentieth century.

The second process unleashed by 1967 was the re-emergence of the Palestinians as an autonomous political force. Prior to 1948 Palestinian politics had been dominated by a loose coalition of religious officials and notables; under the Mandate, they had been able to negotiate in some measure with British officials, but showed no ability to offset or deal effectively with the growing strength of the Jewish community.[34] The war of 1947–9 dispersed this leadership as it did the Palestinian community, and in the ensuing years the Arab states ensured that no independent Palestinian leadership emerged. Only in 1964 was an official organisation,

---

[31] William Qaundt, *Peace Process: American Diplomacy and the Arab–Israeli Conflict since 1967*, Berkeley: University of California Press, 1993.

[32] Fred Halliday, *Revolution and Foreign Policy: the Case of South Yemen, 1967–1987*, Cambridge: Cambridge University Press, 1990.

[33] Oleg Smolansky, *The USSR and Iraq: the Quest for Influence*, Durham, NC: Duke University Press, 1991.

[34] Rashid Khalidi, *Palestinian Identity: the Construction of Modern National Consciousness*, New York: Columbia University Press, 1997.

the Palestinian Liberation Organisation, established by the Arab League, but very much under the control of Arab states, and in particular Egypt. At that point it was a 'non-state actor' only in name.

However, 1967, gave the Palestinian movement room for manoeuvre: the regular Arab armies were discredited, while political mobilisation grew within the newly occupied West Bank and in the refugee camps of Jordan and Lebanon. The new leader of the PLO, Yasser Arafat, an engineer from a modestly well-off family in Gaza, used his own political organisation al-Fath (a reverse acronym for the Arabic HTaF, *Harakat al-tahrir filastin*, or Palestinian Liberation Movement) to represent an independent Palestine voice. While al-Fath and other groups carried out guerrilla actions in areas under Israeli control, the PLO itself came to challenge established Arab states, first in Jordan, up to 1970 and then, from the early 1970s onwards, in Lebanon. If the Jordanian challenge was defeated, by King Hussein in 1970, that in Lebanon was to be a major factor behind the explosion of a brutal civil war there that began in 1975 and was to last until 1990.[35]

Throughout the 1970s and 1980s the Arab states sought to contain and influence the Palestinians. In 1974 at the Fez summit of Arab leaders the PLO was confirmed as the sole legitimate representative of the Palestinian people. While much of the third world gave broad verbal support, the western world sought at first to ignore Palestinian national claims: Israeli leaders dismissed the PLO as 'terrorists', a term that, deliberately, confused tactics with political aim, and others, particularly the USA, sought to keep them at arm's length. But over time the very endurance of the Palestinians, and a shift of opinion not only in the west but in Israel itself, led to a change. By the late 1980s, the PLO came increasingly to be accepted as an independent and legitimate force. Parallel to its military activities, the PLO pursued a diplomatic strategy that led it in 1988 to proclaim its own willingness to accept an Israeli state side by side with a Palestinian one. The history of this process of growing, if unstable, mutual recognition by Israeli and Palestinian leaders, and by some at least of their own people, was complex and incomplete: many layers of prejudice in their own ranks, and in the broader world, against Palestinians on the one side and Jews on the other, remained. Yet the legacy of the war of 1947–9 – Palestinian refusal to accept a Jewish state, Israeli denial of the Palestinian claim to statehood – was in principle corrected by the Oslo Agreement in 1993; in this the Israeli government and the PLO agreed to work for a final, and just, settlement of the dispute.

[35] Yezid Sayigh, *Armed Struggle and the Search for a State: the Palestinian National Movement, 1949–1993*, Oxford: Clarendon Press, 1997.

The realisation, and time-frame, of implementation appeared to remain, however, beyond the grasp of leaders on both sides. Mutual suspicion at the level of negotiation was compounded by continuing and repeatedly inflamed resentment among their peoples, and by the influence of obstructive, and irresponsible, diasporas.

The rise of Islamism was the third underlying social and political process unleashed by the war of 1967. This retreat from secularisation was less immediately evident but was to have long-term consequences for the Arab world, for the Muslim world as a whole and indeed for Israel. Despite the use of some religious rhetoric, Arab socialism was in large measure secular, a local variant of the generic third world populism of the age.[36] Socialism's decline, combined with a broader shift in social attitudes, led over time to a return, by state and social movements alike, to the espousal of a more traditional set of values, associated with religion. This was evident in a country like Egypt where interest in al-turath (heritage), and in Islam became stronger across a broad social spectrum. It was evident too in the influence of states, most notably Saudi Arabia, which sought to increase their own influence by promoting 'Islamic' values, and in the rise of opposition movements, sometimes associated with the Muslim Brotherhood. These Islamist radicals saw themselves both as a challenge to the secular state and as a pan-Arab movement. Here the Arab world matched the process seen in Iran. There was no one cause of this shift, but it reflected a general rejection of the secular modernity associated with radical nationalist politics and with the modernising state. Thus a pattern could be discerned wherein the impact of the secular modern state, whatever its particular ideological orientation, was met by a rising Islamist resistance. The latter interpreted religion, tradition and culture in oppositional form.[37]

For Egypt this shift to religion was stimulated by the 1967 war. Elsewhere, in countries as diverse as Iran and Algeria, strong Islamist movements emerged in opposition to the secular state, the first example taking

---

[36] Adeed Dawisha, *Arab Nationalism in the Twentieth Century: From Triumph to Despair*, Princeton: Princeton University Press, 2002. On populism in general, and with much that is uncannily resonant of Middle Eastern cases, see the essay on Latin American variations (Peronism especially) published in 1977, two years before the triumph of the Iranian revolution, by the Argentinean theorist Ernesto Laclau: *Politics and Ideology in Marxist Theory: Capitalism – Fascism – Populism*, London: NLB, 1977, chapter 4 'Towards a Theory of Populism'. This essay by Laclau, whose analytic themes are paralleled in the classic study by Ervand Abrahamian, *Khomeinism* (London: I. B. Tauris, 1993), sets populism in its *modern* context and in so doing casts more light on the ideology of the Ayatollah, a religious-populist melange, than any excavations of the Quran or *hadith*.

[37] Fred Halliday, *Nation and Religion in the Middle East*, London: Saqi, 2000, chapter 7, 'Fundamentalism and the State: Iran and Tunisia'.

power in 1979, the other from 1989 onwards engaging in sustained violent opposition to the National Liberation Front (FLN). Turkey too was far from immune to this process: those forces opposed to the Kemalist state that had begun to emerge in the 1940s gained ground in the transformed social and economic climate of Turkey in the 1970s and 1980s. Islamists came to office in 1996–7 and again in 2003. This shift in political culture and sentiment, which took different forms in each country, reflected both changes maturing within Middle Eastern states and wider international trends. It was in part a reaction against the kind of state and secular politics that had been generated by the Cold War, in both the pro-western and pro-Soviet blocs, but it was also encouraged by some states as a means of countering left-wing and secular opposition movements.

The most dramatic instance of this promotion of Islamist groups, very much as part of the Cold War, was the US arming of the Afghan guerrillas fighting the Red Army in Afghanistan after 1978. During the 1970s and 1980s, however, many other countries, not only Saudi Arabia but also Turkey, Egypt and indeed Israel, sought to use Islamist groups to diminish the influence of their opponents, only to find that such groups had outlived their initial patronage and become independent, violent actors. In September 2001 this was to reach its culmination in the attacks on the USA. The power of these Islamist movements was, therefore, not a product of the *end* of the Cold War, but a pervasive, influential legacy of *the Cold War itself*, and the ends to which western states and their regional allies, in a policy of world-historical criminality and folly that was to cast its shadow over the onset of the twenty-first century, incited these fanatics and killers. Starting at 8.40 a.m. US Eastern Standard Time on 11 September 2001, the world was to learn what this meant for the century just begun.[38]

The Middle East and the Cold War: regional and global conflict

As we have seen, World War II did not so obviously shape the Middle East as World War I had done. It nonetheless laid the basis for much of what was to come after 1945 as, largely beyond the region, the Cold War unfolded on a world scale. The interaction was not, however, only one way. The Cold War was itself, repeatedly, influenced by events in the Middle East. The most visible of all dimensions of Cold War rivalry was in the case of the strategic rivalry, nuclear weapons. One Middle East state, Turkey, was a full member of NATO. No nuclear

[38] Gilles Kepel, *Jihad: the Trail of Political Islam*, London: I. B. Tauris, 2002.

weapons were used in the Middle East and, in the main, the great powers abstained from deploying them in the region, in contrast to Europe and East Asia. But the USA did deploy intermediate range Jupiter nuclear missiles, capable of hitting targets in the Soviet Union, in Turkey in 1961.[39] As part of contingency planning for a world crisis, Britain designated Masira, off the Omani coast, as a dispersal site for its nuclear weapons.

Moreover, the crises that erupted in the Middle East had their impact on nuclear policies and east–west relations. The Cold War indeed began in the region: the first major Soviet–US showdown was not over Berlin or Poland, but over the Soviet refusal to leave Iranian Azerbaijan in March 1946. On several occasions thereafter the Cold War rivals went on nuclear alert as a result of developments in the region: the Middle East was the cause of nuclear alert on six out of a total of twenty occasions for nuclear alert by the USA, the last and most important being during the Arab–Israeli war of October 1973. The Middle East was also the occasion for the one, and only, time that the USSR itself threatened the use of nuclear weapons, during the Suez crisis of 1956.[40] Both sides supplied their allies with large quantities of weapons during the Cold War period: indeed throughout these years the Middle East was the largest recipient of arms supplies of any region of the developing world.

The region was not the sole or, compared with Europe or East Asia, the *main* locus of Cold War conflict. Yet both blocs saw the Middle East as, in different ways, vital to their security. The series of global security doctrines enunciated by successive US presidents were, to a considerable extent, prompted by, or at least readily applicable to, the Middle East. The Truman Doctrine (1947) applied, in addition to Greece, to defence of western interests in Turkey and Iran. The Eisenhower Doctrine (1957) was explicitly directed at reassuring US allies in the Arab world in the aftermath of Suez. The Kennedy Doctrine (1961), promoting social reform to pre-empt revolution, was applied to land reform in Iran and Egypt. The Nixon Doctrine (1969) encouraged a greater role by

[39] John Lewis Gaddis, *We Now Know: Rethinking Cold War History*, Oxford: Clarendon Press, 1997 pp. 264–5. At the time of writing (2004) it is not yet evident whether the large amount of material thrown up since 1991 from Soviet and, some, western sources about the Cold War in the Middle East has led to any major breakthroughs or revision of established views, compared with what we now know about, say, the Korean war, the Cuban missile crisis, the wars of southern Africa, etc. On the most contentious issues of the time, I would say that 'we', the members of the editorial committee and broader community of MERIP(Middle East Report and Information Project), got it right.

[40] Barry Blechman and Steve Kaplan, *Force without War*, Washington, DC: Brookings Institution, 1978, p. 48. These instances of nuclear alert were: Suez 1956, Lebanon 1958, Jordan 1958, Turkey 1963, Jordan 1970, Arab–Israeli war 1973. The 1970 Jordan incident is not included in Blechman and Kaplan.

influential regional powers including Iran and Saudi Arabia. The Carter Doctrine (1980) was designed to protect US interests in the Gulf. The Reagan Doctrine (early 1980s), actively challenging the USSR through anti-communist insurgency, was applied most vigorously in Afghanistan but, by providing a 'green light' to Israel, also encouraged it to attack Soviet allies, the PLO and Syria, in Lebanon in 1982.[41] A further dimension of US policy in the latter part of the Cold War was the fight against 'international terrorism'; this came to be a central feature of US security policy in the 1970s and 1980s and, while not exclusive to the Middle East, was particularly concerned with actions by Palestinians. Until the unexpected entry of Osama bin Laden, the core concern in the terrorism policy was Palestine.

For their part, the Soviets saw the Middle East in both military and political terms. Their pursuit of détente and strategic agreements with the USA was affected by a wish to prevent US deployment of forces in the region, near their frontier: there was a direct link between their deployment of missiles in Cuba in 1962 near the US mainland and their concern at the US deployment of missiles in Turkey. As Khrushchev inimitably put it, 'We shall put a hedgehog in Uncle Sam's pants!' Like the USA the Soviets also sought to justify their support for regional allies, with weapons and political assistance, in terms of broader doctrines. Thus Arab allies were part of a broad 'national democratic' and 'non-capitalist' bloc that was growing in the third world and which, as seen from Moscow, strengthened the camp of those opposed to the west. This strategy of Cold War engagement was to reach its culmination in the 1980s with the participation of *ogranicchonni kontingent*,[42] the 'limited contingent', over more than nine years, in the war in Afghanistan.

However, for all the incorporation of the Middle East into broader Cold War strategies and ideological visions, there were limits to the fusion of regional and global politics. In the first place, both major powers stayed out of major *direct* involvement in the region. US forces did enter Lebanon unopposed in 1958, and the CIA was active in many contexts, most notably in Iran in 1953; yet the first time that US troops actually fought in the Middle East was after the Cold War ended, in Kuwait in 1991. The USSR deployed forces in Egypt, above all after the June 1967 war, but again avoided overt, direct, involvement. Secondly, each side, for all their use of military supplies and political support for allies, knew these

---

[41] Zeev Schiff, 'The Invasion of Lebanon: Did Washington Give a "Green Light"?', *Foreign Policy*, Summer 1984.

[42] And 'limited' it was: compared with the 550,000 troops that the USA had, at its peak involvement, in Vietnam, the Soviet forces in Afghanistan were, at their maximum, 190,000.

were instruments with limited effect. For example, Soviet air and artillery crews did participate directly in the 'war of attrition' fighting along the Suez Canal after 1967. Yet while western states and Israel knew what was happening, this was concealed from public discussion at the time; as had happened in the Korean war, and in several other conflicts in the third world, for reasons of strategic management and to ward off public pressure for precipitate action, the Soviet role was not challenged by the west.

The Soviets too avoided direct confrontation with the USA, despite repeated warnings, for example, by Brezhnev over Lebanon in July 1982, that they could not 'remain indifferent' to events so near their frontiers. Soviet leaders spoke ominously of the 'smell of oil', but did little to counter western action. The USSR continued to use diplomatic channels to contain conflict in the Middle East: the Arab–Israeli wars were, to a degree greater than those of other regions, discussed and negotiated at the United Nations in New York. In the latter part of the 1980s diplomatic contacts continued on a range of 'regional' matters – Palestine, the Iran–Iraq war, Afghanistan. Moreover, in the overall context of the Cold War, the scale of conflict in the Middle East should be recognised. Total casualties in the Arab–Israeli wars were round 50,000, far less than those in the wars of Algeria or Yemen, or the Iran–Iraq war, and small compared with those of the wars of East Asia and southern Africa.[43] The region knew no Vietnam or Korea, no Angola or El Salvador; Afghanistan in the 1980s was on its margins, its impact all the more muted by the fact that the Iran–Iraq war was raging at the same time. This was, of course, to change later as Saudi Arabia and others were to reap what they had sown.

All of this international rivalry of the Cold War years was shaped by the regional states themselves. Of no little significance for the external powers, and in contrast to the more obedient regimes of other regions (for example, eastern Europe, Latin America), the states of the Middle East displayed an ideological individuality and resilience that made them uneasy partners for both east and west. Of the eighteen Arab states only one, South Yemen or the People's Democratic Republic of Yemen (PDRY), was a full supporter of the Soviet Union, embracing the theory of 'scientific socialism' and modelling itself on the Soviet pattern of political and economic development. For all their temporary alliances with Moscow, the Arab nationalist regimes kept Soviet influence and local commitments

[43] Anthony Cordesman, *Perilous Prospects: the Peace Process and the Arab–Israeli Military Balance*, Oxford: Westview Press, 1996, p. 105, Table 5.1 'Losses in the Arab–Israeli Wars, 1948–1982'.

at bay.[44] On the other side, only Israel had a political system that, for its own Jewish citizens, approximated to the model of western democracy, the remaining allies of the west – in the Arab world, as well as Turkey and Iran – being ruled by various forms of authoritarian regime where the state controlled political and much of economic life. As far as Middle East states were concerned, alliance with the 'free world' was an external, not a domestic, matter. In the most constant Arab ally of the USA, Saudi Arabia, slavery was permitted until 1965.

The Cold War in the Middle East: a balance sheet

The period of the Cold War had, therefore, a profound effect on the Middle East, its states and peoples, and on the place of the Middle East within the international system as a whole. Yet it is important here to distinguish between the Cold War as a global, formative *context*, and the Cold War as a system of *strategic control* which dictated the actions of local states and movements. As states and political movements manoeuvred to take advantage of the global rivalry, that rivalry itself had a profound impact on many parts of the region, inspiring mass movements of left and right. External forces sought allies and poured weapons, advice and in some cases economic assistance into the region. In addition, the Cold War certainly accelerated the transition in international involvement that World War II had begun – pushing out the French and the British, bringing in the Americans and the Russians.

On some occasions, the Middle East could be seen as the focus of the global rivalry: over Iran and Turkey in 1946, in the Arab–Israeli conflicts of 1967 and 1973, and, on the margins, over Afghanistan after 1979. Yet in two respects the independent impact of those forty years of global conflict should not be overstated. In terms of state–state relations, as already noted, the Cold War, unlike World War I, did not alter the state map of the Middle East, with the exception of Israel's expansion in 1967; that delineation of states remained virtually unchanged. Unlike both world

---

[44] The same primacy of regional/local power applied to social forces – be they the Palestinians or the Islamic revolutionaries. My central argument in *Soviet Policy in the 'Arc of Crisis'* was that the upheavals of the late 1970s in the four states concerned – Afghanistan, Iran, South Yemen, Ethiopia – were due not to Soviet instigation but to political revolt within these states – an 'Arc of Revolution', not an 'Arc of Crisis'. For general discussion of Soviet policy see Rolan Danreuther, *The Soviet Union and the PLO*, London: Macmillan, 1998; Galia Golan, *Soviet Policies in the Middle East*, Cambridge: Cambridge University Press, 1990, and *The Soviet Union and National Liberation Movements in the Third World*, London: Unwin Hyman, 1988; Yaacov Ro'i, ed., *The Limits to Power: Soviet Policy in the Middle East*, London: Croom Helm, 1979; Fred Wehling, *Irresolute Princes: Kremlin Decision-Making in Middle East Crises, 1967–1973*, New York: St Martin's Press, 1997.

wars in the Middle East, and in contrast to the later war in East Asia, the Cold War in this region, Suez excepted, was not accompanied by military conflict directly involving major outside states. Also limited was the ideological impact of the Cold War. While in the aftermath of World War II Soviet communism did inspire mass movements in a number of countries (Iran, Iraq, Sudan, Egypt), these did not survive the repression of the Cold War itself. The Arab socialist regimes copied some of the rhetoric and administrative practices of the Soviet system, but they had their own reasons for doing so. As we shall see in chapter 7, the most lasting ideological impact of communism in mindset and vocabulary may turn out to have been in the influence it had, not on the secular left, but on Islamist discourse. On the pro-western and pro-capitalist side, while the attractions of western consumerism and financial security were more widely accepted by the middle classes of the region, this did not lead to a political alignment, in terms either of acceptance of western strategic goals or of the introduction of western democracy at home.

Now that the clamour of these four decades has died down, a balance sheet must, therefore, be cautious. In terms of influence on the course of events it is indubitable that the Cold War did provide the context and spur to many developments in the region: but the initiative all too often lay not in Moscow or Washington, but with the local states. It was part of Cold War, and nationalist, rhetoric to cast all opponents, within the state and outside it, as 'agents', 'puppets' and 'lackeys' of external powers; but the elites of Turkey, Israel, Iran and Saudi Arabia were not simply tools of Washington, any more than were the radical leaderships of Egypt, Syria, Libya, Iraq or the PDRY agents of Moscow. The policies of Egypt towards Israel in, say, 1967, and again in 1973, were by no means directed by Moscow. A striking example of this autonomy, while lacking even a state, was the PLO which resisted for years Soviet encouragement to recognise Israel as part of an eventual peace agreement. Equally, the radicals of the PDRY, albeit dependent on Soviet military and economic support, persisted in their aspiration to spread revolution to Oman and North Yemen. Ideology had its own dynamic, as anyone who knew the revolutionaries of that time can confirm.

Much of what took place in the inter-state relations of the Middle East during the Cold War had, moreover, little to do with the global conflict. Apart from inter-Yemeni rivalry, the major inter-state conflicts – Arab–Israeli, Iran–Iraq (from 1975), Syrian–Lebanese – had only an indirect relationship in their origins and outcomes to the Cold War. If this independence of regional actors was true for states, it was even more so for the social and political forces that states did not control. The upheavals that rocked the region, be they the Zionist drive for a state in the 1940s, the revolutions of Iraq and Iran, or the rise of Palestinian or Kurdish guerrillas, were themselves largely autonomous. The growth of Islamist sentiment from the 1970s onwards was a rejection of both west and east and served to threaten both, in ways peaceful and violent. As much as by the nuclear alerts and inter-state wars of the region, the history of the Middle East in the Cold War was marked by events that states did not control or which struck at states: on one side, military coups (for example, Egypt 1952, Iraq 1958, Yemen 1962, Iraq 1968) and the eruption of social movements (Palestine after 1967 and in 1987, Iran 1978–9, Hizbullah after 1982); on the other, longer-term shifts in the composition and values of society that enabled, or prevented, foreign policy shifts. Here again the narrative of states, global and regional, has to be combined with that of societies and social movements, a topic to which we shall return in chapter 8.

A final verdict on the past may rest not with global strategy, but with international political economy. What was decisive for most people in the region, the pursuit of a livelihood and a measure of economic security, had almost nothing to do with the Cold War: the USSR never offered significant amounts of investment or aid, let alone a viable economic model, whilst the monies coming from the west were largely channelled to elites through the provision of oil revenues from consumers and then recycled back to London and New York. If the Middle East that confronted the changed international situation of the early 1990s, after the end of the Cold War, was very different from that which had faced the world at the beginning of the conflict, in the 1940s, this was as much in spite of, as because of, the four decades of Cold War that had just passed. The most important conclusions by far, however, concern not what the Cold War did to the Middle East but what, as a result of the policies developed in the Cold War, the Middle East was, in the next historical phase, to do to the world. The seeds of the crisis of the atrocities and wars of the early twenty-first century, of 11 September 2001 and all that followed, lay in the Middle East of the 1970s and 1980s, and not in 'Islam', the 'Arab psyche' or any other such vapid hypostatisation. They lay in a concrete, political and socio-economic context that the outside world, in particular the west, had sought to exploit.

5 After the Cold War: the maturing of the Greater West Asian Crisis

'Dear Professor, very nice to see you. But, before you sit down, just one question: is Communism really finished?'

Gulf minister to author on visit to region, April 1999

Into the 1990s: international change, regional consequences

The course of events in the Middle East from the end of the Cold War (1991) to the early 2000s (2003) was, above all, framed by four dramatic, regional and, in their impact, global, developments: the Iraqi invasion of Kuwait on 2 August 1990, the signing of the Israeli–Palestinian Declaration of Principles on 13 September 1993; the al-Qa'ida attack on the USA on 11 September 2001; the Anglo-US occupation of Iraq in March–April 2003.

The first was an act of inter-state war that divided the region itself and drew external forces into regional conflict more directly than at any time since 1918. The Kuwait war of 1990–1, the Third Gulf war, prevented one possible course of history in that it checked Iraqi ambitions and restored the sovereignty of Kuwait. Yet while the immediate occasion for the conflict, the Iraqi occupation of Kuwait, was resolved, with the expulsion of Iraqi forces at the end of February 1991, the aftermath was to leave many issues unresolved. Not least among these was the international standing of Iraq itself, which was subjected to intrusive inspection and elaborate sanctions. The tinder of further conflicts remained, only to be concluded in 2003. The aftermath of the 1990–1 Gulf war also produced other tensions within, and between, the states of the region that were to contribute both to 11 September 2001 and its consequences, and to the 2003 Iraq war. The Palestinian–Israel Declaration of Principles raised hopes that some definitive settlement of the Palestinian question would be reached: indeed they envisaged a permanent settlement by December 1998. Instead, however, as the leadership on both sides faltered, and public support in every camp waned, the dynamic of peace began to unravel, no definitive settlement was reached and in September 2000 a second Palestinian *intifadha* broke out. A decade after the Gulf war, it was to be the tensions unresolved by that event, and a broader pattern of increasingly integrated regional tension which I have termed the 'Greater West Asian Crisis',[1] to which the Palestine issue made a major contribution, that exploded first in September 2001, then in the occupation of Iraq in 2003. The events of 11 September 2001 and the 2003 Iraq war were to be the culmination of tensions inherited from Cold War and post-Cold War alike, and of tensions as much *within* the societies of the region as in inter-state relations.

Central to this course of events was a process, slow but inexorable, whereby a growing *interlocking* of regional crises was taking place.[2] Country-based issues, like Palestine or Iraq, hitherto relatively distinct in origin, were now combined in one broader regional crisis, one that went beyond the Middle East to include Afghanistan and South Asia. Hence the use here of the term 'Greater West Asian Crisis' to designate both tensions between states and, at the regional level (for example, in terms of nuclear competition), from below, a sense of shared popular concern and militancy, one that stretched from Palestine in the west to Kashmir, a region disputed by India and Pakistan, in the east. To offer an example of interlocking at the inner-state level: a country like Iran was affected by the Indo-Pakistani nuclear breakout of 1998, by its own rivalry with Iraq and with, to a lesser extent, Saudi Arabia, and by the Arab–Israeli dispute. At the same time, in the popular mind Palestine, Iraq, Afghanistan were all linked 'causes', and objects of mistaken western policy. Nor indeed was the 'Greater West Asian Crisis' the slimit of strategic interaction: to the east, India's nuclear test in 1998 was justified by its rivalry with China, with which it had fought a war in 1962, while to the west of even the 'Greater' West Asia the disintegration of Yugoslavia after 1991 translated Middle East rivals into the Balkans – Iran, the Arabs and Turkey favouring Muslim forces in Bosnia and Kosovo, whilst Israel and Greece were sympathetic to Serbia; popular imagination did not lag far behind – taking in such disparate questions as the secession of East Timor from (Muslim) Indonesia in 1999, and moving over to the civil war in Algeria after 1991 or the fate of Muslim immigrants in Europe, even the USA, especially after 11 September 2001.

---

[1] Fred Halliday, *Two Hours that Shook the World – September 11, 2001: Causes and Consequences*, London: Saqi, 2001.

[2] In early 2004 Washington, in response to grandiose, but ill-conceived, plans to pursue a wider process of democratisation in the Middle East, started to call for a 'Greater Middle East Initiative', the 'Greater' *excluding* Afghanistan and Pakistan. Europe, bemused and somewhat apprehensive, was to follow (*Financial Times*, 5 February 2004). A few weeks later under Arab *and* European pressure, the 'GMEI' was scaled down.

The end of the Cold War in the Middle East was, however, in large measure the result not of these specific regional crises themselves but of broader changes in the global context that only then had their considerable impact on the region. The abrupt end of the global conflict in 1989–91 transformed the context of Middle Eastern politics, but not in the way that many who envisaged an age of peace and liberalisation might have anticipated. The period from the late 1980s to the 2000s was, above all, not one of a greater interdependence or liberalisation, but one in which patterns of regional conflict and alliance came to prevail over the international rivalry of great powers. The region asserted autonomy, *against* the global trend; this was the significance of August 1990, of the unravelling of the Israeli–Palestinian peace agreement during the later 1990s, of September 2001 and of the slow-moving but ineluctable drift of the USA and Iraq towards war in 2003.

To take the global changes first. Proceeding from the nature of the Cold War itself, as both inter-state and social process, several broad global trends – strategic, regional, socio-economic – followed from its denouement: the end of east–west strategic nuclear and geopolitical rivalry, the dissolution of the Soviet Union itself and the reconfiguring of inter-state and regional relations, the end of the ideological division of the world into capitalist and anti-capitalist forces, and the spread, as a consequence, of a model of supposedly neo-liberal political and economic organisation to new areas of the world.[3] The end of strategic and ideological rivalry was accompanied by, and in some measure served itself to accelerate, a separate process associated with the erosion of barriers between states, termed 'globalisation'. Globalisation and the end of the Cold War were not identical processes: the former reflected the lessening of barriers – economic, political, cultural – between states within the western world, the latter was primarily a strategic and ideological shift.[4] However, together these two trends, reduction in strategic competition and globalisation, defined at the international level the period after 1991 and in so doing did much to shape events, and expectations, in the Middle East.

Yet here the distinctive characters of regional states and societies were decisive. Middle Eastern states reacted to the changes but as much against, as in accordance with, global trends: their policies were, in the main, designed to offset any impact global trends might have, particularly

[3] William Hale and Eberhard Kienle, eds., *After the Cold War: Security and Democracy in Africa and Asia*, London: I. B. Tauris, 1997.
[4] Ian Clark, *Globalization and International Relations Theory*, Oxford: Oxford University Press, 1999; John Baylis and Steve Smith, eds., *The Globalization of World Politics: an Introduction to International Relations*, second edition, Oxford: Oxford University Press, 2001. The Arabic for 'globalisation', *al-'aulama*, is neutral, but Persian has two rival terms, one denoting favour – *jahanishodan*, literally 'world-becoming' – and one commendation – *jahanigiri*, 'world-taking'.

in the reduction of state control of the economy and the promotion of a genuine, as distinct from showcase, democratic process. This state resistance was compounded within regional societies: in much of the region popular responses to the disappearance of the USSR or to globalisation were dominated by suspicion. While keeping the general context in view, therefore, here it is important to avoid, as in earlier phases, excess generalisation: it is not possible to apply, without qualification, world-wide trends to an area that, while not immune to general historical trends, has its own resilient specificity. The reason was not culture or religion as such, or the insecure regional inter-state situation, but the response of states and social movements to these changes. What was striking was how many of the global trends of the 1990s did *not* affect the Middle East; this was as true of political processes, such as democratisation, as of the economic effects of globalisation. The Middle Eastern state, and those who benefited from controlling it, was not about to go out of business. *In sum, states kept control of politics, society and economy, and where necessary took pre-emptive action. The same applied to those social movements which challenged states within the new international context.*

This counter-cyclical Middle Eastern distinctiveness was all the more noticeable because the region was in a key respect already *in advance of* the strategic global trend, as has been suggested: if the Cold War is defined above all as the dominance of international politics by Soviet–US competition, then it had to a large extent ended in the Middle East not in the late 1980s but a decade earlier, with the Iranian revolution and the onset of the Iran–Iraq war (1979–80). The relationship of the Cold War's demise to the most dramatic event that accompanied it in the Middle East, and arguably in the world, the Iraqi invasion of Kuwait in August 1990, and to the subsequent international response, was also far from direct, of one cause followed by one effect. An examination of the three broad *global consequences* of the end of the Cold War – strategic, regional, social and ideological – needs, therefore, to be matched by a discussion of *autonomous trends* within the region in the 1990s.

End of the Cold War: global dimensions

End of east–west strategic rivalry

The pragmatic co-operation of Moscow and Washington in the region, Afghanistan excluded, but evident from 1982 vis-à-vis Iraq, became more comprehensive during the latter half of the 1980s, including above all the moves towards a joint international initiative on the Palestine question at the Madrid Conference in October 1991. With the end of significant Soviet arms deliveries after the collapse of the USSR in late 1991, and with Moscow in effect acting as a very secondary actor, in this context an associate of US policy, the attempt to find a diplomatic solution to the most explosive regional issue was initiated. Yet the impact of the end of the Cold War was not limited to the Arab–Israeli region, since it had important implications for Soviet and US policy on two other areas of conflict, the Iraq–Kuwait crisis and the unification of Yemen.

From the US side, the ending of the rivalry with the USSR, and the apparent lack of major challenges to its Middle East policy from other states, gave it the unprecedented advantage of unipolarity. This meant in the first instance that Washington could devote more attention to its core concern in the field of energy: this interest involved the reliable flow of oil, to the USA and allied economies, and at what were judged to be 'reasonable' prices (say, $20 to $30 per barrel). This energy policy, rarely spelt out in formal terms, or even formally negotiated behind closed doors, but understood by both sides, continued to be successful for much of the 1990s until, in 1999 and 2000, OPEC was able to effect a substantial price increase. This price rise in turn precipitated much more forceful US pressure on oil-producing states, the US Secretary for Energy, Bill Richardson, at one point calling the Qatari delegate on his mobile phone during an OPEC summit meeting to suggest to him what to say. The other focus of US policy after 1999 was securing systems in the Gulf and can be dealt with more briefly. Here the war of 1991 had achieved two of its goals – the expulsion of Iraqi forces from Kuwait, and the longer-term strategic containment of Kuwait. But the Desert Storm campaign of 1990–1 did not lead to a broader resolution of the issues that had underlain the crisis in the first place.

However, despite the fact that US oil policy involved above all a continuation of priorities already established, some major changes in the political economy of oil could be observed. As a direct result of the 1990–1 Gulf war and of alarm about the long-run instability of the region, President Bush and Secretary of State Baker took the decision in 1991–2 to promote more actively the Arab–Israeli peace process. They thereby qualified, but did not abandon, the static, and virtually unconditional, support for Israel that had till then, since 1967 in effect, prevailed along the Potomac.

Beyond Gulf oil, the main political focus of US policy in the region in the early 1990s was therefore on the Arab–Israeli context. In regard to the Gulf states, the initiatives taken in 1991 by the US administration, which led to the Madrid Conference of October 1991, appeared to run aground. No substantive agreement came out of the bilateral talks contained within the Madrid process (Syria–Israel, PLO–Israel). Over time the multilateral committees set up to discuss 'functional' issues, such as trade and water, foundered. A series of conferences held with Israel and

Arab states designed to promote economic integration of Israel into the Middle East led to little, the last, at Doha in 1996, boycotted by Saudi Arabia and Egypt. By the mid-1990s, Arab willingness to go along with this multilateral process had faded; it evaporated entirely when Premier Rabin was assassinated in 1995 and Likud won the Israeli elections in 1996. Attempts to persuade Syria to reach a compromise peace with Israel failed repeatedly; a meeting between Presidents Assad and Clinton in Geneva foundered again after less than half an hour (Clinton, with a heavy cold, mishandled disastrously the opening exchanges with Assad). Without Syrian agreement there was no possibility of a lasting separate peace between Israel and Lebanon. Israel did sign such a peace agreement with Lebanon in 1993, but this was overturned by the latter in 1994.

This failure with Lebanon was without broader resonance; a peace agreement reached with Jordan in 1994 did endure. However, the momentum of 1991 was not entirely lost: in 1991–3, Palestinian and Israeli negotiators continued to hold secret talks separate from the Madrid process. In August 1993 they surprised the region, and the world, by reaching agreement at talks in Oslo on a negotiation procedure: this involved, amongst other things, recognition by Israel and the Palestinians of each other's existence as a nation and implicitly the right of each to their own state. It may have appeared as though Oslo was an alternative to Madrid; but Oslo was not as separate from the official Madrid process, and hence from US diplomacy and power, as it may have seemed. Whilst Norway played an important facilitating role, it was the momentum set in train by 1991 that made Oslo possible. Moreover, after 1992 it was in the main the USA, with support from the EU, Norway, South African president Nelson Mandela and others, that took the process further. Significantly, the final agreement, at which PLO leader Arafat shook hands with Israeli premier Rabin in September 1993, was signed in Washington.[5] There is, needless to say, many a 'contested' IR lesson in this story. Enthusiasts for informal diplomacy, and 'non-state' actors, may claim this outcome as their own. Others, intoning the power of large states and noting their intermittent diplomatic attention, may, sadly, disagree.

The contraction of Russia

Beyond these immediate policy adjustments in east–west strategy following the end of the Cold War, a more specific geopolitical change occurred, namely the strategic retreat of Russia. This was a result not

[5] Mahmoud Abbas, *Through Secret Channels: the Road to Oslo*, Reading: Garnet, 1995; John King, *Handshake in Washington: the Beginning of Middle East Peace?*, Reading: Ithaca Press, 1994.

only of Moscow's reduced international, particularly military, role, but above all because of its geographic retrenchment, with the abandonment of Transcaucasia and Central Asia as well as much of the northern coast of the Black Sea in the latter part of 1991. Gorbachev had, in weeks, reversed the Tsarist gains of 1763–1828. For the first time in two centuries, Russia did not have a common border with the Middle East. While it, and some Arab states, evoked its past strategic role, this was an illusion: Russia became a country with a policy relationship more like that of western European countries – Britain, France, Germany – and more dependent on whatever economic links it could build from afar.[6] For all the changes in modern communication and transport, territory still mattered in international relations – not least for such new 'actors' as illegal immigrants, drug smugglers and cross-border 'suitcase' (in Russian, *chemodan*) traders. The disappearance of the USSR, a vast hegemonic state adjacent to the Middle East, was therefore an event of major importance, particularly for the countries of the northern tier – Turkey, Iran, Afghanistan.

Where Russia retained a vital interest, and where if anything the end of the Cold War created even greater uncertainty, was with regard to new patterns of inter-state relationship. These emerged in the region as a result of the fragmentation of the Soviet state. The end of the Cold War meant that the old controls by the superpowers, such as they were, and the element of predictability involved, had gone. After 1991 Russia was initially alarmed about the revival of Turkish power, something it had fought to oppose and to reduce from the mid-eighteenth century until 1918. To counter Turkey, Russia sought out a pragmatic relationship with Iran, and even Saudi Arabia. For all the 'faultline' rhetoric that here as elsewhere accompanied the end of the Cold War bloc system, there was in any case no reason to suppose that strategic relations between Russia and Turkey, or between Turkey and Iran, would necessarily become antagonistic, let alone lead to war: Turkish construction companies, for example, were more interested in good relations with Russia and Ukraine a short distance across the Black Sea than with distant, impoverished, Turkic states. These developments in Turco-Russian relations required, however, considerable diplomatic management on Ankara's part. This was especially so in regard to the conflicts of Transcaucasia and the Kurdish question. In the course of the 1990s Azerbaijan and the Chechnya rebels sought Turkish support, the PKK sought Russian aid. The pattern already discernible between the 1940s and the 1980s, whereby the regional and internal conflicts of the Middle East attracted international intervention, beyond that which external forces may initially have intended, was thereby reproduced in this new, post-Cold War situation. In the event, and for all the rhetoric of Turkic or Islamic identity, state interest prevailed over ideology and 'culture': neither Turkey nor Iran supported anti-Russian forces in this area.

The dissolution of the USSR in 1991 brought, therefore, a fundamental change in, and reduction of, Russian influence in the region. Russia remained formally part of the diplomacy of the Middle East, through its permanent membership of the UN Security Council and its formal co-chairmanship of the Madrid Arab–Israeli peace negotiations. Later it was, after 2000, to be part of the UN 'quartet' negotiating on Palestine. In some respects, such as direct air connections and people-to-people contacts, the Middle East became closer, as links between Israel and the Arab states on one side, and Russia and the former republics on the other, developed: investment, tourism, trade, narco-trafficking all began to flourish. It took under two hours to fly from Dubai to Baku. Hundreds of thousands of migrants left the former USSR for Israel, many of them, an estimated 300,000, not recognised by the Israeli religious authorities as Jews. At Tel Aviv airport in the late 1990s planeloads of people from Russia and Kazakhstan could be seen heading for the *Zal absorbtsii*, the 'immigration hall'. Yet in other ways Russia's position in the region was weaker. The geographic reduction of Russia in 1991 was compounded by a loss of military presence; while Russia took to selling weapons, this did not yield noticeable strategic advantage. Of the USSR's former allies, Syria, devoid of other options, remained interested in a relationship, whilst the PDRY, encouraged to fend for itself by Gorbachev, disappeared in May 1990 into a disastrous union with North Yemen.

Elsewhere, from 1991 to 2003, Iraq remained isolated by the UN sanctions regime enforced by the USA, Britain and France. The one country with which Russia was able to develop a more substantial relationship was Iran. Despite Soviet hopes in the early 1980s that 'the mullahs will come to their senses', the Islamic Republic never did come to accept the Soviet model of socio-economic development beyond a broad replication of state-run, and inefficient, management. But as Iran came under continued external pressure, it sought in Russia a diplomatic and military partner. This Moscow–Tehran relationship, something short of an alliance, but pragmatically resilient, alarmed the USA which feared Russia was providing Iran with nuclear materials and technology. It made sense for an Iranian state to take strategic precautions. Tehran saw instability all around it and, after 1998, it had two new nuclear powers on its south-east frontier. The fact that the USA continued to

exhibit sustained animosity compounded the sense of regional unpredict-
ability.[7]

Yet there may have been more continuity with the Soviet period than at
first sight appeared, in a paradoxical sense. What is perhaps most striking
about the whole history of Russian involvement in the Middle East during and after the Cold War is not how *much*, but how *little*, Moscow was
able to shape the course of events. Only in the period after the Suez crisis of 1956 was its strategic influence strong, while its political influence
was ever countered as much by the reckless Arab socialist regimes as by
the conservative monarchies. In economic terms the Soviet Union made
almost no impact, beyond acting as a general model for state-run development. If the USSR's period of strongest influence lasted for about two
decades, from 1955 onwards, it is, in this respect, comparable to that of
the two main colonial powers during the 1960s; yet in many ways Britain
and France, while geographically more removed, were able to sustain
a deeper, and more comprehensive, relationship with the region than
Russia. The post-colonial linkages between these states and the Middle
East, backed by interests in oil, trade and investment, were far greater
than those of Russia, as were the links of education, tourism and elite
interaction.[8] Arab princes and merchants and the fashionable elite of the
Islamic Republic shopped in Harrods and lodged in Knightsbridge, not
in the centre of Moscow.

Hegemon without a history: the USA and the region

The history of the Middle East since World War II, before and after the
end of the Cold War, and the dramatic events of September 2001, and
its aftermath, draw attention to an underlying issue, play the role of the
USA. This was often latent in discussion of the region, as to the *why* and
the *ought*, but too rarely did it receive systematic or measured attention
by observers in the region. Everyone who talked about the Middle East
seemed to know how to analyse policy-making in Washington, something
far from the case.[9] A retrospective assessment of external involvement in
the Middle East, especially the Iraq war of 2003, would indeed have
to be forgiven for ascribing primacy for much of the region's modern

[7] Galia Golan, *Russia and Iran*, London: Royal Institute of International Affairs, 1998.

[8] Barbara A. Roberson, ed., *The Middle East and Europe: the Power Deficit*, London:
Routledge, 1998 on UK, French and other west European relations with the region.
For a lively, incisive account of British expatriates in the Gulf in the 1970s see Jonathan
Raban, *Arabia Through the Looking Glass*, London: Fontana, 1979.

[9] The late Professor Edward Said often observed that there was no centre for the study of
the United States anywhere in the Arab world. The Iranians were more vigilant.

history to the USA. The USA was not, except in the Philippines, a conventional colonial power seeking territory, yet throughout modern times it had imperial aspirations, in terms of the assertion, indirect when not direct, of its interests in the strategic and economic fields. It, more than any other country, had since World War II viewed the Middle East as its predominant field of influence, even to the point of quarrelling openly with its European allies, Britain and France, during the 1950s and 1960s over Suez and the Arabian Peninsula.[10] From the end of World War II it provided the most significant military assistance, in terms of weapons, credit and training, to Turkey, pre-1979 Iran, Israel and a range of Arab states, most noticeably Egypt and Saudi Arabia. The USA also for much of recent decades monopolised diplomatic activity in the region, holding, as Egyptian president Sadat once aptly put it, '99 per cent of the cards'. The USA intervened militarily, in Lebanon in 1958 and 1982 and in Kuwait in 1990–1, as well as indirectly, through covert action since the 1940s.[11] In the maelstrom of the Cold War and after, the USA was the object of intense, often divided sentiment; it was the external country to which most inhabitants of the Middle East looked, as an aspiration for life-style, wealth, and possibly residence, and simultaneously as object of denunciation and alleged source of all ills in the region. Apparently either way the USA *could not* win. Either way in fact *it did*. It simultaneously ostracised *and* dominated, the first in life-style and imagination, the second in terms of raw power.

The collapse of the USSR in December 1991, in addition to removing any lingering western fears about Soviet rivalry in the Middle East, also provided a new arena for US diplomacy and economic interest and for co-ordination with regional allies, namely the former Soviet republics. The mix of oil, ethnic conflict, strategic interest and a new ex-*nomenklatura* clientilism, not to say kleptocracy, in Central Asia, all served to draw Washington, and its Saudi, Turkish and Israeli allies, into a new regional configuration, and towards new sources of profit. The old strategic rivalry, and some of the strategic certainty, of the Cold War had passed, but a new, profitable and diplomatically challenging environment had been formed. This new conjuncture was given spurious historical depth by being labelled in a false and inaccurate way, and with reference to the Anglo-Russian rivalry of the nineteenth century, as a new

---

[10] Not only Suez in 1956, but the Buraimi crisis of 1955–9 and the Yemeni revolution of 1962.

[11] See Miles Copeland, *The Game of Nations: the Amorality of Power Politics*, London: Weidenfeld, Nicholson, 1969. A full list of such actions may never be possible: they would include Syria 1949, Iran 1953, various reckless infiltrations in Egypt after 1952 and, some say, the first Ba'thist coup in Iraq in 1963.

'Great Game'. This it was *not*, not least because, in contrast to the late nineteenth century, local states and elites were active, as protagonists and co-conspirators in the plunder of oil wealth, as they were not a century before. In sum that two-thirds of the world's oil and gas were in the Middle East region was enough in itself to guarantee continued US involvement. Two of the three major interests of the USA in the region – protection of Israel, access to oil – therefore remained; the USA was not about to abandon its interest in the Middle East. The events of 11 September 2001 and the subsequent interventions in Afghanistan and Iraq made this even less likely.[12]

In the post-Cold War epoch, America's involvement seemed so predominant, and its motivations so obvious, that further analysis might have seemed redundant. Most commentators were satisfied with variants of either craven, if sullen, loyalty on the one hand, or denunciation of Great Satan on the other. That US policy was never a simple outcome of imperial plan, together with the very bureaucratic and factional diversity of the Washington policy process, seemed a complexity lost on many, not just in the Middle East but among critics in the west. Yet this is far from being such a simple story of grand imperial strategic design. First of all, the American involvement in the Middle East was in its origins slow and fragmented, betraying no grand design. The USA had no colonies in the Middle East, and, prior to World War II, little economic or political interest. Its first diplomatic relationship was with Oman, then a maritime power, in 1833, the year in which a ship from Muscat sailed all the way to New York. But this was a marginal engagement, perhaps symbolically reinforced by the fact that both states were at that time practitioners of slavery. It was only a century later that the modern relationship began to take shape. US oil firms established a foothold in Saudi Arabia in 1933 and President Roosevelt met with King Ibn Saud in 1945. It also gave the USA entry into the semi-independent states of the northern tier, first to Iran, where it was involved in training military and police personnel, and then to Turkey, where the turn to the west coincided with the onset of the Cold War; while not without its crises, the US–Turkish alliance was, over the years, the most stable of all US relationships with the region. Ankara always preferred the distant ally across the Atlantic to the unreliable, sometimes critical, Europeans.

Relations with most of the Arab world followed later: an attempt well after the end of World War II to forge an alliance with Nasserite Egypt, based in part on covert contacts with the Egyptian leadership, foundered

---

[12] For a lucid overview see Richard Crockatt, *America Embattled: 9/11, Anti-Americanism and the Global Order*, London: Routledge, 2003.

in 1955, while the relationship with the conservative Arab states in the Peninsula developed during the 1960s and 1970s, benefiting from the British withdrawal. Even here, in the Gulf, however, the USA found it difficult to reconcile Arab and Iranian aspirations euphemistically designated as the 'Twin Pillar' policy, pillars of an edifice that never coalesced and fell apart in 1979. Given the military predominance which the USA has been seen to have in the region for years, it is worth noting that the first time US forces actually participated in large-scale combat in the region was in Kuwait in 1991, fifty years after the first deployment of advisers in Iran – a marked contrast to the US involvement over many decades in Europe, and to more than a century of intervention in Central America and East Asia.

If history needs correction, equally in need of accurate analysis is the issue of the *sources*, or motives, of US policy. In the eyes of many of those opposed to the USA, this was an all too simple matter, above all dictated by some underlying cultural and ideological hostility to the indigenous peoples of the region, Arabs and Muslims. Such perceptions were, certainly, not hard to find, be it in the views held by successive Christian zealot presidents about the Palestinians and the Arab world in general, or the growing popular dislike of Muslims, be they Arab or Iranian, something enhanced by Palestinian use of terrorism and the Iranian revolutionary seizure of the US embassy in November 1979. Critics of US policy point at the same time to the role of the Jewish lobby in the USA: such a Jewish lobby working through Congress, parties and the media has indeed been a vocal part of the US political system since the 1940s, in common with other ethnic lobbies. Yet this is not the whole story. Sympathy for Israel is far wider than among the 4 per cent of Americans of Jewish origin: it would indeed be more accurate to speak of a 'pro-Israeli' lobby, one that encompasses both Democrats and born-again Christians whose backing for the Jewish people draws on biblical reference.

Those opposed to the USA can equally present its policy as reducible to two self-serving goals – the strengthening of Israel as an instrument of US rule, and the capitalist/imperialist preservation of control over Middle Eastern oil. Yet, here as well, simplification may come too easily. Israel was not created by the USA or, as noted, initially backed by it alone; it was the USSR that first recognised the Jewish state. Israel has been shrewd and insistent in building support in the USA, but has never been controlled by Washington as were client states in Latin America or East Asia during the Cold War.[13] Nor did Israel act as the 'outpost', 'guarantor', 'garrison',

---

[13] For an informative account see Stephen Spiegel, *The Other Arab–Israeli Dispute: Making America's Middle East Policy from Truman to Reagan*, Chicago: University of Chicago Press, 1985.

'satrap' or direct protector of US interests in the region: this role fell to Washington's other allies, Arab, Iranian and Turkish. That Israel did serve such a function was a myth sustained by pro- and anti-Israeli sentiment alike. A simple test: Israel never intervened to prevent the overthrow of any US ally in the region even if it came near to it in regard to Jordan in September 1970. As for oil, this is an important US asset but the Middle East has until recently not been a major source of US imports, its oil representing less than 10 per cent of US consumption; the US usage of Middle Eastern oil, which grew in the course of the 1990s, came in addition to the power which US firms already had through controlling the global market for the region's oil, and the attendant power which the US state, by guaranteeing access to that oil, has over its partners in the developed world.[14]

As with nuclear weapons, so with oil: it is both the object itself *and* the associated political and strategic power, more the latter than the former, which matter, and which gives strategic leverage. Against a climate of simplification, be it indulgence or abuse, the range and development of the US involvement in the Middle East, substantial as it has been, has, therefore, to be seen in the light of a careful, more historically nuanced, analysis of both its evolution and its sources. The first question is that of purpose. In brief, US policy in the region since World War II has been dictated by the three main goals – protection of Israel, guaranteeing the supply of oil, and, until 1991, containing Soviet influence. The ending of Soviet rivalry in 1991, combined with the Gulf war of 1990–1, certainly provided the USA with a new unipolar opening in the region. While such an idea was strongly rejected when articulated by Saddam Hussein during the Kuwait crisis of 1990–1, Washington then came to accept that there was a connection, 'linkage', between the Gulf and Palestine issues. Yet despite its efforts to broker peace between Israel and the Palestinians during the 1990s, Washington remained in the eyes of many in the region irredeemably partisan, in its support for Israel and Israel's new-found regional ally, Turkey, and in its failure to apply to the Arab oil-producing states the supposedly universal panaceas of 'good governance' and respect for human rights that it had so vigorously espoused elsewhere. Talk of 'human rights' and 'democracy', later 'reform', was seen as another pretext for imperialism, a simplification that was encouraged by rather too many, unfocused and irresponsible voices in the west. The end of the Cold War did not, therefore, produce a new, and more harmonious,

---

[14] On the international politics of US oil see Simon Bromley, *American Hegemony and World Oil*, Cambridge: Polity Press, 1991; Joe Stork, *Middle East Oil and the Energy Crisis*, New York: Monthly Review, 1975.

relationship between the USA and the countries of the Middle East. Relations with both Iraq and Iran remained tense, the Arab world as a whole
regarded US policy as overwhelmingly biased towards Israel, and popular
dissatisfaction with US policy, and that of the regimes allied to it, was
growing. This all led to the explosion of September 2001, an event which
itself served to detonate a new chapter of violence, counter-violence and
transnational paranoia, the occupations of Afghanistan (2001) and Iraq
(2003), and an apparently open-ended conflict between 'terror' and the
latest representative of western 'imperialism'. Whatever else, the USA,
its allies and its enemies were in for the long haul.

Festival of state autonomy: the Middle East in the 1990s

Discussion so far has been concerned with the ways in which after 1991
the end of the Cold War, as a global process, had an impact on the region.
Of equal importance, however, were those regional developments that
seemed to be autonomous, or even contradictory, of the global trend
towards tension reduction.

Confrontation with Iraq 1990–1991: the occupation of Kuwait

By far the most dramatic event in the Middle East of the immediate post-
Cold War epoch of the early 1990s, and the one that appeared to challenge
that overall, global trend of negotiation and reduction of tensions, was
the Iraqi invasion of Kuwait in August 1990. Not only did this lead to
a level of external intervention in the region unprecedented since World
War II, but it also divided, at the time and for the ensuing years, the states
of the Arab world in a manner greater than ever before. For the first time
in modern history Arab states fought *with* western armies *against* another
Arab state. This was an inter-Arab division even more profound than that
which had prevailed during the 'Arab Cold War' of the 1960s, or following
on Egypt's opening to Israel in 1977–9. In the end, as has been noted,
beyond restoring Kuwaiti sovereignty, the Kuwait crisis and resulting
war resolved little, for Iraq, Kuwait or anyone else. Over a decade later,
the underlying causes of the 1990–1 crisis remained in large measure
unchanged, US forces remained in the Gulf, and Iraq and Kuwait were
no nearer reconciliation. Only the war of 2003 presaged a new, but itself
unstable, conjuncture as the Arab Ba'th Socialist Party was driven from
power.

The Iraqi invasion of Kuwait came almost like a thunderbolt out of a
summer sky. Iraq had a long-standing claim to Kuwait going back to the
1930s, but few until the last minute expected this to lead to an all-out

invasion, as happened on 2 August 1990. One reason for scepticism was that Iraq was apparently exhausted: it had only as recently as August 1988 ended an eight-year war with Iran. In the course of that war it had received substantial assistance from Kuwait, Saudi Arabia and other Gulf states, estimated at $40–50 billion, or four times its average annual peacetime oil revenue.[15] Its sudden switch to confrontation with Arab countries began in February 1990 when Iraqi president Saddam Hussein made a speech in Amman, Jordan, attacking Arab rulers. This antagonism to the Arabs was, in itself, a surprise, since Iraq had only recently received substantial backing from all the Arab world, except Syria and the PDRY, during its war with Iran.

The invasion was preceded by several weeks of negotiation in which the Iraqis made a number of complaints against Kuwait: that it had lowered the general market price of oil by overproduction and had thus lessened Iraq's income; that it had stolen oil from a field, Rumaila, that lay along their joint frontier; that the frontier was drawn in such a way as to harm Iraq's maritime interests and security; that Kuwait was acting as an 'agent' of imperialism. After the invasion, the outside world at first appealed to Iraq to leave and then imposed sanctions on Iraqi oil exports: much of the Arab world, with Egypt and Saudi Arabia in the lead, Iran and, to the surprise of many, Turkey, which stopped oil passing through its pipeline, supported this move. When, as the months went by, Iraq failed to leave Kuwait and compromise solutions failed, the UN in Security Council Resolution 678 of 29 November 1990 authorised military action. The failure of last-minute US–Iraqi negotiations in Geneva on 6 January and the expiry of an ultimatum for withdrawal on 15 January was followed on the night of 17 January 1991 by the start of a US–UK aerial war against Iraq. Towards the end of February a ground offensive followed and, in a period of 100 hours, after many of the Iraqi forces had been withdrawn or had fled, the remainder were driven from Kuwait.[16] For the Middle

[15] It was often suggested during the Kuwait crisis that one of the factors driving Iraq to invade the country was the level of the Iraqi debt. This may, or may not, have affected Saddam's judgement, but its real import should not be overstated: even if Iraq's total debt to Arab and international creditors was in total $80 billion, eight times its average annual revenue, this is not the crucial ratio in evaluating a country's debt, especially if, as was the case with Iraq, it had enormous proven oil reserves. The crucial ratio is that of anticipated annual debt servicing to exports: here Iraq, which faced no great pressure to repay, had a favourable ratio (around 1:5), much more so than many Latin American states.

[16] Lawrence Freedman and Efraim Karsh, *The Gulf Conflict 1990–1991: Diplomacy and War in the New World Order*, London: Faber and Faber, 1993; Amatzia Baram and Barry Rubin, eds., *Iraq's Road to War*, London: Macmillan, 1994; Saïd K. Aburish, *Saddam Hussein: the Politics of Revenge*, London: Bloomsbury, 2000; Mohammad-Mahmoud Mohamedou, *Iraq and the Second Gulf War: State Building and Regime Security*, San Francisco: Austin and Winfield, 1998; Gregory Gause, 'Iraq's Decision to Go to War, 1980 and 1990', *Middle East Journal*, vol. 56, no. 1, 2002.

East this was the watershed event of the 1990s, equal in magnitude to the crises over Arab–Israeli wars of 1948, 1956 and 1967 and by any measure one of the most dramatic regional events of the late twentieth century. The Kuwait crisis had manifold implications for the region and for its relations to great power politics.

Three analytic questions in particular were raised by this crisis: first, the *causes* of the Iraqi invasion; secondly, the *relationship* between the crisis and the end of the Cold War; thirdly, the *consequences* of these events for the shaping, or reshaping, of international relations in the region. As for causes, the Iraqis themselves, at various points in the crisis, gave four different reasons for their occupation: as we have seen, these included the view that Kuwait was in any case a historic part, the 'nineteenth province', of Iraq, that it had damaged Iraq's economic interest by selling oil above its OPEC quota and consequently pushing down the world market price, that the country was stealing Iraqi oil from the Rumaila field, and that a 'popular movement' in Kuwait had requested an Iraqi intervention.[17] While these claims may not be taken as *explanations* of Iraqi action, they are not in themselves mutually exclusive, nor need it be necessarily doubted that many Iraqis believed some, or all, of them. It would appear that, even among Iraqis who opposed Saddam Hussein, there was wide support for the long-established *national* goal of 'liberating' Kuwait and contempt for Kuwaitis.[18]

What does most certainly require explanation is *why* these reasons had the effect they did and *when* they did; why, in other words, Saddam Hussein invaded in the summer of 1990. Here regional, internal and international factors may all have played a role. Regional factors were certainly relevant: Iraq saw itself in 1990, as it did after Camp David in 1979–80, as bidding for leadership of the Arab world against two other rivals, Saudi Arabia and Egypt, and as using Kuwait to mobilise Arab opinion on its side. It was *qala'a al-thaura al-'arabiyya*, the 'Citadel of the Arab Revolution'. Egypt could be denounced for its 'capitulation' to Israel in 1977–9 and for its continued inability to help the Palestinian people: in August 1990 the Palestinians were at the height of their unarmed but politically effective uprising against Israeli rule, the *intifadha*. In various registers, Saddam suggested that the action against Kuwait was a step towards the liberation of Palestine. Dislike of the oil-producing states, and of their profligate rulers, was widespread in the Arab world. For their part, the Saudis, and by extension Kuwait, were seen as clients of

[17] On the background see Richard Schofield, *Kuwait and Iraq: Historical Claims and Territorial Disputes*, London: Royal Institute of International Affairs, 1991.
[18] During the author's visit to Baghdad in April 1980 there was a football match between the Iraq and Kuwaiti teams. The Iraqis lost and that night the tyres of many Kuwaitis' cars were slashed.

the USA, the country that was protecting Israel even as it looted the oil wealth of the Arab world. Regional and Arab 'paralysis' was to be broken by Iraqi daring and leadership. As an *enabling* condition, the regional 'atmosphere' was therefore important.

The internal Iraqi context was probably more decisive: Iraq had fought an eight-year war with Iran, a conflict everyone knew it had started even if the mullahs had been provocative, and yet had nothing to show for it. There was widespread discontent inside Iraq: hundreds of thousands had died, many tens of thousands were prisoners in Iran. UN Security Council Resolution 598, to which both Iraq and Iran acceded at the end of the war in August 1988, not only called for a return to the pre-existing frontiers, which Iraq had in 1980 contested, but, at Iranian insistence, in clause 7 called for an investigation by the UN to determine the state responsible for the initial aggression. Iraq may well have hoped that a weakened Iran would accept Iraqi conditions in peace negotiations. With Iranian leader Ayatollah Khomeini already in ill health, a power struggle that would benefit Baghdad was, it appeared, in the offing in Tehran. However, as the months elapsed, Iran did not yield to Iraqi pressure in the peace negotiations after the ceasefire of August 1988. When Khomeini died in June 1989, a new, effective, government was formed, amidst a wave of emotional public support for the regime. Faced with an impasse on his east, in regard to Iran, it appears that Saddam turned, for compensation, to the south, to Kuwait. In February 1990, eight months after the death of Khomeini, at the meeting in Amman of the Arab Co-operation Council, of which Iraq, along with Egypt, Jordan and Yemen, was a member, Saddam launched those first polemical shots in what was to be the diplomatic run-up to the invasion that followed in August.[19]

So much for the regional and the internal. The role of the international, non-regional, context was to occasion much speculation at the time. For some analysts, the Kuwait war was the first harbinger of the post-Cold War epoch: this meant that, in effect, Saddam invaded Kuwait *because* the Cold War was over. This argument could be made in structural terms, in the sense that the balance of power, and the constraints it imposed on regional states, no longer operated: the Russians could not discourage Iraq as was the case in the past, for example during the first Gulf war of 1969–75. The connection to the end of the Cold War could also be made in terms of a more immediate, efficient cause: in this latter analysis, Saddam Hussein acted over Kuwait to forestall a challenge, because

[19] For a perceptive analysis of Iraqi calculation and miscalculation leading up to the invasion of Kuwait, and the role of internal factors see Aburish, *Saddam Hussein*, chapter 10, 'The Friend–Foe Game', and Gause, 'Iraq's Decision', note 16.

he foresaw pressure, from the USA and the USSR, to democratise. The fall of pro-Soviet regimes in eastern Europe in the last months of 1989, combined with a broadcast on the Voice of America in February 1990 indicating that Iraq might be another suitable country for democratisation, may have been elements of the post-Cold War world that spurred him to action. For those of a conspiratorial bent, including many outside the region, the USA itself had 'encouraged' Saddam to invade. April Glaspie, US ambassador in Baghdad, had told Saddam that the USA did not have a position on border disputes between Arab countries.[20] This was *not* the same as saying Washington encouraged Iraq to invade, but the distinction was cast aside by many.

For others, the opposite applied: Saddam invaded not *because* the Cold War was over but *because he did not realise* that the Cold War was over. Saddam Hussein's regime was itself an untransformed product of the Cold War, a nationalist military dictatorship forged in the height of the that conflict in the 1960s and 1970s and modelled on Leninist principles of control. Saddam modelled himself on Stalin.[21] Moreover in recent years Iraq had been the beneficiary of US–Soviet competition to sustain Iraq against Iran – the Cold War had acted to his benefit. Most importantly, the decision to invade could be seen as having been taken by Saddam on the understanding that Cold War constraints still applied. The west would not be able to evict him from Kuwait. The USSR, although weakened, would support in one way or another its old Iraqi 'socialist' ally, while the USA had no will to fight, as its retreats from Vietnam, in 1973, and, most relevant for Iraq, from Lebanon, in 1983, had shown; as the taunting Beirut billboard put up for American soldiers to drive past in 1983 said, 'Beirut 15 km. Vietnam 15,000 km.' This latter example of American weakness is believed to have had a particular effect on Saddam. In a meeting with a Cuban military delegation in early January 1991 Saddam proclaimed that he would 'crush the Americans like cockroaches'.[22]

In the event, Saddam Hussein's calculations about Kuwait were partly disproved, but partly vindicated. The western states, supported by some Arab countries, did impose sanctions and, in January 1991, did launch

---

[20] For the text of the Saddam Hussein–April Glaspie discussion see Micah Sifry and Christopher Cerf, eds., *The Gulf War Reader: History, Documents, Opinions*, New York: Times Books, 1991, pp. 122–33. This is based on an Iraqi transcript which has been neither confirmed nor denied by the US government.

[21] While in prison in the late 1950s, he is said to have read three times Isaac Deutscher's *Stalin*, translated into Arabic by the Lebanese Marxist writer, Fawwaz Trabulsi. Aburish, *Saddam Hussein*, also reports a special interest in the Soviet dictator. Saddam is believed to have paid a private visit to Georgia, Stalin's birthplace, in the 1970s.

[22] Information from Cuban Foreign Military official, Havana, November 2000.

a military assault. The USSR did not align itself completely with US policy, and some elements in the Russian military tried to send supplies to Iraq; but it voted for the key UN Security Council resolutions on Iraq and did not provide any significant assistance to Baghdad. The USSR did not even, so far as is known, provide something that would have been of great interest, if probably not a decisive factor for Iraq, namely satellite photographs of the coalition preparations for war. At what point Saddam realised that a military attack was coming, no one can know. What is known is that in late January and early February 1991, as the fighting neared, he withdrew his most important military forces, and their tanks, from Kuwait. The aim was to protect his regime, and here his calculations were more accurate. At the Geneva meeting on 9 January between James Baker and Tariq Aziz, the USA had warned Saddam *not* to use chemical or nuclear weapons; he did not and was thereby implicitly saved from mortal attack. The coalition forces did not, except briefly, enter Iraqi territory; no attempt was made to march on Baghdad or to oust Saddam. When a nationwide uprising against the Iraqi state broke out in March–April 1991 the west did nothing to help the rebels. They did intervene some weeks later to impose a protected zone on the Kurdish region, but this was to stem a tide of refugees into Turkey, and to prevent a humanitarian disaster, rather than as a prelude to challenging the Iraqi regime. On what was *the* most important question, the immunity of his regime, Saddam therefore calculated correctly.

In the aftermath of the Gulf war, thinking in the UN was influenced by an aspiration, or myth, that somehow the response to the Iraqi attack had shown the way to a different, co-operative, dispensation, a 'New World Order'. In the international response to the Kuwait crisis there apparently opened an opportunity for the Middle East to set a precedent for the world. This crisis would provide the occasion for a radically new international and regional system. Freed of Cold War paralysis, the UN Security Council did meet rapidly and effectively to impose sanctions and later authorise military action; hence the belief that a 'New World Order' based on American–Soviet collaboration at the UN and on a more effective peace-keeping and peace-enforcement policy could be realised. Kuwait seemed not only to come after the Cold War but, for the first time, to make possible realisation of the UN's security role envisaged in the Charter before the Cold War commenced. This optimism was all the greater because of the sense of failure which had beset the UN security role in the 1980s specifically for a Middle Eastern reason: the paralysis of the Security Council when Iraq invaded Iran in 1980, following on the 1976 reoccupation of western Sahara by Morocco, had done much to prolong the war, by hardening Iranian distrust of the UN as a whole and of the Security Council in particular.[23] Now both failings, that of the Cold War and that of the Iran–Iraq war, could be cast aside.

However, as the 1990s unfolded, this expectation of global harmony was, in large measure, to be disappointed. The basis of a 'New World Order' was effective American–Soviet collaboration; this ceased to be possible in the latter part of 1991 as the USSR itself disintegrated, leaving Russia as a reduced, and intermittently disgruntled, power. The fate of peace-keeping in the 1990s did little to sustain the optimism of 1991. Successful intervention in Kuwait in 1991 was followed by the failures of Somalia in 1992 and Rwanda in 1994 and by protracted reluctance to intervene in Bosnia up to 1995. The record of UN peace-keeping in the 1990s was far from wholly negative, and its weaknesses were largely those of its leading members, but the momentum for global 'peace-keeping' which Kuwait had unleashed was soon dissipated.

If, therefore, by 'New World Order' was meant the ability of the USA, and its allies and collaborators, to resolve the problems of the world more effectively and jointly, then apart from its limited application elsewhere the slow, agonised progress of diplomacy in the region after 1991 was also sufficient to dent that optimism. For the Middle East, as it eventuated, the end of global rivalry was *not* sufficient to bring regional peace. A decade after the occupation of Kuwait none of the other major inter-state problems of the region had been resolved. If this was a result of the end of the Cold War, it was one that itself presaged a new phase of regional inter-state competition and intransigence. The limits of the *global*, faced with the *regional*, were never more evident. At the same time, the Gulf crisis illustrated how, beneath the appearance of a domain of inter-state conflict, one that proceeded independent of social and internal factors within, these latter forces were of sustained importance. The very decision by Iraq to go to war was driven by two political judgements about social trends: the pressures from society *within* Iraq following from the war that bore on the Ba'thist state, and the sense of widespread popular frustration in the wider Arab world that stimulated animosity against the rulers of the oil-producing Gulf states and which was strengthened by the Palestinian *intifadha*. At the same time, the preparation for and limited scope of the war were shaped by the anxiety of Arab states and western rulers alike about popular support, within their societies, for Iraq, and its potential to explode were the war to be taken, at that point, into Iraq.

It was not arms, but politics, the calculation of states and of their relation to their societies, that shaped the outcome of the Kuwait crisis. As

---

[23] *The United Nations and the Iran–Iraq War*, Ford Foundation, 1987. The report was based on a conference in April 1987 which the author attended.

much as it was a major inter-state crisis, the Gulf conflict also exemplified the limits as well as the effectiveness of armed intervention. The Iraqi state placed its priority on survival. It successfully confined the actions of the coalition to Kuwait, while in the aftermath of war the priorities of the Ba'thist state, and of others in the region, limited all attempts to forge a new regional security system, let alone promote democratisation. Only in 2003, with the US attack on Iraq, was this impasse broken.

There was, finally, one other, at the time unnoticed, consequence of the Gulf crisis that was later to have major consequences: the decision by the Saudi government to invite US forces into Saudi Arabia after 2 August 1990, and to form a coalition with them against Iraq, was to be the breaking point in relations between Riyadh and the militant Islamist current led by Osama bin Laden which the official intelligence services and their associated reckless princes had sustained in the 1980s. This was the turning point that led, a decade later, to the al-Qa'ida attacks of 11 September 2001. This was the first significant 'southern' armed assault on a metropolitan city in the five hundred years since Columbus had unleashed Europe's offensive against the non-western world.[24] The seeds of this may have lain deeper in Middle Eastern history, although such claims of atavistic determination must be viewed with some caution; but it was August 1990 that set the ball in motion.

Regional realignments

As had been the case since 1918, changes in *international* relations between the major external powers were in the post-Cold War context matched by developments in the policies of regional states. In some areas the winding down of the Cold War appeared to lead to a significant reduction of tensions: the Iran–Iraq war ended in August 1988, with both west and east claiming credit; in November 1988 the PLO meeting in Algiers agreed to a two-state solution; the two Yemens agreed to a transition to full unity in May 1990; and in Lebanon a peace agreement between the major factions, signed in the previous year, came into operation in December 1990. At the same time, the long isolation of Egypt from the Arab world, originating in President Sadat's visit to Jerusalem in 1977, had begun to erode during the 1980s and was concluded in 1988 with the return of the Arab League to Cairo, its original headquarters – in the Arab nationalist *qaumi* phrase, the *'auda ila al-suff al-'arabi*, 'the return to the Arab fold' by this aberrant, but rather large, black sheep had been completed.

[24] Peter Bergen, *Holy War: Inside the Secret World of Osama bin Laden*, London: Weidenfeld and Nicolson, 2001, pp. 83–5.

These developments were, however, more than offset by the continuation of conflict or the threat thereof in parts of the Middle East. One
such area was Palestine. The possibility of a just, enduring settlement
had been delineated by sensible observers on both sides for decades.[25]
The PLO accepted an Israeli state in its November 1988 Algiers pro-
nouncement, and the final resolution of this problem had been specified
by the Oslo Accords of 1993. For all their uncertainties and defects,
mainly to the disadvantage of the Palestinians, the Oslo Accords did provide a framework for a permanent peace. The realisation of this involved,
however, three preconditions, none of which was met: a commitment by
Israel to evacuate, without equivocation, the territories seized in 1967; a
clear and sustained commitment by the Palestinians, *and* the Arab world
as a whole, to normal relations with Israel and the acceptance of this
problem as, at least in principle, one susceptible to compromise; and a
sustained and determined engagement by the USA to drive forward a
two-state solution. On all three of these the protagonists wavered and,
as time went by, opinion on each side hardened. Those who opposed any
compromise between Arabs and Israelis had, by the late 1990s, seized
the initiative. Startled into action by the prospect of such compromise in
the early 1990s, religious bigots on both sides proclaimed their intolerant
and maximalist goals. The result was the second *intifadha*, the explosion
in Palestinian–Israeli relations that began in late 2000. To say that the
Palestine issue was the *sole* cause of tension in the Middle East region was
exaggerated. To deny its general inflaming role was equally mistaken.[26]

Even more problematic during the 1990s was the situation in the Gulf
region, where after the war of 1990–1 no progress was made on inte-
grating the three major states – Iran, Iraq, Saudi Arabia – into a new,
mutually reassuring security system. Iran and Iraq were both subjected

---

[25] Two phases of possible Israeli–Palestinian compromise followed the 1967 and 1973 wars,
but were overwhelmed by violence and political obstruction on both sides. In the immediate aftermath of the 1967 war a clear, critical and internationalist position on the dispute
was laid out by two western writers, Maxime Rodinson, *Israel and the Palestinians*, second edition, London: Pelican, 1982, and Isaac Deutscher, 'The Arab–Israel War, June
1967', in *The Non-Jewish Jew*, Oxford: Oxford University Press, 1968. Later, after the
1973 war, a group of PLO officials implemented public discourse with members of
the Knesset. From 1978 they were assassinated on the orders of Saddam Hussein.
These were both chances destroyed. For those of the author's generation and outlook,
Deutscher's interview, given immediately after the 1967 war, is the touchstone, in substance, critique of both sides and tone, for all later discussions. It has never been bettered.

[26] This question, hotly debated by Israelis (who deny any exacerbating role) and Arab
nationalists (who blame everything on 'Zionism'), allows of independent, historically
founded adjudication. The Arab–Israeli issue had nothing to do with the Iranian revolution or the second Gulf war, but did play a role in the rise of Arab nationalism after
1998. A survey of Arab *poetry* in the period since 1948 will illustrate the wider sense of
anger prevalent in the Arab world.

by the USA to a policy of 'dual containment', of economic and diplomatic sanctions.[27] Iran, a third of whose navy was sunk by the USA in 1987–8, was excluded from the post-Gulf war system being evolved by Washington and the Gulf Co-operation Council (GCC), and signalled its refusal to accept it; Washington did not accept the argument that there can be no security system in the Gulf without Iranian involvement, while the Iranians, whatever some leaders may have thought in private, were not willing in public to accept a US presence. In particular, the Iranian leadership, centred not in elected presidents or foreign ministers, but in the unelected power centre around the Spiritual Leader, for a long time, unable to take serious political or economic initiatives within the country, resorted to rhetorical initiatives in foreign policy that would only serve to isolate the country further – demagogy on Palestine, opportunism in Afghanistan, reckless utterances on Salman Rushdie. With the election of President Mohammad Khatami as president in May 1997 this appeared to change. Iran improved its relations with the Arab world and, gradually, with the west, but not that much. Iran still remained opposed to any US presence in the region, and its conservative religious chief, the *rahbar* (leader) or *faqih* (interpreter) of Islamic law, Ali Khamene'i vetoed any direct dialogue, or establishment of diplomatic relations, with the USA.[28]

After the 1991 war, Iraq too remained at odds with its neighbours. It was contained by the third Gulf war and its aftermath, but its relations with Iran, Kuwait and Saudi Arabia were frozen. For their part, while the USA and its allies were able to isolate Iraq, they made no progress on the central question that pre-dated the war, namely that of establishing a minimally secure relationship between Iraq and the other states in the region, *and* better relations between the states and their peoples. Nor was one of the issues underlying the Iraqi invasion of Kuwait in 1990, the level of oil prices, addressed. Iraq resisted the UN inspection regime and in 1998 expelled all UN inspectors. As it had done for decades, Iraq also remained equivocal about the status of Kuwait.[29] Iran, as well as Kuwait, continued to fear Iraq's long-run intentions. For its part, Turkey took advantage of the new strategic context to promote its interests: if its initiatives towards the Turkic republics of the former USSR appeared to have disappointing results,[30] it was more successful in developing a relationship with another

---

[27] Robert Litwak, *Rogue States and US Foreign Policy: Containment after the Cold War*, Washington, DC: Woodrow Wilson Center Press, 2000.

[28] Sharham Chubin, *Whither Iran? Reform, Domestic Politics and National Security*, London: IISS, 2002; Fred Halliday, 'Peril and Opportunity', *The World Today*, vol. 58, March 2002.

[29] Schofield, *Kuwait and Iraq*.

[30] Idris Bal, *Turkey's Relations with the West and the Turkic Republics: the Rise and Fall of the 'Turkish Model'*, Aldershot: Ashgate, 2000.

regional state, Israel. Arab criticism of the Ankara–Jerusalem alliance was brushed aside by Turkish diplomats, who often accused the Arab world of having betrayed them in World War I. While Ankara had long had relations with Israel, it was to develop a more fully fledged military co-operation in the 1990s, to the alarm of many in the Arab world.

These dimensions of inter-state strategic relations in the region were, however, compounded by the return, in accentuated form, of another dimension of inter-state rivalry, namely the arms race. Towards the decade's end, in 1998, the Middle East remained the world's largest non-OECD arms market, its total annual defence expenditure around $60bil-lion, compared with $9.7bn for sub-Saharan Africa, $21bn for Central and South Asia, and $37bn for Central and South America. At 7 per cent of GDP, defence expenditure was the highest for any region of the world.[31] The end of the Cold War may have reduced the supply to the region of arms for strategic reasons, but the continuation of inter-regional suspicion and conflicts, and in some measure the very uncertainties pro-voked within and around the region by the Cold War's end, led to a new round of inter-state regional military competition, especially in the Gulf. The fear that grew with time was of a 'nuclear breakout' whereby states other than Israel would acquire nuclear weapons. That nuclear weapons might be used by states not as possible military instruments, but as mech-anisms for strategies and political bargaining, did not make for greater stability.

In the Gulf this arms race was spurred by the aftermath of the war of 1991: while Iraq was inhibited in its purchases of weapons by UN sanc-tions and inspections, it nonetheless retained substantial conventional forces, and the will to use them. Few doubted that Iraq retained the wish, and some capacity, to produce weapons of mass destruction; there was more doubt surrounding the actual actions taken by Saddam.[32] This in itself was sufficient to occasion a new round of arms purchases by Saudi Arabia and Kuwait, and to ensure that Iran, within the capacities it had, would build its potential as well. This Gulf armament process was overshadowed elsewhere in the region by the continued imbalance between an Israel believed to have up to three hundred nuclear warheads and Arab states which possessed no nuclear capability. For its part, Israel declined to sign the Nuclear Non-Proliferation Treaty. This growing con-cern about the nuclear imbalance within was, moreover, affected by the

[31] In 1997 prices. IISS, *The Military Balance 1999–2000*, London: IISS, 2000, Table 50, pp. 119, 300–5.
[32] This issue became the cause of much controversy before, and after, the fourth Gulf war, that of 2003. For one contemporary, overstated, evaluation of evidence see IISS, *Iraq's Weapons of Mass Destruction: a New Assessment*, London: IISS, 2002.

breakdown of the nuclear non-proliferation regime in a region adjacent to the Middle East, namely South Asia, in May 1998. The demonstration effects of the successful detonation, and retention, by India and Pakistan of nuclear weapons were, in the immediate term, not calculable; but few could doubt that their success in defying the non-proliferation system on the one hand, and the continued inability of Middle Eastern states to discuss, let alone create, a regional security system on the other threatened to unleash new destabilising forces in the region.

In this, as in other ways, the Middle East, locking its own regional conflicts into a mosaic of crises, was drawn more firmly into an international structure of rivalry, that of China and India being continued, via Pakistan, into the Middle East and beyond. Indeed arguably *the* most important consequence of the end of Cold War was the wealth of new, interlocked, sets of crises, each separate in origin, but now linked both by state rivalry at the top and by the transnational conflict of *jihadi* versus the 'west' below. This 'Greater West Asian Crisis' combined, in ways hitherto not the case, Palestine, the Gulf and Afghanistan as well as, on the south-east, the Indo-Pakistani conflict and, on the north-east, the Balkans. The unitary challenge of the USSR had gone; a new mosaic of conflict binding Turkey/Arabs, Israel/Arabs, Iraq/Kuwait and Iran/Afghanistan into one interlocked structure, and extending outward from Sarajevo to Kashmir, had been created. It was the growth, at inter-state *and* popular levels, of this regional crisis that led to the events of 11 September 2001 and their consequences, and to the wars of Afghanistan and Iraq that were themselves subsumed into the new global US strategy of a 'war against terrorism'. It was accentuated inter-state rivalry from above and growing transnational mass recruitment from below that together characterised the onset of the twenty-first century.

The Greater West Asian Crisis and confrontation with 'Islam':
11 September 2001, Afghanistan and Iraq

Hitherto, the focus of analysis has been the 'state' and 'inter-state'. The continuation of inter-regional conflicts was now, however, to be matched by the impact on the global stage of another Middle Eastern political phenomenon, transnational armed violence, or as it came to be known in an ambiguous phrase, 'international terrorism'. On 11 September 2001 attacks were made on the USA by an underground military grouping, al-Qa'ida (The Foundation), which had been formed earlier in the 1990s in Afghanistan. This group had arisen out of the fundamentalist *jihadi* currents that had fought the Soviet forces in Afghanistan in the 1980s, while it drew its support from recruits across the Muslim world and proclaimed a corresponding ideology, so was, at its core, an *Arab Sunni* radical group. It embodied that fusion of different causes – Palestine, Iraq, Saudi Arabia, Kashmir – that formed the popular, lived and west-hating dimension of the 'Greater West Asian Crisis'. Yet for all its appeals to the *umma* and the general war with *kufr* (the infidels), its leaders were Arabs, Saudis and Egyptians, and its goal was political, to take power in Arab states, specifically Saudi Arabia. Confrontation with the west, and a rhetoric of militant *jihad*, was determined by that strategy.

The import of this *jihadi* campaign and its apocalyptic rhetoric need placing in regional context. The disappearance of the Cold War led to numerous attempts by politicians all over the world to promulgate a new logic of global politics: a carnival of new-Hegelian meta-analysis swept the world, with many curious ideas, of a 'New World Order', 'The End of History', 'The Triumph of the West' and, not least, a belief in 'Cultural Confrontation' or 'Clash of Civilisations'. This last was an idea espoused in the Middle East as well as in the west which, for many, became, by the same means, *the* dominant feature of the whole period. Up to two decades before, in a debate that seemed incisive and informative by contrast, the issues underlying international inequality had been framed in terms of the *material* – social, economic, military – inequalities that separated north from post-colonial south. This new theory, however, involved the belief that relations between the Middle East and the west had become those of *civilisational* confrontation, based on a western hostility to 'Islam'. Such diverse developments as western refusal to support a Palestinian state, the opposition to Iraq's invasion of Kuwait, anti-Muslim prejudice in the west and the US response to terrorism after the events of 11 September 2001 were subsumed into this new global pattern. Suitable reference, of blithely ahistorical kind, was made to the 'Crusades' and other antecedents. This was a historical myth sustained after 1991 by some in the west, for whom 'Islam' had become the enemy, and by some in the Middle East, for whom cultural confrontation, or, if one prefers, opposition to 'cultural aggression', with the west was a convenient and popular cause, even as they bought its weapons and medicine and invested in its financial markets.

This idea had been central to the Iranian revolution of 1978–9. For Iran the enemy was *tahajum-i farhangi* (cultural aggression), for the Arabs *al-qazu al-thaqafi* (the same). Intermittently espoused in the 1990s it was to receive dramatic reinforcement in the events of 11 September 2001 and in the actions which the USA and its allies on one side, and its opponents on the other, were to take in response. That this idea had widespread currency was beyond doubt.[33] It received support from remarks by some

[33] For one excellent critique of the idea that there is a coherent US policy on 'Islam' see Fawaz Gerges, *America and Political Islam: Clash of Cultures or Clash of Interests?*, Cambridge: Cambridge University Press, 1999.

western politicians on an Islamic 'threat', and by the theory of a 'clash of civilisations' first propounded by the American academic Samuel Huntington in 1993 and elaborated in a book in 1996.[34] As with all fideistic assertions, the 'clash' theory sailed on over all criticisms only to take 11 September as further indication of its historical perspicacity. Movements in the region did not need Huntington to make their own contribution. They had been saying something similar for decades, if not centuries: it was one of the several deplorable elements in this now international debate of the middle 1990s that the Harvard professor himself, his supporters and his opponents seemed to think he was saying something original.

By its very diffusion, the idea of a civilisational clash certainly acquired some reality: it was part of the post-Cold War political atmosphere, in east and west, a form of east–west shared transnational paranoia. Yet there were several reasons for doubting its validity, as a description of the post-1989 period or of relations between the Middle East and the west more generally.[35] First of all, throughout this period the twenty or more Middle Eastern *states*, and the 50-plus Islamic ones, as distinct from transnational groups, continued to conduct their relations with the west on the basis of broad considerations of national interest – military, political, economic – and as normal bilateral interactions. The Islamic states co-operated with the west where this benefited their interests and opposed western policies where this did not suit them. For all Saddam's posturing about *jihad*, Iraq's hostility to the west derived not from religion at all, but from calculations of state interest, and disputes over territory and power. He was always happy to sell oil. The same centrality of states applied in considerable measure to transnational groups: al-Qa'ida itself had an Arab agenda and needed a state, Afghanistan, within which to operate.

Secondly, for all the babble about civilisational 'faultlines', conflicts between Middle Eastern, and Muslim, countries were at least as significant in the course of international affairs as were those between the Middle East as a whole and the west. In the 1980s and 1990s Saudi–Iranian, Iraqi–Kuwaiti, Arab–Turkish, Saudi–Yemeni, Egyptian–Sudanese relations all lived through tensions as great as any between

[34] Samuel Huntington, *The Clash of Civilisations and the Remaking of World Order*, London: Simon and Schuster, 1996.
[35] These ideas are developed in Fred Halliday, *Islam and the Myth of Confrontation*, London: I. B. Tauris, 1996; there it is argued that the best way to refute culture-based accounts of international and national events is to provide alternative substantial and more persuasive accounts of actual events. See also Fred Halliday, '"Islam" and the "West": Cultural Conflict and International Relations', in Halliday, *Two Hours that Shook the World* and Amin Saikal, *Islam and the West: Conflict or Cooperation?*, London: Palgrave, 2003. See also Gerges, *America and Political Islam*.

these states and the west. Nor could such, in this context, empty terms as 'Islam' and 'culture' explain the international relations of the region. For example, as the Taliban regime fell in Afghanistan, many Afghans turned against the Arabs and Pakistanis in their country. The Libyans and the Iranians, rivals in the market of Muslim radicalism since the 1970s, and particularly in Lebanon, continued to spar over the disappearance in 1978 of the Lebanese Shi'ite leader Musa Sadr, whose fate Tehran blamed on the Tripoli regime.

Thirdly, many of the claims made on both sides about the 'clash' were false: 'Islam', meaning a coalition of Muslim states, did not threaten the security of the west, in military or economic terms – al-Qa'ida could alarm, but not pose a strategic threat; on the other side, the bombastic argument advanced by Islamists that they were now in a position to rival the west was also palpably false. So too was the claim, in varying registers, that all the problems of the Middle East could be blamed on the 'west', a stock-in-trade, with small variations, of all third world regimes. Finally, it was argued that the west had after 1991 promoted 'Islam' as an enemy to substitute for the loss of an external enemy in communism. Although a widely held idea, this argument was, on closer examination, facile. As discussed elsewhere, it was *during* the Cold War itself that the west had encouraged conservative Islam. On top of all this, the west as such did not *need* an 'enemy' – it has wanted since 1500 to create a world market, not a world war – and communism was not invented, as it was a real political threat of a kind Islam never was in modern times.

There was therefore no need for the 'west', accepting for the moment this facile term, to replace communism by Islam. Moreover, if there was an economic challenge to the west in the 1990s, it came not from the, economically weak, states of the Middle East, but from the Asian industrialising states. Until the Asian crisis of 1997 at least, and whatever their short-term difficulties, these presented a low-cost, technological and industrial challenge to Europe and the USA. The latter challenge came, above all, from a resurgent and increasingly confident China, a country which had, until the eighteenth century, an economy in advance of the Atlantic zone. GDP growth rates of 8 per cent per annum from the mid-1990s onwards revealed a huge shift in global economic power. In sum, the illusion of 'Islam' challenging the 'west' was part of the pathology of the post-Cold War epoch, not of the explanation. Yet as 11 September 2001 was to show, this myth was to acquire widespread credence in the region as well as in the west and so to become part of its political reality.

There was, moreover, something mistaken in seeing the issue of terrorism (despite its own vain rhetoric) as, in the proper sense of the term, primarily a *global* phenomenon. Analysis, in a purely strategic or international context, of relations between the Middle East and the west, and of the events of September 2001 and their aftermath, obscured the degree to which Islamist movements were primarily caused by, and directed at, conditions *within* their own societies. Beyond their globally articulated rancour, nationalist and terrorist groups reflected conflicts *within* Middle Eastern societies and generated groups whose primary aim was to take power in their own societies. Their primary foes were their own states, not least the secular forces within their own societies: the National Liberation Front (FLN) in Algeria, the Yemeni Socialist Party (YSP) in Yemen, the People's Democratic Party (PDPA) in Afghanistan. Certainly, the threat to the west was not *invented*: the development of these conflicts after the Cold War was to mark many societies in the Middle East and, in September 2001, profoundly to affect the USA and the developed world. Yet, pervasive and violent as this global *jihadi*–west conflict was, and with uncertain long-term consequences, it did *not* constitute a strategic fissure in international relations, on the scale of colonial rivalries of the nineteenth century or the two world wars or the Cold War of the twentieth century, nor did it unite all, or even most, Middle Eastern and Islamic states in a bloc confronting the west. Indeed most states saw a political and strategic opportunity, not least to crush their own domestic oppositions as 'terrorism', a ruse easily bought by the USA and replicated with equal hypocrisy by the new privatised and criminalised *nomenklaturas* of Central Asia. The dividing line of the post-Cold War world ran as much *within* Middle Eastern societies as along any new international, strategic 'faultline'.

The emergence of this confrontation around *jihad* was, however, stimulated not only by political opportunity but also by socio-economic conditions prevailing within many Middle Eastern states. This is analysed in more detail in chapter 9. In summary form here, in the 1990s Arab state-centred development had failed (Egypt, Algeria, Syria, etc.); however, in the race for competitive capitalist development, the Middle East as a whole, in comparison with other states and apart from its oil wealth, stagnated or receded. Despite its revenues, the region was, on most development criteria, more comparable to Africa than to either Asia or Latin America. Thus real per capita income in Saudi Arabia fell by between a half and two-thirds over two decades. On standard economic criteria, the majority of the regional states were far behind such comparatively disadvantaged third world states as Malaysia, the Philippines and the majority of Latin American states. The excuse of colonial/post-colonial inhibition was wearing even thinner as far less capital-rich states surged ahead in the global market. If the record of a country like Singapore, forty years earlier poorer than most Middle Eastern states, and which by the early 1990s produced half of the computer hard disks in the world, was compared with that of the Middle East states, then the contrast between states, all of which enjoyed some autonomy, was evident.

This economic paralysis of the Middle East in general was replicated in politics. The collapse of the Soviet system was accompanied by much speculation about the global triumph, actual or inevitable, of the western conception of democracy and the free market. At the ideological level there was much truth in the claim, articulated by Francis Fukuyama: there was no global ideological challenge, no internationally accepted alternative, to this model, even if Fukuyama, like many in the west, over-estimated how many states had attained democracy and how securely they had done so. Of course, a region where established elites had for centuries faked piety to the divine was quite able to ape the formal trappings of democracy, focusing narrowly on voting, that the USA required.[36] But as a description of reality, or of the plausible future, the Fukuyama model was mistaken, and simplistic. First, the economic history of few, if any, societies in the world had even approximated to the free market model of liberal theory – the development of Japan, Singapore, Korea, and before that of Germany and Britain relied centrally on state intervention. The state was, with the partial exceptions of Israel and Turkey, dominant in the region's economies. Secondly, democratisation was not a sudden, all or nothing event like building a dam or buying a car, but a gradual process, over decades and centuries: it took Britain and the USA three hundred years and three internal wars between them to move from tyranny to the kind of qualified democracy they now have. Thirdly, liberal politics is not a single act, bestowing finality on a political system. No one can be certain that a democracy is even reasonably stable unless it has been installed for at least a generation – many have appeared only to disappear (Lebanon, Sri Lanka, Liberia in the 1960s to name but three). Moreover, democracy beyond official proclamations about elections, 'civil society' and 'NGOs' can only function if certain real embedded and parallel preconditions prevail: a reasonably functioning economy, reasonably transparent public finances, a degree of tolerance in politics and religion, the prevalence of secular law, and, most importantly, a guarantee for different sectors in society that their interests will not be overridden. Where a state denies

---

[36] In one Arab military regime, a citizen was asked why his country had introduced pluralism, or *ta'adudiya*. His reply was: 'we have introduced *ta'adudiya* because the president told us to do so'. As any student of politics knows, votes mean nothing if divorced from other real conditions – a free press and media that reflect different views, public information on state finances, the right freely to organise parties, an executive that is really subject, and not faking acquiescence, to the elected legislature. Above all, there must be a credible belief on the side of rulers and ruled that the elite can be voted from power. In no Arab state which pretended to hold elections did these conditions prevail.

these conditions, then formal elections mean little, or nothing, and no democracy or attendant free domain of 'civil society' can flourish.[37] The history of the modern Middle East illustrates this. It had in the early decades of the twentieth century some experience of partially liberalised media, political parties and elected parliaments. However, this 'liberal' period, marked at the time by partial democratisation, if that, in much of pre-1939 Europe and Latin America, was to be swept away in the tide of coups, revolts and statist populism after World War II. In the Middle East context the second, post-1991 democratisation process advanced in some respects, but it too faced many obstacles: state *and* popular intolerance within societies, on ethnic, tribal, religious and class grounds; profound economic difficulties; virulent anti-democratic ideologies, masquerading as nationalism or religion; entrenched elites who, by taking control of economic resources, manipulated political and social processes including a charade of 'globalisation'; tensions between regional states that strengthened the repressive and military apparatuses in societies, and prevented democratic evolution. Ideology and nativist relativism also played their part.

The use made of regionalist and religious particularism by regional elites to deny the possibility of democratisation was one means of justifying a continued monopoly of power. The revolutionary rhetoric of some other states – including Iran – served similar purposes: all real opponents were playing an 'American' game. Only the Saudis actually went as far as to claim these Islamic values prevented them from even considering democracy. In the past Cold War regional dictatorships had been invested with a spurious political legitimacy by external powers – be it in myths of a particular 'Arab' democracy propagated in the west, or those of 'socialist democracy', the 'non-capitalist road', propounded in Brezhnevite Russia. After 1991, another range of myths was generated in the region, either to describe as 'democratic' or 'transitional' or 'emerging' processes that were still in their early stages, or quite paralytically in transition to nothing at all (Egypt, Tunisia, Iran), or to erect from within bogus objections to liberalisation on the grounds that such a liberalising process was part of the wider 'imperialist' intervention. On the showing of the 1990s, there was nothing inevitable about democratisation in the Middle East or anywhere else; at best, it would be a slow, sometimes contested, process and would take decades before it can be consolidated on a region-wide basis.[38]

---

[37] Sami Zubaida, 'Islam, the State and Democracy: Contrary Conceptions in Egypt', *MERIP Middle East Reports* no. 179, November–December 1992.
[38] See, in general, Ghassan Salamé, ed., *Democracy without Democrats? The Renewal of Politics in the Muslim World*, London: I. B. Tauris, 1994; Eberhard Kienle, *A Grand Delusion: Democracy and Economic Reform in Egypt*, London: I. B. Tauris, 2001; Amnesty International, *Egypt: Muzzling Civil Society*, London: September 2000.

Equally remarkable, however, was the extent to which the political trends in the region, not only *from above*, from states, but also *from below*, from public opinion and opposition movements, reflected an ideologically particularist and often anti-democratic character. In some countries movements in favour of political liberalisation and greater diversity emerged: this was most evidently the case in Iran, where by the late 1990s, two decades of clerical rule, and the existence of a politically educated population, led to a strong movement for democratisation. A similar maturation could be observed in Turkey in the 1990s. Elsewhere, however, notably in Arab states, the discourse of opposition was increasingly dominated by Islamist rhetoric, anti-democratic, illiberal and, in social and economic terms, regressive. Far too many people in these societies were poring over holy texts and invoking irrational symbols, borrowing when it suited them from the anti-globalisation rhetoric of the west, rather than engaging in an informed and critical manner as their secular and liberal Muslim predecessors had done with the real problems of the modern world – the latter included unemployment, the participation of women in society, economic management, education in information technology, the growth of an independent judiciary, the environment, to name but some theories. It was against this background that a growing body of opinion in the Middle East, incited by confrontational voices in the west and supported by too many renegade ex-secularists, came to argue that the relations of the region with the outside world were, or were about to be, dominated by a civilisational clash pitting 'Islam' against the 'west'.

'Culture', 'civilisation', 'Islam' did not identify the causes of the events of 11 September 2001. The attacks on the USA were political in origin, both regionally *and* internationally. Regionally they reflected the growing strength of armed Islamist groups, committed to extreme violence and enjoying widespread popular support, in sum the maturing of an integrated 'Greater West Asian Crisis'. At the same time there was widespread anger at the USA pioneered by anti-secularist fanatics, themselves having been promoted by the west during the Cold War, like al-Qa'ida or Hamas, who paradoxically drew on forms of guerrilla organisation and popular 'anti-imperialist' ideology, initially pioneered by the secular left. The international context was one shaped by successive phases of colonialism, Cold War and globalisation, as three superimposed periods of asymmetric relation between the region and the west, going back to 1798 at least. The central dynamic of this challenge lay not in tales of history or 'values', but in the contemporary state–society relationship itself, marked by an effective militarisation of opposition in some states where central authority was weak or compliant (Afghanistan, Pakistan, Yemen, Somalia) and a growing Sunni popular resentment in the major Arab states (Saudi Arabia and Egypt in particular).

Moreover, in the two countries occupied and subject to 'regime change' after 11 September, in Afghanistan and Iraq, the US and allied military forces could protect a core administrative state; but the longer-term prospects for the successor regimes would be decided not by force, or external finances, but crucially by the ability of the new political elite to turn their positions rather effortlessly acquired through external imposition into a viable state–society interaction. Thus, how this crisis eventuated might depend, initially, on external military and diplomatic interventions, judicious or not; but in the longer run the decisive terrain of conflict lay in the relation of the Middle Eastern states themselves to their own peoples, restless and increasingly insistent as they were.[39]

A margin of political choice: global structure, regional actors

This analysis of the post-Cold War Middle East has addressed two broad analytic issues. The first is that of how far it is possible to talk in any meaningful sense of a combined *regional* politics for the Middle East or a 'Greater West Asia Crisis'. Each country, and each crisis, has its own character, yet in the 1990s, above all, these distinct conflicts appeared to be drawn more closely together, as their protagonists would not tire of asserting. This was as true at the inter-state level in the alliances and rivalries formed as it was at the level of popular sentiment. The Gulf war of 1990–1 was *not* a direct cause of 11 September 2001. The Palestine issue was *not* the single source of instability in the region. Yet they both played a role. At the level of state *and* society, a 'Greater West Asian' political, strategic and discursive space had been formed.[40]

The other broad analytic issue discussed here is that of the salience of external context. Every phase of the international history of the Middle East, from the assault of Catherine the Great in the 1760s and Napoleon's occupation of Egypt in 1798, to the Iraq war of 2003, raises the issue of *how*, and *how far*, external factors determine the politics and society of the region. The character and history of this external involvement in the Middle East, and the impact of this on Middle Eastern politics and society, posed questions that go to the heart of analysing the modern international system and the socio-economic character of the region. For its part, International Relations theory has, as discussed in

[39] Gilles Kepel, *Jihad: the Trail of Political Islam*, London: I. B. Tauris, 2002; Malise Ruthven, *A Fury for God: the Islamist Attack on America*, London: Granta Books, 2002; John Esposito, *Unholy War: Terror in the Name of Islam*, New York: Oxford University Press, 2002.

[40] For a comparable thesis see Saikal, *Islam and the West*, and his astute 'How These Threats Interlock', *International Herald Tribune*, 29 December 2003.

chapter 2, traditionally divided its explanations into three kinds – those in terms of states, in terms of non-state actors, in terms of structures. As we have seen, each of these has explanatory potential: each can provide a detailed, compelling and as yet unfinished account of the role of external factors in shaping the modern Middle East, and of each of its inter- and intra-state crises. A history can be written in terms of the policies and impact of the major states, the 'great powers': this can be in the form of diplomatic history, bilateral relations, imperialism, post-colonialism, globalisation or, for those so minded, conspiracy theory. An argument can also be made, as in chapters 3 and 4, however, that it was not so much states as others – banks and oil companies, tribes and guerrillas, Zionist colonisers and Islamic radicals, nationalist and social movements, today financiers, migrants and traders – who have played the most important part.

Yet each of these, in themselves rival, actor-based explanations may have to take account of an analysis which stresses the overarching structural context, and inequality. This has defined the relationship between the Middle East and the external world for the past three centuries, as that between an industrialised and militarily powerful west, and an increasingly weak, dependent and fragmented Middle East. It is the multifarious impact of that structural inequality, from the trade and finance of the eighteenth century, the cannon and armies of the early nineteenth-century colonial powers through to the cruise missiles, interventionist armies, Internet, investment houses and modern life-style of the contemporary west, not to mention good governance and 'NGOs', that has most shaped the Middle East. States, ethnic groups, business interests, not to mention individuals, from Muhammad Ali, Sultan Abdul Hamid, Naser-ad Din Shah and Theodor Herzl to Yasser Arafat, Ariel Sharon, Husni Mubarak and Osama bin Laden, have all been subordinated to that continuing, and intensifying, but ever re-defined, international and inexorable, that is structural, differential imegration.

Whatever the assessment of these different forms of determination, this argument still leaves the danger of overstating how far the region has, in its international relations and domestic politics, been determined by these external factors at all. The structural determination may remain, but within that it has always been open to local states, and those that challenge established forms of power, to play an autonomous role. All individuals, and states, are constrained by structure, of time, place, history, capacity, but they also have room for manoeuvre.[41] As seen above, the Ottoman empire was not simply a passive object of western strategic rivalry, but

[41] A few examples of such autonomous choices from the twentieth century: (i) the Young Turk decision to enter World War I in 1914; (ii) the miscalculation by Reza Shah about external forces that led to the Anglo-Russian invasion of Iran in August 1941; (iii) Iranian

made its own shifting alliances. The post-colonial states of Egypt, Iraq, Syria and Israel after 1945 have also had leeway in their foreign policy, as has, on a grander scale, the Islamic Republic of Iran. Even a state such as Saudi Arabia, a military dwarf if a financial and religious medium power, has been able to pursue its own separate interests against, often Arab, resistance.

That this state autonomy was possible during the height of the Cold War is evident from the initiatives which regional states, and social movements, took *against* the wishes of their supposedly controlling external patrons. In the post-Cold War world this may be even more so, and the room for autonomous action and policy all the greater: 2 August 1990 and 11 September 2001 were evident cases of this. Between, on the one hand, the myth of pervasive external control, common in conspiracy theory and nationalist and fundamentalist rhetoric, and in 'anti-imperialist' literature the world over, and, on the other, the illusion of complete independence, at which no state arrives, there lies a more varied world of conflicting, and accommodating, interest, and of choices, be they informed, reckless or fatalistic. Analysis of that relationship involves more, however, than the narrative exposition of forces, regional and global: it requires analysis of some at least of the distinct elements that constitute Middle Eastern states and societies and around which the international context shapes the behaviour of states and non-state actors alike. History having been summarised and to some degree rationalised, we can now turn to these dimensions of international relations.

premier Mosadeq's failure to reach a realistic compromise on the nationalisation of Iran's oil in 1951–3; (iv) Israel's alliance with the UK and France, and against *both* Washington *and* Moscow, in the Suez crisis of 1956; (v) Egyptian president Nasser's reckless request to the UN to withdraw its peace-keeping forces from Sinai in May 1967, a move that enabled Israel to attack on 5 June 1967; (vi) President Sadat's launching of the October 1973 war, to the surprise of both Washington and Moscow; (vii) Syria's invasion of Lebanon in 1976; (viii) Saddam Hussein's invasions of Iran (1980) and Kuwait (1990).

Part III

Analytic issues

6   Military conflict: war, revolt, strategic rivalry

Wars, old and new, and the formation of the Middle East

Armed conflict, social upheaval and the impact of the world economy have constituted the three most important formative influences on the Middle East. In a famous summary of the events of the twentieth century in particular, the German philosopher Hannah Arendt said that it was a time of 'wars and revolutions'. If this is true of Europe, it equally characterises other regions of the world, not least East Asia and the Middle East. Here, as with culture, state and nation, the *appearance* of ancient patterns of conflict, via wars, *reveals* the rupture introduced by modernity. What distinguishes modern history is the *combination* of war with socio-economic change and revolution, and the very different character of the first. Prior to the twentieth century, the role of war was evident in the ways in which the ancient pre-Islamic empires, the Persians, the Greeks and Romans and others, were created by war as well as in how the major Islamic empires were formed: the initial Arab conquests forged an Islamic world that was, later, ruled by the Ummayads, the Abbasids, the Safavis and the Ottomans. It was war too which began to reverse this process, to push back the frontiers of the Islamic empires, from the fourteenth century in Spain and the seventeenth on the western (Austrian) and northern (Russian) frontiers of the Ottoman empire.

Yet important as these wars were in defining territory and elites, war in these earlier centuries was not, as was to be the case in the twentieth century, linked, as consequence and precursor, to social and political upheaval. In the twentieth century it was, as discussed in chapter 3, most obviously World War I, itself the product of upheaval in Turkey and the Balkans, which finally brought the end of the Ottoman empire and led to the designation of the modern Middle East state system. World War I was preceded and to a considerable degree caused by revolts against the established order, the Young Turks in 1908, Serbian nationalism in 1914. World War II and its aftermath revived anti-colonial nationalism and, mediated via the Palestine question and the post-war instability in

Iran, contributed to the broader radicalisation of the region. The anti-colonial sentiment bred in both world wars was accentuated by the Cold War which in the 1950s and 1960s dominated the international relations of the region. The end of the Cold War opened, as discussed in chapter 5, a new phase of conflict, based apparently on 'Islam' and cultural norms.

These conflicts of the twentieth century had, therefore, not merely a *military* dimension, but equally *social*, *ideological* and *political* ones. In these dimensions lay their importance and their distinctiveness. They were in the first instance part of a broader strategic rivalry of 'great', non-regional, powers which had their impact on the countries of the region. However, regional powers themselves never lost their ability to wage war on their own behalf, as the Turks demonstrated throughout the nineteenth century and up to 1923. In the decades that followed World War I the region saw a successful war of national reassertion by Turkey (1920–3), the conquest of four-fifths of Arabia by the Saudi forces up to 1926 and a war with the only other independent Arab state at that time, Yemen (1934), and, following World War II, in 1948 the invasion of Palestine by a coalition of Arab armies. That first Arab–Israeli war of 1948–9, the Israeli war to establish a state, was followed by four others (1956, 1967, 1973, 1982) and by other inter-state wars, most notably the Iran–Iraq war of 1980–8, by far the bloodiest in the history of the region, and by the Iraqi occupation of Kuwait (1990–1).

War has, therefore, in both its pre-modern and modern forms, certainly played an important role in the formation of the modern Middle East, be this in regard to the fall of empires, in the Ottoman, Tsarist, and later British and French, variants, or in creating the context for the redrawing of the territorial map and for changing the very character of states and the political orientation thereof. This was especially so of World War I, which led not just to the detachment of the Arab provinces of the Ottoman empire, and the definition of five new Arab political entities, but also to the emergence, within the Arabian Peninsula, of Saudi Arabia, as it also transformed the political character of Iran and Turkey by occasioning the emergence of modernising military regimes. World War II led to the emergence of Israel and, combining the nationalism incubated in the war with the humiliation of defeat by Israel, to the overthrow of the monarchies of Egypt and Iraq. Here war was not a consequence of political change, but its catalyst.[1]

Other regional wars also had their impacts, if not one which those who launched them anticipated. The 1956 tripartite attack on Egypt led not to Israeli or Anglo-French domination of the region, but to an

---

[1] Fred Halliday, *Revolution and World Politics*, London: Macmillan, 1999, especially chapter 1, 'Introduction: Revolutions and the International'.

Israeli withdrawal, the effective end of British and French colonialism, and to the introduction of the two main protagonists of the Cold War, the USSR and the USA, into the Middle East. The 1967 Arab–Israeli war was prompted by an Egyptian miscalculation when Nasser took a gamble vis-à-vis Israel: it led not to vindication of the Arab position but to another defeat. Strategic miscalculation was not, however, an Arab monopoly after 1967. The Israelis failed to detect Sadat's plan to launch a surprise attack in 1973. For its part the 1982 Israeli invasion of Lebanon was designed to root out the PLO and finish the Palestinian question on Israel's terms; instead, it led to Israel's first military failure and to strengthening of the PLO's political, if not military, position internationally and in the region. Miscalculations in other wars were legion: most spectacular were Iraq's two military adventures, against Iran in 1980 and Kuwait in 1990. Neither succeeded: instead, both imposed heavy strains on Iraq, reducing it from being arguably the most advantaged and economically best-endowed Arab state to a position of penury and fragmentation. On one estimate, per capita GDP in Iraq stood in 1979, on the eve of the war with Iran, at over \$2,400; by 1995 it had shrunk to \$350.[2]

About the only war launched with a clear political goal that was attained was the Egyptian attack on Israel in October 1973: designed by Sadat not to defeat Israel but to redeem Egyptian prestige and force Israel to the negotiating table, it attained these goals. It had, by 1982, secured the evacuation of all Egyptian territory occupied by Israel in 1967. Even here, however, Egyptian president Sadat failed in one of his key goals, that of using the war to bring the Egyptian, and Arab, public with him: this did not succeed. For many his trip to Jerusalem in 1977 was *khiana*, 'treason'. Arab political victory in 1973 was followed by food riots in 1977 and a growing alienation between the Egyptian autocrat and his people.[3] Despite his success on the battlefield, and in subsequent negotiations, Sadat died in 1981 a rejected man, a *bahlawan* or 'clown', detested by his own people and the Arab world alike for the concessions he had made to the 'Zionist' enemy.[4]

This Middle Eastern martial record can be expanded from inter-state wars in the normal sense to include other forms of conflict – military coups, civil wars, guerrilla opposition and terrorism: each has been a recurrent feature of the politics, and international relations, of the area.

[2] Estimates in constant 2002 US dollars. Source: Iraq, Ministry of Planning, 2003, cited in Mary Kaldor and Yahia Said, 'Regime Change in Iraq', London School of Economics, Centre for the Study of Global Governance, November 2003, p. 17.

[3] The 1977 rioters chanted the rhyming slogan: *Ya batal al-'ubur, feen al-futur?* ('Oh, Hero of the Crossing [a military title referring to the crossing of the Suez Canal in 1973] where is the breakfast?').

[4] On the atmosphere just preceding Sadat's death in 1981 see Mohamed Heikal, *The Autumn of Fury: the Assassination of Sadat*, London: Deutsch, 1983.

Of the Arab states, no fewer than seven were in the post-1945 period ruled
for significant periods of time by military regimes that issued from coups
d'états: Egypt, Libya, Tunisia, Sudan, Yemen, Syria, Iraq.[5] Some of the
Arab monarchs were also in large measure leaders of praetorian military
regimes (Morocco, Oman, Jordan), while all other Arab states, with the
partial exception of Lebanon, relied on military and security apparatuses
for overt retention of power. The Turkish state was formed in the military
rising of 1920–3 and the Turkish military thereafter intervened repeatedly
to reassert control. In Iran the Pahlavi dynasty was created by a coup,
in 1921, out of which emerged the regime of Reza Khan, while Reza
Khan's son, Mohammad Reza Pahlavi, was restored to power in a military
coup three decades later, in 1953. Yet the Iranian military were, perhaps
surprisingly, less of a force thereafter, and were unable to prevent the
success of the Islamic revolution in 1978–9. In some way similar to the
Russian officer corps, before and after communism, the Iranian military
had little inclination to take power. In November 1978 an attempt at
military rule and martial law was made, headed by General Azhari, but
it proved ineffectual and two months later the armed forces, of 400,000
men, virtually disintegrated.

Israel might appear to be an exception, its army always having been
under civilian control. Yet Israel was far from being that exemplary state,
envisioned in the hopes of Theodor Herzl in his original programme of
1896, *Der Judenstaat*, in which the soldier would stay in the barrack just
as the rabbi would stay in his temple.[6] Both before and after the creation
of the Israeli state in 1948, the armed forces, and support for them, have
played a major part in Israeli politics, society and economics; the defence
budget has been amongst the highest in the world in the 1990s, at 12 per
cent of GDP, and all Israeli men have been liable to military service up to
the age of forty-five. Israel is often referred to as 'a nation in arms'. The
fact that three influential generals became prime minister, Yitzhak Rabin
in 1992, Ehud Barak in 1999 and Ariel Sharon in 2001, is an index in
itself of how influential the military as a socialiser had become.[7] Equally

[5] Barry Rubin and Thomas Keaney, eds., *Armed Forces in the Middle East: Politics and Strategy*, London: Frank Cass, 2002.

[6] *Theodor Herzls Zionistische Schriften*, ed. Leon Kellner, Berlin-Charlottenberg: Jüdischer Verlag, 1912, p. 122.

[7] The argument made in the 1950s and 1960s that the military were 'new men', modernisers with a national interest, has petered out. In general see Alan Richards and John Waterbury, *A Political Economy of the Middle East*, second edition, Boulder, CO: Westview Press, 1998, chapter 13, 'The Military and the State'. Also Anouar Abdel-Malek, *Egypt: Military Society*, New York: Random House, 1968; Stuart Cohen, *Democratic Societies and their Armed Forces*, London: Frank Cass, 2000; Michael Barnett, *Confronting the Costs of War: Military Power, State and Society in Egypt and Israel*, Princeton: Princeton University Press, 1992.

relevant, perhaps, is that of the nine Israeli premiers from 1948 to 2001, no fewer than four had, in their earlier careers, been involved not just in security but in the covert world of assassination or terror – Begin, Shamir, Barak and Sharon.[8]

On the other hand, there has also been recurrent and influential armed activity *against* states. The later history of the Ottoman empire was one of nationalist revolt against central government by Greeks, Serbs, Armenians. From 1918 to the 1960s, the colonial powers faced, as we have seen in chapter 4, repeated challenges to their rule, in Egypt, Syria, Iraq, Palestine, South Yemen, Oman. The experience of the post-colonial region has been little better. In the case of two peoples this has involved sustained, if intermittent, challenges by nationalist movements claiming their own states or significant autonomy: Palestinians against Israel, Kurds against Turkey, Iraq and Iran. Palestinian resistance was crushed in 1948–9 amidst defeat and dispersal, but revived in 1964 and continued thereafter. Kurdish opposition to the new centralising states was crushed in the 1920s but revived in Iraq after 1958, in Iran after the revolution of 1979 and in Turkey in the insurrection of 1984–2000.[9] Separate from these wars of national assertion have been situations in which countries have been riven by civil war: Lebanon between 1975 and 1990, Sudan intermittently from 1956, Yemen between 1962 and 1970 and in 1994 for 'the war of seventy days', Algeria from 1991.

While there were several nationalist and popular revolts earlier in the century, the rise of Islamist movements in the 1970s opened a new chapter in the incidence of violence within Middle Eastern states.[10] Some Islamist movements did not advocate violence but sought to pursue their goals through peaceful, if not always constitutional, means: the Reform Party in Turkey, the Islah in Yemen, the Labour Party in Jordan, the Muslim

---

[8] Menachem Begin had in the 1940s been leader of the Irgun, a breakaway armed Zionist group that killed Arab civilians, executed some captured British soldiers and blew up the King David Hotel killing forty-seven people. Yitzhak Shamir had a murky past the terrorist group *Lehi*: and in the darker reaches of Israeli covert operations. Ehud Barak had, as a regular soldier, taken part in secret operations in Lebanon, at least, that killed Palestinian leaders in their homes.

[9] For a marvellous pictorial survey of the modern history of the Kurds, documenting these dawns and disappointments, see the photograph collection, a portable museum of Kurdish history, by Susan Meiselas, *Kurdistan: In the Shadow of History*, New York: Random House, 1997.

[10] See, *inter alia*, Gilles Kepel, *The Revenge of God: the Resurgence of Islam, Christianity and Judaism in the Modern World*, Oxford: Polity Press, 1994; Edward Mortimer, *Faith and Power: the Politics of Islam*, London: Faber and Faber, 1982; Mohammad Hafez, *Why Muslims Rebel: Repression and Rebellion in the Muslim World*, London: Lynne Rienner, 2002.

Brotherhood in Egypt, the Nahda in Tunisia. But elsewhere Islamists did seek to use violence, often against governments they considered to be tyrannical and allowing no space for non-violent dissent: in Iraq Shi'ite guerrilla groups challenged the Ba'thist state from the 1970s onwards; in Egypt the Islamic Jihad engaged in assassination and armed attacks in the 1980s and 1990s; in Syria the Muslim Brotherhood staged an insurrection in 1982; in the Arabian Peninsula several organisations took up arms against local states; amongst Palestinians some groups advocated violence against Israel even when the dominant, secular PLO called for a ceasefire; in Algeria a widespread insurrection broke out in 1991. Most dramatic of all, in international impact and mobilisatory appeal, was the growth during the 1980s in Afghanistan, and in Yemen and Somalia, of the army of transnational *jihadi* Muslims, mainly Arab militants, fighting first the left and its Soviet allies, and, after 1991, the regional states and the west. These actions were often accompanied by a rhetoric that exalted violence in the cause, be it noted, *both* of national goals ('independence', 'liberation', expulsion of the 'oppressors') and of religious ones (*jihad*).[11] The levels of violence ranged, therefore, from full-scale convulsion of societies in civil war (as in Lebanon, Yemen or Afghanistan) to protracted guerrilla opposition (Palestine, Turkey, Egypt), to individual but recurrent acts of violence.

For all that they may have appeared, or at times presented themselves, as being separate from the international politics of the region, these armed actions *within* states were always intertwined with external context. The central goal of these movements was to take and retain state power; this necessarily entailed control of *both* dimensions of the two-faced state: society within, inter-state and transnational relations without. In many of these cases, therefore, just as in inter-state wars themselves, these internal revolts had their international dimensions. This was partially so as far as the cause of the conflict and support for participants were concerned: while in some cases these movements were opposition movements acting on the basis of resources drawn from within their own societies, in others assistance came from outside, either from other states or from transnational networks of support built up by these oppositions. Thus in the 1960s and 1970s the Palestinians received aid from Arab states, the Iraqi Kurds from Iran after 1958 and the PKK from Syria, while the Islamists across the Middle East were at least until the early 1990s aided by Saudi

[11] *Jihad* literally means 'effort', but such effort can, across a history of centuries of religious, social and political change, mean anything from individual prayer to collective social action to war. This last interpretation 'holy war', is, of course, a doctrine shared, and mutually reinforced, by Christianity and Judaism.

Arabia. Iran too, committed to *sudur-i inqilab*, the 'export of revolution', provided aid to the Shi'ite opposition in Lebanon in the 1980s and 1990s, while Iraq, for a time, to counter Syria, backed the Maronite breakaway General Aoun. Whatever the international dimension of *cause*, however, it was in *consequence* that these conflicts within states compounded that militarisation of the region already forged by the conflicts between states themselves.

Even if the incidence of inter-state war is taken as the sole basis of comparative judgement, of any region of the world, the Middle East had the most conflict-ridden record in the second half of the twentieth century. This importance of inter-state conflict will be all the more evident once the influence of general security threats, and the military competition associated with it, on the internal politics and on the society of each state, are also taken into account. If the Middle East state was, therefore, held in being by military power, indigenous up to World War I, predominantly external thereafter, it remained an area where military issues, and also what is subsumed under the vague term 'militarism', had a preponderant impact: military budgets took up much of state expenditure, arms purchases were, for decades, the highest for the non-developed world. States came therefore to be controlled by military and security elites whose preoccupations, and mode of government, dominated society as a whole. Although formally controlled by elected presidents and ruling parties, Egypt and Iraq were good examples of such militarised societies: civilian ministers could come and go, but it was the top officers who called the shots. This military influence was, however, also evident in the political culture of these states, as the cult of military strength, and belief in deliverance through war and conflict, pervaded states and opposition movements alike.[12] The titles given to state leaders illustrated this: Atatürk was the *gazi*, in Turkish the 'Islamic conqueror'; Sadat was *batal al-'ubur*, 'hero of the crossing' (i.e. October 1973); Saddam was *al-faris*, the 'knight on horseback'. Here a vicious circle was forged, in which the prevalence of violent conflict between states, and within them, promoted a social, political and ideological context that could itself come to rely on continued conflict and on fear of others. That the military elite also used this stimulated legitimacy to make money and corner business deals should be no surprise.

---

[12] One, to any reasonable outsider, objectionable practice was that, found with the PLO and Arab regimes, of parading very young kids in military uniform, brandishing guns. These were the *ashbal* (Young Lions) – a repugnant practice and a clear violation of the rights of the children concerned.

Armed conflicts: strategic, regional, internal

Against this background it is now possible to turn, in greater detail, to the impact on the Middle East of the three kinds of armed conflicts already mentioned – strategic and global, regional inter-state, and internal.

Strategic

As chapters 3, 4 and 5 have shown, the Middle East was, for much of the twentieth century, dominated by external, global rivalries. In the nineteenth century it was clear how the strategic rivalries of the European powers shaped the region. Both major Islamic states, Ottoman Turkey and Qajar Iran, were caught in these strategic contests. While European states sought to encroach on the Ottoman empire, they were also capable of allying with it against other European powers; this was notably so when Britain helped defend the Ottomans against France in 1838, and fought with them against Russia in the Crimean war (1853–5), just as the Germans fought with Istanbul in World War I. The outbreak of this last war in August 1914 had, however, been preceded by years of conflict on the borders of the Ottoman empire, the occupation of Egypt in 1882, the Balkan wars of 1912–13, and the violent Italian occupation of Libya in 1911. Throughout the nineteenth century Qajar Iran was less able to serve as an ally of European powers: defeated by Russia in the first decades of the nineteenth century, and backed by Britain against Russia in the 1850s, it was progressively encroached on by Britain and Russia around 1900. It was then carved into spheres of influence in 1907, only to be occupied by a variety of armies in World War I. However, in 1919, when Britain sought to impose on Iran an agreement that would have made it a *de facto* protectorate, popular opposition inside Iran, and the opposition of France, the USA and Russia, led London to withdraw this proposal.[13]

The post-1918 settlement temporarily froze conflict between Middle Eastern states: in World War II Turkey remained neutral, until the last moment, February 1945, while Iran was occupied by Russia and Britain in 1941. The Arab world was largely untouched by conflict, though not, as in Syria, by food shortages, with only North Africa serving as a theatre of active war. But as World War II ended so the Cold War came for forty years to cast a shadow on, if not determine, the politics of the region. The Cold War indeed began in the Middle East, with a dispute over the withdrawal of Soviet forces from Iran in March 1946. This was followed by the

---

[13] Peter Avery, *Modern Iran*, London: Ernest Benn, 1965, pp. 202–9.

proclamation of the Truman Doctrine, covering Greece and Turkey, but with implications for Iran, in 1947. While the crises that followed, notably the Arab–Israeli war of 1948–9, the Mosadeq crisis in Iran 1951–3 and the Egyptian revolution of 1952, were not directly caused by the Cold War, they did attract greater international attention, as regards both the dangers and opportunities which the region presented. The Cold War came, however, to the Arab world with the US attempt to forge a pro-western military pact in the region in 1953–4 and the Arab nationalist turn to the USSR in 1955. The supplies of arms, the endorsement of regimes and the diplomatic alliances involved, all reflected Cold War concerns: thus Egypt, Syria and Iraq became allies of the USSR, and their military leaders were hailed as progressive, 'national democratic' patriots by Moscow, while the monarchies of Jordan, Saudi Arabia and Iran, and the military in Turkey were regarded as defenders of a 'free world'. As has been discussed in chapter 4, the impact of the Cold War on the region was, therefore, not just on formal alliances or arms supplies, but also on state–society relations. By forging external alliances Middle Eastern regimes sought to meet internal needs, to reinforce themselves as much vis-à-vis their own societies as vis-à-vis their neighbours.

Many of the wars that divided the region in these decades had, there-fore, a Cold War character. This was true of the 1967 and 1973 Arab–Israeli wars, of the conflict between Iran and Iraq between 1969 and 1975 and of the Yemeni civil war of 1962–70. The Cold War also accounted for the increased provision of military advice and aid to allied states, and for the political, diplomatic and intelligence support provided to these states by their strategic patrons. The impact of the Cold War was seen not only in the ways in which these conflicts reflected global tensions, but also in the language used, in which each side painted the other as an 'agent' or 'puppet' of the opposed strategic camp. Quite apart from the impact on the region, however, was the way in which the Middle East contributed to great power conflict itself; how, in other words, it fuelled the Cold War: if this was not so for the first Arab–Israeli war, it most certainly was the case for 1956, 1973 and 1982. The Arab–Israeli war of 1973 in particular came at a very dangerous moment in world history: in its final hours the USA went on a calibrated nuclear alert, DEFCON 3, while the USSR was believed to be preparing to send troops to protect Egypt from Israeli advances.[14]

Yet even during the Cold War, that is up to 1989, it would be mis-taken to overstate the degree of responsibility of this conflict for these

---

[14] The retrospective US view was that DEFCON 3 (one of five stages) was still well short of being a direct threat to act. Author's interview with Henry Kissinger, New York, April 1995.

Middle Eastern regional wars. First of all, the external powers did not in any simple way control regional states as the USSR did in eastern Europe.[15] A striking example of this was the inability of either side to get their Arab allies to recognise the state of Israel, and the failure of the Soviet Union to control their Arab nationalist allies.[16] Secondly, while they remained committed to regional allies, the external powers did not become directly involved in Middle Eastern conflicts: American forces entered Lebanon in 1958, but they were not involved in fighting there or elsewhere, until their re-entry to Lebanon as part of an ill-conceived peace-keeping operation in 1982–4. British forces fought colonial wars in Palestine, Egypt and South Yemen, but their Cold War actions were also without violent consequences. Compared with East Asia, Africa or Latin America, and amidst all the clamour of the times, it is striking *how little* the Cold War brought in armies from the outside into the Middle East. Moreover, even during the Cold War, there were many conflicts that did *not* have a Cold War character: the 1956 Suez war, for example, in which the USA and Russia both supported the Arabs; above all the 1980–8 Iran–Iraq war which broke out and was waged independently of Cold War. Only in the closing stages of the Cold War did either the USSR or the USA become directly involved in large-scale combat deployments

---

[15] Two authors who shrewdly contest the external determination in favour of regional forces: Bassam Tibi, *Conflict and War in the Middle East, 1967–91: Regional Dynamic and the Superpowers*, London: Macmillan, 1993 and Fawaz Gerges, *The Superpowers and the Middle East: Regional and International Politics 1955–1967*, Boulder, CO: Westview Press, 1994.

[16] Raphael Israeli, *PLO in Lebanon: Selected Documents*, London: Weidenfeld and Nicolson, 1983, pp. 34–73, chapter 5, Document 7.1, 'PLO talks with Kremlin leaders'. Conservative Arab states, especially Saudi Arabia, were forever criticising American support for Israel. On the other side, the author can recall from his own experience many cases of Arab radicals disparaging the apparent timidity, or capitulation to western influence, of the Soviet leadership. Visiting the more radical arena of the Arab world after the 1967 war – Egypt (1968), Jordan (1969), South Yemen and Dhofar (1970) – I was struck by the recurrence of radical denunciation of the USSR, now irrevocably associated not with communism but with the evident failure to 'confront' Israel in 1967 and later. A certain verbal if not organisational association with the then militant model of Mao Zedong's China was evident. *Tasqut al-tahrifia*, 'Down with Revisionism', a favourite Chinese term of denunciation of the Russians, was an official slogan in Dhofar, although I was not sure if the militants proclaiming it knew exactly *who* the 'revisionists' were. In 1972 I met in London with a senior member of the South Yemen ruling party. He had just been receiving treatment in the special CPSU Central Committee hospital in Moscow. I asked him how he had found it, and he replied that it was fine, but that, as an Arab revolutionary, he had been shocked to find a whole suite in the hospital occupied by the Queen of Afghanistan and her retinue. When he asked 'Soviet comrades' about this, they told him that the then King of Afghanistan, Amanullah, had in 1921 been the first leader in the world to recognise the Bolshevik state and that Lenin had left instructions to pay special attention to the needs of Afghanistan. This in 1972 – six years *before* the communists took over in Kabul. In the light of subsequent events, an ironic incident indeed.

in the region – the former, after 1979, in Afghanistan, the latter, in 1990, in regard to Kuwait. In both cases allied regimes were threatened with, or had already faced, annihilation.

The limited impact of the Cold War on the region was evident in one other, important, respect, namely in the efforts both blocs made throughout the Cold War to find negotiated solutions to Middle Eastern conflicts. One of the striking features of all five Arab–Israeli wars, in contrast to many other conflicts of the latter half of the twentieth century, was how they were taken to the Security Council and ended with UN resolutions. In the UN Security Council debates in New York there was acted out an often dramatic combination of regional military and political issues on the one hand, with great power rivalry and the nuclear arms race on the other. The contrast between these Arab–Israeli wars and the Iran–Iraq war is striking: in the latter case the UN Security Council was powerless, as first Iraq and then Iran rejected it as an authoritative negotiator. Only in July 1988, when Iran was exhausted by war and its leadership at last realised they had failed in their goal of ousting Saddam Hussein from power, did they come to accept the UN resolution stipulating terms for peace. The Middle East was, therefore, in the Cold War, as it had been in the nineteenth century and in both world wars, a site of great power rivalry. This was, however, a rivalry tempered both by the autonomy which regional states and movements had, and by the calculation, in Washington and Moscow, of the risks involved in a direct confrontation in the region.[17]

Regional rivalries

If it is impossible to detach regional conflicts from external context, it is nonetheless possible to look at wars between regional states as in some degree separate from these broader internal pressures and restraints. Indeed, since the collapse of the Ottoman empire the region has been the scene of wars in which local states have, while hoping to use external support for their war aims, nonetheless exercised considerable independence from their patrons, with varying degrees of success. This pattern of autonomous inter-state war was already set in the inter-war period, when the rising state of Saudi Arabia took power by conquering much of the Arabian Peninsula with the sword and then, in 1934, fought a war with the only other independent Arab state at that time, Yemen. At the Treaty of Taif (1934), the Saudis prevailed, but in imposing a peace on Yemen

---

[17] Steven Spiegel, ed., *Conflict Management in the Middle East*, Boulder, CO: Westview Press, 1992.

that forced the latter to cede three provinces hitherto considered as part of their national territory ('Asir, Jizan, Najran), they laid the basis for a Saudi–Yemen conflict, and much Yemeni resentment, that was to last for decades. Only in June 2000, at a summit between Prince Abdullah and President Al-Abdullah Salih, was a comprehensive agreement on this frontier, the longest undelineated one in the world, reached. That very night all Saudi aid to the Yemeni opposition was stopped, and various media activities associated with them, and based in London, abruptly interrupted.

In a later case, British withdrawal from Palestine after World War II precipitated the Arab–Israeli war of 1948–9, out of which Israel emerged as an independent state and the Palestinian lands were taken by Israel and Jordan. That, first, Arab–Israeli war was caused by the default of the colonial power, Britain, while Israel enjoyed the active support of external patrons, both the USA and the USSR, at that time more the latter; but it was prompted above all by a regional conflict, indeed between two 'non-state' forces, that between the Zionist movement aspiring to statehood on one side, and the Palestinians on the other. The 1948 conflict was an example of a relatively autonomous, regional war, both in terms of the factors provoking it and equally in terms of its course and outcome. Not that the participants saw it that way – heaven forbid! The Zionists believed that Britain was behind the Arab states, especially Jordan and Egypt, whilst the Arabs felt the USA and the Soviet Union were manipulating the Israelis.

The claim of autonomy could not be made to the same degree of later Arab–Israeli wars. That of 1956 would have been impossible without the direct involvement of two external powers, Britain and France, on the side of Israel. In 1967, and in terms of political direction, Israel acted on its own: it did not attack Egypt on America's orders, let alone with direct American air support, although this is what was widely believed at the time in the Arab world. (Even the USSR, which, to its later regret, broke off relations with Israel at the time – a move that was to cost it dearly in subsequent decades, as it thereby excluded Moscow from a role in regional diplomacy – long repeated this exculpatory myth of US participation in the war.) But in 1967 external *context* mattered greatly: Israel was able to take the decision to launch a pre-emptive strike on the Arabs because it was confident, amidst a climate of heightened east–west tension, of the backing of the USA. Pro-Soviet leaders had been ousted in Indonesia (1965) and Ghana (1966). Fascist colonels had just come to power in Greece (April 1967). Washington was preoccupied by the war in Vietnam and therefore saw the Arab–Israeli conflict, where the USSR backed the Arabs, more in bipolar terms than in 1948 or 1956.

Permissive context is as important as imperialist command. A comparison may, indeed, be made between *Israeli* calculation of general USA backing in 1967, and the *Iraqi* estimate in 1980 that the USA, then preoccupied by the Iranian detention of US hostages in Tehran, would turn a blind eye and then support Baghdad's invasion of Iran. It is irrelevant to ask whether Israel in 1967 and Iraq in 1980 were *instructed* by Washington to act – there was no need for such explicit endorsement. The same was true for the Israeli invation of Lebanon in 1982.

The 1973 Arab–Israeli war was one in which the autonomy of local actors was similar to that of 1967 but in reverse: Egypt planned its counter-attack on Israel in secret and, whilst acquiring Soviet weapons, did not take the USSR into its confidence. This is not what the Israelis, or many Americans, said at the time; they claimed that Egypt had attacked at the behest of Moscow, in line with some broader Soviet-backed offensive then underway against western positions in the third world, from Vietnam to Angola to Nicaragua. As in 1967 the Cold War context, and suspicion, understated the degree of autonomy which local states in fact enjoyed in launching the wars, but rightly highlighted the ways in which, once fighting had begun, the leading Cold War states did act to impose negotiated settlements on both sides.

The Cold War also played a role, but a more rapidly diminishing one, in war between Iraq and Iran. Prior to the Iraqi revolution of 1958, Iran and Iraq, as two monarchies formed after World War I, enjoyed reasonably co-operative relations, even if there remained the issue of the territorial dispute between them, concerning the division of the Shatt al-Arab river (Persian Arvand Rud), which runs for sixty miles to the Persian Gulf. At that time a combination of shared monarchical political system and British influence in Iraq kept conflict under control. The Iraqi revolution of July 1958, which brought a radical nationalist regime to power in Baghdad, destroyed all that: the two countries then found themselves involved in competitive interference in each other's internal affairs, backing dissident forces (Kurds in northern Iraq, Arabs in the southern Iranian province of Khuzestan), and in a more active dispute over the riverine frontier.

Prior to 1969 Iraq had asserted a predominant position on the Shatt al-Arab but in that year the Shah repudiated the Iraqi position; at the same time a low-level border conflict developed, with shelling across the frontier and a substantial Iranian involvement in support of the Kurdish guerrillas in northern Iraq. Iran and Iraq had, certainly, their own reasons for fighting this, the First Gulf War, which expressed, beyond the territorial issue itself, a conflict over political system, between the radical republicanism of Baghdad and the monarchical conservatism of Tehran.

The Cold War certainly added to Iraqi–Iranian tensions, as the USA encouraged the Shah to put pressure on a pro-Soviet Iraq while Moscow sought to promote its relations with an anti-imperialist Iraq. In contrast to the Arab–Israeli wars, however, the ending of this war was largely the work of the regional states themselves: in 1975, after six years of intermittent conflict, the Shah and Saddam Hussein reached agreement on delineating the border and, most importantly, on ceasing interference in each other's internal affairs. Nevertheless, and once again, regional perception suggested a major external 'hand': Saddam Hussein, in private, blamed the USSR for staunching his arms supplies, while his Arab critics saw Saddam's acceptance of a compromise with Iran as evidence of the Ba'thist government's subservience to the west.

The outcome of secret negotiations between the Shah and Saddam, the Algiers Agreement of April 1975, appeared to put an end to the conflict between the two states in that it settled *the* most important issue between them, interference; yet just as the Iraqi revolution of 1958 had opened one chapter of conflict between the two states, so the Iranian revolution of 1979 initiated a new, far bloodier phase.[18] In the period between the accession of Khomeini to power, in February 1979, and the outbreak of the war, in September 1980, conflict developed along several fronts: there were clashes on the frontier, mutual denunciations of each government by the other, and, most important of all because it violated the core understanding of the Algiers Agreement, growing involvement of each side in the internal affairs of the other. The Iranians, in particular, seem to have believed that, with the successful fall of the Shah in Iran, they could extend their Islamic revolution to Iraq and that there was a favourable situation in Iraq for this, given the large numbers of Arab Shi'ite Muslims and Kurds, in all over two-thirds of the population, whom they believed could support a rising against the secular state. When Saddam Hussein launched the war against Iran, on 22 September 1980, he also repudiated the Algiers Agreement, including the stipulations concerning the division of the Shatt al-Arab waterway; but it was not the frontier issue as such, so much as broader political calculations – the threat which the Iranian revolution posed to Iraq on the one hand, the opportunity for Iraq to assert itself in the Gulf and in the Middle East as a whole – which would appear to have determined his course of action. Much has been made in subsequent years of who 'started' the war. In the sense of who fired the first shots, in September 1980, this was certainly Iraq. But responsibility

---

[18] Ralph King, *The Iran–Iraq War: the Political Implications*, London: IISS, 1987, Adelphi Paper 219, chapter 1, 'The Causes of War'.

for the deterioration of relations in the preceding year and a half was as much Iran's as Iraq's, as any reading of the radio broadcasts of both sides will show.

The Iran–Iraq war lasted for eight years, far longer than any other modern Middle Eastern war between states, and involved hundreds of thousands of casualties. At its core, and despite major mobilisations on both sides, it remained a conflict along the frontier, backed up by air and missile attacks on each other's capitals. Neither side won a decisive breakthrough, as in World War I. From 1984 the war also spread to the waters of the Persian Gulf: Iraq attacked Iranian offshore oil-drilling and oil-loading facilities, and tankers carrying Iranian oil, and Iran, in retaliation, attacked tankers carrying oil from the two main supporters of Iraq in the Gulf, Kuwait and Saudi Arabia. It was this 'tanker war', the extension of the war to sea, which increased the external involvement in the war, but also highlighted an external dimension that had already been present: from the beginning of the war, Iraq had benefited from external support. This was evident at the UN, where the Security Council, under pressure from Ismet Kittani, Iraq's envoy, and with the connivance of the USA and the UK, delayed for days before ever addressing the outbreak of the conflict, and even then did not call for an Iraqi withdrawal to the pre-conflict frontiers. External support was also evident in the provision of arms, agricultural credits and intelligence to Baghdad by both east and west. The tanker war led, in 1987, to the arrival of US, British and other ships which in effect protected Iraq's allies from attack and engaged with the Iranian navy. Soviet military aid, the core of Iraq's logistical system, was limited in the period up to mid-1982, when Iraq was seen as the aggressor, but plentiful thereafter. There can be little doubt that this external contribution played its part in sustaining Iraq and, thereby, in forcing Iran, after eight years of war, to accept the ceasefire in August 1988. As in the Arab–Israeli wars, therefore, it is possible to identify an element of external participation in the course and conclusion, but not the causes, of the war. Yet in contrast to most Arab–Israeli wars, and to the first Gulf war of 1969–75, all of which took place within a Cold War context, that between Iran and Iraq was very much not along Cold War lines, for one reason above all: from the summer of 1982 when Iran advanced into the Fao Peninsula, east and west, far from backing or finding competitive sides in this conflict, both blocs backed the same side, Iraq, against Iran.

Other examples of 'autonomy' were to follow. As discussed at greater length in chapter 5, the Iraqi invasion of Kuwait in 1990, in effect the start of the *third* Gulf war, was equally independent of the preferences, let alone instructions or promptings, of external powers.[19] Iraq does appear to have been influenced by two external considerations: one the view that, following the collapse of the communist regimes in eastern Europe, there would be increased pressure for a change of regime in dictatorial Middle Eastern countries like Iraq; the other that the USA would not have the will to fight, as borne out by its withdrawal from Vietnam in 1973, and its departure from Lebanon in 1984. However, what would appear to have been most decisive for Iraqi strategy was its calculation that the Arab world would accept the occupation of Kuwait and so restrain any concerned international response. In this it was, of course, fundamentally mistaken, a mistake held to by many Arab countries as well. The USA, Britain and their allies were able to secure UN Security Council agreement for a counter-attack, to bring in a number of Arab states, and in January 1991, to launch a successful war to expel Iraq from Kuwait. Here the calculation, and miscalculation, of regional states, in its early stages largely independent of global politics and external influence, led to the reverse outcome. From 1991 onwards, not only during the war but for the years to come, an external, US and British, military and diplomatic presence was implanted firmly in the region. The international did *not* therefore cause this war to occur; but, as with successive Arab–Israeli wars, the August 1990 invasion of Kuwait did have significant, and enduring, long-term outcomes.

Internal warfare

This recurrence of external, great power military involvement in the region and of war between regional states has been accompanied by irregular war *within* states, the actions of opposition forces contesting external involvement and local states alike. The spectrum of such actions has ranged from substantial guerrilla campaigns, involving the mobilisation of thousands of armed men and the occupation of territory, as in Algeria (1954–62), Turkey (1984–98), Iraq (intermittently 1958–2003) and Yemen (1962–70), to war between confessional groups within one country (Lebanon, 1979–90), to lower-level campaigns of bombing and assassination (Egypt, 1990s; Iran from 1981 onwards), through to a more sporadic set of armed actions linked to political campaigns (second Palestinian *intifadha*, 2000 onwards). Actions of the irregular kinds have not been specific to the Middle East; yet the combination of such

---

[19] Lawrence Freedman and Efraim Karsh, *The Gulf Conflict 1990–1991: Diplomacy and War in the New World Order*, Part I; Amatzia Baram and Barry Rubin, eds., *Iraq's Road to War*, London: Macmillan, 1994.

irregular actions with the broader context of international and regional
military action, and with the invocation of particularist Middle Eastern
justifications, be these nationalist or religious, has done much to
shape external perceptions of the region as it has to inflame relations
between states and peoples, and between different peoples themselves,
in the region.

If rural uprisings against the state were recurrent in 1918–39, the use by
nationalist forces of guerrilla warfare became more common after 1945:
the Zionists in Palestine used this against British and Arab foe alike from
1946 to 1948, but it was as an instrument of struggle by Arab nationalists
that guerrilla warfare has become best known in this region. In the early
1950s Egyptian *fedayin* carried out raids against British forces stationed
in the Suez Canal zone. The Algerian war of independence, fought from
1954 to 1962, saw a high level of mobilisation for nationalist guerrilla
war, in which hundreds of thousands of Arabs were killed.[20] The 1960s
were a high point for guerrilla war world-wide; in the Middle East this
found expression in two radical nationalist campaigns: the launch of the
movement against British rule in South Yemen, in the Radfan moun-
tains, October 1963, and the launch of the al-Fath guerrilla campaign
against Israel, in January 1965. Each, Palestinian and Yemeni, was to
have wider consequences after the cataclysmic year of 1967: the British
departure from Aden in November 1967 led to the taking of power by
the National Liberation Front, later (1978) the Yemeni Socialist Party,
one of the guerrilla factions, which then proceeded to promote a guerrilla
organisation in the neighbouring Sultanate of Oman, the People's Front
for the Liberation of the Occupied Arab Gulf (PFLOAG), with the aim
of liberating 'the occupied Arab Gulf'. For its part the Israeli victory in
the war of June 1967, and the crisis of the Arab regimes that followed,
opened the way for a much more active campaign, against Israel and Arab
states alike, by the Palestinian resistance.[21]

While the Palestinian guerrilla resistance had begun in January 1965,
prior to the war of 1967, this latter conflict created a context in which
much more extensive operations could be carried out: Israel had now
occupied Gaza and the West Bank, territories hitherto held by Egypt and

[20] On Algeria's independence war see Alistair Horne, *A Savage War for Peace: Algeria,
1954–1962*, revised edition, London: Papermac, 1987, and the recollections of an FLN
mujahid in Mahfoud Bennoune, *Le hasard et l'histoire. Entretiens avec Belaid Abdesselam*,
2 vols., Reghala: ENAF Editions, 1990.
[21] On South Yemen see Fred Halliday, *Revolution and Foreign Policy: the Case of South Yemen,
1967–1987*, Cambridge: Cambridge University Press, 1990; Vitali Naumkin, *Red Wolves
of Yemen*, Reading: The Oleander Press, 2003; on Palestine see Yezid Sayigh, *Armed
Struggle and the Search for a State: the Palestinian National Movement, 1949–1993*, Oxford:
Clarendon Press, 1997.

Jordan respectively, while in Jordan itself the *fedayin* were, temporarily, able to establish a separate military and political apparatus, a state within a state. When in September 1970 King Hussein decided to end this situation of, in effect, dual power within Jordan, the focus of Palestinian resistance activity, and of the construction of a separate political-military apparatus, shifted to Lebanon. The presence of these Palestinian forces, to some degree encouraged by Arab nationalists among the Lebanese Muslim population, together with the provocations they caused, contributed to the outbreak in 1975 of the Lebanese civil war: this was to provoke interventions into Lebanon by Syria, in 1976, and Israel, in 1982, and was to last, at enormous cost to Lebanese and Palestinians alike, until the peace accord of 1990. Mao's 'single spark' had lit a prairie fire, if not the one the PLO had expected.

In the Middle East guerrilla warfare was not, however, a prerogative of the Arabs alone. Kurdish nationalists also took up arms, when circumstances allowed, against the various states that controlled them. The 1958 revolution in Iraq was followed by a Kurdish uprising led by the Kurdish Democratic Party of Mustafa Barzani, a phase that was to end only in 1975 when the Shah of Iran abandoned his Kurdish allies and the areas were reoccupied by the Baghdad regime. In 1991, following the Iraqi defeat in the war over Kuwait, a new Kurdish uprising took place in northern Iraq and, following western intervention on the side of the Kurds, a protected area that was to last through the war of 2003 was created. In Iran Kurdish guerrillas were active against the Shah in the 1960s, but it was the revolution of 1979 that provided a context for a full-scale emergence of Kurdish opposition, only for this to be bloodily crushed by the Tehran government in the early 1980s.[22] The most sustained Kurdish uprising was to be in Turkey: arising in part out of the formation of the Turkish left as a whole in militant armed actions against the state in the 1970s, the PKK launched a struggle in 1984 that was to last for fifteen years, lead to the deaths of many thousands and the displacement of tens of thousands, and, by forcing some greater recognition of a distinct Kurdish identity, was profoundly to affect Turkish society as a whole.

Guerrilla activities involved, at the least, the organisation of groups of armed men, and some women, by political movements, and their retention of some territorial control. The late 1960s Arab phrase, 'organised revolutionary violence', *al-'unf al-thawri al-munadhdham*, in contrast to violence that is 'spontaneous', *'afawi*, that is tribal, and so *not* revolutionary, captures this point well. This contrasted also with less systematic,

---

[22] Reza Farzad, 'The Kurdish Question in Iran,' Ph.D. thesis, University of London, 1997.

but recurrent, forms of violence practised by opposition groups from the 1970s onwards, involving bombing, hijacking of planes, assassination of political leaders. While from the 1980s onwards these actions were most readily associated with Islamist groups, the resort to such irregular low-level acts of violence was by no means confined to religious-oriented organisations. In the Iran of the 1970s left-wing opponents, notably the Fedayin-i Khalq, were as prominent amongst the perpetrators of assassination and kidnapping as their religious counterparts, Fedayin-i Islam, and Mojahidin-i Khalq.[23] The first wave of Palestinian aeroplane hijackings, in the period 1968–70, was carried out by secular, Marxist-Leninist groups within the resistance movement, the PFLP in particular.[24] It was with the rise of Islamist opposition in the 1970s, in Egypt and Iraq, that groups with a religious identity came to use violence in this war. The high point of such armed opposition was in the 1980s and 1990s: in Egypt, Iraq, Algeria and elsewhere religious groups turned to violence in the name of Islam, and in the name of a particular rendering of the Islamic concept of struggle or *jihad*. As discussed in chapter 8, the term 'terrorist', legitimate if carefully used, has not only descriptive, but also normative, uses. Whatever the declared justifications for such actions, their import and extent were, however, far less than the violence of the states against which they were directed. Indeed, for all the publicity associated with guerrilla actions, in general, it is striking how rarely they were able successfully to challenge the states they were pitted against. Over the sixty years or so since the end of World War II, only in Israel (1948), Algeria (1962) and South Yemen (1967), where the colonial power withdrew amidst mass upsurge, did guerrillas attain their goal. The outcome of the fourth such conflict, Palestine, one colonial in form if not, given the origins of Zionism, in historic formation, is, after close on sixty years, as yet undecided.

The failure of negotiation

Reason, and some intellectual order, can only be restored if, after this overview of terror and violence, we take the argument back to the question of the state. Without this anchor, all analysis, and moral judgement, runs adrift. Despite appearances, in all forms of Middle Eastern conflict, international, regional and internal, the core actors have been regional states. This conclusion, relating the recurrence of war in the Middle East

[23] Fred Halliday, Iran: *Dictatorship and Development*, Harmondsworth: Penguin, 1978.
[24] See Sayigh, *Armed Struggle*, pp. 213–15. See also interview with Ghassan Kannafani, PFLP leader, *New Left Review*, no. 67, May–June 1971. Kannafani was killed in a car bomb explosion in Beirut a year later.

to the nature of states, has implications not only for analysis but also for the future of the region itself. The continued incidence of war is not, necessarily, something that belongs to the Middle East of the past. The less emphasis is placed on strategic factors, be these the struggle against colonial rule or the Cold War, and the more on the dynamics, and choices, of regional states, and of revolt against them, the greater the prospect becomes of a continuation of war between these regional states. Put another way, if war is a product of two factors, state–society relations within and state–state relations without, then it is evident that, for all the changes in the global situation since 1991, and the impact of globalisation, these two factors have not been fundamentally changed. On the one hand, the majority of Middle Eastern states remain authoritarian, prone to repression, scapegoating and nationalist rhetoric, while those that are not so dictatorial, notably Israel and Turkey, exhibit strong nationalist, and at times chauvinist, attitudes towards their Arab neighbours, this fuelled by popular sentiment. In this internal dimension, the twenty-first century has brought, as yet, little or no change. If anything 11 September 2001, by what it symbolises and in its consequences, has accentuated the problem. The contemporary Middle East thus perpetuates the domestic preconditions for insecurity and belligerency – this, not the ever-plotting 'west', is the root, causative and moral, of the problem.

On all major axes of conflict, there was only limited progress in the 1990s and, in some individual cases, a net deterioration. The external, regional situation remained unstable. As it took shape after 1991, the 'Greater West Asian Crisis' rattled all state structures. In the Arab–Israeli arena, the endurance of the peace between Egypt and Israel, signed in 1979, was matched by that between Israel and Jordan in 1994; but, as we have seen, there was no Israeli peace with Syria, or Lebanon, and the overall state of relations with the Arab world, somewhat more positive after the Oslo Accords of 1993, had turned to renewed rancour by the end of 1999. In the Gulf, the defeat of Iraq in 1991 had led to no political or diplomatic progress: Iraq had remained in confrontation with the USA, the UK and their Arab allies, evasive about recognising the independence of Kuwait, and seemingly committed to new confrontations; in the end, in early 2003, the USA and Britain invaded and toppled the leadership of the Ba'thist state. Few believed that this marked the end of the story: there was no quick fix in *bilad al-nahrain*, Mesopotamia. At the same time, after 1991, Iran, which was able to improve its relations with Saudi Arabia, remained wary of Iraq and in protracted confrontation with the USA, slipping the straitjacket of dual containment.

Meanwhile relations between the Arab world and Turkey, never of the warmest, deteriorated in the 1990s, in part because of Turkish plans to dam the waters of the Tigris and the Euphrates, which run into Syria and Iraq, in part because of a much closer military collaboration between Turkey and Israel. The incorporation into the Middle East of the wars of Afghanistan, and the instability of Pakistan, only compounded this problem. One example among many: the conflict between the radical Sunni Taliban in Afghanistan and their Shi'ite, Tajik and Hazara opponents. The Middle East was, therefore, structured by at least four distinct and major inter-state rivalries that allowed, it seemed, of little political or strategic amelioration, as, over the 1990s and beyond, the world elsewhere apparently moved on; from the agenda of the Cold War years these rivalries fed on each other and led to sharper inter-confessional relations throughout the Arab world.

Unsettled as these conflicts were at the political level, they were, moreover, as discussed in chapter 5, exacerbated by the development of capability at the military level, and in particular by the growth of a regional arms race. As of early 2004, no state in the region other than Israel had acquired a nuclear capability, but it was known, on the basis of evidence gathered by UN inspectors after 1991, that Iraq had earlier been seeking to develop such a capability. A decade later, and on the eve of the US attack in March 2003, it still in theory possessed the experts and the financial capability to do so. Other countries, notably Iran and Saudi Arabia, were believed to have shown interest in longer-run acquisition of such a capability. This was in both cases not only in response to the Israeli nuclear force, but also out of concern about what, in the future, Iraq might do. This incipient nuclearisation of the region was not encouraged by external powers. The one external state that did promote this was Pakistan, which cheerfully, and under US protection, proliferated nuclear potential to Iran and Libya, as well as North Korea. European states, however, were concerned about the possible threat to their territories of intermediate-range missiles based in the Middle East, while the USA took the possibility of attack from the Middle East as legitimation of its national missile defence programme announced by President Bush in 2001. The occupation of Iraq, in 2003, an action that had other strategic purposes, was justified as an outcome of this concern.

These developments in the late 1990s and later did not, on their own, entail an increased likelihood, let alone probability, of conflict in the Middle East. Arms races do not, in themselves, lead to war; some elements of deterrence, or caution, may result. Arms purchases also keep armies, and middlemen, happy. What was most alarming, however, about these developments in military capability were, however, two other accompanying factors. First, in contrast to the strategic climate of the Cold War, which, in large measure, involved a rivalry of two strategic blocs, led by the two major states, the USA and the USSR, the security situation within the Middle East was *multilateral*, involving several areas of conflict and so much harder to control and mediate. Iran, for example, was seen by Israel as a possible threat, yet its military programmes were determined, in the first instance, by its concerns with Iraq and by the growing nuclearisation on its south-east flank, in Pakistan and India, following the explosion of nuclear weapons by those two countries in 1998. The other particular reason for concern was the failure to build even the most minimal levels of confidence, and negotiating, machinery, between the competing states, of the kind that had been built up in Europe from the 1960s and which had, as in the Four-Power arrangements for Berlin, themselves built on a basic set of understandings inherited from the establishment of the post-war order in 1945. The lack of such diplomatic and confidence-building activity reflected, in the end, not some timeless political culture of suspicion, but the character and priorities of states, contemporary, coercive and calculating as they were.

War and the politics of the region

Little wonder then that the all-embracing explanations in terms of 'history', here taken as transhistorical continuity, should seem so appealing. Even the staunchest, most anti-atavistic, modernist and well-versed *fedayi* of historical sociology might be tempted to conclude from a history of war, and conflict, in the Middle East that violence between and within states was endemic to its age-old past, contemporary politics and culture. The phrase 'the only language they understand is force . . .' can itself be found in many languages. Certainly this is how it has appeared at certain times in recent years, be it with regard to the Arab–Israeli conflict, Lebanon or the wars involving Iraq. This is also the way in which some within the region chose to present the evidence, invoking as they do the values of struggle in defence of national and political goals and, almost automatically, a long antecedent and legitimating history of struggle against oppressors, regional and global.[25] This is, of course, not a

[25] This invocation of a long nationalist past sometimes had unanticipated consequences. On one occasion in 1973, during a visit to the 'liberated areas' of Dhofar, southern Oman, I was assigned a bodyguard of eight fighters. It was a time of sudden raids by British SAS units on the rebel areas and, as we settled down for the night on the side of a mountain, I noticed that the unit commander appeared to be very young. 'Had he had any combat experience?' I gently enquired. The reply was not reassuring: 'Our people have been fighting imperialist intervention for over four centuries. We defeated the Portuguese. We defeated the Dutch. We defeated the Iranians. Now we shall defeat the British and their other Arab mercenaries. Ours is a collective national struggle. We do not believe in the individual.' I did not sleep well that night.

sign of historical fidelity, let alone of courage, but a surrender to the easy option, and to nationalist demagogy.

The *causes* of violence are also not a sufficient explanation. That violence, once engaged in, does have a dynamic of its own is indisputable: states locked in military rivalry reproduce conflict, while a culture, and politics, of violence within states reproduces itself, crushing alternatives. Leaders also make money out of war. Atavism will retain its hold, but a closer examination reveals a less clear-cut picture as far as both the history and international relations of the Middle East are concerned.

To recognise the importance which wars have had in the formation of the modern Middle East is not, therefore, to treat their role here as in some way distinct from that elsewhere, or to see the incidence of wars as an expression of something peculiar to the politics of the Middle East. In its pre-modern form, war has been a formative influence, on the map of states as on their internal composition, in many parts of the world: war shaped Europe, between 1870 and 1945, as it shaped Latin America in the early nineteenth century and East Asia in the period between 1894 and 1975. From the 1960s onwards much of Africa was also ravaged by wars, with outcomes yet to be ascertained: the final death throes of South African racism, from 1945 to 1994, were brought on by regional wars. In terms of intensity it is questionable how great the impact of war on the Middle East has been in modern times. With the exception of the Russo-Turkish front in World War I, the two world wars involved very low military casualties, on any side, though civilian deaths through hunger, for example in Syria in World War II, may have been high.

The most costly inter-state wars of the post-1945 period were the Algerian war of independence, in which up to one million people are believed to have been lost, and the Iran–Iraq war, the Second Gulf War: casualties in the latter were in the hundreds of thousands. By contrast the Arab–Israeli wars have involved relatively low numbers of casualties, the total between 1948 and 1982 for Israelis and Arabs, and including civilian casualties as a result of Israeli raids into Lebanon, being around 50,000.[26] Similarly the war over Kuwait in 1990–1, although heralded as involving the risk of major casualties, and reported by some afterwards as having done so, involved rather low casualties, a few hundred on the Kuwaiti and Allied side, around 15,000, civilian and military combined, on the Iraqi side.[27] The Iraq war of 2003 had casualties of a similar magnitude.

[26] Anthony Cordesman, *Perilous Prospects: the Peace Process and the Arab–Israeli Military Balance*, Boulder, CO: Westview Press, 1996, p. 105.
[27] Patrick Cockburn, *The Independent*, 5 February 1992; and John Heidenrich, 'The Gulf War: How Many Iraqis Died?', *Foreign Policy*, no. 90, Spring 1993. It would seem that for 1991 *both* Iraq *and* the west allowed inflated figures, of up to 200,000, to go unchallenged for, contrasted, political reasons.

Compared with the costs of the wars after 1945 of China, Korea and Vietnam in East Asia, or the wars of southern and later central Africa after 1961, these were relatively low figures.

Proportion aside, however, the analytic, theoretically informed question of why war affected and may well still continue to affect the Middle East as it did needs to be addressed. Here three broad kinds of explanation present themselves. One attributes the incidence of war to the political systems in the countries concerned, above all their authoritarian character, and the reliance of these on belligerent nationalism. A second form of explanation is in terms of culture, in particular the shaping of perception and foreign policy by religion and of political ideas that may follow from this, be this with regard to the illegitimacy of separate states, or of frontiers, or the sacred character of struggle against unbelievers. A third explanation is in terms of the impact on the region of external factors, imperial or Cold War.

None of these explanations is necessarily exclusive of the other,[28] yet each needs to be treated with some caution. As we have seen, the last of these, in terms of global structures of power and impact of very real global conflicts, world wars and Cold War, did have their impact on the region, if only in the most general sense that each bloc had its allies in the region, and these local allies knew they could rely on the great powers to protect them if they got into trouble. There are, however, two problems with this emphasis on the international as an explanation. One is that explanation in terms of structural factors all too easily degenerates into simplistic explanation, a reduction that dissolves all agency, or human choice, whether of states, classes or individuals, into a determinism if not into a conspiracy theory according to which all states, and opposition forces in the region, act at the behest of external powers. It is not only the initial causes, but the subsequent course of the war, its very start, duration, end, that reflect the decisions, or better, long-laid 'arrangements', of great powers. In some cases this may be an accurate account, Suez in 1956 being a case in point, but in general this invocation of embedded determination, of the 'structura ex machina', is an insufficient explanation. Equally, culture, be it nationalism or religion, is certainly deployed in war, and can provide justification for both great sacrifices and great cruelties. Culture also acts to legitimate demands for territory and to justify intransigence in negotiation. But, again, 'culture' cannot explain

---

[28] As the Arab saying goes, 'success has many fathers', *lil-nijah aba kathirun*, initially an ironic comment on the way different people all claim credit for the same thing, but then a general observation on the multiplicity of causes of a particular event, and, by further extension, a rebuttal of attempts to claim that a particular cultural phenomena – the *'oud* or lute, *humus* or *raksh baladi*, oriental dancing – had a particular country of origin.

the why and the how of specific wars. If religion can lead to great intolerance and violence, it can as easily justify fatalism, acceptance of the
given. Non-Muslim communities lived for centuries under Ottoman rule
without complaining – though they all, especially the Serbs, now deny
it. Religion is also, for all its transnational appeals, organised within specific, delimited countries. As we have seen, the concept of *jihad* in Islamic
thought can mean military struggle, but it can also mean mobilisation for
social ends, or individual effort and prayer. The Jewish, and Christian,
traditions contain sufficient elements that can be used for the bloodthirsty
and the militant, but plenty of others legitimating the opposite; as discussed in chapter 7, the choice of how to use text or tradition to justify
actions depends not on the holy text but on the wishes of the modern
interpreter.

We are left, therefore, with an explanation that goes beyond 'structural' and 'cultural', to one within historical sociology in terms of the
political and social character of the countries involved, the nature of their
Janus-like states, the priorities of their rulers, and the broader domestic context in which foreign, and military, policies are made. There is
much to recommend the argument that dictatorial states, reliant on public support and benefiting from the states of emergency occasioned by
war, seek such confrontation with the outside world, not necessarily war,
but a convenient, prolonged, state of emergency. This may be true of
Iraq under Saddam and Syria under Assad, *père et fils*. The very social
and political privileges which the military and other security forces have
enjoyed in these countries point to the same conclusion. Their populations are to a considerable degree fed on nationalist accounts of enemy
plots and threats: anecdotal evidence suggests that, however much people
distrust their rulers, they keep a good bit of suspicion in reserve for for-
eigners as well. To this analysis of the political character of the states
must be added the broader historical context, not so much of great
power rivalries, but of the tensions associated with modernisation, which
have been evident in other areas ravaged by war in modern times. The
wars of twentieth-century Europe were not a result of violence *endemic*
to modernity, or capitalism, but due to a particular, historically limited
phase of Europe's development. It is as much because the Middle East
shares so many common features with other areas of the world, and has
been so influenced by them, as because of some supposed differences
of ideology, state or culture, that war has been and may for quite some
time remain so central to the international relations and politics of the
region.

Here, to emphasise again, analysis needs to return to the core category of Middle Eastern, and all other, politics: the state. This emphasis

on the state is, however, not merely a matter of internal dynamics, of the interaction of state and society; the two-dimensional character of the state is particularly relevant here, in terms of the way in which it is state–society tension on the one side, and state–state rivalry on the other which, together, determine this outcome. Middle Eastern wars have been initiated as a result of *political* pressures, of discontent and nationalism from within, *combined with opportunities for enhancement of state power without.* In launching their respective wars, the Israeli leadership in 1967, Sadat in 1973, Turkish premier Ecevit in 1974, Saddam in 1980 and 1990, all knew that very well. The insecurity has not, therefore, been one born of strictly military or state interest alone: it has been because of the combination of domestic impulsion *and* regional opportunity, the latter enhanced, but not defined, by strategic context. The revolts of modern history, the actions of Palestinian and Kurdish guerrillas, not to mention the transnational *jihad* of al-Qa'ida, reflect calculations of state–society relations. This is, equally, why the Arabs attacked Israel in 1948, Israel attacked the Arabs in 1956 and 1967, Egypt attacked Israel in 1973, Iraq attacked Lebanon in 1982, and Iraq invaded Kuwait in 1990. In the Middle East, at least, this unstable sociology of the state, internally and externally, may not have exhausted its deleterious potential.

7 Modern ideologies: political and religious

'How much does the future now being constructed correspond to the popular hopes of the past?' (John Berger, 1979) Any serious discussion of 'alternative development' – i.e. one that seeks to go beyond technocratic social engineering – must attempt a meaningful answer to this question. It is necessary, however, to qualify that the 'hopes' are not really of the 'past'. Their expression is frequently, and inextricably, laden with the values, yearnings, and images of the past; but they are intrinsically existential hopes, induced and augmented by the contemporary crisis. For example, the often publicized ideological traditionalism of Third World people (the media spoke as much about 'resurgent' Buddhism in the early 1960s as it does of Islam in the late 1970s) is a product of excessive, uneven 'modernization'. In the so-called 'transitional' societies, one judges the present *morally* with reference to the past, to inherited values; but *materially* in relation to the future. Therein lies a new dualism in our social and political life; the inability or unwillingness to deal with it entails disillusionment, terrible costs, and possible tragedy. One mourns Cambodia, fears for Iran.

Eqbal Ahmad, Lecture, 'From Potato Sack to Potato Mash: an Essay on the Contemporary Crisis of the Third World', Transnational Institute, Amsterdam, April 1980.

'Agents' and 'plots': values, explicit and implicit

No preconception about the Middle East is more prevalent, in east and west alike, than the idea that the politics of the region need to be seen in terms of enduring and all-explaining 'cultural' values. Culture, normally a vague term at the best of times, is now used to cover various phenomena in political culture, for example, attitudes to power and wealth as well as trust, all this subsumed under 'Islam'. All analysis of politics, and power, does and should involve attention to the question of values and perceptions. But any attempt to analyse the region in terms of political or sociological categories runs up against this phenomenon not of a measured use of culture, but as a total explanatory framework. Moreover such supposedly all-embracing concepts are espoused as much in the region as by outside observers.

'Islam', Arab identity or ancient rivalries between peoples are prime candidates for this explanatory role.[1] The ominous phrase 'You must understand the X's mentality' stalks any student of the region – usually followed by the words 'The only thing they/we understand is force', or something to that effect. In much Middle Eastern rhetoric it is also claimed that the 'west', treated as a unitary category, is endemically hostile to peoples in the region – Arabs, Muslims, Jews, Turks. All that has happened since 1945, or 1918, or indeed 1492, 1683 or 1798, is part of a single 'western' plan. Al-Qa'ida dates its current *jihadi* war to some unspecified event eighty years ago, presumably around the time of the end of World War I, possibly the Balfour Declaration of 1917 or the abolition of the Caliphate in 1924. It is certainly not possible to go far in the study of the international relations of the Middle East without coming across a variety of such apparently cogent explanations in terms of political values and symbols. 'Religion', often a term requiring some specification, is one such analytic recourse, but these essentialising discourses, above all else about 'Islam', range from various conceptions of political leadership and legitimacy, through to national stereotypes. The fads of the 1990s, 'a clash of civilisations', and the epistemological jungle of the debate on 'Orientalism' were but the latest in a long line of such aberrant idealist and unanchored elucubrations.

Many of the most influential studies of Middle Eastern politics, and international relations, are rightly concerned with the role of culture and ideology in shaping the region. The classic debate on capitalism in Islam, be it in Max Weber, Karl Marx or Maxime Rodinson, addresses this question.[2] Some writings are properly histories of ideas, particularly of nationalism, or Islamic political theory.[3] More recently in IR 'constructivist' writers on the region have argued that it is through value systems that the policies of regional states can be understood.[4] But here, if anywhere, the

---

[1] The work of L. Carl Brown, *Middle East Politics: the Rules of the Game*, London: I. B. Tauris, 1985, falls into this category. V. S. Naipaul, *Among the Believers*, New York: Knopf, 1981, and Samuel Huntington, *The Clash of Civilizations and the Remaking of World Order*, New York: Simon and Schuster, 1996 are two widely diffused variants of this argument.

[2] Bryan Turner, *Marx and the End of Orientalism*, London: Allen and Unwin, 1978.

[3] Examples of this would include the classic statement of Arab nationalism, George Antonius, *The Arab Awakening: the Story of the Arab National Movement*, 1938, and subsequent editions, and later, less favourable accounts, such as Fouad Ajami's *The Arab Predicament: Arab Political Thought and Practice since 1967*, Cambridge: Cambridge University Press, 1981, and *The Dream Palace of the Arabs: a Generation's Odyssey*, New York: Pantheon, 1998. Significantly, there has not, as yet, been a serious general study of Iranian nationalism, as idea or movement. For one reading see Firoozeh Kashani-Sabet, *Frontier Fictions: Shaping the Iranian Nation 1804–1946*, Princeton: Princeton University Press, 1999.

[4] See chapter 1, pp. 30–45; Richard Cottam, *Nationalism in Iran*, Pittsburgh: University of Pittsburgh Press, 1964.

debate becomes obscured: there is a contrast between cultural essentialism, or unitary culture as core, and sociological focus on the interrelation
of culture with state, class and international context. As against such
simplifications, there is a need for a critical, historical and sociological,
analysis of how ideas are shaped and how they have an impact, one that
goes beyond the acceptance of religious or cultural conventions as independent forces operating across history. Faced with such claims, no one
should forget the words of the great historical sociologist Barrington
Moore, writing in 1966:

Culture or tradition is not something that exists outside of or independently of
individual human beings living together in society. Cultural values do not descend
from heaven to influence the course of history. To explain behaviour in terms of
cultural values is to engage in circular reasoning. The assumption of inertia, that
cultural and social continuity do not require explanation, obliterates the fact that
both have to be recreated anew in each generation, often with great pain and
suffering. To maintain and transmit a value system, human beings are punched,
bullied, sent to jail, thrown into concentration camps, cajoled, bribed, made into
heroes, encouraged to read newspapers, stood up against a wall and shot, and
sometimes even taught sociology. To speak of cultural inertia is to overlook the
concrete interests and privileges that are served by indoctrination, education, and
the entire complicated process of transmitting culture from one generation to the
next.[5]

Taken together with the emphasis of other historical sociologists such
as Theda Skocpol, on the persistence of social conflict, and of state–
society tension, then 'culture' becomes not a given, a constant source,
but the object of change, struggle and multiple, instrumental definition.
The scope of historical sociology pertains as much to this question as it
does to the analysis of the state. It can, in effect, provide an antidote to
the claims of cultural 'substrata', 'faultlines', 'mindsets' and the like, that
became so prevalent in the late twentieth century. Indeed, to escape from
the simplifications of 'cultural' determinism, we need not ignore culture
in the name of supposedly more 'material' factors, like state and class,
but draw on an informed and creatively theorised analysis of culture, of
which latter scholarly category we already have a distinguished body in
regard to the Middle East (Abrahamian, Zubaida, Rodinson, etc.).

This topic matters even more than may appear since it is not just domestic politics or social relations that are framed as ideology by participants
and analysts. International relations, like all politics, is also most vividly
interpreted, as much as anything, through what people think and believe.
People, and leaders, interpret the world through sets of beliefs, hopes and

[5] Barrington Moore, *The Social Origins of Dictatorship and Democracy*, London: Allen Lane,
1967, p. 486.

antipathies, which order and give value to life: herein lies the international importance, and impact, of ideologies – sets of belief about how the past shapes the present, its triumphs and, never far away, its treacheries, how the world works, and, equally important, about *how it should* work. States cannot leave such interpretation to chance: this is why rulers, and those contesting them, seek to use ideologies and values about the international system to strengthen their positions and to discredit their opponents. Unconscious but faithful followers of Barrington Moore as they are, states formulate these value systems and take care to instil them in their populations to justify what they are doing. States are also eager, through their educational systems, to construct a legitimating history of the nation; in so doing they too often cast other peoples in a negative light. Thus Iraqi education long promoted stereotypes of Persians, while Iranian education under the Shah, like too much twentieth-century Iranian literature, disparaged the Arab world. Such values range from invocations of the virtuous people – Arabic *sha'ab*, Persian *mardom* and *khalq*, Turkish *hulk*, Hebrew *am* and *leum* – to words for homeland – Arab *watan*, Persian and Turkish *vatan* or 'homeland', *eretz israil*, 'the land of Israel'. They also include the myriad terms of delegitimising opponents at home and abroad of whom the speaker or movement disapproves.[6] No words have been more frequently used in the modern political discourses of the Middle East than 'agents' and 'plots', both serving to delegitimate the policies of others. The very words used to describe states and their corresponding territories, arbitrary as the latter are, now acquire emotionally charged, 'sacred', meaning.

In a narrow sense, ideology refers to sets of *explicit*, or systematic, beliefs about politics: typical examples would be political ideologies of the twentieth century – socialism, communism, fascism, populism – and also broader sets of political beliefs such as nationalism or religious fundamentalism. Of considerable importance to the Middle East, these ideologies may be those of groups resisting established states, and calling for alternative forms of government, or those of established states, seeking to reinforce their claim to legitimacy. Some ideologies, especially in the mid-twentieth century, have been secular, drawing on modern concepts of the state, people or community. For all their local variants, these nationalist and contemporary value systems have core, shared components: there is, there has to be, a modernist ideological module, just as there has to be a flag, a capital city, a football team, an airline. Others, especially from the 1970s, have been religious, using terms from the Islamic tradition, or those of various forms of Christianity or of Judaism, to answer these

[6] E.g. *'ajam* (for Persians), *shu'ubi* (a medieval term for treason to Islam, reheated by Saddam), *kuffar* (infidells), etc.

recurrent, modular questions.[7] In a country like Iraq, for example, distinct Islamic factions have, since 1958, formulated ideological programmes, each built around the ideas taken from the different forms of *secular* politics.[8]

Ideology in this sense is *not* something specific to the Middle East. Because these political ideas are modular, they address a number of questions to which individuals and collective groups anywhere in the modern world have to give at least some working answer: to which community one belongs, what its historical origins are, who is authorised to rule it, its territory, who is, and who is not, a member of this community, and, not least, who its enemies are. As much as having a national currency, an anthem or air traffic controls, all necessary for modern states but unknown to earlier ages, such ideas are modern inventions but functional necessities. History, identity, authority, community, fear and affection all combine to answer these questions; the content may be arbitrary, but the boxes have to be filled, answers there must be.[9]

However, as noted already, to recognise this cultural dimension of politics and international relations is not, necessarily, to argue that we should ascribe prime causative importance to these, at the expense of other factors such as the interests, of class, ethnicity, social elite, or, say, water carriers, sheepherders, sharecroppers, or of history or structures of political power; herein, as discussed in chapter 1, lies the limit on the ideological or, as it is more recently presented, 'constructivist' approach. It may be as much in the ways these beliefs are themselves shaped by those with power and money, or successfully formulated precisely because their proponents do not have these assets, that ideas matter. For example, state power gave particular resonance and a new form to the ideas of Khomeini on Islamic government hitherto regarded, including by many Iranians, as medieval speculations.[10] The influence of the Saudi interpretation of Sunni Hanbali Islam, within its myriad princely subsections, would have been much less if they had not had plentiful oil revenues to disperse.

---

[7] Dale Eickleman and James Piscatori, eds., *Muslim Politics*, Princeton: Princeton University Press, 1996; James Bill and Robert Springborg, *Politics in the Middle East*, fourth edition, New York: HarperCollins, 1994, chapter 2, 'States, Beliefs and Ideologies'; Fred Halliday and Hamza Alavi, eds., *State and Ideology in the Middle East and Pakistan*, London: Macmillan, 1988.

[8] Faleh Jabar, *The Shi'ite Movement in Iraq*, London: Saqi, 2003.

[9] All of this draws heavily on the two classics of the 'modernist' school of nationalism studies: Ernest Gellner, *Nations and Nationalism*, Oxford: Basil Blackwell, 1983, and Benedict Anderson, *Imagined Communities: Reflections on the Origin and Spread of Nationalism*, second edition, London: Verso, 1991.

[10] Sami Zubaida, *Islam, the People and the State*, London: Routledge, 1993, chapters 1 and 2; Fred Halliday, *Nation and Religion in the Middle East*, London: Saqi, 2000, chapter 7; Ervand Abrahamian, *Khomeinism*, London: I.B. Tauris, 1993, chapter 3.

Apparently constant values, implicit as well as explicit, are like the institutions of state themselves, not therefore timeless givens: they are the product of identifiable historical forces, and usually rather recent ones at that. Modern political context is, therefore, what gives ideas their meaning and force. Herein lies the fallacy of explanations in terms of ahistorical words like 'Islam', or the 'Arab mind', or in terms of some underlying civilisational clash or animosity. While all such ideologies, be they nationalism or forms of religious fundamentalism, *claim* to be returning to some earlier, and legitimating, past the reality is that these are modern creations, using, inventing or ransacking the past, for contemporary purposes.[11]

As with individuals, so with nations, real trauma experienced earlier in life can, if not dealt with, cause paranoia later. Four obvious examples of how modern history has shaped political culture in this way: the Iranian concern with alien 'conspiracies' in their modern history; the Arabs' concern with foreign attempts to partition or divide them; the Israeli concern about anti-Jewish prejudice, anti-Semitism and its murderous potential; the Turkish sense of Arab 'betrayal'. These are products not of a timeless and continuous culture but of the history through which these people have lived in modern times and, to some degree at least, in living memory, *and* of the deliberate, political reproduction of such ideas by political forces.

More specifically, ideologies have to be looked at not as emanations of some collective psyche in regard to what, as argued in chapters 1 and 2, has, in the Middle East and elsewhere, come to be the central organising element in modern politics, the state. Far from being anterior to, or independent of, the modern state, ideologies are in considerable degree creations of these new states. Arab nationalism was shaped by Egypt, Zionism by Israel, Iranian nationalism by Shah and Ayatollah alike. In sum, ideas are creatures of historical and sociological forces. If ahistorical 'history' as explanation is, therefore, one trap which ideology lays for the student of the Middle East, the second claim, of historical continuity and autonomy of cultures, masks contemporary differences of interest and interpretation, and the role of states in shaping their ideological values. For example, in the 1950s and 1960s most Arab states proclaimed their support for 'unity', yet each provided its own, individual statist interpretations of this. In the 1980s the same was true of states promoting 'Islam' – Saudi Arabia, Iran, Libya, Iraq all built mosques and *madrasas*, not to unify the *umma* but to recruit the faithful to their

[11] For the classic statement see Eric Hobsbawm and Terence Ranger, eds., *The Invention of Tradition*, Cambridge: Cambridge University Press, 1984.

own particular, and factional, state interests. Equally, there is the trap of essentialism, the assumption that there is one *true* variant of the national or religious identity, which the speaker claims to represent and which others are in error by rejecting; this is exactly what authorities, including states, want to assert. Hence the discussion of who is *really* a true 'Arab', or 'Jew', or 'Muslim', as if any such identities allow of precise definition, something any knowledge of *fiqh*, text, history or DNA would refute. The definition of 'one' Islam, of a 'True Path' beyond a few bare articles of common faith, is equally spurious. National and religious values are, on closer inspection, immensely flexible and allow of different interpretations. Here *one* transhistorical claim is valid. The search for the one 'true' variant, of religion, nationalism or whatever, is a universally recurrent form of claiming power, if not on political then on gender or racial lines, but is just as universally misleading.

These general reflections on the historical sociology of 'culture' broadly understood may, therefore, serve to introduce a more detailed examination of the three major variants of political ideology in the modern Middle East – secular nationalism, religious fundamentalism, and everyday political culture itself. If the study of ideologies is essential in any discussion of international relations, it needs, therefore, to be *sociological*, in the sense of looking at the relation of ideas to political and social interest. It needs to be *historical*, in seeing how, whatever their claims to being frozen by history, contemporary values are shaped by contemporary context. It needs also to be *contingent*, in the sense both that the particular set of cultures and states we have today is only one, accidental, outcome of past possibilities, and that it is aware of the many varieties of interpretation of national or religious resources that are possible for states and other political actors. We have twenty-five or so states in the Middle East today, yet the briefest look through the histories and sacred texts of the region suggests there were hundreds of other possibilities for modern statehood. The queue of disappointed nations is a long one: Samaritans and Nabaeans, Jephusites and Hadhramis, Sumerians, Sabaeans and Sassanians, and many, many more.

Nationalisms

The modular, *menu fixe*, claims of nationalism are straightforward: that *all* people belong to a distinct community, that this community has a right to self-determination and that a distinct, determinable, territory belongs to each such nation. Distinct peoples and cultures have existed for centuries but *nations* as political entities are products of modernity, that is, to put a date on it, since 1780. The claim of nationalists, in the terms of their respective ideologies, is, however, that nations, at least their own nations, existed long before that, since the 'dawn' of time or thereabouts. Indeed, national legitimacy is guaranteed and their identity defined by this very historical antiquity. Claims of others are rejected on the grounds that these nations are 'artificial'. This claim rests, however, not only on the projection of the present back into the past, but also on a confusion, replicated the world over, between *states* and *nations*: the institutional concept of the state permits analysis that distinguishes between the history of states, which may, as in the case of Egypt, Yemen or Iran, indeed have long histories on one side, and the creation of modern political communities, 'nations', on the other.

It is the impact of modernity that once again explains the story. Nationalism as an ideology developed in Europe in the early nineteenth century but, although an alien import, it has, in modern times, become the dominant political ideology in the Middle East and has served to express the feelings of peoples, and the wishes of states. All the countries of the Arab world have experienced the force of nationalism. All the independent Arab states that have ruled have espoused broad nationalist goals, combined to varying degrees with religious themes and, except for Saudi Arabia, convenient bits of the pre-Islamic heritage. Egypt invokes the Pharoahs, Iraq Mesopotamia, but also Bahrain cites Dilmun, Yemen Saba/Sheba, and Tunisia Hannibal and his father, Amilcar, Phoenician warriors. There is one exception: Saudi pre-Islamic antiquities are housed in unpublicised, state and private collections, relics of a time of *jahiliya* or 'ignorance' which more austere Wahhabi Islam seeks to deny. This dominance of nationalism is also as evident in Turkey and Iran, as it has been in Israel, this last including claims, vigorously asserted, as to the ancient Hebrew origins of various foods and herbs. It is equally true of peoples who have not achieved, or who claim to have lost an earlier, statehood, the Kurds and Palestinians, and, until 1991, the Armenians.

The consequences of these nationalisms, as movements and ideologies, for relations between states have been multiple. First of all, nationalism, like the state, is two-sided – while it is directed *inwards*, at the construction of a community and the legitimation of authority, it is also directed *outwards*, towards co-operation with allies, and against enemies, far and near, real, exaggerated and imagined. Twentieth-century nationalism in the Middle East was concerned, first and foremost, with foreign, western, domination, sometimes in countries under formal colonial rule, such as the majority of Arab states between 1920 and, say, 1950. However, it has also been concerned with indirect, 'neo-colonial' or 'post-colonial', informal, but still supposedly effective, forms of external domination, as in Turkey, Iran and independent Arab states. In Arab rhetoric Israel is also cast in a similar way as but an 'agent', or tool, of western, specifically US, imperialism. In addition to the denunciation of direct rule there has, therefore, been a continuing nationalist critique of what are taken, by nationalists of different kinds, to be the longer-term consequences of foreign domination, and the creation of 'dependent' if formerly autonomous economies, ruled by client elites. In much of the Middle East, the spread of 'globalisation' in the 1990s and beyond prompted a new version of such nationalist themes, with globalisation seen as a continuation of earlier western domination. From the Crusaders to the World Bank and the WTO, it is, it would appear, but one uninterrupted line.

Variations on these general nationalist themes have been shaped by specific state contexts. In the case of the Arab world there have been three major themes in nationalist critique: the partition, *taqsim*, of the Arab world by colonialism, after World War I, the establishment and maintenance of client regimes, therefore, and the creation and continued support of Israel by the west. For the Turks, suspicion of the 'Sèvres Syndrome' of 1920, the western design to partition and subjugate Turkey, has also been recurrent. In Israeli nationalism major themes have included gentile, especially European, hostility to Jews, seen as itself perennial and, even if quiescent, ready to flare up again, and western collusion with the Arabs, as, allegedly, by the British in 1948.

Since 1918, in the Iranian case, earlier, and very real, cases of external manipulation and conspiracy have fostered a nationalism within which alien 'hands', *dastha*, not least those of the British, are often seen as present.[12] Perhaps the most common term used to discredit anyone seen as hostile to Iran has been *vabaste* ('linked'), to what is not always clear. It was said by his critics of Ayatollah Khomeini that, if you lifted his beard, it read, 'Made in England' underneath. The nationalisms of Middle Eastern peoples are, however, directed not just at those outside the region, but often at those within: for example, in the Iran–Iraq war of 1980–8 both sides mobilised nationalist and religious rhetoric against the other. The Iranians talked of the example of Karbala (680), where the Sunnis under Caliph Yezid had defeated the Shi'ites and killed their leader Hussain, grandson of the Prophet, while the Iraqis invoked the Battle of Qadisiya (639) when the Arabs captured a strategic Iranian fortress and marched

[12] On my first ever night in Iran, in August 1965, travelling by bus from Turkey, we stopped at the village of Khoi; the owner of the *mehmankhane* or inn, when he heard I was from England, treated me to a long lecture on the role of British-manipulated freemasons in modern history. As I was, nearly forty years later, writing this book, various friends assured me that the new UK ambassador was socialising with bazaar merchants in Tajrish, as a century before.

on into Iran.[13] This use of historic symbols is made easier by the ways in which other peoples, be they other states or minorities within states, are so often cast as the 'agents' of foreign powers: the Kurds have repeatedly been denounced in such terms, and the Jewish communities in Iraq, and some other Arab states even more so.

Yet while this predominance of nationalism has been self-evident, the challenge of analysing and explaining this protean force is far less easy. The study of nationalism is indeed, the world over, one of the most complex and contentious in modern social analysis.[14] The problem starts with the fact that we have to distinguish between what nationalists proclaim and what the reality may be, and, equally, distinguish between meanings of the terms 'nationalism' and 'nation' themselves. This complexity is by no means peculiar to the Middle East, but it has nonetheless, in practice and analysis, taken some particularly difficult turns in regard to this region. This is especially because, as already noted, the term 'nationalism' covers the two distinct, if related, phenomena – nationalist *movements* and nationalist *ideology*.[15] Usually these core, modular claims are embellished with claims, of more or less explicitness, about how this nation or that is superior to others, or entitled to more territory than it currently occupies, or has suffered from conspiracy and oppression more than others. The claims of nationalism do not stop with conquest and history but extend into food, where particular dishes are claimed as part of this particular nation's heritage, or should be cooked in a particular manner.[16] Arguments about who invented *humus* or a particular kind of kebab may last forever. Here at least conflict resolution is, for those who wish to accept it, at hand, in the Arabic saying 'success has many fathers'.

Middle Eastern variations

The rise of nationalism, in movement and ideological form, is, as we have seen, a result of political upheavals following from the revolutions of the late eighteenth century, in the Americas and in Europe, east and west. A foreign idea undoubtedly, this value-system had no difficulty at all in

---

[13] For comparison of the Iranian revolution with other revolutions in this regard see Fred Halliday, *Revolution and World Politics: the Rise and Fall of the Sixth Great Power*, London: Macmillan, 1999.

[14] For an excellent overview of the debates on nationalism see Umut Özkirimli, *Theories of Nationalism*, London: Macmillan, 2000.

[15] Anthony Smith, *Theories of Nationalism*, second edition, London: Duckworth, 1983; p. 21 gives the core definition, in seven themes.

[16] Sami Zubaida and Richard Tapper, eds., *A Taste of Thyme: Culinary Cultures of the Middle East*, London: I. B. Tauris, 1994; second edition 2000.

finding support in the Middle East – not much evidence for incompatible value-systems here. The ideas of nationalism found an early echo amongst some intellectuals and reformers in the Middle East, but it was only in the late nineteenth century that the nationalist movements that were to shape the modern state system emerged.[17] The impulsion was both ideological, in terms of the influence of movements developing in Europe, and strategic: faced with the encroachments of more powerful European states, officials of the Middle Eastern states began, as did their counterparts in China and Russia, to call for a modernisation of their countries along European lines. In Iran and in Turkey, writers began to express the need for a reform of the state, education and economy, while within the Arab states dominated by the Ottomans, the British and the French, resistance to external control began to take a more nationalist form: reformers such as Malkum Khan (d. 1908) in Persia, Ziya Gökalp (1876–1929) in the Ottoman empire, writers associated with the renaissance or *nahda* of Arab nationalism in Syria, military and political militants in Egypt, all contributed to this early development, a product of inter-state competition rather than any change of heart at the centre.[18]

Outside the Middle East, but with momentous long-term implications for it, Jewish intellectuals in Europe formulated the idea of the creation of a Jewish state, for which they took the term Zion, in the Middle East; Theodor Herzl published his *Der Judenstaat* in 1896, not, as it is often mistranslated, *The Jewish State*, but a stronger claim, *The State of the Jews*. The Zionist movement was formally inaugurated at Basle in 1897. Zion, literally one of the hills on which King David built Jerusalem, long a spiritual concept, was in accordance with the very normal procedures of nationalist ideology, here transformed into a modern territorial entity. Herzl's claim was not that the Jews were different; rather it was precisely a modular nationalist one, partly a response to European anti-Semitism, but also a claim that *the Jewish people were a people like any other*. Hence they were entitled, on universal principles, to a territory and a sovereign, national state – all this without at this stage the paraphernalia of God's will. In all these cases, a modernist analysis shows how nationalist myth and political reality diverge: nationalists, exponents to the last ideologue of the 'sleeping beauty' theory of nations, would in each case term such a process

[17] Bernard Lewis, *The Emergence of Modern Turkey*, Oxford: Oxford University Press, 1961; Albert Hourani, *A History of the Arab Peoples*, London: Faber and Faber, 1991, chapter 30; Reinhard Schulze, *A Modern History of the Islamic World*, London: I. B. Tauris, 2000, chapter 1; Adeed Dawisha, *Arab Nationalism in the Twentieth Century: from Triumph to Despair*, Princeton: Princeton University Press, 2002, chapter 2.
[18] For the classic discussion of Arab ideas in this period see Albert Hourani, *Arabic Thought in the Liberal Age 1798–1939*, Oxford: Oxford University Press, 1967.

an 'awakening'. That is, of course, to presume that the nation already existed, rather than it being itself the creation of ideology, movement and modernity.

If 1789 introduced nationalist *ideology* for the region, World War I ushered in the epoch of nationalist *movements* in the Middle East. The Arab world was rid of Ottoman rule only to fall under that of the British and the French. The only two independent Arab states in the inter-war period were two very conservative if new monarchies, the Imamate of Yemen (1918) and the Kingdom of Najd and Hijaz (1926), later Saudi Arabia (1932). In the new Mandates, and in the already colonised Egypt and in North Africa, there was widespread opposition to colonial rule, and to the partition of the Arab world, of what was, in nationalist aspiration, a single Arab nation or *umma*, the later term interchangeably secular (Arab) and religious (Muslim). In the initial period after 1918, up to the 1940s, some of this Arab nationalism was of a broadly liberal kind, espousing independent states, with secular law and parliamentary government; but there were always challenges, from Islamist and communist groups who had their own definitions of history and national identity. In the aftermath of World War II the tone of Arab nationalism became more militant: leadership was taken by various forms of authoritarian socialist nationalism, be it that of Nasser in Egypt, from 1952 to 1970, or of the more bloodthirsty Arab Ba'th Socialist Party, which ruled Syria from 1963 and Iraq from 1968.

Nasser propounded an Arab socialism and Arab unity. His ruling parties – three in all from 1954 to 1961 – were never very organised affairs, the core 'vanguard' remaining the *military* elite. The Ba'th espoused a harsher variant of the same: their slogan was *wahda, hurria, ishtirakia* – 'Unity, Freedom, Socialism'. They took eclectically from fascist and communist forms of organisation, but their concept of freedom, the second of their three core principles, was not that of political liberty *within the nation*, but of the freedom of the state from *external domination*. The waning of the Arab socialist tide in the 1970s and 1980s allowed the more specific *qutri* (local) nationalisms to advance and gave to nationalism in many countries a more conservative, and Islamic, form, with modernity replaced as the goal by *turath*, a term that, as elsewhere in the world, was held to denote another essentialist and ahistorical given, 'heritage'. The apparent failure of the socialist projects to resolve the problems of the countries they ruled in the 1960s and 1970s, and their inability to confront either Israel or the west, opened the field to the new nationalism framed in terms of religion, heritage and identity.[19]

---

[19] See Ajami, *Dream Palace*.

Elsewhere in the region, and in variant forms, nationalism as ideology if not as political movement also reigned supreme. In Iran earlier upheavals of 1891 and the Constitutional Revolution of 1905–8 were strongly nationalist. Indeed Iran saw the first nationalist popular mobilisations in the region if not in all of Asia. From 1925, the Pahlavi monarchy espoused a form of conservative, but secular, modernisation, based on the idea of Iran as a historic nation, an Aryan people distinct from the Arabs, herein lying the switch from the name Persia, associated with weakness, to Iran. The Shah's title was indeed 'The Light of the Aryans' (*Aryamehr*). In Turkey, Kemalism became the official ideology of the new political entity that emerged from World War I, *Türkiye*, a term not much used before 1914: *melliyet* or 'nationalism' was one of the six core tenets of Kemalism. The slogan on the Anitkabir, Atatürk's tomb overlooking Ankara, is *hakimiyet milletinder*, 'Sovereignty to the People', a new statement of legitimacy. In Palestine the Zionist movement organised, and fought, for the establishment of a state, a goal achieved in 1948, even if this was not, as Herzl had hoped, the *state of the Jews* but something less, a *Jewish state*, incorporating less than half of the world's Jews, the majority of whom chose to remain in the gentile world.

This prevalence of nationalism as a principle of identity and statehood was not only a cause of inter-state conflict but was also often disputed within each state in terms of definition and precise goals. For example, in Syria during the 1930s the radical Syrian nationalism of the Parti Populaire Syrien explicitly rejected *Arab* nationalism as it also called for the separation of state and religion. In addition the PPS exhibited a particular anti-Persian strand, from which Iraq after 1941, through its educational system and its use of Syrian teachers, later borrowed. This anti-Persian strand was in part an effect of the need to define a new identity: Syria presented itself as the inheritor of the first Arab empire based in Damascus, the Ummayads, which had been replaced by the more Persian-influenced Abbasid empire in AD 750. In Egypt there was in the 1920s and 1930s a widespread tension between the claims of an *Egyptian* nationalism and a pan-Arab variant.[20] In Iran, especially after World War II, a militant secular nationalism from below, organised by the National Front and the pro-Soviet Tudeh (Masses) Party, challenged both the Pahlavi state and Islamic sentiment.[21] In Yemen a liberal Islamic strand, *al-yamamiin al-ahrar*, the 'Free Yemens' group, critiqued the 'clerical' *kahnouti* regime

[20] James Jankowski and Israel Gershoni, eds., *Rethinking Nationalism in the Arab Middle East*, New York: Columbia University Press, 1997.
[21] Ervand Abrahamian, *Iran Between Two Revolutions*, Princeton: Princeton University Press, 1982.

of the Imams, called for Yemeni unity and in 1948 attempted an uprising known later, in modular modern national-democratic language, as
al-thawra al-dastouria, the 'Constitutional Revolution'.[22]

However, these variations in nationalist theme did not prevent the general repetition of those modular claims common to all such ideologies and
movements. All these nationalisms had a clear idea of the *people* to whom
they were supposed to refer and represent. All staked claims to *territory*.
All invoked a continuous *history*, going as far back in time as possible, to
legitimate what they did: some Arab states went back to early Islam and
before, the Zionists to ancient Davidic Israel (even though this state lasted
only eighty years), the Iranians to pre-Islamic empires, the Turks to the
Hittites. In the most visible conflict, but not the most costly in terms of
human life, Arabs and Jews argued that in some way or another they could
claim not only historical, but divine authority, for their identity and aspirations, and claims to land.[23] As in Ireland and the Balkans, all engaged
in derogation of others with whom they were in conflict, even as everyone upheld the universal principle of self-determination *for themselves*. In
these respects Middle Eastern nationalisms of the twentieth century were
as modular as other aspects of modernity, be they the components of their
national airlines, or the format of their television news programmes. As
elsewhere, for example, in the Balkans and Transcaucasia, grandiosity
of claim for one's own nation was counter-balanced by meanness and
prejudice towards others: the opt-out formula was itself modular – the
principle of self-determination holds, it is just that *they* are not a nation,
being just 'settlers', 'agents', fascists or something of a lesser-than-nation
breed; or, if they *are* a nation, the land they are living on, or claiming, was
not given to them by 'history', 'God' or whatever passed for authority in
those parts.

In all countries, European, American north and south, and in the
Middle East, the state is legitimated as being the resultant, the representative and expression of an already existing nation or people. Yet the
history of modern nationalism in the Middle East is as much as anything,
not that of peoples seeking to mould states to conform to the nation,
but of states creating, shaping, inventing nations through intervention in
society and polity alike, not to mention using their economic powers to
forge communities defined by, and dependent on, the state. It is states
which not only reproduce the idea and identity of the nation, through

---

[22] J. Leigh Douglas, *The Free Yemeni Movement 1935–1962*, Beirut: American University of
Beirut, 1987.
[23] The Bible asserts Jewish claims to the land of Palestine. The Covenant of Hamas, the
Islamic group, says Palestine is an Islamic trust (*waqf*).

---

education, official culture, military service, law, a good dose of coercion and much else besides, but which also in large measure *define* it – that is, define identity, territory and citizenship. States therefore write the history textbooks, establish the national symbols, define the proper way of writing the language, sometimes of dressing through a virtually compulsory dress code introduced in the 1990s (for example, in the Arab Gulf where citizens, men and women, are enjoined to wear local garb). These textbooks make the history and fight the battles that make up the national history itself, as well as keep quiet about those chapters of the past, often quite long ones, about which modernity prefers to not to speak.[24]

Here we come to another significant, and shared, feature of these nationalisms that is of particular concern for international relations, namely territorial expansion. In regard to territorial claim, nationalism almost always appears to be maximalist: it has, as movement and ideology, a tendency to make as wide demands for territory as possible. Since 1918 Arab states have intermittently claimed parts of Turkey (Syria), Iran (Iraq), Ethiopia (Sudan). After 1967 right-wing Israeli nationalists became increasingly keen to include in their national or 'ancestral' territory the West Bank, what they termed Judaea and Samaria, and the Golan Heights, which were not originally part of *eretz*, the 'Land of Israel'. There are also inter-Arab territorial claims: the Syrians have claimed Lebanon, Egyptians the Sudan, Iraqis Kuwait. Some Yemenis (actually almost anyone you talk to in Yemen) have argued that their legitimate 'historic' territory, *al-yaman al-tabii*, 'Natural Yemen', goes as far north as Mecca or Ta'if and, citing the medieval geographer al-Hamdani, as far east as Muscat; indeed the Prophet is said to have stood on a hill outside Mecca with his back to the West – all to his left was *sham*, in a loose sense 'Syria', and to his right was, in Arabic, *yamin*, or *yemen*.

Turkey might appear to be an exception to the nationalist territorial delusion. Atatürk's great achievement after 1923 was to reject empire and pan-Turkic aspiration alike, even at the price of severing a link to the past. Turkey also said little of the killing and forced deportation of millions of 'Turks' from Transcaucasus and the Balkans in the first two decades of the twentieth century. But from the 1970s Turkish nationalism, partly impelled from below, reanimated, in qualified form, expansionist themes, towards northern Iraq, ceded in 1926, and northern Cyprus, occupied and in effect annexed in 1974. There has also since the 1970s been a

---

[24] In Egypt and Bahrain, for example, much is made of the ancient pre-Islamic period, and of the Islamic, but much less of the Christian centuries in between. The Yemenis are, in this respect, exceptional, recording without apparent reserve not only their Christian (Abyssian) but also their Jewish rulers (notably Dhu Nawas, AD 517–25). Few, if any, states draw attention to episodes of *radical* Islamic movements like the Qarmathians.

neo-Ottoman sentiment in Turkey that is often cultural but can take geopolitical form. Although they do not have a state of their own, the Kurds have also made wide demands, claiming large parts of Turkey, Iraq and Iran. For their part, Armenians claim parts of Turkey, on the grounds that they have lost twenty-eight of their historic provinces, the current Republic of Armenia ('Eastern Armenia') with its capital at Erevan being but the twenty-ninth. The one country which, despite some excellent historical pretexts, for example, Russian annexations in the early nineteenth century, has not raised this is Iran.

These apparently extensive territorial claims masked, however, something else which they also held in common, namely exclusion of the 'non-national' or alien: these nationalisms were designed to consolidate an identity uniting all within the confines of the new state, and so exclude other ideological, and by implication territorial, options. Linguistic 'purification' was very much part, again a modular one, of this process. As in Europe, where German nationalists in the nineteenth and twentieth centuries tried to replace French words by 'genuine' German ones, so in the Middle East linguistic nationalists sought to rid, respectively, Persian of Arabic words, Turkish of Arabic and Persian words, and Arabic of Ottoman, that is, Persian and Turkish, influences. Atatürk went furthest and promoted a wide-ranging lexical revolution to go 'back' to Öztürkçe, or 'pure Turkish', and, when this was not possible, claimed the 'foreign' words were really Turkish in origin anyway.[25] In yet another bizarre case of the oppressed imitating the oppressor, Kurdish officials in northern Iraq began, in the 1990s, to purge Kurdish of unwanted 'alien', that is, Turkish and Arabic words, with the result that for many Kurdish listeners Radio Suleimaniye became unintelligible. Hebrew, for its part, claimed to be *ivrit tanakhit*, or biblical Hebrew, but it too was in realistic terms a new modern language: contemporary Hebrew is an idiom reformulated by modernisers, notably Eliezer Ben Yahuda (d.1922), and borrowing heavily from Aramaic and Arabic, but without the corruptions of Yiddish, a version of German using Hebrew script. The nationalist *claim* was that the historic and the traditional, the sleeping *ethnos*, shaped the present; but in language as elsewhere, the *reality* was, again, that states intervened to define what the tradition was, and exclude what they did not like.

This delimitation of what was 'genuine' and what 'alien' by nationalist ideology was also evident in regard to 'identity', that is, to which

---

[25] Geoffrey Lewis, *The Turkish Language Reform: a Catastrophic Success*, Oxford: Oxford University Press, 1999. The Turks scored a world first in proposing the 'Sun Life Theory' (*Güneç Dil Teorisi*), according to which all languages in the world were derived from Turkish. The fact that the Turkish for man is *adam* was often cited as evidence.

community people belonged, another protean but inescapably modernist requirement. The Kemalist Turkish definition of Turkey thereby
excluded at least three other identities that were possible, and espoused
by other factions within Turkey: pan-Islamism, that is, definition of the
Turks as part of a wider Islamic community; pan-Turkism, which could
have included other peoples speaking, or supposedly speaking, Turkic
languages in Transcaucasus and Central Asia, as well as peoples of Turkic
culture in the Balkans; and pan-Turanism, a territorial idea covering
much of northern Iran and Afghanistan, based on a mythical ancient
land of Turkish character, 'Turan'. Pan-Islamism had been promoted in
the late nineteenth century by the Ottoman state, but had yielded after the
Young Turk revolt of 1908 to a more secular, 'national' politics.[26]

In the Zionist case, the establishment of a Hebrew-speaking community in Palestine also involved a break with a wider diaspora, even as
the support of that broader community remained instrumental to Israel;
other forms of Jewish culture, notably those based on Yiddish and Ladino,
the languages of western Ashkenazi and eastern Sephardic Jews, and on
features of Jewish life in Europe and the Americas, especially those associated with *shtetl* and the ghetto, were necessarily rejected in favour of this
new formal identity. After 1948 the Israeli state promoted the slogan *ivrit,
daber ivrit*, 'Hebrew, Speak Hebrew'. Somewhere on the way to modular nationhood the Jewish sense of humour also seemed to have become
rather attenuated, this too a functional requirement of the national. This
Zionist redefinition was accompanied by renaming, so that those who
came to Israel as refugees exchanged diaspora identities for new Israeli
ones. This was an old practice, common among Jews, but not specific to
them. This transition involved, among other things, rejecting names associated with the diaspora and adopting more 'positive' Hebrew names.[27]

For the Arabs and Iranians too, whatever their broader aspirations of
influence, this modern national identity was based on secular and limited
concerns, of language and territory, not primarily on that of any broader
Islamic identity, except in so far as this enabled Arab nationalists, including many Christians, to argue that they had a special relation to Allah by
dint of his speaking in Arabic. Both these Middle Eastern peoples were
rather free with disparagement of each other, not to mention of Muslim
peoples elsewhere. Some sense of wider Islamic solidarity remained, particularly on the issue of Palestine, and the wider 'Islamic public', identified

---

[26] Lewis, *The Emergence of Modern Turkey*; and Jacob Landau, *The Politics of Pan-Islam*, Oxford: Clarendon, 1989.

[27] E.g. Ben Ami (son of the people), Amiad (my people forever), Eytan (firm), Tamir (towering), Barak (lightning) (from Amos Elon, *The Israelis*, Harmondsworth: Penguin, 1981).

by Reinhard Schulze, but at least until the rise of *jihadi* transnationalism
in the 1990s the claims of the *umma* were always weaker than those of
the new, delimited 'national' communities. In foreign policy there was no
room for confusion: state interest prevailed, even when espousal of the
wider Islamic *umma*, as with Saudi Arabia and revolutionary Iran, was
adopted as official policy.[28]

The dominance of state interest in domestic and international politics ensured therefore that political purpose rather than historical 'sub-
stratum' or cultural accuracy determined how these national ideologies
were formulated. Equally it was such considerations of state interest that
defined answers, then allowed for the resolution of ambiguities or uncertainties within the nationalism of each country. From the perspective of
inter-state relations, two of these ambiguities merit particular attention.
One area of uncertainty is that between multiple layers of possible national
identity. For an Arab there are at least three possible forms of identity –
'religious' or confessional (Muslim or Christian or, till the 1940s not
to be forgotten, Jewish); 'pan-Arab', defined in terms of the whole Arab
umma or nation; and local, defined in terms of particular states, for example, Egyptian, Palestinian, Lebanese, Kuwaiti or whatever. The tension
between these second and third options, often referred to as *qaumi* and
qutri, that is, 'national' or pan-Arab and 'local', is present in all Arab
countries and within their respective ideologies of nationalism. It is not,
however, a tension peculiar to the Arab world (one need only think of
the tension between being 'English' and being 'British', or a hyphenated
American-US citizen). Nor indeed is such plurality of identities necessarily a negative tension – it may, instead, provide a wider reserve of symbols
and legitimation for political leaders and states to draw on. Thus Arab
leaders and nationalist movements have quite easily espoused both forms
of nationalism and varied the relationship between them at different times.
When co-operation with other Arab states is the priority, or when a state
wishes to legitimate its intervention in the affairs of another state, the pan-
Arab or *qaumi* predominates. When a state wishes to downplay the shared
interests of the Arab world, or justify confrontation with another state,
the local or *qutri* comes to the fore. President Nasser of Egypt was not
more, or less, an Arab and Egyptian nationalist, when in the 1950s and
1960s he stressed the *qaumi* than was President Sadat when in the 1980s
he laid emphasis, in his appeals to the 'Sons of the Nile', *ibn al-nil*, on the
qutri. Abroad, at least, many Egyptians when asked if they were 'Arabs'

[28] For the 'statist' argument see James Piscatori, *Islam in a World of Nation-States*,
Cambridge: Cambridge University Press, 1986. On Iran in particular see the fascinating study by Wilfried Buchta, *Die Iranische Schia und die Islamische Einheit* 1979–1996,
Hamburg: Deutsches Orient-Institut, 1997; any student of the French, or Russian, revolution would easily follow the story.

would say, no, they were Egyptians. The Libyan leader Mu'ammar al-Qaddhaffi, who began life after his 1969 'revolution', in effect a military coup, as a young son to Nasser, had by the 1980s and 1990s lapsed into denunciation of other Arabs in general.

A second recurrent ambiguity already alluded to on several occasions in the state–ideology link is the relationship between the ideology of the modern nation and the pre-modern past. In one sense, there is never a problem since nationalism uses, or often ransacks, the past to legitimate the present; but the question is always *which* past. Here selection, when not invention, occurs: for Arab Muslim states, for example, the pre-Islamic past presents a problem, since in Islam all that is prior to Islam is from the period of 'ignorance' or *jahiliya*. This has not, however, prevented Arab states from using this pre-Islamic reserve to strengthen their specific, *qutri*, identity. Thus, as we have seen, Egyptians invoke the Pharaonic period, Iraqis the Sumerian and Mesopotamian, Yemenis the kingdoms of Saba and Himyar, Tunisians and Christian Lebanese the Phoenician and so forth.[29] Even some of the smaller Gulf states, happily contingent excisions of the Arabian Peninsula, boast some ancient stones, even as some also unearth, with some embarrassment, churches from before the time of Islam. In the Arab world of the 1980s and 1990s, where the search for an official 'heritage' became more widespread, every state produced a historical narrative, a narrative of the past, to give it legitimation. An example was Oman whose history leapt from Sultan Said the Great (d. 1856) to the advent of Sultan Qabus in 1970. In some cases this involved the contradictory use of historical legacy: thus in Lebanon, the Phoenician period was used by Christians to define their separation from Arab and Islamic identity, whereas in Libya it was deployed to reinforce claims of the historic character of a Libyan people, continuous from ancient African to modern Arab and Islamic times. In Malta, a Christian country with a derivative of Arabic as its language, the need to repress the centuries of Islamic rule lead it to block excavation of the rather visible archaeological sites in the centre of the mainland. Once again, in regard to 'identity' and history as well as actual people, nationalism *excludes* as well as *includes*.

Fundamentalisms: modernity and the state

In apparent contrast to nationalism, with its predominantly secular approach, religious fundamentalism espouses a politics that claims

[29] For general discussion see Jankowski and Gershoni, *Rethinking Nationalism*; for Iraq see Amatzia Baram, *Culture, History and Ideology in the Formation of Ba'thist Iraq, 1968–89*, London: Macmillan, 1991.

legitimation and derivation from the texts and concepts of religion. 'Fundamentalism' itself is a usable if inevitably loose term, as one among social categories, for example, state, nation, power, originating in regard to US Protestant groups who opposed the teaching of evolution in schools in the 1920s, and called for a return to the foundations of religion, the holy text and the literal reading thereof. Some authors object to the use of this term in regard to Islam given the several major differences between the two religions. But, for all the objections to a general usage by reasonable extension, it can be applied to other religions where similar political appeals are made – Judaism, Christianity and, with some greater problems, Hinduism. In such ideologies authority is derived from divine legitimation, all problems are to be resolved by reference to the holy texts, and particular places, of pilgrimage and worship, are given special importance. In regard to politics, however, the term as used concerns not just such a religious appeal, the return to a pure definition of the religion, or a literal reading of the text (although you do not have to be a postmodernist to see that there is no such thing), but something further, a more immediate, *and political*, claim, that the teachings of these holy texts can be applied to contemporary society and contemporary political life, indeed that these texts contain the solution to the world's problems. Fundamentalism, here, is about law, education, social conduct, including dress, the position of women, and, most important of all, about the organisation and legitimation of the *state*. In its concern with personal matters, including dress, hygiene, food, it is more concerned with *orthopraxy*, 'right doing', than with *orthodoxy*, 'right teaching', the interpretation of texts and doctrine.[30]

As with nationalist ideology, there is a recurrent element of distortion, if not illusion, involved in the way fundamentalist movements present themselves. They *claim* to be returning to the past, and to one 'true', given, interpretation of identity and community. In reality they are *modern* movements that *select* and *reformulate* elements from the past to meet contemporary purposes. A good example of this is the Muslim claim that their societies should return to *shari'ah* law, this being seen as an existing body of holy law. This is a myth, at most a return to a revered tradition, when there is almost no legal content in the Quran, the source of sacred authority. Other examples can be taken from the symbolism of Israeli and Palestinian nationalism. Jewish tradition has two main symbols

---

[30] Zubaida, *Islam, the People and the State*; Gilles Kepel, *The Revenge of God: the Resurgence of Islam, Christianity and Judaism in the Modern World*, Cambridge: Polity Press, 1994; Fred Halliday, 'Fundamentalism and Political Power', in *Two Hours that Shook the World*, London: Saqi, 2001.

of religious and ethnic continuity, the seven-branched *menora* or candelabra, and the six-pointed 'Star of David', known in Hebrew as *magen david*, 'the shield of David'. The *menora is* an ancient symbol: a second century AD synagogue excavated at Katzrin in the Golan Heights shows the candelabra clearly on the wall. On the other hand, the 'Star of David' is a modern invention: it has nothing to do with the historic King David, as star or shield; it is a symbol of the mystical unity of being, used until the late nineteenth century by Muslims, Christians and Jews and found to this day in many paintings and mosque decorations of the Persian artistic world. It was only claimed as Jewish by Herzl in 1896.[31] On the Palestinian side the symbol is the red headdress or *kaffiya*. This too is a modern invention, even as it draws on the already existing indigo-stained Palestinian head covering. After 1920 the British created the Arab Legion in Jordan and commissioned a new uniform, from textile manufacturers in Manchester, the Dweik; like dozens of other textile merchants in Lancashire at that time, they were Sephardic Jews from Aleppo. From Jordan this symbol has moved to Palestine.

Locating fundamentalist movements in their political, and contemporary, context and their ideologies and symbols as modern constructs therefore overturns both external and self-proclaimed images. The religious movements that have shaped Middle Eastern politics present themselves as given by the past. They are in fact part of, not an alternative to, the modern politics and international relations of the region. This is evident both in regard to the context in which they operate – decades of foreign domination, the growth of the modern state, the location of that state within the international context, and the influence of what has been termed the 'Islamic public' – and to their very vocabulary and political practice. They are political movements which seek to deploy religious claims to challenge those with power, or, when they have gained power, to use religion to justify their retention of it. Thus Muslim fundamentalists denounce rulers they oppose both in Islamic terms, as *dhalimin* (oppressors), or, for Shi'as, modern versions of the Sunni tyrants Mu'awiya and Yazid, but equally as 'agents', 'tools', 'clients', 'stooges' of foreign powers. Fundamentalisms have borrowed heavily from modern discourses, socialism and nationalism, and radical anti-'Islamic' imperialist movements for their language.[32]

Khomeini, for example, talked of revolution, an unheard of concept before then. He proclaimed 'revolution', *inqilab*, and built a republic,

---

[31] Joseph Gutman, 'Magen David', in *The Encyclopaedia of Religion*, London: Collier, 1987, vol. IX and Gerscholm Scholem, 'Magen David', in *Encyclopaedia Judaica*, 1938. New York: Macmillan; Jerusalem: Keter, 1971.
[32] Abramahian, *Khomeinism.*

jumhuri, modern political goals. His concepts of imperialism, *istikbar*, and of the oppressed, *mustazafin*, used Quranic terms but with modern connotations.[33] In August 1979 I witnessed a demonstration in which 100,000 people, men and women separated, marched past shouting 'Death to Liberalism', *marg bar liberalizm*, the latter a term taken straight from the Stalinist vocabulary of the Tudeh Party. Significantly, fundamentalisms, be they Muslim or Jewish, resort to terms signifying 'traitor', a term of nationalist disapprobation, when they wish to oppose the politics of their rulers. What is at stake are issues shared with nationalist and other opposition movements – power, relations with the outside world, interest and, never to be forgotten, the subjugation of women.[34] The same modular, modern logic applies when Islamic fundamentalists come to power, as they did in Iran (1979–), Sudan (1986–) and Afghanistan (1992–2001): now it became those who opposed them who were cast as enemies of the state and nation, agents of foreign powers, as well as being corrupt, 'hypocrites' (*munafiqin*), a Quranic term for traitors to Islam.[35]

This flexibility of inherited discourse applies also to the many debates held *within* supposedly unitary or monolithic 'faiths'. In Israel, for example, those who argue, as do *Gush Emunim* (Block of the faithful), that a Jewish state *cannot* give away Jewish land are countered by those who argue the opposite, citing the case of King Solomon who, in reciprocating the supply of cedar wood by King Hiram of Tyre to build the First Temple, gave him twenty villages in Galilee.[36] In the Arab world in the 1960s and 1970s there was a lively debate on which economic system, or, in Marxist terms, 'mode of production', was enjoined by Islam, socialism or capitalism. Suitable verses from the Quran and *hadith* of the Prophet were mustered by both sides, and even other contenders, feudalism and slavery, joined the fray. The same applies to the alternatives of nationalism or cosmopolitanism: religion is not 'for' or 'against' either, is not an endorsement or an obstacle, but can be interpreted to support either. On a more practical issue, the initial revolutionary ban in Iran on caviar after 1979 was soon lifted by the regime. These matter and others are resolved by history and interest, not text alone.

---

[33] Ibid.; Daniel Brumberg, *Reinventing Khomeini: the Struggle for Reform in Iran*, Chicago: University of Chicago Press, 2001.

[34] On the use by Islamism of the modern concept of the state see Aziz al-Azmeh, *Islam and Modernities*, London: Verso, 1994.

[35] For a chilling account of the use by the modern state of Islamic law and custom to terrorise its people, see Ervand Abrahamian, *Tortured Confessions: Prisons and Public Recantations in Modern Iran*, Berkeley: University of California Press, 1999.

[36] Tanakh Kings III 9:11; alternatively in the Bible at Kings I 9:11.

Fundamentalism and international relations

In the matter of international, and as we shall see 'transnational', relations the modernity of fundamentalism is equally evident. First of all,
these movements arise and develop in a context shared by other political
forces, that of the external political and economic domination, formal
or informal that goes back two centuries; in order to construct a history
and a politics of opposition to this international domination they, therefore, borrow extensively from secular ideologies. For Islamic movements
the reserves for such a legitimating history are plentiful: the Crusades,
the loss of 'Arab' Andalucia, the erosion of the Ottoman empire, the
machinations of the British and French in World War I, colonial rule,
Suez in 1956, support for Israel, and, most recently, all that is subsumed
under 'globalisation'. The rhetoric of Islamists, from the 1920s onwards,
easily fuses attacks on imperialism, colonialism, Zionism in creating its
international vision. The denunciations of the west by al-Qa'ida in the
conflict of 2001 drew on a range of such modular excoriatory themes.
For Jewish fundamentalism, the history of persecution of Jews, culminating in Nazism, but reflecting a belief in a deep enduring anti-Semitism,
represents a specific source for constructing an antagonistic international
perspective.

As we shall see in more detail in chapter 8, these movements also
operate in what is termed the 'transnational', the arena of relations
between societies and peoples. While in pre-modern times linkages
existed between Muslim communities and centres of learning, the development of modern society has produced a new context for such inter-
relationships. In his *A Modern History of the Islamic World* the historian
Reinhard Schulze has written of the 'Islamic public', which has grown
up over the past two centuries, accompanying the rise of nationalism
through communications, the media and movement of ideas and people.[37] These publics react to, and are inspired by, movements and events
in other countries: Palestine, Bosnia, Afghanistan, Kashmir, even the
Moro Islands of the Philippines or Sinjiang, serve as catalysts. The comparison is often made between Islamic transnationalism and that of communist internationalism. While this comparison is overstated in terms
of organisational links, or common politics, it is valid in terms of the
ways in which particular issues (the 'struggle' of Muslims in Palestine
against Israeli occupation, in Kashmir against Indian occupation) or particular terms, such as the invocation of *shari'ah* law, or the need to create a *dawla islamiya*, an Islamic state, are diffused from one country to

[37] Schulze, *A Modern History of the Islamic World*, pp. 46–8.

the other. Here again al-Qa'ida was an illustrative, but far from original, case. The growing campaign among some Sunni Muslims to restore *al-khilafah*, the Caliphate, is another example of this emulative transnationalism. Although even inter-Arab Islamic relations are quite compartmentalised, long before al-Qa'ida there has been interchange between Arab and South Asian Islamism, most evidently in the interaction of the Egyptian Muslim Brotherhood ideology (Sayyid Qutb) and the Pakistani Jamaat-i Islami.

Thirdly, this context produces a conceptual framework, an international perspective or vision, one of the struggling Muslim community, or *umma*, its unity sundered by its enemies, oppressed by infidels the *kuffar*, and generic enemies of Islam. The term *umma* is used sixty-two times in the Quran, where it can denote, among its twelve different meanings, a community of believers. In contemporary discourse, appeals to the *umma* about such modern themes as economic exploitation, political domination, the promotion of partition and secession apparently combine with the global 'conspiracy', in Arabic *dasisa* and *mu'amara*, to undermine Muslim society itself: here what are strictly international themes, concerning relations with other states, join with what are essentially nationalist claims about the subversion of domestic society by 'external' forces. For transnational Muslim activists, the *umma* is not, however, just the object of external pressure; it is also a unit of resistance and struggle itself, organised in solidarity with other oppressed Muslims and committed to fighting this external domination.[38]

Beyond such claims of a distinctive God-given or religious politics, domestic and international, there therefore emerges a picture of an ideology, and movement, that is in important respects akin to other, secular forms of modern politics. Study of the discourses, and practice, of fundamentalist movements reveals another modernist phenomenon, a set of tightly organised, political organisations devoted to mobilising support in pursuit of declared political goals. In each case, moreover, the starting point is not a pre-modern *umma* but the compartments of modernity, that of a particular society and states. The Muslim Brotherhood never replicated the global discipline of the Comintern (1919–43). Even al-Qa'ida, a body with definite transnational appeal and participation, was still based during the 1990s in specific countries where it enjoyed the protection of the state, notably the Islamic Emirate of Afghanistan. It

---

[38] Walid Abdelnasser, *The Islamic Movement in Egypt: Perceptions of International Relations, 1967–1981*, London: Kegan Paul International, 1994, Part IV, 'Elements for a Global View of International Relations'.

aspired and aspires to take power in specific Arab states, particularly Saudi Arabia.[39]

The most striking case of a successful Islamic revolution in the Middle East, that of Iran after 1979, illustrates this combination of symbolic invocation of the *umma* and modern state context, that is, of transnational appeal and national location. While Ayatollah Khomeini called for a return to a model of government proclaimed in the seventh century AD, he came to power through modern forms of political action, the mass demonstration and the political general strike. For all its retrospective ideology, in its *organisational form* the Iranian revolution was the most *modern* in world history, contrasting with forms of other revolutions – coups, peasant movements, guerrilla war and so forth. Khomeini's appeal was as much to Iranian nationalism, and the rejection by the mass of the population of both a century of foreign domination and of corrupt 'foreign-connected' government, as it was to a generic, ahistorical or transnational, Islamic model: the slogans of the revolution were *istiqlal, azadi, jumhuri-yi islami* – independence, freedom, Islamic republic; two and a half of these terms were secular in origin. Khomeini's denunciation of the Shah as a tool of foreign interests, and his attacks on *istikbar-i jahani*, (world arrogance), replicated broader third world attacks on western imperialism of the pre-colonial period. Equally a part of the modular modernity embraced by Islamists was his call for the promotion of revolution in other oppressed countries, especially Afghanistan, Iraq and Lebanon. This policy of exporting revolution was one shared with other modern revolutions; in this respect too the Islamic Republic *conformed* to the pattern of its predecessors.[40] But as with the USSR it made sure to control any radical clients for its own state purposes.

This intrusion by the secular into the apparently timeless world of text and *sunna* is also evident in the way interests of state, and other distinctions based on community and nation, shape the claims of identity based on religion. All states in the region profess, to a greater or lesser extent, support for the identity and heritage of their nations. This may appear simple enough, yet in international relations these states face a double, often contradictory, challenge, that of proclaiming solidarity with others, while at the same time promoting the interests and identity of their own particular peoples; Islamic states, of which there are over fifty, have to reconcile, but can also use, these divergent discourses. The most obvious example of this is that of Arab states which

---

[39] Gilles Kepel, *Jihad: the Trail of Political Islam*, London: I. B. Tauris, 2002, chapters 9 and 13.
[40] See note 13.

proclaimed support for Palestine, but did so in such a way as to promote their own state interests: when espoused, militant solidarity with Palestine also served to strengthen the legitimacy of states at home, and to project the influence of that state across the region. This was the case with Nasser's Egypt in the 1950s and 1960s, and Saddam Hussein's Iraq in the 1970s and 1980s, when Baghdad was announced to be the *qala'a* or citadel of the Arab revolution. Yet Iraq did not help the Palestinians when they clashed with King Hussein in Jordan in 1970, and in the late 1970s Saddam ordered the killing of PLO representatives in Europe who favoured negotiation with Israel. For its part Syria always said it was the 'beating heart of Arabism' (*qalb nabid al-'uruba*). In 1976 it invaded Lebanon to crush the PLO and shot and starved to death thousands of Palestinians at Tel al-Zaafar. At the same time as they announced solidarity, Arab states not surprisingly sought to shape, and limit, their support for the Palestinians in such a way that they protected the interests of their own states.

Iran, after 1979, proclaimed itself the bastion of a new pan-Islamic revolutionary movement, yet it was careful about which Islamic causes it espoused: it gave great rhetorical, and some material, support to Hizbullah in Lebanon and Islamic Jihad in Palestine, but was restrained in the extreme with regard to some other 'Islamic' causes where its state interests dictated alliance with the state against which the Muslim forces were fighting (Russia in the case of Chechnya, India in the case of Kashmir, China in the case of Xinjiang). For its part, especially when rivalling Nasserism in the 1960s, Saudi Arabia long proclaimed itself to be the protector of international Muslim interests and spent much money in pursuit of this goal, backing Islamist groups, the construction of mosques and sympathetic media. This too was directed by the interests of the Saudi state. When in 1965 it set up the World Islamic League (*al rabita al-alimiya al-islamiya*), a counter-revolutionary propaganda body in Mecca, it did so for state reasons as much as to resist the pressures of Arab nationalism coming from Egypt. Saudi Islamic solidarity served, therefore, as much as anything, to further state interests against those of rival claimants for Islamic and regional influence – secular rivals such as Egypt and Iraq, religious rivals such as Iran – and, never to be forgotten, to engage, or as it turned out, appease, Islamist critics at home.

Equal in importance to divisions of state were those of nation and country – not only the divisions within the Muslim world between Turks, Iranians, Arabs, Kurds and others, but also those between different Arab peoples themselves. It would be a mistake to assume that the path of inter-Arab brotherhood, *shiqaqa*, is always strewn with flowers and mutual trust. Since there is nothing inconsistent within nationalist ideology in proclaiming multiple identities, a sense of Arab solidarity can co-exist with a sense of distinct Egyptian, Iraqi, Palestinian, Yemeni or other Arab local identity. In line with the modular requirements of modernity, Arab nationalism claimed that a single Arab people already existed in the early twentieth century; also, and equally untrue, that there existed *one* Arabic language. In reality, the division of the Arab world into distinct state entities, ones largely formed by colonial rule, produced a set of peoples who, for all their common identity and sense of shared history, were also conscious of the differences, and sometimes rivalries, between them. Some of this sense of difference, for example, between Egyptians and Syrians, or Saudis and Yemenis, or Iraqis and Kuwaitis, drew on regional distinctions evident in earlier periods, and revived, or stimulated, by modern nationalism. If this was true for relations between Arab peoples, it was even more so for the inter-ethnic nationalist sentiments that divided Arabs from their own Muslim neighbours, Turks and Iranians; here any amount of historical legacy, the scattered debris of past conflicts and resentments, was available for modern nationalists to play upon. The speeches of nationalist politicians, school history textbooks and the press of each state made sure that the differences, with all their supposed historical weight, were reproduced, if not intensified, between the generations. The outside observer could also note something else: while the elites of these states did learn much about, and travel in, the west, they all showed scant interest in the countries nearer to home. Less open to documentation, but informed by an endless flow of anecdote, were popular attitudes to neighbouring minority communities, part of a political culture of unchecked historic resentment and ethnic stereotyping alike.

The Iran–Iraq war of 1980–8, the most bitter in the modern history of the Middle East, would appear to have given support to this view of atavistic determination. It was, as we have seen, the second, more brutal, chapter in a four-part Gulf conflict that had already seen a first war in 1969–75. Modern nationalism will have it that the Iranians and Iraqis are secular enemies, their conflict a result of superimposed layers of rivalry going back at least to the split between Sunni and Shi'ite Muslims in the seventh and eighth centuries AD, if not to the pre-Islamic rivalries of the Medes and the Persians.[41] Yet, much as they conflicted over centuries and speak different languages, Iraqis and Iranians share much in common and have co-existed at least as much as they have fought. The source

[41] For a fascinating study of how Iran framed its religious justification for the war against Iraq see Saskia Gieling, *Religion and War in Revolutionary Iran*, London: I. B. Tauris, 1999.

of their modern wars lies not in history, or disputed frontiers, or irreconcilable cultural differences. It lies in the way in which *modern* political regimes (Iran since 1921, Iraq since 1932) have sought through indoctrination and political rhetoric to demonise the other and have sought to promote their own interests by intervening in the affairs of the other. The Shah and Saddam Hussein fought each other between 1969 and 1975 making use of Cold War rivalries. Saddam fought Khomeini from 1980 to 1988 because the latter's revolution threatened the stability of the Iraqi regime. The war gave Iraq a chance to supplant Iran as the dominant power in the Gulf. In sum, religion influences and provides a language for, but does not determine, the international relations of the Middle East. *There is no such thing as the 'international relations of Islam'* any more than there is such a thing as *'Islamic art'*, a fabrication of curators and auctioneers.[42] Uses, and abuses, of Islamic values and terminology in international relations are, and probably long will be, legion; there is no reason for social scientists to endorse the collective delusion.

Informal ideologies: perception and beliefs

The ideologies considered so far have been ones that take a relatively explicit form, being articulated by leaders, parties and states, and using a vocabulary that is expounded in the speeches and writings of the movements; hence 'imperialism', 'Zionism', the 'nation', 'heritage', 'treason', 'plots' and much else besides are part of a discourse that serves to shape domestic and foreign politics. Anterior terms of religious disapprobation, such as Hebrew *rodef* (defector) and Islamic *mofsid* (spreader of corruption), were given a new lease of life, and people were killed as a result as they were in the name of equally blown-up Marxist categories like 'enemy of the people' (USSR) and 'capitalist roaders' (China). The question of how far the mass of the population of any country believes in these ideologies is an open one; but as with religious belief itself, and with the hold of communism for several decades in the countries where it was the official ideology, too much scepticism may be as mistaken as too little. Human beings may respond to the appeals of leaders, the socialisation of education and the media and the global illusions of their time. They may believe, at least in part and for some of the time, what they hear, even if, once they have abandoned these beliefs, they deny that this was ever the case. For example, the Palestinians in Jordan in 1969 believed in creating a

---

[42] See the regular Saturday contributions of Souren Melikan, art critic and historian, to the *International Herald Tribune*.

'Second Hanoi'. The fact that some of the working classes from these states benefit through economic redistribution, and that some are prepared to fight and die, is not to be forgotten. The fact that beliefs are ancient or modern, 'authentic' or invented, is of no relevance as to how far people adhere to them or, for that matter, kill for them.

Modern ideologies *do* matter. The hold of beliefs, and perceptions, on a people may, however, be all the greater where the ideas in question take the form not of formal doctrines, or novel political terms, but of more everyday and unquestioned assumptions that nonetheless affect political values and choices; here the issue is more one of political culture, a set of underlying beliefs and ideas, than of explicit doctrines.[43] These are here termed 'informal ideologies'. Four recurrent dimensions of such assumptions merit special attention. The first is the resort, in all discussions of conflict, and the rights and wrongs associated with conflict, to the past as an explanatory factor; this, as illustrated before, is not history as rational explanation, of how one set of events led to another, let alone of any discontinuities, but is history selectively defined both as the source of legitimation, in terms of claim to land or specific places and the heroism of ancient leaders, and as the explanation for why nothing has changed, or perhaps can. Thus, within the Middle East region as much as without, generalisations about other peoples combine with assertions that such-and-such a conflict has endured for centuries or more and will continue to do so:[44] Jews and Arabs, Muslims and Crusaders, Turks and Kurds, Arabs and Iranians, and so on. People seem to like saying that the Arab–Israeli conflict, for example, is 'age-old', 'ancestral', 'biblical', 'primordial', has been going on for centuries or millennia. This is, of course, nonsense. It began in the 1920s as a conflict between two communities that were to be formed, over the decades, in conflict with each other. An Alevi Turkish cab driver in London once told me that the Kuwaitis were all murderers because they had killed the Shi'ite martyrs Ali (AD 661) and Hussein (AD 680). I did point out that this had taken place a while ago, and that Ali had not, on the available evidence, been killed. A Kuwaiti academic, for her part, told me not to trust Yemenis because their Queen Bilqis, the Queen of Sheba, had gone to Israel and married Solomon, ignoring the fact that in addition to being King of the Jews Solomon was also a Muslim prophet.

---

[43] On the implicit, everyday, character of ideology see Louis Althusser, 'Ideology and the State', in *Lenin and Philosophy and other Essays*, London: NLB, 1971; Michael Billig, *Banal Nationalism*, London: Sage, 1995.

[44] A new code of nationalist enmity was also coined: Saddam's uncle Khairullah wrote a book entitled *Three Things that God Should not Have Created – Persians, Jews and Flies*, but note the order.

The seduction of such explanations is that they *appear* to give educated, informed support to the explanation of contemporary processes. All too often, they do the opposite; any person, such as the author or reader of this book, who resists such invocations is, of course, regarded as a dupe. Yet reason should hold its ground. In the Middle East as elsewhere, even if a particular conflict did subsist in the past, this is no reason in itself as to why it persists today. 'History' on its own explains and legitimises nothing. It should be discounted until and unless it can prove that it is indeed relevant to explanation or claim.

Equally, explanations of why a particular state, or people, values a piece of land may be assisted by historical evidence; but for all the talk of 'ancestral' land or the heartfelt 'yearning' for this and that, it may just as easily be distorted by historical material. The case of Jerusalem, more often a spiritual rather than a geographic goal for Jews throughout the centuries, and a secondary, intermittently important pilgrimage site for some Muslims, is an obvious example. In the late twentieth century both sides have, in a grotesque tango of bombast, talked it up.[45] A sceptical, but historically literate observer might conclude that it is the three great

[45] For two telling critiques of the exaggeration of 'Jerusalem': Abraham Rabinovich, 'The Truth About Jerusalem: It's Partly Holy but Mostly Not', *International Herald Tribune*, 31 July 2000: 'Today's Jerusalem is more than 100 times the size of the Old City. The sanctity conferred upon the modern city in all its girth by political rhetoric accounts for much needless passion. The boundaries of modern Jerusalem were set not in antiquity but only 33 years ago, and not by holy writ but by a committee of midlevel Israeli government officials and army officers. Their mandate immediately after the Six Day War was to draw boundaries that would, among other things, include defensible high ground and ensure that medium artillery could not reach the heart of Jewish West Jerusalem. Given that there had been a bitter battle in the streets of the city and that there had been an even bloodier battle only 19 years earlier, during Israel's war of independence, these were not frivolous concerns. But God had no place at the committee's map table. The 18,000 acres (7,300 hectares) of former Jordanian territory that Israel duly annexed tripled the size of the city. Only 1,500 of these acres had been part of the Jordanian Jerusalem, a small backwater left under Jordanian rule in a state of benign neglect. The rest of the annexed area was made up of parts of 28 Arab villages between Bethlehem and Ramallah. Around the outer perimeter of the new territory, Israel subsequently built a string of massive housing developments which, in effect, created a new city wall – demographically and even tactically. Inside this wall, and occasionally poking through it to touch the West Bank, are homogeneous Arab neighbourhoods whose 200,000 residents comprise close to one-third of the city's population. These neighbourhoods have less claim to sanctity than much of the West Bank territory already ceded to the Palestinians.' Also Henry Siegman, 'The Truth About Jewish and Muslim Claims to Jerusalem', *International Herald Tribune*, 10 August 2000: 'This radical fragmentation of the city is the predictable consequence of a sterile Israeli policy denying manifestations of Palestinian sovereignty. The consequences of Palestinian rigidity are equally predictable. Today, Palestinian Muslims enjoy largely unfettered access to the Haram al Sharif. But absent a peace agreement, and most certainly after a unilateral declaration of Palestinian statehood, Palestinian access to this area will be curtailed by Israel. In the case of violence, it may well be halted entirely. In the name of protecting the unity of the city and guaranteeing access to holy places in East Jerusalem, both sides are in fact accomplishing

religions which are the root of Jerusalem's problems and that the city would be best off without them. Rather than taking political culture as given, across the centuries, it is necessary to ask why such values persist, or are created, today: it is modern nationalism, no doubt using bits of history that come to hand, but not history itself, that invests places and borders with such importance. 'Land' – that is, soil, stones, weeds and hills – has no intrinsic value or meaning. It is humans who chose to give such things to it. If land is 'sacred', it is because humans have lived, worked and died on it and for that reason alone.

A second much espoused dimension of political culture is the belief in an external, 'western' hostility to the peoples of the region, supposedly manifested over centuries in a series of plots. This is an important component of the nationalisms of the region, and, with the 'Clash of Civilisations' of the 1990s, has become a guiding myth of contemporary discourse. Two obvious points need to be made at the outset. One is that such views are to be found in many other parts of the world, be they the Balkans, Ireland or China. There is nothing specifically 'Islamic' in this mindset; indeed some have been known, on equally flimsy grounds, to explain the Persian addiction to such as ideas as a reflection of the earlier Zoroastrian world view of a war between Good and Evil. Secondly, as already noted, conspiracy theory, while false, is not always *irrational*. If we examine historical formation we can find some reason as to why these peoples should, respectively, hold the views they do. As with individuals who sustain paranoid fantasies through their later life, the explanation for what seems to be paranoia may be found in very real experiences earlier in their existence. Nations do not become paranoid without reason; the problem is that, because irresponsible politicians and idle intellectuals make political profit out of it, they go on complaining for ever more. The Arab world *was* partitioned after World War I; the Armenians and Kurds *did* see their aspirations for independence thwarted and their peoples crushed in the same period; the Turks *were* the victims in 1920 of an attempt to impose a humiliating peace on them; the Jewish people *was*

the opposite. It is clear that only by reaching an agreement that creates new levels of sharing can the unity of Jerusalem and access to its holy places be enhanced. Which brings us to the dirty little secret about Jerusalem. Both Islam and Judaism have managed quite well over the centuries (in the case of Judaism, for two millennia) even when they did not exercise political sovereignty on the Temple Mount, as they call the Haram al Sharif. They would undoubtedly continue to manage well without such sovereignty in the future. What neither side can apparently imagine is yielding sovereignty over its shrine to the adversary. It is Jewish sovereignty over the Haram al Sharif and Muslim sovereignty over the Temple Mount that most outrages the religious/national sensibilities of Muslims and Jews, not the absence of their own sovereignty. This unpleasant truth suggests the solution – both sides deferring indefinitely the issue of sovereignty over Temple Mount/Haram al Sharif.'

repeatedly (but not necessarily perennially) betrayed and massacred by modern gentile society, above all in World War II.

If there are beliefs among peoples according to which all events can be explained by conspiracy, this is therefore in part because, at distinct moments in the past of these peoples, there *were* conspiracies. The modern history of the Middle East offers numerous examples of these, if not as many as conspiracy theorists might suggest: the Anglo-French Sykes–Picot Accords in 1916, the CIA-backed coups in Syria in 1949, the overthrow of Mosadeq in Iran in 1953, the preparations for the tripartite attack on Egypt in 1956, the US connivance at the UN with Iraq's opposition to a ceasefire and return to pre-existing borders after its attack on Iran in September 1980.

Turned on its head, to allow reason to prevail, the past could provide not a prison, as it often is, but an exit, an explanation, rather than an ahistorical legitimation, some unlimited claim on the world's conscience. This would be true, at least, if political leaders saw themselves as having an interest in taking such an explanatory route. Usually they do not. Nor indeed do many of the region's intellectuals who, taking that tribe as a whole, to cover historians, clergy, journalists and creative writers, nearly all see it as their duty to join the factional clamour as loudly and opportunistically as they can. The lachrymose, but also cynical, endorsement by some Arab intellectuals of Palestinian suicide bombers after September 2000 is but the latest example of this self-indulgence. Here again the Middle East should not be singularised: in the third world, the role of chauvinist intellectuals in the 1990s Balkan wars gave plenty of evidence of this, as did the ultra-nationalist ravings of Hindu intellectuals in the India of the same decade, while in the first, narcissistic denials of imperial and Cold War responsibility for the travails of the contemporary world are of equal calibre. A rethinking of history could provide an exit, rather than a confirmation, if the (fewer) real plots are separated from the (many more) invented ones.[46] However, reasons of state, and political interest, mean that they will never happen: the political sociology of half-truth has yet to be written.

Closely linked, therefore, to the sense of external hostility, and endemic to the view of external powers and international relations, is the belief in these wide-ranging conspiracies, plots and secret plans as explanatory causes, as determinants of foreign policy. No one dealing with the politics of the region, the speeches and press coverage it occasions, let alone the perceptions of people themselves, can fail to notice the recurrence of this. Everybody is planned, arranged, 'stitched up' long in advance.

[46] Abrahamian, *Khomeinism*, chapter 5, 'The Paranoid Style in Iranian Politics'.

Too often present events are 'explained' by archives from decades before. Moreover, not only is there a sinister motive behind almost every action and statement, but all events are to be explained in terms of these external machinations. As we have seen, the words in Arabic, *dasisa* and *mu'amara*, have a magic effect across the minds of the region. Thus, to take some obvious examples, the establishment of a Jewish community in Palestine, and of the state of Israel in 1948, was, in much Arab nationalism and Islamic discourse, a product of a deliberate western attempt to divide, and colonise, the Arab world. The Iranian revolution of 1978–9 was, in the eyes of its opponents, including the Shah himself, a result of British and American intervention. An alternative, very Iranian, view is that it was all carried out by Afghans whom the mullahs bussed in to demonstrate. For Iranian revolutionaries, the Iraqi attack of September 1980 was a result of imperialist, British and American, and Israeli, encouragement of Baghdad, and nothing whatsoever to do with the taunting radio broadcasts from Tehran in previous months. In 1990 many Saudis saw the Iraqi invasion of Kuwait as part of a Hashemite encirclement, encompassing Iraq, Jordan, recently reunited Yemen and, not least, the PLO.

From the perspective of any one country, other states, especially those outside the region, do not even have policies as such; they have 'plots' and secret 'plans'. Conspiracy theory, like all forms of paranoia, and like that most successful paradigm for explaining human behaviour, astrology, is also irrefutable – any alternative explanation merely shows the naivety of the person offering it. The western listener who questions such analysis is the object of a special pity. Yet such visions are, in addition to being simplifications of reality, also self-defeating: peoples and states, as individuals, that remain prisoners of such visions are themselves paralysed by them.[47]

A fourth area of political value where much generalisation and ahistorical claim is made is in regard to violence, and cultural and moral values surrounding this. No one can contest that the incidence of violence, but also the justification of it, has been prevalent in much of the modern history of the region. This is, be it noted, as much a matter of the use of violence by rulers, indigenous and foreign, against the ruled, as it is

[47] There is little adequate discussion of this important but sensitive issue. Daniel Pipes, *Hidden Hand: Middle East Fears of Conspiracy*, London: Macmillan, 1996, has some good examples but the overall analysis is unsatisfactory, and lacking in any historical, or comparative, perspective. In chapter 14, 'The Trauma of Modern Islam', Pipes also, without second thoughts, ascribes to *Islam* paranoid analyses which could just as easily be ascribed to nationalism in, for example, its Chinese or Serbian form. A methodological corrective is provided by Abrahamian, *Khomeinism*. Anecdotal evidence from Iran in 2000, two decades after the (very paranoid) Islamic revolution, is that, among young people at least, conspiracy theory has significantly *declined*.

of the resort to violence by those who are ruled. The history of Islamist violence after 1980 is inextricably tied to western instigation. The ascription of responsibility for Islamic terrorism *solely* to Arab society, after 11 September 2001, is an act of grotesque western amnesia.[48] Images of oppressive, tyrannical sultans and amirs, and of bloodthirsty external powers, collide with those of assassins, bombers and terrorists seeking to challenge states. Its undemocratic rulers, traditional and modern, have been as cruel and despotic as those elsewhere.

However, here too, an element of comparison and caution may be in order. It should never be forgotten that the bloodiest wars have been in modern Europe and North America. The first industrial war was the American civil war in which 600,000 people died. As already suggested, and the second Gulf war aside, the Middle East has been far from being the most sanguinary region of the world in modern times, or in the Cold War. Casualties in the Arab–Israeli dispute from 1948 to 2000 were a fraction of those in, say, Vietnam or southern Africa. The modern republican rulers, in the Middle East (Saddam, Asad, Khomeini) as in Europe and East Asia, have on balance been far more brutal than the traditional monarchical ones; this fact alone should give pause to any argument about the *endemic* roots of violence. At the same time the forms of violence associated with modern politics – aggression and subversion by states, terrorism and revolt by the ruled – are ones which originated in, and have been borrowed from, other regions in the world. These contemporary crimes are legitimated in a modular modern discourse – 'liberation', 'identity', 'revolution' and so on. Saddam Hussein's brutal treatment of his own people, as in Operation *Anfal* of 1988, for example, and his attacks on neighbours, in Iran and Kuwait, were imitations of what dictators elsewhere in the twentieth century perpetrated – Stalin and Hitler in particular. Both the Shah *and* Khomeini were inspired by forms of modernist illusion – grandiose economic development in the former case, national-cultural counter-revolution in the latter. The resort to terrorism by fundamentalists and nationalists, be they Islamist guerrillas or the Stern Gang in Palestine, replicates that which, for a century prior to this, other terrorist groups in Armenia, Ireland, India and elsewhere carried out. Some foreign examples, notably everyone's favourite the IRA, inspired both sides in the conflict, the Jewish Irgun and the Palestinian al-Fath.

When it comes to the relation between religion and violence, a similar modern and contingent relationship applies. All religions, their texts, traditions and myths, can, if conveniently interpreted, justify the killing of civilians and other violations of the rules of war; but it is in the *selection* of

[48] Thomas Freedman, *International Herald Tribune*, 20 March 2004, for one egregious case.

that interpretation, a conscious political act, not in the universal injunctions of religion itself, that the resort to violence, and the justification of it, consist.[49] Much is made of the bloodthirsty passages in the Quran, especially chapter 5, 'Sura of Ma'ida', which rails against Jews, Christians and Sabaens, and chapter 9, the, 'Sura of Tauba' or repentance (verses 3, 5, 14, 29, 30, 123). However, Jews and Christians should feel little better: if they choose the Old Testament Book of Deuteronomy, this happily enjoins the chosen people to commit genocide, slaughter civilian captives, and pursue ethnic cleansing (chapters 7, 12 and 20). As for Hindus, who in the immediate post-1945 epoch were held up as models of non-violence, 'ahimsa' as preached by Mahatma Gandhi, they have subsequently more than caught up, in their militarist pursuit of nuclear weapons and chauvinist attitudes, modelled on European fascism, towards Muslims. The cannibalistic goddess Kali yields little in regard to international humanitarian law.

This brings us back to the central argument in this chapter, the relation between, on the one hand, an apparent *autonomy of* ideas and, on the other, their *sociological and (real) historical formation*. The *impression* given by the discourses of Middle Eastern politics and international relations is one in which ideology, in the sense of various competing explicit doctrines, and a range of assumptions about one's own and other peoples, determine much of the domestic and international relations of the region. It cannot be stated too often: *this is* the view most widely held in the region. Taken further, such a world view can easily lead to a set of claims about how distinctive, and unchanging, the region is; it is dominated, so it can be argued, by undemocratic, conspiratorial, religious and other values. There will never be progress, or peace, or democracy; all the more foolish, therefore, are those who think there could, or ever should, be such respite. As with all value systems that aspire to be dominant, the ideologies of the Middle East, formal and informal, in large measure support this claim of a static, perennialist region. These ideologies of timelessness are therefore tempting. They appear to provide a framework that is as enduring as it is inescapable. More difficult, but more revealing, is an approach which recognises the importance, indeed necessity, of such value systems in communities and nations, but which takes a historical and sociological distance and sets these systems within a triple, explanatory context: first, that of *socialisation*, one that follows the agenda of Barrington Moore and looks at why and how ideas are transmitted, or adjusted, by successive generations and by competing groups of political leaders; secondly, that of *comparison*, whereby claims as to uniqueness of Middle Eastern politics

[49] Walter Laqueur, *The Age of Terrorism*, London: Weidenfeld and Nicolson, 1987.

and discourses are tested against examples of other regions of the world, developed and developing; thirdly, that of *historical context*, whereby the social, and perhaps historical, sources and appeals of these ideas are examined.

The ideologies of the Middle East are not on their own an explanation for its international relations. They are shaped by, even as they serve to reinforce and to mobilise, international powers and by the political and social forces that seek to maintain power in this region. As we have seen, this is, of course, *not* what many, perhaps most, people in the Middle East will say. But even their fondly proclaimed and deeply felt assertions need to be, and can be, tested before the tribunals of historical sociology and comparative reason.

8   Challenges to the state: transnational movements

The state and beyond: three general perspectives

It did not take the growth of the Muslim Brotherhood after 1928, the rise of the Palestinian resistance movement in the late 1960s or the events of 11 September 2001 to show that, as agents of political change in the region, Middle Eastern states are far from being alone. This was a recurrent theme in the earlier chapters of this volume on history, and on war and conflict. As with those elsewhere, Middle Eastern states may aspire to control relations between themselves and to limit the influence of other states on their own. The very incidence of war and the salience of security concerns ensure that this is so. However, forces other than the state, the non-state and the 'transnational', in the sense of that which links societies without going through states, are recurrently important, and indeed seek to use states, regional and international, to further their ends.

In pre-modern as well as contemporary periods, transnationalism is therefore an integral part of the regional politics. It is also central to contemporary debate in IR. International Relations has, in recent years, been increasingly concerned with the issue of transnational forces and movements, understood therefore as those which, beyond the domain of the state as normally construed, influence the policies of states and their outcomes.[1] This has been part of the critique of realism as a theoretical framework, but it is also an engagement with the new forms of politics (for example, diasporas, religious networks) and social interchange accompanying globalisation. Discussion of transnationalism has, therefore, important, interdisciplinary consequences for the study of a range of issues, among them globalisation, diasporas, non-state actors and the transnational constitution of societies. This approach allows discussion

---

[1] For general IR background, Peter Willetts, 'Transnational Actors and International Organization in Global Politics', in John Baylis and Steve Smith, eds., *The Globalization of World Politics*, Oxford: Oxford University Press, 1997; Katerina Dalacoura, 'Transnational Islamic Actors', in Daphne Josselin and William Wallace, eds., *Non-State Actors in World Politics*, Basingstoke: Palgrave, 2001.

of the ways in which a 'non-state' and transnational perspective may enhance, or revise, conventional views of the IR and politics of the region. Moreover, it also allows analysis of the ways in which the Middle East may pose its own more general challenges to social and political analysis. As suggested in earlier chapters, this kind of critical reference also suggests ways in which not only the politics of contemporary societies, but also their historical development, may be rethought. As a testing ground, the Middle East can, in this way, serve wider, theoretical ends.

Most work on the international relations of the Middle East has certainly focused on the actions of states, and on the manner in which they are able to dominate and control relations between different societies. It is this focus on states which allows for the discussion of war, diplomacy, international agreements and the like. Indeed, as we have seen, much of the study of the international relations of the Middle East has been concerned with 'great' external powers while regional states have been allotted a secondary role. This emphasis on external states can lead to an awareness of how Middle Eastern states are vulnerable to, and permeated by, external influences. It does not always enhance an understanding of how indigenous social forces may act, within and between societies.

There may be, moreover, a 'first world' bias in this focus: much academic literature focuses on the erosion of state power in the developed world. It might be thought, therefore, that transnationalism applies to relations between developed, open and democratic states, *not* to the authoritarian Middle East.[2] However, not just in the era of globalisation, but throughout history, in the Middle East as elsewhere, there have been significant actors which are not directed by states. These challenge states and qualify any view we may have of politics or international relations as merely the domain of states. Indeed, in the contemporary world as in previous epochs, it is open to question how far it is states at all which are the dominant actors. The Egyptian political scientist Nazih Ayubi's argument about the *weakness* of Arab states in the domestic sphere can equally apply to the international: the very aspiration of states to control so much reflects their concern at not being able to manage events. As Ayubi writes, the 'fierceness' of states is not to be confused with the capacity to implement policies.[3] The frequency with which opponents are accused of being 'agents' of external powers is testimony enough of this disquiet on the part of the authorities.

[2] For classic statements, not subsequently surpassed, see James Rosenau, ed., *Linkage Politics*, New York: Free Press, 1969; Robert Keohane and Jospeh Nye, eds., *Power and Interdependence*, Boston: Little Brown, 1977.

[3] Nazih Ayubi, *Over-stating the Arab State: Politics and Society in the Middle East*, London: I. B. Tauris, 1995.

To elaborate further, the challenge to a state-centric approach to international relations arises from three concerns. The first is a challenge to the idea of relations between states and societies as *international* in the sense of inter-state: here the argument is that those forces which cross frontiers and which have a significant impact on the politics and societies of other countries are not necessarily, or not always, states, hence *transnational*. Such actors may be opposition political movements, movements of national revolt, transnational tribal or ethnic groups, religious sects and confessions, or groups engaged in terrorism. Transnational actors may also be economic: large corporations, investors with oil money, migrants remitting funds to their families at home.

In intra-regional terms, ties of finance and patronage (for example, between the Saudi and Syrian elites, or before 1958, at least, between Iraqi and Jordanian rulers, or between Saddam Hussein and his myriad clients, recipients of 'oil coupons' in the Arab world and beyond) may well accord with links of ethnic or sectarian origin, or with ties of kinship and marriage. In regard to opposition, one does not have to go far in the Middle East to find such apparently transnational actors: guerrilla movements like the PLO and various Kurdish groups, Arab nationalist underground organisations in the 1950s and 1960s, notably the Movement of Arab Nationalists, Islamist groups in the 1980s and 1990s, al-Qa'ida thereafter. In the field of international political economy, there are oil companies, Arab investors, and millions of migrants who have moved from one society to another. This balance of state/non-state is an issue in, for example, evaluating the formation of oil prices. It is quite misleading to present OPEC, the Organisation of Petroleum Exporting Countries, as a 'non-state' actor since it is a cartel of member states; but it is a moot question whether the price of oil is determined more by states, producer (OPEC) and consumer (IEA, International Energy Agency), or by the impact of transnational forces – shifts in demand, speculation on markets, business confidence, not to mention that most transnational force of all, climate. OPEC fixes a price, but it can only do so in a context created by the market.

The second general concern that has led to the discussion of the transnational challenges the premise, methodologically central to much social science, that takes the domestic as a bounded, closed domain.[4] Here analysis of what was previously seen as the largely contained *internal*

---

[4] This has come under increased attention in recent years, e.g. in Michael Mann, *The Sources of Social Power; vol. I*, Cambridge: Cambridge University Press, 1986, and in the growth of 'world' history. I have discussed this in *Rethinking International Relations*, London: Macmillan, 1994, pp. 1–4, and, extensively, in *Revolution and World Politics*, London: Macmillan, 1999.

or *domestic* politics of a country is now set in a broader context, where cross-border connections or linkages bypass state controls and, in turn, shape the domestic. It is recognised that it is not possible, nor was it ever so, to insulate any one society: the spread of ideas, of political and social currents, of issues of public concern, of responses within a society by state and society alike to external economic processes are to a considerable degree affected by external context. Thus the history of the spread of political ideas in the Middle East – of nationalism, socialism, Marxism, Islamism – has been a transnational one, often operating by way of example. This openness is evident in the conflicting responses of these societies to the modern world outside – to technology, to changing gender and generational roles, and, more recently, to what is termed globalisation. Given the recent, and contested, nature of the Middle East state system this permeability of society, sometimes real, sometimes feared and imagined, is especially relevant.[5] The critique of globalisation that developed in the Arab world in the 1990s, a mixture of nationalist and religious themes, made much of the 'cultural aggression' of western imperialism, this latter including McDonald's, pop music, Formula One racing and St Valentine's Day.[6]

'Transnational' here identifies the ways in which, not just recently but in all of history, no single society and no process within it can be insulated from the broader international context in which it is located: the Middle East was from 1800 onwards influenced by the rise of Europe; more recently no Arab society is immune to the Palestine issue, just as no Muslim society was insulated from the Iranian revolution. 'Transnational' may also identify activities, or what are sometimes called 'spaces', within society that are not controlled by the state and which derive much of their strength and character from interaction with the external: if this was true in times past of groups of merchants, or intellectuals or Sufi mystics who were linked to similar groups elsewhere, it may, in the contemporary period, relate more to political and social groups that are outside state domination – of what is, often rather generously, termed 'civil society'. These social, 'non-governmental' groups have operated in some contexts, such as Palestine in the late 1980s. The programmes, forms of organisation, aspirations, sometimes funding of such groups may owe more to their transnational connections than to anything within the society in

---

[5] I have discussed this in *Rethinking International Relations*, chapter 1.

[6] St. Valentine's Day was a particular target of Islamists on Bahrain in 2004, along with Formula One racing, when a major competition was organised on the island in April of that year. On the other hand some solace might be gained from one headline in the local English language paper, in a story datelined Karachi, 'Islamists Welcome Return of Indian Cricket Team'.

which they operate. The same challenge to the bounded society is even more evident in the realm of ideas – these honour no frontier, even as they are subtly changed, and used, by context.

Thirdly, and most recently, the term 'transnational' is used to denote effects of globalisation. Globalisation is understood as the opening of economies and societies (of which more in chapter 9).[7] Grasping what 'globalisation' means anywhere, including in the Middle East, is difficult: it involves multiple dimensions of activity, and the degree of change, or its novelty, may be overstated. In economic terms Middle Eastern states have tended to resist pressures to open markets and ownership. Yet the cultural and social processes associated with globalisation have become particularly strong in the last quarter of the twentieth century. The spread of the Internet in the late 1990s is one striking example of this.

These changes of the 1980s and 1990s challenge not only the role of states, and the insulation of societies, but some of the very categories of space and time in terms of which people, in the Middle East and elsewhere, have hitherto organised their lives. While there were always migratory communities in the Middle East, in a world where some people at least travel, or migrate, with greatly accelerated speed, space or location is no longer so clear: individuals and families may be bilocal, or have strong links both to their countries of origin, to their place of residence and to others in their own diaspora.[8] Some second-generation migrants may have no fixed sense of origin, or identity. Dispersal may be voluntary, for work, but may, not least in the Middle East, be a result of expulsion (Palestinians 1948–9), or fear or desperation resulting from political change (Iraqis from 1958 onwards). Time has been affected by the rapid, indeed instantaneous, movement of ideas, images, money across the globe. Identity, once apparently more secure, is less so: people have different layers of identity, and each of these – religious, political, national, regional – may be changing.

All of this challenges established power – political and social. The response, from those aspiring to authority within states, societies, religions or families, may well be to try to reassert an identity and place that is fixed and supposedly static; but this is often accomplished by even greater, and probably ineffective, assertions of control and dogmatic definition.

[7] Toby Dodge and Richard Higgott, eds., *Globalization and the Middle East: Islam, Economy, Society and Politics*, London: Royal Institute of International Affairs, 2002; Hassan Hakimian and Ziba Moshaver, eds., *The State and Global Change: the Political Economy of Transition in the Middle East and North Africa*, London: Curzon Press, 2000; Clement Henry and Robert Springborg, eds., *Globalization and the Politics of Development in the Middle East*, Cambridge: Cambridge University Press, 2001.
[8] For general discussion see Steve Vertovec and Robin Cohen, eds., *Migration, Diasporas and Transnationalism*, Cheltenham: Edward Elgar, 1999.

Cultural nationalism is one response to globalisation, the claim that the 'national' or 'true' culture of a people is being threatened by external forces. Such assertion is evident in attempts to freeze vocabulary, or to impose one interpretation of religious text over others. In both Iran and the Arab world secular left nationalists *and* Islamists have resorted to this for decades. Prevalent phenomena such as censorship, calls for a return to tradition and authenticity, and outright violence against those who break with orthodox belief and behaviour, by states and families alike, are indices of such a defensive response. So too is the sustained restriction, and persecution, by Middle Eastern states of NGOs and intellectual dissent. The two simplest ways to try to reassert control, of course, are to say that the activity in question is either in contradiction with tradition, variously interpreted in religious and national idioms, or a result of external interference, or, of course, both. Two examples among many provided by the Middle East: the repeated closure by conservative courts in Iran of independent newspapers that began publishing after the election of President Khatami in 1997; the prosecution of the Egyptian political sociologist, and director of the Ibn Khaldun Centre in Cairo, Saad al-Din Ibrahim in 2000 on charges of having received money from abroad. In both cases the fear of the authorities was of independent expression; 'external connections' were an inflated pretext. These coercive actions are, therefore, an attempt to restore power, where it is being eroded, and to re-establish certainty, where it has been called into question. It is doubtful whether the Middle East has heard the last of these apologetic justifications.

The 'transnational' in question

Seen in this light, as an enduring, if reshaped, 'non-state' force, the question posed by transnationalism may not be where the power of the state *ends*, but where it *begins*. Despite the brief historic interlude of the modern state, when this institution arrived to dominate society, the pertinence of the reverse has more often been the case. Yet, for all the recognition of its salience, there are a number of difficulties with this emphasis upon the transnational as 'non-governmental' and with the argument that it has displaced the power of states. First of all, and as suggested already, all that appears to be 'non-state' may not, in fact, turn out to be so. It is sometimes argued that forms of international organisation – the UN, the EU or in the Middle East such bodies as the Arab League, the Gulf Co-operation Council or the Organisation of the Islamic Conference – reflect the growth of 'supranational' bodies. These entities do certainly serve functions which states acting alone cannot perform; but they are

their ends. The rise of Arab nationalism in World War I relied militarily, once the world inter-state war began, on the backing of the British and the French in the conflict.[13] The Arab League, itself a body composed of states, was established in 1945 with strong backing from Britain.[14] The PLO was set up in 1964 by the Arab League; it subsequently sought, with the temporary crisis of the Arab states after 1967, to increase its autonomy of the League, and of the more powerful interested parties (Egypt, Syria, Jordan, Iraq). In Jordan from 1967 to 1970 and in Lebanon thereafter, it took advantage of the weakness of the state to establish its own military and political apparatus. Yet, while it had an independent financial base, throughout its tortuous history the PLO never broke free of the political constraints of the Arab inter-state system.[15] As for the Middle Eastern state system a local representative, Jordan, in time reasserted its predominance, expelling the PLO from its own territory in 1970–1, as the latter was from Lebanon in 1984.

When we come to other radical or anti-state groups the same applies. The Algerian FLN was able to operate against the French in Algeria from 1954 to 1962 because of support from Morocco and Tunisia. The Popular Front for the Liberation of Oman fought in dhofar with the backing of South Yemen up to 1975. Each of the three main Kurdish nationalist movements – in Iran, Iraq and Turkey – has sought support from other states, even though these latter have themselves been oppressing their own Kurds. Thus Iraq supported the Kurds of Iran, Iran supported the Kurds of Iraq, and Syria, and to a lesser extent Iran, supported the Kurds of Turkey. Time and again opposition forces within one country end up being controlled by the forces of a state opposed to their own: thus Egypt came to control Arab nationalist groups in much of the Arab world in the 1950s and 1960s, Iraq did the same in the 1970s and 1980s, and the Iranian opposition group, the Mujahidin-i Khalq, which began in the 1960s as an independent underground group within Iran, had become, by 1986, when its leadership took refuge in Baghdad, an appendage of the Iraqi state.[16]

[13] Though this should not be exaggerated: the total forces were 3,000 irregular Arab fighters as against 250,000 British-officered troops. A similar politically charged exaggeration applied to the role of Saudi forces in the war in Kuwait 1991. Many more Arabs fought in the Ottoman ranks.
[14] Robert MacDonald, *The League of Arab States*, Princeton: Princeton University Press, 1965.
[15] Yezid Sayigh, *Armed Struggle and the Search for a State: the Palestinian National Movement, 1949–1993*, Oxford: Clarendon Press, 1997; Barry Rubin, *The Transformation of Palestinian Politics: From Revolution to State-Building*, Cambridge, MA: Harvard University Press, 1999.
[16] For a revealing, and terrifying, account of life inside this organisation see Masud Banisadr, *Masud Memoirs of an Iranian Rebel*, London: Saqi, 2004.

A similar caution applies to the most controversial of all nationalist movements in the modern history of the region, that of political Zionism, understood as that movement which from 1897 to 1948 sought to set up a Jewish state in Palestine and which, on that latter date, achieved its goal.[17] Here ideological representation and misrepresentation apply from two directions. On the one hand, Zionism itself claims that it was independent of states, an autonomous nationalist movement beset by gentile states hostile to Jews and with the aim of achieving what all other nationalist movements do, namely creating an independent state. In the case of Zionism this involved a particular set of nationalist challenges, not least the migration of large numbers of Jews to Palestine from the 1880s onwards, and the promotion within that community of a modernised language, Hebrew, that was not used for everyday purposes. Those opposed to Zionism claimed, by contrast, that it was not an autonomous movement at all: it was a creature of the colonial powers, a 'stooge', 'outpost', 'agent', created and designed to weaken the Arab world and establish a pro-western state in the region. This is, in the view of Arab nationalist critics, the role which Israel has continued to play since 1948. Zionism therefore stressed its transnationalism as a sign of authenticity; its opponents saw it in realist terms as an instrument of states, a *kian* or 'entity', not a normal state, or, in an overused idiom, as a 'cancerous' growth in the region.

The truth about Zionism may, however, lie somewhere between these two, ideologically constituted claims, as it does with other cases of nationalism. Indeed by posing the question in terms of the roles of states and autonomous transnational forces a more accurate rendering of this normally highly charged issue may be possible. Zionism in its origins – a response to the rise of Jewish sentiment in Europe, itself promoted by the rise of anti-Jewish racism, or anti-semitism – was not the creation of states (except in so far as it was the discriminatory policies of the Russian state that promoted this, after 1881); Zionism was, in a manner similar to that of other nationalist movements, a result of activity, mobilising, writing and general political action carried out by first a small, and later a wider, circle of supporters. It became evident, however, to the organisers of the Zionist movement from early on that, in order to promote their goals, they had to form alliances with states that might be sympathetic to them; prior to 1914 this was above all the Ottoman empire, then it became Britain, and later still, in the midst of World War II, the USA and the USSR.

[17] Walter Laqueur, *A History of Zionism: From the French Revolution to the Establishment of the State of Israel*, London: Weidenfeld and Nicolson, 1972; Shlomo Avineri, *The Making of Modern Zionism: the Intellectual Origins of the Jewish State*, London: Weidenfeld and Nicolson, 1982.

After its establishment, the new state of Israel sought to form alliances with whoever would support its goals – the USA, France and the USSR initially, then, while losing the USSR and later France, Britain and, from the 1980s onwards, China. From the 1960s onwards the key alliance was with the USA, from which Israel received unique levels of political, financial and diplomatic support; yet here was a clear example of the two-sided, international and internal, balancing act of states. If the Israeli state remained keenly aware of the need to sustain US backing, it was also subject to the pressures of Israeli domestic opinion. Where external 'support' from America ended and control by Washington began is an open question; it was never, however, a matter of Zionism/Israel having complete autonomy or complete subservience. Distinct in its origins, and antagonistic in its relation to other Middle Eastern nationalist movements and states, Zionism nonetheless acted as other transnational movements do. It sought to maximise support from other states in pursuit of its own, autonomously defined goals.

One further point needs emphasis here: the goal of nationalism is not the 'non-state', but precisely to establish a state. While opposition groups are by definition not part of the state they contest, their existence and programme are usually not indices of the rejection of the state as such, since what these groups aspire to themselves is the control of the state. The PLO has wanted to create a Palestinian state for Palestinians, not dissolve Palestinian society into transnational community, let alone have the Palestinians fall under the control of the other states that sought to dominate them – Israel, Syria and Jordan. Kurdish groups have aspired to self-determination for their peoples, either through the establishment of separate states or, more frequently, through claiming rights and a share of power within the states where they are located. Once established, states then become the determinants of national ideology and identity: they promote, define, organise nationalism even more than they express it. Henceforward, it is states that form nationalism, and nations, as much as the other way around.

(ii)   *Islamism: the return of the state*

When it comes to the Islamist groups that emerged in the 1970s and later, a similar ambivalence prevails. At first sight, Islamist movements are *par excellence* ones that defy the state and are transnational in ideology and organisation. Al-Qa'ida, an organisation based in Afghanistan but with recruits and activity across the Arab world, is a clear instance of this. One of the most common claims of Islamist movements is that they reject the division of the Muslim world into different states and peoples: the state in its modern form is an alien, western creation, and all Muslims share a common identity as members of the *umma* or community of believers. The Quran provides a sound basis for rejecting nationalist categories and fragmentation: it states that all believers are brethren (49:10), condemns division among peoples (49:13) and attributes sovereignty over land to God not man (38:65–6). Many modern Islamists have cited classic sources to 'prove' that ethnic and national divisions are the creation of the 'west'. Moreover, there is no doubt that Islamist groups *have* acted transnationally: they have inspired each other by ideology and by example, 'struggling' *jihadi* Muslims have gone from one country to another to participate in the struggle. Many have been explicitly members of organisations that incorporate groups in more than one country. The Muslim Brotherhood, al-Ikhwan al-Muslimin, was founded in Egypt in 1928 and set up branches in several Arab countries which have survived to this day, among them Palestine (Hamas) and Jordan. These *ikhwan* groups operate within a shared political framework, but without centralised coordination of the kind that used to operate in the case of the communist movement. Yet in the Arabian Peninsula they came over time to infiltrate ministries and government offices significant to them, such as censorship boards and the media (including by 2004, Qatar's al-Jazira TV). The radical Hizb al-Tahrir, or Party of Liberation, founded in Jordan in 1953 also has branches in several Arab countries as well as among Muslims in the west; it too calls for the unification of the *umma* under a new Caliphate.[18] The Afghanistan conflict of the 1980s mobilised support from Muslim volunteers throughout the Middle East as did, later on, the war in Bosnia of 1992–5 and the conflict in Chechnya. Out of these distinct but increasingly fused conflicts came al-Qa'ida, officially announced in February 1998.

To these linkages across Middle Eastern boundaries must be added those which involve Muslim, and specifically Arab, migrant communities in Europe and North America. It has often been possible outside the Middle East for opposition groups, not only Islamist but also Kurdish and Palestinian, to build supporter networks, accumulate funds and negotiate for weapons provision. It has also been possible here to build broader political coalitions, as other diaspora communities, be they Irish, Armenian, Cuban or Jewish, have done. Here, historically as well as in the contemporary whirl of the Internet and satellite TV, is that globalised, ever-changing and instantaneous transnational world which political, and security, experts have in vain tried to monitor, and social theorists have, equally vainly, sought to analyse. The attacks on the USA

---

[18] Suha Taji-Farouki, *A Fundamental Quest: 'Hizb al-Tahrir' and the Search for the Islamic Caliphate*, London: Grey Seal, 1996.

on 11 September 2001 arose from just such a process of transnational recruitment and organisation.

That there is an 'Islamist transnationalism' is, therefore, unquestionable: it has existed in some form through history, was reconstructed by Schulze's 'Islamic public' in the nineteenth and twentieth centuries and has found a third form in the era of mass migration and the Internet from the 1980s onwards. Yet despite appearances of autonomy from the state, and the very claims which such movements themselves assert, this distance needs to be questioned. In the first place, if we examine the origins and bases of such forms, and in particular seek to chart the rise and fall of Islamist movements, these in one sense lie very much *within* the specific societies in which they originate. The overall context is certainly international, that is the subordination of these societies to the west, and the rhetoric is gloriously eclectic, but the form the revolt takes is primarily revolt against the local state. Whatever the transnationalism of disclosure, the internationalism of symbol and appeal, and a floating cadre of mobile *mujahidin*, the factors that lead to the rise of an Islamist movement in, say, Iran, Algeria, Afghanistan, Pakistan or Palestine are those located within that society. In particular they are a reaction to the character of the secular state against which these movements revolt and of the reforms, of an interventionist and secular character, which these states have sought to implement. It was, in particular, the secular state's intervention in control of law, education, family policy, or the very reaction of society against the state's domination of the economy and its associated corruption, which explains the rise of Islamist movements in these societies.[19]

In explaining their advance, the *modernity* of these Islamist movements also needs to be recognised. In several cases, Islamism was not the first resort of a rebellious populace: they had in the 1940s and 1950s first turned to secular ideologies, of nationalism, populism, socialism or communism. Only when these latter had been discredited by their relation to the state, either because they had come to power and instituted tyranny, or because, as in Iran after 1953, they had been defeated, did Islamism emerge as an oppositional tendency with mass appeal. This pattern of country-specific revolt is evident as the movements themselves unfold: for all the transnational linkages that may exist, they confine their activities, and build their support, as much as nationalist movements do, within particular spaces, that is, the boxes that are modern states. Analysis over the 1980s and 1990s of, say, the Palestinian Hamas, or the Algerian armed groups, the Lebanese Hizbullah, or the Egyptian Jihad, shows that these were based in their respective countries. They may have involved

[19] Sami Zubaida, *Islam, the People and the State*, London: Routledge, 1993.

pan-Islamist symbols, such as the struggle against 'Zionism', or they may
have had funding and arms procurement, and propaganda, networks
abroad, but their emplacement was within their particular countries.
Al-Qa'ida was an exception, in some measure, to this; yet it too had its origins in revolt against specific states, notably Egypt and Saudi Arabia, and
was able to base itself in another state, Afghanistan, because of the alliance
it formed with the regime in that state, namely, from 1996, the Taliban.
This connection to states was even more evident when it came to the
way these forces appropriated state power itself: the Iranian revolution
embodied the tension which is present in all revolutions, that, in ideology, between internationalism and nationalism, and, in practice, between
state interest and international solidarity.[20] Khomeini proclaimed that
'In Islam there are no frontiers.' He denounced nationalism as a block
to the development of Islam, and a result of colonialist fragmentation
of the Muslim world. The Iranian revolution, as much as its predecessors, also inspired movements in other countries. Yet this revolution was
perceived elsewhere as an Iranian when not a Persian or Shi'ite process,
especially once war with Iraq, a country ruled by a Sunni elite, broke
out in September 1980. The movements that followed it in the Muslim
world were charged, rightly or wrongly, with complicity with Iran. For
its part, Iran came more and more after 1979 to direct its diplomacy,
and the management of its international appeal, to meet the needs of the
Iranian state. The greatest challenge the Iranian revolution faced was the
invasion by Iraq in September 1980: this led to eight years of inter-state
war. In its turn, Iran called for the Iraqi people to rise up. Yet the Iraqi
state held and there was no replication of the Iranian Islamic revolution
in Iraq.

Later, while the Islamic Republic of Iran pursued solidarity, in word
and with arms and financial support, with the Islamists in Lebanon,
notably Hizbullah,[21] it was careful to avoid involvement in other conflicts

[20] Wilfried Buchta, *Die iranische Schia und die islamische Einheit 1979–1996*, Hamburg:
Deutsches Orient-Institut, 1997; Fred Halliday, 'Iranian Foreign Policy since 1979:
Internationalism and Nationalism in the Islamic Revolution', in Juan Cole and Nikki
Keddie, eds., *Shi'ism and Social Protest*, London: Yale University Press, 1986.
[21] During an interview with the author in February 2004, in his headquarters in the Beirut
suburb of Harit Hreik, the deputy leader of Hizbullah Sheikh Naim Qasim talked openly
of the close links between his organisation and Iran and stated, in particular, that the
'main lines' of party policy were laid down in Iran. In response to a question about
the decision taken by Hizbullah in 1992 to make the transition from being a guerrilla
to being a political organisation within the Lebanese context, Sheikh Naim stated that
Hizbullah had set up a twelve-person committee to study the matter and that this report
had then been sent to Tehran; the final decision, he stated, seated beneath portraits of
Ayatollahs Khomeini and Khamenei, had been taken by Iran and in particular by the
faqih, or leading juridical and spiritual figure, Khamenei. The links between Lebanese

where this might have weakened its state interests by provoking friendly states (for example, Kashmir, Xinjiang and Chechnya). Like all revolutions the Iranian therefore appeared to lend credence to the transnationalist argument, but could also be seen as reinforcing a statist, realist case. By the twentieth anniversary of the revolution in 1999 Iranian diplomats were stressing 'national interest' as a guiding concept, and repeating Khomeini's categorisation of Iran as a 'Great Nation' (*millat-i bozorg-i Iran*).

If the fate of Islamists replicated that of communism in one respect, namely the yielding of revolutionary regimes to the pressures of state interest, it also echoed communism in another regard, namely in the manner in which established states sought to direct transnational contestatory movements. Here, again, the appearance of transnational autonomy often belied a more statist reality. From the 1970s onwards rival Muslim states sought, in varying ways, to exert control over the Islamist movements operating in other states. In doing this they replicated not only what the Soviet Union, China and Cuba had done with regard to their own revolutionary followings, but also what secular Arab states had sought to achieve in the 1950s and 1960s. If Nasser's Egypt had managed the nationalist groups of those years, particularly the Movement of Arab Nationalists (MAN), a pan-Arab party largely controlled by Egypt in the 1960s, such states as Saudi Arabia, Libya and Iraq all had relations with Islamist groups from the 1970s onwards; they tried to use the latter to prosecute their influence. Saudi Arabia in particular used its financial and political patronage to build a network of dependent groups across the Muslim world.[22]

That this attempt at international control was fragmented, competitive and often, as in the aftermath of the Iraqi invasion of Kuwait in 1990, ineffective, did not diminish the reality of attempted state control.[23] In this, of course, these states were replicating what many were also doing at home, accommodating to, and trying to control, internal Islamist forces: such control was both a means of diminishing their appeal and a counter to secular opposition forces, often of the left, which were challenging these states. Indeed the whole history of Islamism in the Middle East from the 1970s onwards has a strong state component: it is inextricably bound up with, while not reducible to, this move by states to promote Islamism as

and Iranian Shi'ism go back many decades but it was the events of the late 1970s (the first Israeli invasion of Lebanon in 1978, the Iranian revolution of 1979) that turned this largely religious and educational connection into a form of militant political solidarity.

[22] Malise Ruthven, *A Fury for God: the Islamist Attack on America*, London: Granta, 2002.

[23] James Piscatori, ed., *Islamic Fundamentalisms and the Gulf Crisis*, Chicago: The Fundamentalism Project, University of Chicago Press, 1991.

a rival to the left. During the 1980s in Algeria the FLN, in Turkey the military, in occupied Palestine the Israeli military, in Jordan the monarch and in Egypt the Sadat and Mubarak regimes all sought to use Islamists against nationalist oppositions and the left. So too did the ruling militant elite in Yemen in the 1980s and 1990s and, most spectacularly, Pakistan and the USA in the Afghan war of the 1980s. These patrons did not always succeed, and at times these Islamists escaped the controls of their sponsors. This process of state manipulation of Islamist symbols and groups did, however, once again underline the complex and mutually reinforcing, as opposed to exclusive, relationship between transnational Islam and the modern Middle Eastern state.

(iii)   Political violence

Widely associated with the activities of opposition movements in the Middle East, and sometimes taken as the quintessential 'transnational' activity, is the subject of unlawful political violence, often termed 'terrorism'. By this is conventionally meant a group of activities by armed groups that violate the rules of war, by using tactics that include hijacking of aircraft, assassination, bombings of civilians and kidnapping.[24] Such activities by opposition groupings have certainly been part of the modern politics of the Middle East. They have also spread, most notably through the activities of al-Qa'ida, to targets outside the region, culminating in the attacks of 11 September 2001. Violence, like nationalism, is a viscous concept, combining a moral and legal stance with an attempt to analyse a particular kind of political and social behaviour. Like nationalism, however, it is an important feature of modern life, can be defined and merits attention in its own right.

Any discussion of terrorist movements as an index of transnationalism has, however, to take note of two important qualifications, which establish a statist, domestic context. The term 'terrorism', in its original sense taken from the French and Russian revolutions, refers to abuses of the rules of war *not by rebels*, but by *states*: in the annals of the modern Middle East, and in relations between the region and the west, violations of humanitarian norms, or terrorist acts, by states far dwarf those of opposition groups, in terms of attacks on civilians, killing of prisoners, use of illegal weaponry and the use of terror for political ends. Ba'thism in Syria and Iraq has committed large-scale massacres of its own people, Israel has

---

[24] The best workable definition of such activities is given in Additional Protocol II of 1977 to the Geneva Conventions. For further discussion see chapter 4 of my *Nation and Religion in the Middle East*, London: Saqi, 2000.

used violence widely against the populations of Palestine and Lebanon, the Iranian revolutionary regime waged a reign of terror against its own people from 1979 through to, at least, 1988.[25] If terrorism is taken as an index of transnationalism it has, however, to take the actions of states into account.

The second major qualification to any discussion of illegal use of force concerns the actions of armed groups in situations of inter-ethnic and communal violence: in the Middle East as elsewhere, it is in such contexts, such as the civil wars in Algeria, Lebanon and Sudan, that the greatest atrocities are seen. The culture that leads to criminal violence at the international level is often bred within such contexts.

Conceptual confusion also stalks this debate. The whole discussion of the illegal use of force, and in particular the use of the term 'terrorist', may, if unclarified, do more to confuse than to elucidate. Generic use of the term may indeed reinforce not the transnationalist but the statist argument: the charge of 'terrorism' is frequently used automatically, as in the phrase 'state-sponsored terrorism', to ascribe responsibility for a particular violent action to another state. It is here that the analytic, as well as moral, assessment becomes even more clouded. However, as with nationalist movements in general, there is a tendency to exaggerate this linkage of terrorist action to other states. The Zionists who committed atrocities against British troops and against Palestinians in the period 1946–9 enjoyed international support but were not acting at the behest of a state. The Palestinians who hijacked aircraft and committed other terrorist acts in the period 1968–74 were, likewise, independent actors, even as they enjoyed widespread sympathy in the Arab world.[26]

Yet from the 1970s onwards there was also a tendency for Middle Eastern states to become more involved in such activity, both to gain advantage from it and to control the activities of the groups involved, particularly Palestinians. It was here that the term 'state terrorism' came increasingly to be used, not to denote the original sense of that term, that is, violence *from above* against the state's own population, but to denote the promotion by states of armed activities, apparently from below, within

[25] Human rights organisations such as Amnesty International and Human Rights Watch have published extensively on these issues. On Iraq see Middle East Watch, *Human Rights in Iraq*, London: Yale University Press, 1990; Samir al-Khalil, *Republic of Fear: The Politics of Modern Iraq*, London: Hutchinson/Radius, 1989; on Iran Ervand Abrahamian, *Tortured Confessions. Prisons and Public Recantations in Modern Iran*, London: University of California Press, 1999. On Israel, for example, Amnesty International, *Israel and the Occupied Territories: State Assassinations and Other Unlawful Killings*, 21 February 2001.

[26] For an engagement with the arguments of one such group see Fred Halliday, Interview with Ghusan Kannafani, PFLP leader, *New Left Review*, no. 67 May–June 1997.

another state, that is, internationally or transnationally. In practice, where state power was weak, as it was in Jordan between 1967 and 1970, in Lebanon in the 1970s and 1980s, or in Afghanistan in the 1980s and 1990s, it was possible for armed groups to operate in an autonomous manner. Elsewhere such activities were carried out across frontiers with more or less active involvement of state authorities. Syria, Libya and Iraq all backed factions of the Palestinian movement that used criminal forms of violence, Israel supported Maronite militias who carried out massacres of Palestinians in Lebanon (most notably the killing of several thousand Palestinians at the camps of Sabra and Chatila in 1984), Iran supported radical Shi'ite groups in Lebanon and elsewhere who resorted to bombings and kidnapping of civilians.[27] The level of state involvement was frequently exaggerated, for polemical reasons, to pin the blame for all violence on other states. But equally the appearance of freedom or autonomy of such groups was, like that of other transnational social movements and political actors, often overstated.

In this debate on terrorism the partisan interests of states are assisted by one further, normative confusion. Here, the use of the term 'terrorism' is made more complex by the fact that it is often employed for factional political purposes, not to identify a particular act, but to deny the legitimacy of any political claims made by the group in question. Yet to identify an action by any group, state or non-state, as in violation of the rules of war is not the same as to disqualify the *legitimacy* of the political claims such a group is making: for sure, acts of criminality lead inevitably to a decreasing sympathy for the causes of a group, but this distinction between method and legitimacy stands. The state wanting to condemn 'terrorism' cannot so easily deny legitimation by concentrating on the *methods* of its opponents. To say that Palestinian nationalists, or Zionists, or Shi'ite guerrillas in Lebanon, or opponents of a despotic military regime, have committed acts of terrorism is not the same as saying that their cause is invalid, let alone that their enemies are justified. The term 'terrorism' can, therefore, have precise, legal and military usage. However, 'terrorist' is used too often in regard to Middle Eastern politics not to denote a class of acts by armed groups, but as a coded means of dismissing the validity of a political cause. That assessment has, however, to be based on other grounds.

As on so many other topics, there is also a risk in singularity, in seeing terrorism as something unique to the Middle East. The events of 11 September 2001 were in many respects a hitherto unique event, in scale and impact. But terrorism, in the sense of the use of criminal violence

---

[27] Patrick Seale, *Abu Nidal: a Gun for Hire*, London: Hutchinson, 1992.

for political ends, from below and from above, is a product of modern politics, the increasingly violent clash of authoritarian institutions with challenges from below, the world over. The incidence of terrorist activities in modern politics is by no means specific to the Middle East, let alone to Muslims: terrorism has been carried out in the politics of Russia, Japan, Ireland, America to name but some. To singularise it in Middle Eastern terms is to distort its causes and consequences. The term 'international terrorism' may, moreover, obscure the degree to which acts of criminal violence have their origins within specific political contexts, such as the Palestine–Israel conflict, Lebanon or Sudan, or, outside the Middle East, Sri Lanka or Kashmir, and only later acquire international or transnational character.

Even more so is it mistaken to singularise terrorism in religious terms. Islam, like all religions, provides means both of limiting the impact of violence and of validating violence against opponents.[28] Terrorists in Muslim societies have used convenient texts for their purposes, as have Zionist Jews, Armenian Christians and Hindu chauvinists. Religion is not the determinant, but the dependent variable. Moreover, many of the most prominent acts of terrorism in the Middle East have been carried out by groups with a secular ideology, be it Palestinian 'Marxist-Leninists' (PFLP, PDFLP, al-Saiqa) in the late 1960s, or various forces of the far left (PKK) and far right (MHP) in Turkey. Suicide bombings were pioneered not in Palestine, but in secular politics in Sri Lanka by the Hindu youths of the Tamil Tigers. In Lebanon, mass kidnapping of members of another confession was part of the civil war, and an estimated 17,000 people disappeared; when it came to such a sustained and widespread form of barbarity, there was nothing to choose between Sunni and Shi'ite, Maronite and Druze. Every belief was plunged into a grotesque, and retaliatory, cycle of violence.

(iv)   Culture and media

The extent, and also state-imposed limits, of transnationalism are equally evident in regard to the question of culture. As noted this term 'culture' relates not just to separate domains of literature, language and social custom. It also refers, as in political 'culture', to the very fraught areas of who is entitled to hold power, in state and society, who is, and equally who is not, part of a community, and ultimately to the varied forms of legitimacy that every society has to define and seek to uphold. In certain respects, this was ever so: the great empires, pre-Islamic and Islamic, ensured that

---

[28] Ruthven, *A Fury for God*, chapter 2, 'Jihad'.

language formed part of their hegemony and that culture defined those who were to be included in the body politic. Traditional Arabian poetry praised the deeds of the tribe and celebrated the defeat of others.[29] Places, of rule and worship, as of pilgrimage, always had symbolic importance: this is why all three major religions have asserted, and often exaggerated, the importance to them of the city of Jerusalem. Culture, in a broad sense, and power have, in that way, always been linked. In modern times, however, this relation has, if anything, become more important: as has torture, or education, so has cultural legitimation become more important because states fear they will lose control.[30] The people have become less submissive. Just as those with power have sought to shape and control culture, so those opposed have sought, within their own societies but increasingly from without, to deploy culture in pursuit of their goals. This is simply a requirement of the modern, authoritarian or democratic state.

The most obvious example of the linkage of politics to culture is found in nationalist movements. The rise of Arab nationalism in the middle of the nineteenth century was closely tied to the *'asr al-nahda*, 'The Age of the Renaissance', the revival of interest in the Arabic language and in Arabic literature, including that of the pre-Islamic period, a project with a strong commitment to preparing the Arab world for secularism. Later Arab nationalists established a special link between the particular character of the Arabs and the fact that the Quran, the word of Allah, was written in Arabic: thus Abd al-Rahman al-Kawakibi, a Syrian cleric working in Cairo, writing in 1931 of the twenty-six ways in which the Arabs were distinguished, argued that the Arabs, by dint of language and of religion, should lead other nations to Islam.[31] In Turkey the emergence of Turkish nationalism was associated with a similar 'rediscovery'. In both the Arab and Turkish cases this combined with the attempt, a modular requirement of modern nationalism, to cleanse the language of foreign accretions – Persian in the case of both Arabic and Turkish, Arabic too in the case of Turkish.[32] Within Zionism, the recreation of a modernised Hebrew, in any objective philological terms a new language, by Eliezer

---

[29] In the fine words of a medieval Arab historian: 'There are three things that bring joy to the heart of the Arab – the birth of a son, the foaling of a mare, and the arrival of a poet.'

[30] Torture, in the form of acts of cruelty against individuals, has always existed, but its incidence as a means of state control and deterrence is also a product of modern politics because of rising popular pressures from below.

[31] Abd al-Rahman al-Kawakibi, 'The Excellences of the Arabs', in Sylvia Haim, ed., *Arab Nationalism: an Anthology*, Berkeley: University of California Press, 1964, pp. 78–80.

[32] Geoffrey Lewis, *The Turkish Language Reform: a Catastrophic Success*, Oxford: Oxford University Press, 1999.

Ben-Yahuda from the early 1890s onwards was, after initial hesitation, to become an essential part of the rise of a Jewish national movement.[33] These linguistic revivals served, moreover, to promote a renewed interest in the written word – with the emergence of a national press in these languages, and of a modern literature. This was, of course, something lived by each national movement as particular to it; but seen world-wide from the mid-nineteenth century onwards, it was very much part of the broader nationalist upsurge. This was a transnationalism of form and content in which groups in one country drew inspiration from others – every nationalism was in this sense modular.[34] This was not a free-floating 'renaissance', an autonomous cultural process: it was connected to the possibilities for power, in political terms and in control of natural resources, which independence, the ultimate goal of most nationalists, appeared to offer.

In the post-1945 period the Middle East, as elsewhere, entered the epoch of the radio. From outside the region, the BBC, Voice of America, Radio Moscow and a host of other stations broadcast to the region, although in entertainment terms for the Arab world one of the most influential external stations was that of at best a very tiny state indeed, almost a one-street NGO, Radio Monte Carlo. Within the region, the Egyptian revolution of 1952 led to the launching of Saut al-Arab, 'the Voice of the Arabs', a station through which Nasser appealed to all Arabs and which did more than anything to spread his message. His followers listened to the denunciations of imperialism, Zionism, Arab reaction and the like, while his opponents complained. 'Why do you fill the atmosphere with abuse? . . . Why do you shout over the microphone with every discordant voice?' enquired, in a critical poem, the Imam of Yemen in 1959.[35] Not only political propaganda and news, but also music served to attract listeners: the most popular Arab of the twentieth century was, arguably, not a political figure, nor a man, but the female Egyptian singer Umm Kulthum, whose broadcasts on Thursday evenings were listened to throughout the Arab world; when she died in 1975 it was said that more people had attended her funeral than that of Nasser five years before.[36] Her songs celebrated the tensions of love, but also, implicitly, those of

---

[33] When I asked one Israeli how, given that Hebrew was a sacred language, they could use swear words, he replied: 'No problem: we use Arabic and Russian.' No such inhibition has, of course, ever affected Arabic itself.

[34] Benedict Anderson, *Imagined Communities: Reflections on the Origin and Spread of Nationalism*, second edition, London: Verso, 1991.

[35] Said al-Attar, *Le Sous-développement économique et social du Yemen*, Algiers: Editions Tiers Monde, 1964, pp. 83–4.

[36] Virginia Danielson, *The Voice of Egypt: Umm Kulthum, Arabic Song, and Egyptian Society in the Twentieth Century*, London: University of Chicago Press, 1997.

modern Arab nationalism.[37] Other states also sought to win influence through the airwaves. Thus Kol Israel commanded an audience in Iran and in the Arab world, partly because its news tended to be more accurate than that of Arab state stations, partly because it employed Jewish émigrés to produce humorous and literary programmes.

The radio was, of course, also available to opposition groups, but, given the technology involved, only with the agreement of other Middle Eastern states. Thus Arab states would permit the PLO to have radio facilities, but in conformity with their policies. During the Cold War communist parties broadcast from the Soviet bloc, again in conformity with their hosts. In the 1980s there were over thirty opposition or clandestine radio stations operating in the region, some with the favour of Arab states, some run by western intelligence agencies.[38] Communist parties – from Turkey, Iran, Iraq – had use of facilities in the Soviet bloc, Berlin or East Berlin, while other left sects, intermittently, found a voice on Radio Tirana and Radio Beijing. Where no state was willing to provide it with radio facilities, an opposition group was limited; despite claims by many in Iran that the Persian service of the BBC had brought down the Shah in 1979, this station had pursued a cautious policy. During the revolutionary period from September 1978 to February 1979, news of the opposition movement was broadcast, but Khomeini's voice in interview was only broadcast once by the BBC Persian Service, in 1978. Less controllable was, from the 1970s onwards,

[37] E.g. *Thawrat al-shikk*, 'The Upsurge of Doubt', written by a Saudi prince, and *Uli Zaman*, 'Bring Back the Old Times', a taunt to a nostalgic former lover.

[38] The clandestine radio was a feature above all of the Cold War years. Prominent among the stations broadcast to the region were those of the Persian Tudeh Party (Peik-i Iran), which broadcast from Baku, in Soviet Azerbaijan, of the Omani guerrilla movement (Saut al-Thawra, 'the Voice of the Revolution'), which broadcast from Aden, and of various other stations promoted by left-wing (Egypt, South Yemen, Iraq) and right-wing (Saudi Arabia) regimes. During the Suez crisis of 1956 the British government, abusing the BBC Arabic Service staff, set up a covert station in Cyprus, Muhattat al-Sharq al-Adna, 'the Station of the Near East', in an attempt to confuse the Arab public. A BBC listing of the mid-1980s gave more than thirty such stations. Their role was parallel to, but probably much less influential than, the over transmissions of the major powers to the region – Voice of America, BBC, Deutsche Welle, Radio Moscow, to which were joined, for brief periods of regional aspiration, such competitors as Radio Tirana and, for music and news, Radio Monte Carlo. One radio station that commanded a considerable audience in the Arab world was Kol Israel, if only for the political jokes which it retailed. Among the more bizarre was a short-lived transmitter named 'The Voice of the Satanic Verses' that came on air in 1989 during the controversy over Khomeini's condemnation of the novel of that name written by Salman Rushdie. Khomeini had denounced the novel for blasphemous and obscene passages, so the promoters of this station, believed to be based in Iraq, and having a good sense for the curiosity of the Iranian listening public, took to broadcasting the most salacious sections of the novel interspersed with which they delivered their political message. In the 1990s the clandestine radio went into decline: the end of the Cold War, and the emergence of new information technologies, notably the Internet, reduced the role of such transmitters.

the cassette, a technology suited to the mass distribution of speeches through underground channels; this was the ideal instrument for the Islamist movement, with sermons and denunciations of corruption being made widely available. Here the Islamic revolution in Iran was able to make good use of the opportunity. The late 1980s and 1990s brought a further development, that of broadcasts from independent bases, notably western Europe. Several Arab satellite TV stations were set up in London – MBC, al-Jazira and ANN. Opposition groups, including the Turkish PKK and the Iranian Mujahidin-i Khalq, established, or gained control of, such broadcast outlets in Britain and Germany.

Objective reporting was not the priority here. What this multiplicity of voices did was greatly to sharpen the level of political awareness within Middle Eastern states as discussions, ideas, debates and, not least with TV, images of conflict were brought onto the screens of viewers of the region. The most spectacular case of this was during the outbreak of the second Palestinian *intifadha* in the autumn of 2000 when, for the first time, and in emphatic mode, with solemn commentary and emotional music, the resistance of Palestinian society to Israeli occupation was reported night after night on television screens. One clip in particular, showing the death by Israeli bullets of a twelve-year-old boy, Mohammad al-Durra, in October 2001, was repeatedly transmitted on Arabic television. This served to mobilise Arab public opinion in a manner hitherto not seen and, in so doing, to constrain the policies of states themselves.

Here apparently was a transnational media world, of political influence and autonomy, that challenged the power of states. It made frontiers permeable to external political and cultural influences. While some states, Syria for example, sought to ban satellite dishes or restricted Internet access, such attempts to control these intrusions were, to a considerable degree, unsuccessful. Yet while the Middle East was, especially from the early 1990s onwards, thereby opened up to a range of influences and flows of information, there were, as far as the relative powers of states and independent transnational actors are concerned, two important qualifications to this picture, of a media-based transnationalism.[39] First, much of the broadcasting carried out in and to the Middle East remained under the control of states. This applied not only to state-run radio and television services, but also to the patronage by states of the opposition groups that worked in this field. Whatever the pretence, the reality was that any group operating from a Middle Eastern capital was an arm of the state that gave it the relevant facilities. When the group defied this state, or when the

[39] *The Middle East Journal*, vol. 54, no. 3, Summer 2000, 'Special Issue: The Information Revolution'.

state's policy changed, then the radio station was silenced, often from one day to the other. The same applied, albeit in less overt form, to the satellite TV stations operating from western Europe: all the major Arab stations based in London or Paris were owned by prominent political figures from Middle Eastern states and followed the appropriate guidelines. MBC TV, based in London in the 1990s, was owned by Khalid bin Sultan, a Saudi prince and Minister of Defence at the time of the Kuwait war of 1991 (whose book on the Kuwait war was banned in GCC countries), al-Jazira TV was owned by the Amir of Qatar, and so forth. In 1996 the BBC Arabic TV service, a supposedly independent channel enjoying the protection of the British state, was closed immediately because its Saudi transmission partner, Orbit TV, owned by the al-Mawarid Group, disapproved of a programme, already shown on domestic BBC, that it had broadcast on Saudi Arabia. What was true of satellite TV was equally true of the press: the main Arab newspapers produced in Europe were, as with the TV stations, owned and controlled by political interests in the region.[40] They were displaced from, but not out of control of, the states concerned. The formula was clear: apparently daring and critical international coverage, evasion or plain censorship of domestic affairs of the founder state.[41]

Here a Middle Eastern mirage of freedom needs correction. Beyond the ordinary control of states, a diversity of voices cannot in itself be equated with democratisation or even liberty. The very fact of a multiplicity of voices on Arab TV does not guarantee freedoms. It is mistaken to confuse plurality of voices, and information, with a genuinely free or freer audience. Moreover, the transmission of any information, or symbol, depends not only on the transmitter, but also on the reception. The impact of information or other programmes is, in large measure, a function of the culture and outlook of those who access it. In a region where

[40] It is in this context worth noting that perhaps the most spectacular case of a press leak in modern Middle East politics, that by the Lebanese paper *al-Shira'a* in November 1986 of secret US–Iranian contacts, later known as 'Irangate', was also a result of state calculation: the paper was controlled by Syria and the leak was either a deliberate act by the Syrian government itself, or the result of factional differences within the Syrian and/or Iranian regimes. The one thing this leak did *not* reflect was independent investigative initative by the paper concerned.

[41] The Arab Gulf press is rich in reports on western slander of Islam and the details of the politics of Nepal and the Philippines, but in other respects limits prevail: the 'red lines' included corruption, dynastic succession problems, the rise of *salafis*, treatment of migrant workers. In 2000 a world-renowned sociologist was invited to a Gulf university to lecture on globalisation. It was his first time in the Arab world. As the plane came in to land, two colleagues, with some knowledge of the region, advised him how to proceed: give the standard public lecture on globalisation, but with three items removed – secularisation, the decline of the nuclear family and new transgressive sexual identities.

free discussion is not permitted, where because of censorship suspicion and conspiracy theory are rife, and where there is a widespread disbelief in the integrity of any source of information, a plethora of broadcast or newspaper outlets does not correct for the prejudices of those who access them. It may well reinforce these prejudices, producing a carnival of non-sense and myth. Producers, anchormen and funders are well versed in how to take advantage of this. What this yields may be not a more open, or autonomous, informational space, but a plurality of half-truths and competing state or opposition ideologies. Conspiracy theory also flourishes in such an environment. The preconditions for a more open, questioning, cultural and information life lie as much as anything in the domestic conditions prevailing within a country – a democratic culture, the rule of law, and a free, and critical, spirit in education. Here the priorities of the modern state reign supreme; it is, moreover, difficult to blame all this on the 'west', though this has not stopped many from trying.

(v)   Diasporas

Diasporas, that is communities of people originating in one country and living in another, are the quintessential 'transnational' grouping.[42] They are transnational in the straightforward senses that their activities – social, economic, political – are independent of states and cut across frontiers. They are also transnational in the more abstract sense, to which 'post-modernism' draws attention, that their sense of location, time, identity may be more multi-layered and fluid than that of either their fellow nationals at home or the society within which they reside. Here again some forms of transnationalism may pre-date modernity. Such communities have, in some respects, been a feature of Middle Eastern society for centuries, if not millennia: the Prophet Muhammad, himself a merchant involved in long-distance trade, began his political challenge to the rulers of Mecca by engaging in a flight, a *hijra*, to the neighbouring city of Medina; communities of traders, religious disciples or soldiers from one city or region residing in others were very much part of the urban culture of the Islamic empires. The cosmopolitan intelligentsia of modern cities – Cairo, Tangiers, Istanbul, Beirut, Baghdad, to a lesser extent Tehran – were the product of centuries of such movement and interaction. In an extreme case, the dispersal of Jews around the world that is attributed to the destruction of the Second Temple in AD 70 formed part of such a transnational exile, so much so that the community in the country of historic origin virtually disappeared. In the case of the Muslim world,

---

[42] Vertovec and Cohen, *Migration*.

some Jewish communities were long-established, such as those in Iraq and Iran which dated back over two thousand years, and were the longest continuous communities in the world, while others were Jewish communities expelled from Spain in the sixteenth century, what were later termed Sephardim.[43]

In the modern politics of the Middle East diasporas ranging from a few individuals to larger communities have been crucial in the politics of the home country: the rise of Turkish, Armenian and Iranian nationalism in the late nineteenth century is closely related to the activities, in publishing and political engagement, of exiles in Europe. Those who have migrated for economic reasons – the Lebanese from the latter part of the nineteenth century, the Yemenis from the early decades of the twentieth – have maintained links with their homeland that have also contributed politically, as well as financially. The first mosques and the first Arabic newspaper in Britain (al-Salaam) were founded by Yemeni exiles in the 1940s.[44] The rise of modern guerrilla nationalisms in the Middle East has also been located to a considerable degree within émigré communities. Thus after the defeat of 1948 Palestinian nationalism began to revive in Lebanon, Egypt and Kuwait, amongst Palestinians studying and working there: al-Fath was founded in 1957 in Cairo by diaspora Palestinians resident in several states. In the showdown at the end of the Algerian war in 1962, it was the exiled, regular, army of Oujda, in Morocco, that prevailed over the forces of the interior.

The origins of the guerrilla movement in the Omani province of Dhofar, which fought the Sultan's forces between 1965 and 1975, lay in the Dhofari emigration in the Gulf. In the 1980s and 1990s the PKK was able to sustain its activities in Turkey in part because of the contribution of finances from Kurds living in western Europe, who gave a percentage of their earnings to the organisation (as did Eritreans in Saudi Arabia to their liberation fronts). Every significant political movement of opposition within the Middle East has sought to mobilise support in exile, be it from students, as in the time of the Iranian opposition to the Shah, or migrant workers, as has been the case with both the secular left and Islamist groups in the 1980s and 1990s. An apparent exception, the Iranian revolution was not, in the main, based on the diaspora, but

---

[43] The term 'Sephardi', from a Hebrew word used for Spain, has come to have a much broader usage in modern Israeli and Jewish parlance, to encompass all eastern Jews. But as the examples of Baghdad and Iran show, this is an inaccurate usage as these communities did not came from Spain after the late fifteenth-century expulsion, but were established much earlier in the time of the Babylonian captivity.

[44] Fred Halliday, Arabs in Exiles: Yemeni Migrants in Urban Britain, London: I. B. Tauris, 1992.

Ayatollah Khomeini, by dint of his being in exile, was able more freely to direct the movement at home. In the 1990s al-Qa'ida recruited some key personnel amongst Arabs living in Europe and the USA.

To identify the role of diasporas is, however, not to argue that these émigré communities have become in some way the dominant factor in the opposition movements affecting their country. In the case of Zionism up to the establishment of a political leadership in Palestine in the 1920s, or later the Palestinian movement after 1948, this may for a long time have been so; in these cases the diaspora led the home community. In the main, however, control has lain with the political leadership located in the home country, very much as it has done with other homeland–diaspora linkages, such as that between Irish republicanism and its support community in the USA and Britain. Indeed, as the home-based movement becomes stronger, it comes more and more to direct, and exert control and surveillance over, the diaspora. What may appear in the country of emigration as an autonomous, transnational, multi-local community is, in terms of political orders, flows of money and general control, very much a sub-section of the organisation at home; the latter, as is only natural, does not leave much to chance. Here the PKK and al-Qa'ida were no exception.

States too are far from being indifferent to diasporas. In the first place, precisely because of the activities, real or potential, of opposition groups within the exile communities, states, through their embassies, not least their visa sections and education attachés, seek to monitor what is taking place. Middle Eastern states are not slow to protest to host countries about what they consider to be unfriendly or illegal activities by their own nationals abroad. This political concern is matched by an economic one – the wish to mobilise émigré funds for domestic financial needs, be this a development fund or project, or, as is too often the case with states without oil revenues, the current expenses of the head of state and his associates. Many states set up organisations to 'represent', but also control, those living abroad; these may be linked formally, or informally, to ministries at home. Much effort is put into inviting back delegations of visiting émigrés and publicising their loyalty to the homeland. On the other side of the coin, those who do not conform in exile may not receive re-entry visas. In the case of Israel, because of the historic direction of migration and political influence, this involves a particularly difficult interaction. Here the Jewish diaspora clings to a considerable degree to its claim on the homeland, while within Israel itself those who chose not to live within the state, diaspora Jews, are regarded, despite the fact that they still claim to be Zionists, as having a decreasing claim on the political, cultural and religious life of the state itself.

Cultural and 'post-modern' approaches are right to draw attention to diasporas, but they run the risk of downplaying the material factors shaping the relation to home communities. Diasporas are, like other transnational phenomena, not just forms of identity and hybridity; they are also social contexts in which the conflicts over wealth and power remain central, and in which those challenging states seek to build support even as states, therefore, seek to intervene and control. Undoubtedly, the large increase in the numbers of migrants from Middle Eastern states to western Europe and the USA since the 1960s, the availability of new wealth and the spread of more rapid mechanisms of communication have increased the potential, for both non-state actors and states alike, to pursue their goals in the new transnational context. The very multiplicity of linkages with the host society, combined with change at home, has led to new political ideologies, new forms of identity and innovative forms of cultural expression. Yet despite these changes in the scale, and quality, of diaspora–homeland relations, these remain, to a perhaps greater degree than is always acknowledged, subject to more traditional forms of interest and control – state, family, political leadership and, yes, class and gender. Once again, all that is transnational is not so new, so independent of the state, or of already established forms of power.

The state in question: long-term transnationalism

This chapter began by asking not what theories of transnationalism could do for the Middle East, but the reverse. The challenge of assessing the relationship between the inter-state and the transnational in the Middle East is not, therefore, merely a question of adjudicating, on the basis of some at least workable criteria, how far a particular movement, group or process is independent of the influence of states. It also forces, or allows, us to question the very analytic framework in terms of which the question of transnationalism in general is itself posed by IR and sociology. In particular, there are three questions which, for the Middle East as for elsewhere, return the question of transnationalism to the analytic framework of the state.

First, most discussion of transnationalism comes out of a liberal, western context. It assumes a unilinear historical progression, from a world that was divided up into separate national and political entities, and where relations between these were controlled by states, to one where the non-state, or transnational, came to be more significant. Ultimately we are moving towards a new 'global civil society'. This is, in large measure, the assumption of the English-speaking literature that developed from the 1970s onwards; but this may reflect a particular Anglo-Saxon, that is, British and North American, view of the world, not invalid or 'Orientalist', but partial, in so far as these countries, almost alone in the world, have escaped external domination and formation in modern times.[45] Moreover, even for these countries transnationalism is not just a product of the late twentieth century. The timescale, if lengthened, may illustrate a different sequence, one in which, far from transnationalism being *subsequent to* nationalism, the opposite may also apply. In this perspective earlier forms of linkage between societies, of a kind we could term transnational, were in time supplanted by more fragmented, national forms: this would be true in terms of religion, language, migration, political authority. *It is fragmentation by these contemporary states, communities, nations, that is modern, not linkage.*[46] The rise of the modern state involves as much as anything the sundering of links that hitherto existed, over centuries in Europe and North America, over a much more accelerated timescale in the colonial world, including the Middle East, and the promotion of an ideology, nationalism, that normalises and legitimates this division. The same process, of parcellisation of political and social life by modernity, applies to the Middle East.

In the case of the Middle East this alternative historical perspective provides a different insight into the contemporary relation of the inter-state to the transnational. It also opens the question of how far, and in what ways, pre-modern forms of linkage can, in a similar or transformed manner, play a role in contemporary relations, within and between states. One form of pre-modern transnational organisation is the Sufi *tariqa*, 'way' or order, a body of people, active in everyday political and economic life, who, in addition to their religious activities, sometimes co-operate to further their joint interests – for example, trade, employment – in the secular world. Claiming a line of succession back to the Prophet, and originating in the earlier centuries of Islam, but suppressed by the modernising state, these *tariqat* have revived in recent decades to play an important role in the business and political elites in such countries as Turkey and Egypt. Examples of such groups are the Qadiriya, Naqshbandi and Tijaniya. A dramatic area of their revival has been the northern Caucasian region of Russia, especially Chechnya where *tariqat*, loosely linked to those in other independent states, have been influential in the revival of nationalist politics. It is not a question of asserting that the *tariqat* of today are the same as those of centuries before; rather they have survived, and changed,

---

[45] Robert Keohane and Joseph Nye, *Transnational Relations and World Politics*, Cambridge, MA: Harvard University Press, 1970; James N. Rosenau, *The Study of Global Interdependence: Essays on the Transnationalism of World Affairs*, London: Pinter, 1980.

[46] This is what Michael Mann, in *The Sources of Social Power*, has termed 'casing'.

to meet new challenges and opportunities, but within a transnational context.

'Identity', construed as being the way in which an individual asserts primary loyalty and identifies the prime object of legitimacy, provides another dimension of this shift from transnationalism to a more national context. Prior to the modern period, most inhabitants of the Middle East claimed a geographic identity, as coming from Cairo, Beirut or Baghdad, but they identified also in terms of their religion, Islam, Christianity, Judaism, or in terms of the multinational empire to which they belonged. Within the cities of the Ottoman empire there was a cosmopolitan mix of peoples but each community was aware of its own place, and limits.[47] Modern communications and transnational politics served in the nineteenth century and after to create the modern 'Islamic public': this involved a press, links of scholarship and political activism, and a growing sentiment.[48] Yet, the hold of this shared identity, the *umma*, was limited. For all the claims of a pan-Islamic community today, the *umma* has become less important than the identities formed by the modern state system; education, national politics, conscription, not to mention national interest, have eroded, rather than strengthened, this wider identity. Two examples will suffice: in the Iran–Iraq war each national community rallied to its own state leaders; in the 2001 campaign in Afghanistan many Afghans turned against their Arab and Pakistani *jihadi* associates. The revival of appeals to the *umma* by radical Islamists in the 1990s appeared to go against this. But it is questionable how effective these appeals to a transnational *umma* were, and how far their resonance, as on Palestine, was with an enduring *Arab* nationalism, as opposed to dissatisfaction with the rulers of their own particular state. If never completely, the national continued to displace the transnational.

A second issue called into question by the examination of inter-state–transnational relations in the Middle East is that of the boundaries between state and society itself. The distinction inter-state/transnational presupposes that it is clear where the distinction between the two lies. Yet even in more developed societies this boundary may be less clear than is conventionally assumed: business interests, family ties, networks of sentiment and class, lobbies may all play a role. In the Middle East, the distinction may be much harder to draw. Thus in non-democratic countries, the power of the political elite extends into much of the economy, either through appropriation of production or, as in oil-producing

[47] Sami Zubaida 'Cosmpolitanism in the Middle East', in Roel Meijer, *Cosmopolitanism, Identity and Authenticity in the Middle East*, Richmond: Curzon Press, 1999; Albert Hourani, by origin a Lebanese Protestant, once remarked that in the *millet* system you never knew when people would 'turn nasty'.

[48] Reinhard Schulze, *A Modern History of the Islamic World*, London: I. B. Tauris, 2000.

states, through control of rent. A business project that is funded by state revenues is, to a large or total extent, part of the state even if it is legally and in public terms separate. Where there is no income tax, and rather generous credit, the 'private' sector may appear rather less private. In the case of Saudi Arabia, for example, it is a matter of analytic discretion, not fact, whether to include within the state the thousands of princes who received allowances and other concessions from the state. In Saudi Arabia too, there is also the adverse factor of there being such fragmentation within the state, between different princes, that it might be better to talk of not one but, say, seven states. In Israel, the inter-relationship of the state bureaucracy with much of society, including the Histadrut trade unions, the arms industry and the banking sector, long made this distinction harder to draw, even if in more recent times market liberalisation has to some degree modified the picture.[49] The very extension of the state, the lack of a clear non-state economic sector as much as of a clear non-state political sector, thereby renders the very category of the transnational less clear than might at first sight appear.

Beyond these two questions of history and state–society relations, there lies, however, a challenge that confronts all analysis of transnationalism, namely the relation of both forms of actor, state and non-state, to a third dimension of power, that of structures.[50] Structures may include the global financial system, the strategic balance of power, the climate of ideas, the shifting character of technology. In their broadest sense structures determine both state and non-state behaviour and give them meaning and direction. In both historical and contemporary periods, the Middle East has, if anything, been influenced by these structures as much as by any particular states and transnational actors: the shifts in the world economy from the sixteenth century onwards, the rise of the European democratic and liberal movements, imperialism, the spread of nationalism and communism, industrialisation, the end of the Cold War, then globalisation, go a long way to explaining how the Middle East developed. The impact of these structures was addressed in the earlier historical chapters. It is a matter not of reducing what occurred in the Middle East to these external structures, but of showing how they shaped the changes, and outcomes, of the region as a whole.

In contemporary times, the analysis of structures takes the form of what is loosely termed 'globalisation', the increasing volume and rapidity of exchanges in finance, trade and information between societies. Examples of such a process with regard to the Middle East would include the

[49] Keith Kyle and Joel Peters, *Whither Israel? The Domestic Challenges*, London: RIIA and I. B. Tauris, 1993.
[50] For a stimulating overview see Susan Strange, *States and Markets*, London: Pinter, 1988.

variations of the oil market, the movement of millions of dollars in oil rent from the region, the Internet, pressures of privatisation and trade liberalisation, and the clash of ideologies in a post-Cold War world. It is possible to analyse globalisation in terms of the activities of states, which seek to promote or limit changes in terms of their own national interest. Equally, globalisation allows for new and accelerated forms of activity by non-state actors – be these banks, satellite TV companies, terrorist groups, or consultants. Yet both states and non-state actors are themselves to some extent formed by the structures, ever-changing, associated with globalisation – be this shifts in information technology, changes in world demand for oil, or political and media representations of relations between the Muslim and non-Muslim worlds. At the same time, states and non-state actors alike are not superseded by globalisation; they can adapt, and so derive advantage from, as well as adjust to, much of what globalisation involves. The whole process of globalisation rests, moreover, on the underpinning, in terms of military security, rule of law and regulation, provided by states. Yet the latter, and their non-state counterparts, are at the same time forced to respond to changes over which they may have only limited influence. For the Middle East, as for the rest of the world, it is here, in the interaction of state with non-state actors, but within a context shaped by broader structural processes over which each may have only limited influence, that the impact of the transnational, necessarily multi-faceted and ever changing, is decided.

9   International political economy: regional and global

The essential story then, as it appears to me, is that in the process of the economic development of the past 200 years the Arabs have gone through a thorough process of metamorphosis which one may call Westernization. This is not something one can easily describe as good or bad, but it is, to say the least, highly dramatic. Only an economist can respond to this drama by counting the costs and benefits. This response is particularly lamentable since the economist has in his box of tools one particular hypothesis which should have protected him from falling in his error. This is the old hypothesis in welfare economics that it is illegitimate to make interpersonal comparisons of utility, that is, it is not right to compare one person's welfare with that of another . . . I personally dislike the change, which is usually called Westernization, but this is a matter of temperament and I am not going to try to force my opinion on anyone. I will only attract your attention to the fact that this Westernization is itself changing, so much so that it may really have become something very different from what it was when the Arab–Western encounter started 200 years ago.

> Galan Amin, 'Two Centuries of Arab Economic Relations with the
> West: 1798–1997', in Derek Hopwood, ed., *Arab Nation: Arab Nationalism*,
> London: Macmillan, 2000

In the kingdom of international political economy

The formation and current condition of the modern Middle East exemplify even more in the interaction of political and economic factors. Whether or not the Muslim Middle East is *dar-al-islam*, the House of Islam, it is most certainly, in the sense of a domain where economics and politics interlock, the kingdom of international political economy.[1] In pre-modern times an earlier version of this was evident, be it in the role

---

[1] For general background see Alan Richards and John Waterbury, *A Political Economy of the Middle East*, second edition, Boulder, CO: Westview Press, 1998; Clement Henry and Robert Springborg, *Globalization and the Politics of Development in the Middle East*, Cambridge: Cambridge University Press, 2001; Hassan Hakimian and Ziba Moshaver, eds., *The State and Global Change: the Political Economy of Transition in the Middle East and North Africa*, London: Curzon Press, 2000.

of the merchant class and trade routes in the early history of Islam or of the military landowners of the major Muslim empires. Economic factors shape, and underpin, all political systems, pre-modern as well as modern, but in the case of the Islamic Middle East this is reflected, perhaps more than in any other major civilisation, in religion itself. Islam does not just permit trade and property, it positively enjoins it.[2] The beliefs of other trading communities – Armenian or Maronite Christians, Jews, Zoroastrians – have, on the evidence, not inhibited commercial activity either.

Political economy asserts an indissoluble interconnection of political factors – states, conflict, ideology – with the economic – production, finance, technology. It is, indeed, only since the late nineteenth century that the conceptual, and academic, separation between them has been enforced. In every region of the world economic issues, domestic and international, are inseparable from politics. Yet this is perhaps nowhere more true then in the Middle East. In republics and monarchies alike politics and political aspiration, not to say fantasy, are the key, *inter alia*, to the economic projects, supposedly 'planned', 'constructed' and the like, which are promulgated by sometimes megalomaniac rulers through their industrialisation and other programmes. In a story that could stand for all modern Arab and Iranian rulers, the distinguished Palestinian economist Yusuf Sayigh retailed the story of a meeting he had, in the mid-1970s, with Iraqi President Saddam Hussein. Saddam wanted to be told about 'economic development' and Sayigh, summoned with a group of other visiting Arab economists late at night to an unknown destination in Baghdad, tried to respond. He soon realised that this was a waste of time: the president had no education with which to comprehend the issues involved and only looked at economic factors in so far as they could strengthen the power of his state.[3] Its economic resources enabled Iraq to play the role it did. What was true of Saddam is true to a considerable degree of other Middle Eastern rulers: whether it be the Shah's drive for a 'great civilisation' in the 1970s or the lavishly funded but ultimately unachievable projects of Gulf rulers for higher education, the same factors, of elite vanity, manipulation of state–society relations, and inter-state competition, apply.[4] This is, however, far from saying that politics and economics can be dissolved into each

[2] Maxime Rodinson, *Islam and Capitalism*, London: Allen Lane, 1974, pp. 16–17.
[3] Professor Yusuf Sayigh, conversation with the author, London, *c.* 1985.
[4] A similar pattern of behaviour can be observed far from the Middle East, and its supposed singularity, in the oil-producing state of Venezuela. Here, when faced with rising opposition in 2003–4, the radical populist president Hugo Chavez, elected in 1998, launched a programme of radical state expenditure, using the revenues of PDVSA, the state oil company, for spending on health, education and other social services. These programmes,

other: if economic considerations alone predominated, then the degree of
co-operation between Middle East states would be all the greater.
However, despite fitful attempts at economic integration, the states of
the region resist, for political reasons, any real attempt at unity. What is
evident, by contrast, is how the interaction is often contradictory, how in
particular political concerns override economic ones, but in a relationship
that is none the less intense for that.

Historians, even some IR specialists, like to talk in general terms of
'the expansion of the west', or the interaction of 'Islam' and the 'west'.
But these are more often than not vague if not misleading terms, con-
cealing the concerns of military power and commercial profit that have
driven the subjugation and reconstruction of the non-European world
since 1600.[5] The western impact on the Ottoman empire in the nineteenth century was determined by the political economy of imperialism,
western imperial strategy on the one side, and concern for trade, debt
repayment and raw materials on the other. As discussed in chapter 3, this
expansionary process was multi-dimensional: no reduction to one concern – strategy – or another – profit – is possible. In modern times two
dates stand out: 1869, the year of the opening of the Suez Canal, which
gave the region a new strategic importance; 1914, when the British navy
converted to oil. After World War I the Middle East became important
because of its reserves of oil (first discovered at Masjid-i Suleiman, Iran,
in 1908), a factor that led to closer integration of the region with the outside world. During the Cold War, strategy and a political commitment to
allies in that struggle (notably Israel, Iran) reinforced this integration. In
the 1980s and 1990s other dimensions of this international political economy developed. Sanctions were imposed on certain states (Iran, Iraq,
Libya) by the west, and support was provided in financial and material
terms to others (notably Israel and Egypt). Egypt received 25 per cent
of its total food supply from the USA, including up to 50 per cent of its
wheat and flour.[6] In the latter part of the twentieth century, and again

termed *missiones*, served to win him popularity amongst the population and survive a
referendum calling for his resignation in August 2004. It is estimated that such expenditures rose 70 per cent in 2003 and over 90 per cent in 2004. This was a most dramatic
case of the 'distributive state' in action: in an echo of his Middle Eastern counterparts,
Chavez also made many references to the will of God and to a nineteenth-centry monastic
campaign against the devil, but, for all his military manner and demagogy, he continued,
in the main, to respect formal democratic norms, and maintain good commercial relations
with the USA.
[5] The narrow 'economic' theory of imperialism has been disproved, most notably in the
work of the economic historian P. K. O'Brien. The problem with much more recent
political or cultural analysis is that it has forgotten the economic, i.e. profit, altogether.
[6] Richards and Waterbury, *A Political Economy*, p. 147; M. A. Cook, ed., *Studies in the
Economic History of the Middle East*, Oxford: Oxford University Press, 1970.

for political reasons, relations between the states bordering the eastern and southern Mediterranean and Europe came to be concentrated in the Barcelona process, formalised in 1995.[7] This process, a way to reconstitute an economic space sundered since the fall of the Roman empire in the fifth century AD, was built around a range of social and economic issues that were shared by developed and Middle Eastern states alike – most prominently access to EU markets, the environment and migration. Security, or border insecurity, however, stalked in the wings.

Yet this international inter-relation of politics and economics, and its impact on the policies of external powers to the region, was, particularly with the globalisation of the 1990s, in some respects not matched by a corresponding prominence of the Middle East in the contemporary world economy.[8] In one respect the region *was* of crucial economic importance for the rest of the world: oil. In 2000 the Middle East accounted for almost a third of the world supply and almost two-thirds of known reserves.[9] All indications suggested, despite the talking up, often for political reasons, of Caspian and Russian potential, that this reliance on the Gulf would become *more* important by 2010 and 2020, not least as demand from China, scheduled to rise from 2 mbd in 2000 to 10 mbd in 2020, increased. Moreover, as a consequence of oil revenues unspent, the Gulf producer states also had a large international financial role, in that they had revenue surpluses which they invested in western banks and companies; the size of the latter was unknown, by far the biggest financial or politico-economic secret in the world. But the scale, thousands of billions of US dollars, a third or perhaps a half of US GDP, was not. On other indices, however, the Middle East lay largely outside the global economy. It simply mattered much less. In the post-Cold War context, Middle Eastern economies, with the partial exception of Israel and Turkey, were not participating in that neo-liberal privatisation and opening up of markets, in response to globalisation, seen in eastern Europe, Latin America and the East Asia. Oil production and processing apart, there was, for example, relatively little high technology industrialisation in the Arab world or Iran. In what was widely taken as the key index of participation in the global economy, *exports by these states of manufactured goods* to OECD markets were inconsequential. Closely related to this was the fact that the Middle East was scoring very poorly on the other most visible index of international economic performance, its ability to attract foreign direct investment (FDI): the Arab world and Iran were almost entirely outside of

[7] On the Barcelona process see the journal *Mediterranean Politics, passim.*
[8] Hassan Hakimian, 'From MENA to East Asia and Back: Lessons, Globalization, Crisis and Economic Reform', in Hakinian and Moshaver, *The State and Global Change.*
[9] See Tables 2–4, pp. 336–7.

the flow capital to developing countries that marked the 1990s. Of a total world FDI in 1999 of $900 billion, $200 billion of which went to developing countries, the region, Israel apart, attracted around $8 billion.[10] On the basis of one calculation, in income terms the population of the Middle East and North Africa had, in the early 1990s, per capita annual income little more than a tenth that of the European Community: $2,124 as against $20,738. If Israel and the oil-rich GCC countries were factored out of the figure, the former figure fell to $1,489.[11] On index after index, the region was not just behind but falling further behind not only Europe but also significant parts of the developing world.[12]

If this international political economy characterised the external relations of the region, it also operated *within* the region as well: as a result of the oil boom of the 1970s, substantial flows of money and labour crossed regional frontiers. For their part oil-producing states used money not for an intelligent or managed economic independence of the region but for political purposes, often arbitrary or short-term, through military purchases, and through subsidies to friendly states and client movements. Agricultural self-sufficiency was down, and great changes were limited by the restrictions on water.[13] For example, Iran's repeated attempts, under Shah and Ayatollah alike, to boost agricultural output and non-oil exports showed how difficult this was. Per capita incomes in some countries may have been at high or medium levels in the 1970s and early 1980s in particular; but this apparent growth was largely due to oil revenues, directly earned or reallocated by inter-state flows. These oil revenues too were in long-run real decline, particularly when rising population, as in Saudi Arabia, was taken into account.[14] Indeed, beyond all of these phenomena lay another, inexorable trend, in part a consequence of rising welfare resulting from the oil boom – population growth. This, the one reasonably predictable aspect of the Middle East of the early

---

[10] See Table 6, p. 337.

[11] John Roberts, *Visions and Mirages: the Middle East in a New Era*, Edinburgh: Mainstream, 1995, p. 24.

[12] Arab Human Development Report 2002, Geneva and New York: UNDP, 2002, http://www.undp.org/rbas/ahdr

[13] For an alternative, well-informed analysis of water see Thomas Naff, 'Hazards to Middle East Stability in the 1990s', in Phoebe Marr and William Lewis, eds., *Riding the Tiger: the Middle East Challenge after the Cold War*, Boulder, CO: Westview Press, 1993, and Tony Allan, *The Middle East Water Question: Hydropolitics and the Global Economy*, London: I. B. Tauris, 2001.

[14] On Iranian agriculture under the Shah see Afsaneh Najmabadi, *Land Reform and Social Change in Iran*, Salt Lake City: University of Utah Press, 1987; Fred Halliday, *Iran: Dictatorship and Development*, Harmondsworth: Penguin, 1978, chapter 5, 'Agricultural Development'; Keith McLoughlin, *The Neglected Garden: the Politics and Ecology of Agriculture in Iran*, London: I. B. Tauris, 1998; Richards and Waterbury, eds., *A Political Economy*, chapter 6, 'Water and Food Security'.

twenty-first century, did not bode well for stability, or equity, within or between states.[15]

As the 1990s and 2000s wore on, this lack of external competitiveness was therefore matched, and compounded, by a growing *internal* regional socio-economic crisis. Within these countries themselves factors of an economic and social kind came to exert a growing pressure on states: demographic rise, pressure on employment, urbanisation all contributed to political tension, to shifts in state policy and to the strength of contestatory movements, now of a mainly religious orientation with, nonetheless, material issues like employment or trade rules underpinning them. The most pressing question facing states in the region was that of how to manage the pressures from below for employment and distribution of wealth. The growing requirement, from international financial institutions (IFIs) and domestic opinion in the Gulf, was for *shafafia*, 'transparency', that is, on where the money had gone, and where current income from oil and investments was going. Only one thing was beyond dispute: no one but a handful of the elite knew, and they were most certainly not saying.

This set of trends in society was accompanied by a paralysis of political will and a lack of vision at the top of the state. One official of a radical Arab state, faced with violent Islamist opposition at home, summed up the situation to me as follows: 'We have been in power for thirty years, and have run out of ideas. Everyone knows this. The opposition also has no ideas, but people do not know this yet. We need to find a way to employ 10 million young people, and fast.' Across the region, the state–society relation, which had on successive occasions in the twentieth century exploded, most spectacularly in Iran in 1979, remained the decisive concern of states. For a number of states oil had bought time, but it had also exacerbated problems; in some countries (for example, Bahrain, Oman) declining output, and the challenge of other non-Middle Eastern producers, was initiating a post-oil epoch for which the region was ill-prepared – according to one Scottish expert, real per capita income from oil in 1995 was around one-eighth that of its peak in 1980.[16] Amid rapidly expanding populations, the possibilities of employment were falling: in the 1990s national labour forces were growing at an average of 3.2 per cent per year, the highest rate anywhere in the developing world.[17] Thus, the state apparatuses that had controlled the region for the previous decades were facing increased pressure from within, for transparency in fiscal and economic matters, even as they sought more and more to transfer

---

[15] See Table 1, p. 335.   [16] Roberts, *Visions*, p. 202.
[17] Richards and Waterbury, *A Political Economy*, p. 91.

onto their populations the costs of maintaining their political and social systems. The glamour of oil of the 1970s and 1980s, itself transient, had therefore concealed a set of tensions, and degradations, that boded ill for the future, domestically and internationally.[18] And all of this in countries that had, by the standards of the rest of the third world of the latter part of the twentieth century, enjoyed a marvellous windfall in the most important of normal constraints on growth, capital, had levied no income or meaningful corporation tax, and had greatly expanded welfare systems. Incomes had, for a time and for some, risen. Expectations had risen even further. This was, on any normal comparative social science criteria, a recipe for catastrophe.[19]

Onslaughts of the world market: the impact of modernity

If, therefore, there was *one* pervasive and ultimately constitutional 'Middle East crisis', it lay here, in inter- and intra-state political economy, not in Palestine or Iraq. The roots of the Middle Eastern economic impasses lay in the pattern of incorporation into the world market in regard both to the economies themselves, in my phrase 'differential integration', and also in the very pattern of formation of these modern states.[20] As discussed in chapters 3 and 4, the formation of the contemporary Middle Eastern economies has been determined by the rise of an expansive European modernity as a whole, and in particular by their interaction over the previous two centuries with the industrialised states of Europe, in large degree since 1798.[21]

[18] Jahangir Amuzegar, *Managing the Oil Wealth: OPEC's Windfalls and Pitfalls*, London: I. B. Tauris, 1999; Roger Owen and Sevket Pamuk, *A History of Middle East Economies in the Twentieth Century*, chapter 9, 'The States of the Iranian Peninsula 1946–1990'; Nawaf Obaid, *The Oil Kingdom at 100: Petroleum Policymaking in Saudi Arabia*, Washington, DC: The Washington Institute of Near East Policy, 2000.

[19] For one informed, if alarmist, warning see Cassandra, 'The Impending Crisis in Egypt', *Middle East Journal*, vol. 49, no. 1, 1998.

[20] This draws on an earlier discussion: Fred Halliday, 'The Middle East and the Politics of Differential Integration', in Toby Dodge and Richard Higgott, eds., *Globalization and the Middle East: Islam, Economy, Society and Politics*, London: Royal Institute of International Affairs, 2002. This is arguably preferable to the more classic term 'imperialism', first because the latter is now associated, with a particular assumption of the global market as inhibiting development, something that understates the contradictory, in some ways dynamic, impact of capitalism; and secondly because it is in twentieth-century political discourse associated with a now discredited view of historical progress, with which an inevitable 'anti-imperialism' carries progressive meaning.

[21] Roger Owen, *The Middle East in the World Economy 1800–1914*, London: I. B. Tauris, 1993, and Charles Issawi, 'Middle East Economic Development, 1815–1914: the General and the Specific', in Albert Honrahi, Philip Khoury and Mary Wilson, eds.,

The 'rise of the west', an indisputably unique event, was, in economic as in military, as well as in philosophical terms, a rather recent phenomenon.[22] Prior to the eighteenth century the economies of the Middle East, and of the major Islamic empires, had for centuries been more than able to hold their own against their competitors, Europe to the west, and India and China to the east: for all the exactions of despotic rulers and recurrent disease alike, they traded on equal terms, fed their populations, developed textile and other urban mills, produced a sophisticated and diverse artistic output, and most importantly, sustained strong and militarily effective states. All this was to change, however, with the industrial revolution in Europe at the end of the eighteenth and beginning of the nineteenth century: while the Ottoman empire enjoyed considerable economic growth in the nineteenth century, it was unable to compete with the west, economically or militarily. Istanbul sought, in the face of challenges from Russia, France, Austria and Britain, to modernise its state and economy, but, as in Manchu China, this was a fitful and unsuccessful process; the verdict of world history, slow in execution as it may have been, was inexorable. No Middle Eastern state, indeed no other state in the world, was able to duplicate what Japan had achieved in turning a non-western state and economy into one that was internationally competitive. With the cataclysms of revolution and war that burst over the world in 1900–20, and as the Chinese numarilly fell in the east, and the Romanovs, Habsburgs and Wittelsbachs in the west, so too did the Ottoman and Qajar domains in the Middle East.

Already by 1904, when the Japanese were able to defeat Russia and established their claim for inclusion into the ranks of the most powerful modern states, parts of the Middle East had succumbed to economic pressure from outside. Oman, in the early nineteenth century a major maritime power in the Indian Ocean, had in 1856 lost its African territories and its trade, remaining formally independent, but in effect becoming till 1970 a backwater of the British empire. As the nineteenth century wore on, the Ottoman empire, like China, became afflicted with debt, its trade and customs administered by western nominees; the Ottomans declared themselves bankrupt in 1875, the Egyptians in 1876, both declarations being followed by increased external control, in the Egyptian case this

---

The Modern Middle East, London: I. B. Tauris, 1992. On the political economy of regional states see the pioneering study of Simon Bromley, *Rethinking Middle East Politics*, Cambridge: Polity Press 1994.

[22] On pre-modern economic structures see Rodinson, *Islam and Capitalism*; Marshall Hodgson, *The Venture of Islam*, vol. III: *The Gunpowder Empires and Modern Times*, London: University of Chicago Press, 1974, 'The Islamic Heritage in the Modern World'.

leading in 1882 to direct occupation. The imposition of external, western financial control was more a matter of economical, specifically fiscal, than of direct political and military rule, and in some respects prefigures the power of IFIs in the late twentieth century.[23] But political reason was not long in coming. In Iran, from the 1870s onwards, nationalist sentiment grew in response to external economic intrusion. The first significant chapter of modern Iranian nationalism was written by the country-wide protest in 1891 at a concession given to an English firm authorising it to monopolise the processing and marketing of tobacco in the country. The Anglo-French invasion of Egypt threw up the first icon of modern Arab nationalism, Urabi Pasha.

In so far as the very imperfect statistics allow judgement at all, it would seem that the record of this impact of modernity on the Middle East was, however, not one of unrelenting or general decline.[24] In the nineteenth century the textile industries of the Middle Eastern cities were facing increasing competition from western imports, but also higher demand for silk products. Moreover, in some areas agricultural output – cotton above all, but also cereals and tobacco – grew in response to European demand. In three particular respects, moreover, the external European impact not only put pressure on but to a significant degree transformed society. First, along a wide swathe of the Mediterranean coast, running from Morocco in the west to Palestine in the south-east, settlers from Europe were establishing themselves in control of the lands or in domination of urban finance and trade; this was particularly the case in Algeria, and after 1900, in Egypt, Libya and Palestine. In contrast to Latin America, Africa or Australasia, these settlers came not so much from the colonial power itself as from other Mediterranean states – Italy, Greece, Malta – whereas in Palestine the settlers were mainly from the eastern European Jewish diaspora. Secondly, in one country, Egypt, the loss of American cotton supplies to British mills, as a result of the US civil war, led in the late 1860s to the transformation of much of the countryside to meet European demand for cotton.[25] Elsewhere, notably in Syria, there were significant exports to Europe of wheat, fruit and tobacco. Finally, this agricultural change coincided with the opening of the Suez Canal in 1869, an event that bound the Middle East into the communications system of the British empire in an era of growing world trade. The Middle East was, therefore, given the limits of colonisation and the lack of plantations or mining, less incorporated into the world economy than many

[23] Owen, *The Middle East*, chapters 4 and 8 (the Ottomans), chapters 5 and 9 (Egypt).
[24] Ibid., chapter 12, 'A Century of Economic Growth and Transformation', 'Conclusion'.
[25] Roger Owen, *Cotton and the Egyptian Economy 1820–1914*, Oxford: Oxford University Press, 1964.

other areas of the colonial world, but by 1900 it had nonetheless been profoundly affected, in political and economic terms, by the latter's impact on it.

The aftermath of World War I and the establishment of the modern state system provided a context for much greater and more diverse external intervention in the economies of the region, as well as for their modern separation from each other. The fragmentation of the Middle Eastern economies into distinct boxes is, as with the map of 'nations', a product of externally imposed modernity. In Turkey, and to a lesser extent Iran, independent military regimes promoted industrialisation, above all for reasons of arms production and 'national', that is, state, security. Yet, in the main, as far as economies were concerned, the post-1918 colonial impact was limited, focusing on the construction of effective state machineries, and on some selected development projects; with the exception of Egypt, Palestine and Algeria, where European colonisation affected urban and rural areas alike, there was no major transformation of the agricultural character of these societies, let alone any promotion of industrialisation. The Middle East exported to Europe certain traditional products – carpets, handicrafts. It did not, however, serve, as did Latin America, India, Indo-china, as a major source of primary products for European consumption, such that its own agriculture would be transformed by the external demand. In sum it can be said that, while the transformative *political* impact of British and French colonialism on the region was considerable, before and after 1918, in the institutions, administrative and coercive, it founded and in the animosities it fuelled, the *economic* impact was, with the exception of the process begun in Egypt in the 1860s and the Europeanisation of parts of Palestine, far less.

The curses of black gold

The one exception to the enduring pattern of global marginalisation in the late twentieth century was, of course, oil, the basis of global industrial activity across the twentieth-century world and the largest commodity, in value terms, traded in the world market.[26] Middle Eastern oil was discovered first in southern Iran in 1908, then in Iraq, and Arabian Peninsula countries; production in Saudi Arabia began in 1939, in Kuwait in 1946. In the late 1990s the Middle East accounted for 30 per cent of world output, but 65 per cent of world proven reserves (the latter, be it said, a far

[26] Peter Odell, *Oil*, Harmondsworth: Penguin, first edition 1970, and subsequent editions. For a Saudi view of the industry's political economy in the 1970s see Alawi D. Kayal, *The Control of Oil: East–West Rivalry in the Persian Gulf*, London: Kegan Paul, 2002.

from precise figure). While producers outside the region appeared, these
tended to produce oil that was more expensive than that of the Middle
East, and also to be drawing on wells that had a much shorter prospec-
tive life: in 2000, the reserve/production ratio in the Middle East was
88 years, compared with a North American ratio of 16 years and a
Latin American one of 37.[27]

Oil certainly transformed the place of the Middle East in the world
economy, and, whatever else, guaranteed a continued attention by the
outside world to the affairs of the region; in particular, as the United
States, which had earlier been largely self-sufficient in oil, became from
the 1970s a major energy importer, so the power of the Middle Eastern
producers in the world market became stronger.[28] Several consequences,
across the range of international political economy, followed from this oil
boom. In the first place, oil shaped the social character of the state and,
by derivation, of the economy. The states which possessed oil derived
from it an increasingly important income, and came to depend largely
on that income; they were what were termed 'rentier' or, more respect-
fully, 'distributive' states.[29] While these revenues greatly strengthened
the states, and enabled them to increase imports, this reliance had, as
we shall see, other, negative consequences, ones that any economic historian or social scientist, writing about any state or society in the past
five hundred years, could have anticipated. In all cases where unearned
income has come to dominate state revenues, a pattern marked by par-
asitism *and* factionalism has emerged.[30] Secondly, while it was not, in
itself, a source of conflict, oil did provoke a political reaction within these
societies:[31] the development of the oil industry and the issue of ownership
of oil became objects of great dispute within Middle Eastern countries,
as well as between these countries and the west. As western policy in the
Middle East was increasingly seen as dictated by the desire to control oil

[27] See Table 2, p. 336.
[28] US output fell from 8.87 mbd in 1992 to 7.7 mbd in 2002, while consumption rose from
17.03 mbd in 1992 to 19.71 mbd in 2002: *BP Statistical Review of World Energy*, 2003.
[29] For a critique of the concept 'rentier' as opposed to 'distributive' see Dirk Vandewalle,
Libya since Independence: Oil and State-building, London: I. B.Tauris, 1998, chapter 2. For
a classic statement see Hossein Mahdavy, 'Patterns and Problems of Economic Development in Rentier States: the Case of Iran', in Cook, ed., *Studies in the Economic History
of the Middle East*, 1970.
[30] Terry Lynn Karl, *The Paradox of Plenty: Oil Boom and Petrostates*, Berkeley: University of
California Press, 1997.
[31] Much has been made in policy and press discussion of oil as a *cause* of inter-state conflict.
This is rarely the case: for all the claims to this effect, oil has no significant causative relation to, e.g., the Arab–Israel conflict, the Iran–Iraq war of 1980–8, the conflict between
Yemen and Saudi Arabia, the war between (oil-rich) Azerbaijan and Armenia, or the
wars of Afghanistan 1978–2001. The *delimitation* of the Rumala field was used as one,
among several, pretexts for the Iraqi invasion of Kuwait in 1990, but was not a real cause.

production, this led to strong nationalist reaction. The crisis in Iran between 1951 and 1953 was precipitated by the attempt by the prime minister Mohammad Mosadeq to nationalise oil. This attempt was followed first by an international boycott of Iranian oil that weakened the Iranian economy, and then by the overthrow of Mosadeq in the 1953 coup organised by the USA and Britain.

The enduring controversy surrounding oil had, however, a much wider impact: something mysterious and menacing seemed to attach to this commodity, perhaps as a result of it being so vital and so valuable. In his speeches, the Soviet leader Leonid Brezhnev used to say of the Middle East, 'here, it smells of oil'.[32] For once, an element of psychopathology or paranoia may indeed also be relevant here: unique among traded commodities, it should be noted, oil, throughout its production process, from well-head, through refinery, tanker, distribution and petrol pump, remains *invisible*. In developed countries too, oil firms were associated with a special degree of conspiracy and backdoor politics, in the USA as much as in the Middle East, and in more recent times with dubious environmental policies. From Texas to Azerbaijan, from 1900 to 2000, and beyond, 'Big Oil' was associated, often rightly, with corruption.[33] The oil magnate was, in US lore at least, the quintessential crook and vulgarian, an association reproduced in Russia after 1991. This further charged the atmosphere in which the issue of oil, the management of which was vital to developed and developing economies alike, was discussed.

For all the imposition of myriad actors in a complex marketplace, the determinant actors in Middle Eastern oil production were, necessarily, states, producer and consumer. This had long been so for the great powers. Britain made control of oil a strategic priority when, in 1914, the British navy switched from reliance on coal to reliance on oil. While oil and the attempt to control it were not *causes* of global or regional conflict, they were significant factors in the definition of strategy in both world wars: the British drive through Iraq in 1915–17 and the German attempt to break through Soviet lines to the Caucasus in 1941–2 were results of the wish to monopolise oilfields. So too was the Japanese drive through China and South-East Asia in 1941–2. In the post-war epoch it seemed that imperial hegemony over oil prevailed securely. In the 1950s Mosadeq failed to consolidate Iranian ownership of its oil. In 1960 it was the Cuban government's nationalisation of a Standard Oil refinery in Havana that

[32] In Russian *zdes nafti pachnit*, probably a play on a sentence from Pushkin: 'Here, it smells of Russia.'
[33] Daniel Yergin, *The Prize: the Epic Quest for Oil, Money and Power*, New York: Simon and Schuster, 1991; Harvey O'Connor, *World Empire in Oil*, London: Elek Books, 1962 gives a critical variant of this approach.

gave the USA the pretext on which to break diplomatic relations with Castro. But in 1960 something else happened: the Middle Eastern oil producers, and other states, such as Venezuela, set up the Organisation of Petroleum Exporting Countries (OPEC) with the aim of negotiating jointly with the oil companies over prices. It was to be another decade before, in 1971, OPEC was able significantly to alter the price of oil. In 1973, however, in conjunctural conditions of a global shortage and of a political crisis precipitated by the Arab–Israeli war in October, OPEC members were able to raise prices by 400 per cent. The December 1973 price of $14 was equal, in terms of the late 1990s, to $90 per barrel. In the same period, and reflecting a shift in attitudes in both the region and the west, the oil-producing states were able to take over, in effect nationalise, the oil companies. The concessionary state had now become the producer, and rentier, state. Mosadeq had been twenty years too early.[34]

The changes of the early 1970s did not, however, end political controversy over oil. The cartel of producer states in OPEC still had to operate within a framework of other, stronger, consumer states and of a shifting global structure, the energy market. In the first place, the oil-producing states remained almost wholly reliant on the international oil companies for downstream, or marketing, operations. Amazingly, three decades after the OPEC price rises of 1971–3 none of its Middle Eastern members had been able significantly to break into the downstream and retail directly in the developed states with a major retail chain identifiably its own. The inter-state body set up after 1973 by consumer states, the International Energy Agency, worked through building up reserves and supply co-ordination to lessen OECD vulnerability. The ability of OPEC to determine prices turned out, moreover, to be limited. It had, in the early part of the 1970, been hoped that OPEC's success could be generalised to cover other third world primary product producers – such as those of rubber, copper, bauxite. This led to a campaign to reform the world market, proclaimed at a Non-Aligned Summit in 1973, entitled the New International Economic Order. No such generalisation of OPEC's success occurred. Nor was OPEC's success in raising prices sustained: rising from $10 per barrel (in constant 1997 prices), which they had been from 1930 to 1973, they rose temporarily to over $50 in 1981, but from 1982 they began to decline and had fallen to $20 at the end of 1997 and another 40 per cent by the end of 1998.[35] In its entire industrial history, from 1861 to 2002, oil prices had known only *three* major

---

[34] Although twenty years before him, in Mexico in 1937, President Cárdenas had been able to nationalise and survive. A different geopolitical place and time may account for this.

[35] BP *Statistical Review of World Energy 1998*, p. 14.

spikes: in 1862 (during the US civil war), in 1973, during the October war, and in 1979–80 as a result of the Iranian revolution and the Soviet drive into Afghanistan.[36] For the remaining period the producers were held in check by consumer states and markets alike.

There were several reasons for the inability permanently to sustain high prices after 1973. Increased conservation in the importing states after 1973, itself a response to OPEC price rises, was one factor. In the 1980s divisions developed within OPEC between population-rich countries (e.g. Iran, Iraq), which wanted to maximise output, and low-population states (e.g. Kuwait, Abu Dhabi), which wanted to conserve oil resources. At the same time, while OPEC held 73.5 per cent of proven world reserves in 1998, the rise of non-OPEC producers, such as Mexico, Norway, Russia and Colombia, led OPEC's percentage of the world market to fall from its height in the early 1970s to 42 per cent in 1998. In the 1990s technological change also significantly reduced the place of energy in economic growth. Politics and state intervention by OECD members were also evident in the downstream sector. There could be no more obvious indicator of the enduring role of *political* factors in the downstream oil market than the differential between petrol pump prices in different OECD countries: in 1997 the price in the USA was around a half that in Britain and France, and less than a third that in Norway.[37]

After 1973 OPEC states encountered policy obstacles, the limits of *political* economy, both internationally and internally. While they found it difficult to convert their market control of the early 1970s into a permanent international lever, they found it even harder to use their natural wealth to further broader foreign policy goals. In the first place, the common possession of oil did not produce a common foreign policy: Iran quarrelled with the Arab world, and Iraq with Kuwait. Much was made in 1973, and after, of the 'Oil Weapon', but this was simply a mirage, albeit one sustained by both self-vaunting producers and alarmed consumers; in reality it meant, and achieved, zero. Those states, notably Saudi Arabia, which sought to use their oil wealth to win influence in the Arab world found this to be a dubious weapon. Egypt, whose break with the Soviet Union was in part financed by the Saudis in the early 1970s, defied Saudi advice in making peace with Israel in 1977–9. Yemen, itself without significant resources, was more antagonised than reconciled by Saudi supplies of funds to state and tribal leaders alike. In 1990–1 many of the Islamic militants who had till then been funded by Saudi Arabia defied Riyadh and supported Iraq in the confrontation over Kuwait. To the chagrin of the Kuwaitis, the three largest recipients of Kuwaiti

---

[36] *BP Statistical Review*, 2003, p. 4.   [37] *The Economist*, 26 July 1997, p. 114.

funding before 1990 – Sudan, Yemen, the Palestinians – all inclined to Iraq in that conflict.

If this limitation to the 'Oil Weapon' applied to the Middle East, it was even more evident in relations with the outside world. During the crisis of 1973, following on from the Arab–Israeli war, the Arab producers reduced output by 25 per cent and vowed not to supply the USA or Holland, two states considered most sympathetic to Israel, until Palestinian demands had been met. In the end, and despite much alarm in the west at Arab 'blackmail' (as if all market relations were not based on conflicting pressures), this concerted Arab action achieved nothing. In early 1974 the boycott ended: not a single positive political result for the 'Arab cause' resulted, then or in the rest of the century. Many outside the Middle East seemed to think that western policy faced a split, between its inclination to Israel on the one hand, and its relation to the Arab oil producers on the other; this was a concern often voiced by those sympathetic to Israel itself. But this dilemma was largely illusory, in that on closer examination western relations with the oil producers were not at all affected by the Israeli connection. Moreover, after 1973, the 'Oil Weapon' itself was never used or seriously contemplated again. Indeed close on two decades were to pass before, for different reasons, an Israeli–Palestinian compromise was to be worked out at Oslo in 1993. After that Arab economics and their financial support to the PLO, eroded by Palestinian backing for Iraq in 1990–1, had no impact on peace negotiations, or on the conflict.

In the retrospect of the three decades, however, from the the Arab–Israeli war of 1973, and the Anglo-US occupation of Iraq in 2003, it transpires that, while oil producers were able to use their income and reserves to *commercial* and *investment* advantage, they were not able to do so for political ends. Indeed, after 1975 in many ways these states became *more* not *less* vulnerable: later events were to illumine how far this vulnerability had gone. After 1973 it was not in the exacerbation of *inter*-state relations that oil was so important, but in the sharpening of *state–society relations within states*. The revolution in Iran of 1978–9, the rise of Islamic fundamentalism in Algeria in the late 1980s, and the 1991 upsurge against Saddam Hussein in Iraq, upheavals in three large rentier states, showed how the misallocation of oil revenues could fuel a social tension that in the end challenged apparently strong states. Yet the Iraqi invasion of Kuwait in 1990, following which Kuwait and Saudi Arabia were forced to call for international help, showed how little oil rent could be converted into military security. Despite the shift in ownership and apparent market influence that began in the early 1970s, the oil states were not, therefore, in foreign policy or strategic terms, more powerful. Politics and economics were interwoven, but the strength of one was not necessarily convertible, or to use the economics term 'fungible', into strength in the other.

The state in command: political economy within

Oil pervaded the economies of Middle Eastern producer and non-producer alike, but in so doing it as much exacerbated existing weaknesses and hierarchies as it reduced them. In regard to pressure for sustained regional growth, oil did not integrate the economies of the Middle East, except in terms of financial flows. Rather, it reinforced the fragmentation, and suspicious bitterness, of producer states. Indeed oil itself had a relatively limited direct impact on the economies of the countries in which it was produced. The 'linkages' oil established between mineral extraction and the rest of the economy – labour, agriculture, industry – were weak. It employed few people overall, and many of the skilled and managerial personnel were brought from other countries. The physical inputs – drilling equipment, pipelines, pumping and loading stations, storage units – were not manufactured in these countries. Even the housing and food were often imported. Decisively, oil affected the economies of the oil producers not directly, but as a form of rent paid to states, that is, through the mechanisms of state expenditure. On the other hand, oil affected the non-oil producers, in which the majority of the population of the Middle East lived, even more indirectly – through state-to-state monetary transfers, through labour migrant remittances, through provision of services such as tourism.[38] Above all, it generated rancour not amity.

In terms of a simple model of economic growth, it might have appeared from the 1973 OPEC rises onwards as if oil-derived rent would solve the central problem of Middle Eastern, as of other, development, namely lack of capital. This was what development theory of the 1960s, for example Walt Rostow's classical development study *Stages of Economic Growth*, identified as the main obstacle to what was then naively thought of as a single goal, 'development'. Yet this did not occur. Oil could be used for certain political purposes – purchasing weapons, inflating employment, subsidies to political clients at home and abroad. Oil had certain other evident and positive social and therefore economic consequences, not least in the development of education which, in the longer run, could enhance economic growth. Yet the record of the quarter century after 1973 showed that, wastefully used, or used for predominantly short-term political purposes, above all used by ill-educated, whimsical and grandiose leaders, be

---

[38] Richards and Waterbury, *A Political Economy*, chapter 15, 'Regionalism, Labor Migration and the Future of the Oil Economies'.

they monarchs or tribesmen, oil, as much as it promoted it, also inhibited growth. First of all, oil was used within producer countries to increase employment of nationals, without consonant insistence on work or qualification by those so employed. The result was a tendency, to put it gently, for public administration and state-subsidised economic activity to conceal semi-unemployment and an inhibition of a commitment to work.[39] Most nationals of GCC states had, at best, an intermittent attitude to work. When in the 1990s states began to promote employment of their nationals in the private sector – 'Arabisation', 'Omanisation', etc. – it was local employers who were most reluctant to comply. Secondly, oil was used time and again not to promote growth but to substitute for failures in other branches of the economy: nowhere was this more evident than in regard to agriculture, where oil revenues served to subsidise large imports of food rather than boost indigenous production. Iran was a striking, and enduring, example of this avoidance.

Where oil did play a decisive role was in regard to the state itself. Here politics and economics were tied. It was not that oil rent as such shaped or distorted the state; rather the impact of this rent was determined by the already existing character of the state, and society, into which it was paid. Ten million dollars paid to the state of Norway, or Texas, had consequences different from that paid to Iraq or Saudi Arabia. The very fact that oil revenues were paid to the state meant that it was those who controlled the state, ruling families in the Gulf and military elites in Iraq, Libya and Algeria, who disposed of the money: a combination of an established clientilism, and the refusal of authoritarian regimes to submit their accounts to public scrutiny, led to a situation in which a considerable proportion of oil revenues was, in the euphemism of the US embassy in Saudi Arabia, 'off budget'. A rough rule of thumb, as applicable to republics (Iraq, Yemen) as to monarchies, was that a third of income from oil, and a larger percentage of revenue from foreign investments, went to the ruling family. In a country like Iraq during the 1980s even such a figure as oil output not only was not published, but was a state secret. Saddam Hussein and his associates used their oil revenue to enhance their own security, and life-style, in addition to the economic development they promoted.

In Saudi Arabia it was reckoned that, in the mid-1990s, the state budget of, in an average year, $28 billion was $14 billion short of the

---

[39] One friend, an intellectual of a similar generation to mine, from a smaller GCC country, was asked by his ruler in the late 1990s to become Minister of Information and reluctantly agreed. Upon taking up office, he discovered he had 18,000 employees. This was only the beginning of his problems. In the end, exasperated by the inertia of his staff and harassed by *salafi* critics without, he one day took a plane to Beirut and resigned.

full revenue from oil. The gap between the two figures was made up by a combination of disbursements: subsidies to Islamic activities to further Saudi aims, arms-for-oil swap arrangements with the UK under the al-Yamama deal, and private income for the several thousand princes and, not to be forgotten, *their wives*.[40] Each of the Saudi princes was, it was believed, entitled to a starting sum of a $500,000 per annum *khasusia* or personal income, free air travel and telephone, and privileged access to land, business and import commissions. Little wonder that as oil revenues fell in the 1990s there came to be increasing demand from within producer states for transparency, rendered by the Arabic term *al-shaffafia*. One other consequence was too easily slid over in the 1990s neo-liberal euphemism: *there was, in effect, no such thing as a private sector in these societies.* Herein lay, of course, the large, only slowly glimpsed, challenge of WTO membership and other forms of agency up to the world market and globalisation. This patrimonial appropriation of revenue led to misconceptions about the 'private sector' in such states: there was no taxation, all lived on contracts handed out by the state. So much of business was subsidised by cheap or free credit and by the activities of the ruling family in business that it was impossible to say where, if at all, the 'private' sector began. In reality, it never did.[41]

It was, however, the *political* costs of oil dependency that as much as anything cast doubt on oil as being a beneficial source of capital. Internally, states that obtained revenue from oil were, in varying degrees, able to fend off pressure for sharing of wealth or meaningful democratisation: oil consolidated oligarchic control by enhancing both the distributive, welfare and coercive power of the state. This was as true in monarchical Iran, Saudi Arabia and the other GCC states as in the republican states of Iraq, Libya and Algeria, although the population was many times higher in the latter. Patronage and subsidies on the one hand, repression on the other, combined to paralyse the political system in a range of countries, even as it promoted longer-run social changes, and resentments, that were to challenge these regimes.[42]

---

[40] Communication from Saudi economist, September 2001.

[41] Israel was, of course, different, but not that different: as a result of the earlier Zionist history of socialist state control of the economy, and in line with much of what had happened in other semi-democratic Mediterranean countries such as Greece and Italy, economic practice even into the 1990s continued to follow clientilist practices. In a situation where the financial sector was dominated by two banks, credit was allocated on political or clientilist bases. Over the two decades up to 2004, 70 per cent of all loans were given to 1 per cent of borrowers, and up to 10 per cent of these were likely to be written off (Daniel Doron, 'Middle East Peace? It's the Economy, Stupid', *Wall Street Journal Europe*, 11 August 2004). In some respects, Israel was also to some degree a rentier state, since its economy depended to such an extent on state and private financial flows from the USA.

[42] Richards and Waterbury, *A Political Economy*, chapter 12, 'Solidarism and its Enemies'.

The consequences for international relations were also far-reaching. Despite much rhetoric to this effect, *oil as such* does not promote conflict, any more than does water, or wheat, or, for that matter, frontiers or religion. The impact of oil in international relations, as it does internally, depends on the policies of states and of those who challenge them. It is nationalism and social conflict, driven by calculations of power by states and their rivals, that convert oil into controversy. Resentment at external, or oligarchic, control of oil and oil rents has been a recurrent feature of Middle Eastern politics. So too has conflict in which a threat to oil fields, and wealth, is perceived. During the Cold War, much was made by east and west alike of the enemy's drive to control Gulf oil – true as regards the west, not so as against the self-sufficient Soviet bloc. In regional relations too, the possession of oil was on occasion itself a source of particular anxiety, evident in the 1960s in Saudi fears of Egyptian advances through Yemen, through to the Iran–Iraq war that broke out in 1980, when Iraq made an attempt to seize Iran's oil fields, and the Iraqi invasion of Kuwait in 1990, an adventure itself encouraged, in part, by an Iraqi desire to control Kuwaiti oil resources. An Arab diplomat who spent three hours with Saudi King Fahd in August 1990 found the monarch talking for two of the three hours about a 'Hashemite encirclement', involving Iraq, Jordan, the PLO and Yemen, and their desire to seize Gulf oil. But such anxiety, related to the protection of an immovable resource, combined with the fear of pressure from within, led these states to engage in substantial purchases of weapons, and hence to a regional arms race, that grew, from the early 1970s, in parallel to the rise in oil revenues.

In the end, after decades of speculation and ballyhoo about oil, there were two most tangible results of oil revenues. One was the increased import of arms into the region, and the consequent reduction in the security, domestic and international, that the importing states now felt. The other was the concern showed by the industrialised states, and in particular the USA, to ensure reliable and uninterrupted access to the oil of the region. Neither did much for the long-term social and economic development of the region.

Political economy in the international arena: regional and strategic

In analysing the international dimension, we return to the inextricable combination of politics *and* economics, of states, on one side, and production and finance on the other: this interaction of political and economic issues at the international level is evident in relations between Middle Eastern states themselves, and also in relations between these states and the outside world. In both cases, regional and international, economic relations affect, but have to a large extent been controlled by, political relations, the latter not excluding relations between individual leaders and elites. Here the world of discourse may mark, rather than explain, the world of politico-economic power. In both regional and extra-regional relations power, shared values or 'Arabness' ('*uruba*) has been at least as important as the case for co-operation. Yet political considerations of a supposedly co-operative or supportive kind have been accompanied by other strategic concerns, of subordination and, repeatedly, sanction and embargo, not to omit whim. Hegemony and coercion are as important a part of international political economy as interdependence, in south as in north. An examination of first regional and then external dimensions of this, the power politics of international political economy, will hopefully make this clearer.

In regional economic terms, modern politics has, indeed, as much divided as united the region. Prior to the creation of the modern state system the region had a pre-modern, but enduring transnational economy: what are today the separate Middle Eastern economies were able to trade with each other, within the Ottoman empire and with its neighbouring states. Modern state-building, and economic development, with frontiers, excise officials and control, have inhibited this, just as they have fractured political and cultural contact between peoples and tribes. The result has been that intra-regional trade as such has been much less important than trade with more developed countries. In part this stems also from the belief that trade with more developed, and powerful, states may have other benefits for the Middle Eastern state concerned: an obvious example is in US–Saudi relations, where stronger co-operation is the guiding principle. This politicisation of trade to exclude regional economies has been taken further by the stress on import-substitution industrialisation. For all the talk of Arab, or sub-regional economic integration, in the early 1990s intra-regional trade was only 10 per cent of the total.[43] It is, however, important here as on other issues not to singularise the region. Such trading preferences are, indeed, not specific to the Middle East. The relatively low level of regional integration in the post-1945 period is by no means unique to the Middle East, a similar phenomenon being observable in Africa and Asia. This limited regional trade was, however, compounded in the Middle East by the fact that non-oil exports from these countries were, in the main, at relatively low levels, that is, they had relatively little to trade with each other.[44]

[43] Ibid., pp. 366–7.
[44] Victor Bulmer-Thomas, *Regional Integration in Latin America and the Caribbean: the Political Economy of Open Regionalism*, London: Institute of Latin American Studies, 2000.

Some degree of integration began to develop with the growth of the oil revenues in the 1970s. After 1973 especially, labour from population-rich countries, above all Egypt and Yemen, worked in the Gulf states, and money, in the form of workers' remittances and capital, flowed from the oil producers to other Arab states and to Turkey: at their peak in 1980 official remittances from the oil producers to the labour-exporting countries exceeded $8 billion. In this way, from the 1970s until the end of the 1980s, a greater degree of Arab economic integration took place. At the same time Turkey began to play a more active commercial role in the Arab world, exporting to Arab countries food and meat, as well as consumer goods, and participating in the extensive construction boom of the 1970s and 1980s. Middle Eastern trade rose to over half of all Turkey's exports, and capital from construction enhanced the Turkish economy: this was, perhaps, the most successful case of regional integration based on comparative advantage. Egypt too was a beneficiary, earning from remittances, from Arab tourism, from investment, to add to its revenues from the Suez Canal. Egyptian earnings from remittances rose from $123 million in 1973 to $6,104 million in 1992.[45] Israel had had, of course, plans to play such a regional role, best known through the ideas of Shimon Peres, but politics put a clear stop to that.

Yet even in the 1970s and 1980s the politics of integration prevailed over economic criteria. In the words of the noted Iraqi economist Mohammad Salman Hassan: 'In the Arab world there are no state-to-state economic agreements, only person-to-person ones.'[46] Individual rulers – the Shah in the 1970s, Qaddhaffi in the 1980s, Amir Abdullah of Saudi Arabia in the 1990s – gave loans on the basis of individual trust to rulers in other states. Arab states, or more accurately Arab rulers, invested and loaned for political purposes, supporting regimes they favoured or wanted to influence. They denied support, or removed it, when they did not favour recipients. Thus Egypt found to its cost in 1977 that what the oil-producers could offer they could also take away. Similarly Yemen found Saudi support intermittent, the flow depending on political circumstances. In Yemen Libya switched arbitrarily from North to South Yemen, totally indifferent to the consequences of its actions on poor Arab states. Most dramatically, Iraq decided in 1990 that, after a decade of receiving financial support from Kuwait and Saudi Arabia, to a sum believed to be over $40 billion, it would renounce this in pursuit of other political goals, in this case a confrontation with the Arab world and the west over Kuwait. The integration of the labour market also proved to be a

[45] Richards and Waterbury, *A Political Economy*, p. 379.
[46] Conversation with the author, London, 1972.

short-lived affair. In general from the mid-1970s the oil producers turned away from the Arab labour market, preferring Asian labour that was both clearly imported on a temporary basis and often more skilled and more politically controllable. As early as 1980 the majority of the expatriate labour force in the Gulf states was non-Arab.[47] After 1990 this trend was reinforced across the GCC.

The story of programmes of economic integration, and of the creation of an Arab common market, is itself a limited one, projects for economic co-operation or integration being prompted, and then paralysed or cancelled, for political purposes. Thus Gulf Airlines, set up by the smaller GCC states in 1980, contracted after a few years as individual states founded their own carriers – Qatar Airways, Oman Air, Emirates. In the late 1980s three different political and economic groups were apparently in operation within the Arab world – the Gulf Co-operation Council, the Arab Maghrib Union and the Arab Co-operation Council. The GCC had been founded in early 1981, for political and security reasons, after the outbreak of the war between Iran and Iraq the previous September. The Arab Maghrib Union involved a low-level set of economic arrangements. The Arab Co-operation Council, comprising Egypt, Jordan, Iraq and Yemen, broke apart in 1990 when Iraq sought confrontation with its Arab neighbours and invaded Kuwait. For reasons of politics *and* economics, the prevalence of a pan-Arab sentiment in the popular mind, coupled with continuing flows of remittances and funds, was not accompanied by any sustained, let alone institutionalised, integration of the Arab economies. State interests, and the allocation on general grounds of security and profitability of resources in a global financial and investment climate, prevailed. Here much was made of 'western' inhibitions of Arab economic development, but the choices were those of rulers and investors in the region. This was a point made by the US ambassador to Manama at an investment conference in Bahrain: 'You are asking me to invest in the region,' he said. 'We will invest when you do!'

In two further respects, the pattern of labour migration confirmed both the extent, and the limit, of this integration. As we have seen, in the 1970s and 1980s, millions of Arabs moved in intra-regional migration to work in oil-producing states, and sent back remittances to their countries of origin. These remittances compounded those which Arab workers, mainly from the Maghrib, were sending to their home countries

[47] On migration see Richards and Waterbury, *A Political Economy*, chapter 15, and J. S. Birks and C. A. Sinclair, *International Migration and Development in the Arab Region*, Geneva: International Labour Office, 1980. For a more benign view than mine, Sharon Stanton Russell, 'Migration and Political Integration in the Arab World', in Giacomo Luciani, ed., *The Arab State*, London: Routledge, 1990.

from European states, above all France and Germany, to which they had migrated. But this flow of labour and money was not necessarily beneficial for development and was itself subject to enduring limitations. On the one hand, the work which these Arab migrants performed in the oil-producing states was, with the exception of Palestinian professionals, largely of an unskilled character. It involved no skill acquisition, of the kind that tended to occur in Europe; one of the prime developmental benefits of labour migration, longer-run enhancement of the skills of the labour-exporting country, was not, therefore, realised. On the other hand, this financial integration through remittances did not provide longer-run security: conditions of employment in the oil-producing states were subject both to economic fluctuations and to political considerations. In contrast to the rhetoric of Arab and Muslim fraternity, harassment and expulsion of workers en masse was a recurrent feature of regional labour relations; thus Libya expelled hundreds of thousands of Tunisians and Egyptians, following political disputes, in 1986; in 1990 Saudi Arabia expelled 800,000 Yemenis, many resident in the country for decades; at the same time Iraq expelled hundreds of thousands from Kuwait when it occupied in 1990, as well as Egyptians who had been working in Iraq itself; Israel repeatedly banned the 120,000 Palestinians who worked there from crossing the dividing line. The political economy of integration in discourse was, it could be said, accompanied by the political economy of expulsion in reality.[48]

There was, and remains, however, one further consequence of this conflictual inter-state regional political economy. This has been inherent in much inter-Arab tension from the 1960s onwards, and it promises to continue to be so in the future: this is the *antagonistic perception* in the Arab world of the differences between oil-rich and non-oil states, a feeling present in public attitudes in oil-rich and non-oil states alike; long marked by nationalist hostility to the west over its exploration of Middle Eastern oil, this is a major factor in Arab politics. Those in the states with oil, and particularly those such as the GCC states with small populations, perceive themselves as under pressure, if not siege, from their poorer, and more numerous, fellow Arabs. Here again, the rhetoric of Arab solidarity, of other states as *shaqiq* or 'brotherly' is not matched in reality. It is this concern which explains much of the GCC states' policies in regard to Palestine, migration, economic aid, all issues conceived of in terms of limiting the demands which others without oil may make on them. On

---

[48] Roger Owen, *Migrant Workers in the Gulf*, London: Minority Rights Group, 1985. The general humanitarian, legal issue of migrant workers in these countries has been treated with almost complete neglect, not least by their countries of origin who want to ensure a smooth flow of remittances.

the side of the non-oil states, there has, since the 1960s, developed a growing resentment at the oil-rich countries. This is based on evident inequality but it is a resentment exacerbated by the treatment of migrant workers in these states and by the behaviour of some of the richer Arab tourists when out of their countries (Saudis in Egypt, Kuwaitis – before 1990 – in Iraq.) Where and when this resentment finds expression in political form is an open question, but this was most certainly a factor in the widespread Arab sympathy for Iraq, and dislike of Kuwait, before and after 1990. That such resentment is a constant of Arab political life – in security terms, or in the form of wry inter-Arab jokes – is evident. Oil has, in this sense, had pervasive consequences for the economic politics of the region. It has done to relations *between* Middle Eastern states what it has done *within* them, to create new hierarchies and new divisions. Nor will time and the onus of unemployment and contraction of real revenues make things better; in many cases they may make them worse.

The economics of coercion

The political, or, better, 'politicised', economy of the Middle East's relations with the rest of the world has, if anything, been more dramatic than those within the region itself. In the first place, over more than a century states external to the region have repeatedly intervened to secure their own economic interests, often in conflict with local states and political forces: the most dramatic moments of this would include the British occupation of Egypt in 1882, to enforce debt repayment, the oil boycott and then overthrow of Mosadeq in 1951–3, to challenge his nationalisation of Iranian oil, and the Anglo-French invasion of Egypt in 1956, following the nationalisation of the Suez Canal Company, not to mention the US threat in 1973–4 to seize Gulf oil fields if the 'Arabs' did not back down. The longer-term commitment to Gulf security evident over Kuwait in 1990 was in international law and its commitment to maintaining state sovereignty quite justified but reinforced, to a considerable measure, but not solely, by external interest in Gulf oil. This willingness of the USA and its allies to come to the aid of Kuwait in 1990, when it had a legitimate case for protection against aggression, was not solely determined by the issue of oil, but this latter factor certainly served to concentrate the minds of western decision-makers, and of their publics.[49] In general, the

---

[49] The most publicised *inconsistency* of western policy has lain not in defending Kuwait in 1990, but in *failing to defend* sovereignty elsewhere, where no such material interest existed – Tibet (in 1950), East Timor (in 1975), Eritrea (in 1961), Western Sahara (in 1975), Kurdistan (in 1920+), Palestine (in 1948+).

evolution of British, and then American, security relations with the Gulf states and their indulgence of local elites has long been based on the local states' possession of so much of the world's oil reserves – a sycophancy reproduced across the private sector – press, publishing and, it has to be said, not least, some universities.

Political factors have therefore played a formative role in the policies of western states over recent decades and, in its day, of the USSR towards the Middle East. As a result, they repeatedly practised a political economy of economic assistance, money for military influence. This is most evidently the case in regard to the US support for Israel: in the 1990s US financial assistance each year amounted to around $1,000 per Israeli resident, or $4.2 billion, to which was added money from Jewish fundraising and German war reparations, totalling between them around $1,500 billion:[50] since Israeli annual per capita income was around $15,000 this represented an external subvention of around 10 per cent. Elsewhere, in the period after 1945 western states, where political priorities dictated, offered development advice, and limited quantities of aid, to other Middle Eastern states: thus Turkey and Iran received aid in the 1950s, to bolster them against the Soviet Union, and other states later received credit support. Little wonder that they had a tendency to exaggerate a Soviet 'threat'. During its war with Iran in the 1980s, Iraq did not obtain direct supplies of US arms, as it did from the USSR and some European states, but it benefited from US agricultural credits, enabling it to divert funds to purchase military equipment. From the 1970s onwards politically motivated aid to Arab recipients was most evident in the context of the Arab–Israeli dispute. From the Camp David agreement onwards Egypt received around 2 billion dollars worth of food aid, the better to sustain it in support of peace with Israel. It was calculated that in the early 1990s official development assistance to Egypt from the USA, the IMF, the World Bank and other agencies amounted to 9 per cent of GDP.[51] In the aftermath of the Oslo Accords of 1993, the Palestinian Authority was promised significant economic aid from the European Union and the USA, in the hope that this would stabilise it and allow the Palestinian leadership to continue the peace process. The fact that the PLO had a large offshore investment portfolio, valued in 2001 as high as $50 billion, did not deter such politically motivated subventions.[52] Sadly, if not surprisingly, the Palestinian Authority soon began to replicate the spending

[50] Roberts, *Visions*, pp. 32–3.
[51] Richards and Waterbury, *A Political Economy*, p. 229.
[52] Loretta Napoleoni, *Modern Jihad: Tracing the Dollars Behind the Terror Networks*, London: Pluto, 2003, pp. 34–6.

and elite appropriation patterns of other Arab states, charges of corruption from within and without being met by tired nationalistic bluster, not least from the ever-indignant Chairman himself.

During the Cold War the USSR too sustained this kind of politically determined economic policy, albeit on a much smaller scale: Moscow provided substantial economic aid to its Arab allies, most notably helping Egypt in the construction of the Aswan Dam after 1956, as well as providing aid to South Yemen in the 1970s and 1980s. It also provided arms on long-term credit that was never repaid. Yet, if calculation of these nebulous figures is ever possible, it would seem that Soviet aid was a fraction of that of the west.[53] The political economy of aid from both Soviet and western donors was, however, significantly different in this region from that in other parts of the third world for two reasons: first, the availability of large amounts of *regional* capital, from oil; secondly, the recalcitrance of regional states when faced with great power pressures to alter their policies. The USA could not, for all its largesse, control Egypt in 1955–6, or, in the 1990s, push Cairo further than a minimal peace with Israel. Soviet aid, for its part, brought no *economic* benefit to the donor, and, in the end, proved incapable of sustaining the political allegiance of the recipients to Moscow. As the USSR fell apart in 1991, the Syrians, Iraqis, Yemenis and Libyans owed it many billions of dollars for arms deliveries. As in inter-Arab relations so in the US–Arab and Soviet–Arab context, the political economy of aid demonstrated the political *purposes*, but also the political *limits*, of inter-state financial influence, and, not least, the margin of manoeuvre, of regional states. If this was the master–client relationship, it was not entirely clear which one was the master.

A parallel story of *political* economy and state resistance is evident in the contrary field, that of the use of economic instruments as a form, not of co-operation or aid, but of confrontation: set against the history of inter-state economic support and subvention, since World War II, this is the other recurrent dimension to the international political economy of the Middle East. Confrontation, through financial instruments, and the resort to forms of economic pressure and warfare in pursuit of strategic goals, have been as important as support. The most obvious and enduring dimension of this was the Arab boycott of Israel which, from the war of 1948–9, continued unbroken until Egypt signed the Camp David Accords

[53] Cissy Wallace, 'Soviet Economic and Technical Cooperation with Developing Countries', unpublished Ph.D. thesis, London School of Economics, 1990; Quintin S. Bach, *Soviet Aid to the Third World: the Facts and Figures*, Lewes, Sussex: The Book Guild, 2003; on the PDRY, Fred Halliday, *Revolution and Foreign Policy: the Case of South Yemen, 1967–1987*, Cambridge: Cambridge University Press, 1990.

in 1979.[54] Even after 1979 the majority of Arab states continued their boycott of Israel, and Egypt, while formally open to trade and investment with that country, had, in effect, little economic interaction with it. In another example, already noted, the international oil companies, backed by their respective governments, imposed the embargo on Iran after the oil nationalisation of 1951 which contributed, in time, to undermining the elected Mosadeq government.

A quite different form of economic warfare came to be waged from the 1970s onwards, that of the USA against states deemed to be inimical to it, be it through the promotion of what Washington deemed 'international terrorism',[55] or through actions such as those of Iran in seizing US diplomats as hostages in 1979, or the enduring confrontations with Libya (up to 2004) and later Iraq (up to 2003). In the 1990s, policy towards Iran and Iraq of 'dual containment' put both under the pressure of a strategic confrontation. Here sanctions on oil exports, the seizure of financial assets held abroad, and, in the case of Iraq, an attempted invigilation of all foreign financial transactions, were part of a general policy of political and military pressure on the Middle Eastern regimes in question.[56] In the case of Iran this policy was in some ways most stringent, limiting investments by US companies to $40 million and making it illegal, in contrast to Iraq from which the USA continued to import oil, to purchase any Iranian oil. Such US pressure was designed to persuade target states to change their policies on international security issues: indeed the sanctions policy of the 1990s came to take the place of those economic issues, debt and nationalisation, which had a century earlier provoked an interventionist military response against Egypt in 1882. Instruments of economic coercion changed, but the underlying structure of global economic and military inequality, and the political use of economic instruments, nonetheless endured across the centuries of a brutal, resiliently unequal, international system.

The economic record: competing explanations

The combination of international tension and distorted domestic growth that characterises the political economy of the Middle East has invited several, contrasting explanations. Yet if the record of Middle Eastern

---

[54] Sarah Graham-Brown, *Sanctioning Saddam: the Politics of Intervention in Iraq*, London: I. B. Tauris, 1999; Gil Feiler, *From Boycott to Economic Cooperation: the Political Economy of the Arab Boycott of Israel*, London: Frank Cass, 1998.

[55] The problem with this category was not so much what it *included*, as what it *excluded*, most notably US and Saudi aid to the *mujahidin* in Afghanistan, 1978–92.

[56] Robert Litwak, *Rogue States and US Foreign Policy: Containment after the Cold War*, Washington, DC: Woodrow Wilson Center Press, 2000.

political economy is evident, the reasons for its persistence, above all the continued domination by the state, are less so. One, that of the conventional economics of development, is in terms of low factor endowment: insufficient cultivable areas, weak domestic demand, inadequate capital, underdeveloped transport. A related, more historically speculative, explanation is in the terms of 'oriental despotism', a historically formed and geographically determined state structure and attendant set of political and social norms that inhibit growth and entrepreneurial activity; in this form of society the state, as a result of the arid and harsh natural conditions in, for example Egypt or Iran, in which centralised control of water is essential for life, comes to have an enduringly authoritarian and inhibiting role in the economy. Some variants of this 'oriental despotism' theory could, in addition to explaining earlier state forms, claim to explain the modern economic history, and contemporary state forms and political cultures, in terms of the need for strong states to control and distribute water in arid societies.[57] This explanation has already been touched on, and contested, in chapter 3. Invocation of an ancient, timeless state structure or despotic political culture derivative of it is, questionable. 'Oriental despotism', for all its recurrent fascination, can be historical sociology at its worst – neither historical, in that it denies change, nor sociological, in that it abstracts the state from social context, and contemporary international connection.

The states and economies of the region are, as discussed earlier, *modern* creations. Whatever the merits of the first argument, that from lack of growth in resources in the pre-oil period, this cannot be a sufficient explanation for what has happened since the 1960s. Indeed it is precisely in this period, when the Middle Eastern economies, in the main, continued to stagnate, that those of other countries such as the industrialising states of East Asia, ones without comparable supplies of capital, experienced sustained growth. As for the general thesis of oriental despotism, one not specific to the Middle East (it could be applied to China, Sri Lanka and pre-Colombian America), it is in several respects flawed: above all, it *assumes* a degree of paralysis that does not accord with the actual history of these societies, and a state that can resist pressures, from within society and from the international context, to change. In sum it misrepresents the history of state and society, and in positing a continuous state and cultural form it assumes that which it sets out to prove.[58]

[57] Homa Katouzian, *The Political Economy of Modern Iran 1926–1979*, London: Macmillan, 1981, explores the continuity between 'oriental' and 'petrolic' despotism.
[58] Brendan O'Leary, *Asiatic Mode of Production: Oriental Despotism, Historical Materialism and Indian History*, Oxford: Basil Blackwell, 1989.

A second broad explanation of Middle Eastern economic performance is in terms of culture, and more specifically, 'Islam'. This might seem to be a strong correlation and, for all its western overtones, it is one that many writers in the Middle East themselves offer. Yet this is far from being an explanation: Islam did not, in pre-modern times, inhibit considerable economic achievement, being comparable at that time with Europe, in its history and doctrine, as observed above, being more favourable to trade and profit than any other major religion; nor has it constituted a block to sustained growth in other, non-Middle Eastern, states, such as Malaysia. Most importantly, as the great French writer Maxime Rodinson has shown in his definitive, if widely ignored, *Islam and Capitalism*, it is not possible to see how a value system such as the Muslim religion can, in terms of autonomous ideological or textual impact, *explain* the history of economic behaviour; as explored at greater length in chapter 7, Islam, like all religions, has no definitive economic, financial or fiscal implications, and is compatible with a ranges of values and social practices. It cannot therefore explain why one economic system or another is adopted. Islam can sanction collective ownership, from that by nomadic tribes to that by modern workers' collectives, but it is equally compatible with private property, accumulation of wealth and trade. Far from necessarily entailing hostility to economic growth, it can, indeed, be interpreted to entail precisely capitalist values, those attitudes to saving and limited consumption that were associated with Protestantism and the rise of capitalism in Europe.[59]

Much was made in the 1990s about something called 'Islamic banking'. Institutions with names, sacred if the interpreter so wishes, like Baraka, Ikhlas and Ijma began to emerge. Like Islamic 'art', *hizbullah* chic and the Islamic theory of the environment, it was, on closer examination, a form of modernist packaging. Like any body of religious thought, Islam can be interpreted to validate a range of different economic and social practices; that particular interpretation which it yields depends, therefore, not on the religion itself but on other, secular factors in the society and political system. The argument, sometimes made by Muslims to non-Muslims, that their religion prohibits taking of interest (*riba*), and hence modern banking, is not however valid, since, apart from the fact that *riba* can be interpreted to mean only 'profiteering' or 'usury', not normal interest, other forms of service charge can be, and are, introduced. The market, not *sunna*, governs the flow of money. Islamic banking is indeed a

---

[59] Rodinson, *Islam and Capitalism*, chapter 2 where he cites from the Quran, the *hadith* and the Sunna in favour of traders and profit; Rodinson, *Marxism and the Muslim World*, London: Zed Books, 1979, chapter 8, 'Islam and the Modern Islamic Revolution'.

rather unoriginal venture, a project by local elites and national financiers, comparable to the promotion of 'national' or 'regional' banks in the west, to attract funds that would otherwise go to international banks, and to bring into circulation local money that would otherwise be kept out of general circulation, not least for fear of the investor being asked to account for the provenance of the funds in question. Marked in many cases by a lack of regulation, 'Islamic banking' is a political and financial emanation, not the expression of some authentic or distinct cultural system, no more than a bank called 'Bradford and Bingley' or 'First San Francisco' or 'Dresdner' has some special regional method of investing and lending.[60]

A third form of general explanation of the Middle Eastern economic record is in terms of the external context, historically in the impact of western industrial society on the region, before and during the colonial period, in the period after World War II through a structural, 'imperialist' domination of the economies of the region, and after 1990 through 'globalisation'. This argument, from global structure, antagonistic and all-pervasive, rests as much upon a general claim, that it is the industrialised west which has promoted the poverty and underdevelopment of the third world, as it does on a particular reading of the Middle East's economic history. For the non-oil producers this relates to the discouragement of agricultural and industrial growth; for the oil producers it relates above all to the unfavourable terms of trade, whereby oil prices are in real terms depressed, Middle Eastern imports are purchased at increasing prices and FDI is prevented. Underlying this explanation in terms of external structural constraint is often a political judgement, a suspicion that the industrialised west wants to keep the Middle East weak, its economic policies compounding those of military predominance on the one hand, and support for pro-western states, be they in Israel, pre-1979 Iran or the Arab world on the other.

The historical argument, on the disruption of previously organic Middle Eastern economies, has, as we have seen, some force. So too do arguments about the restrictions placed on Middle Eastern agricultural and other exports to the developed world, in colonial and globalised times alike. The argument from external inhibition is, however, inadequate. In its most widely diffused form, as 'dependency' theory of the 1970s, it has been shown in comparative terms to be of limited relevance, as the success of other third world countries, notably the Asian industrialising countries, from the 1960s onwards demonstrated. At the same time theories of external determination remove from consideration the role of factors internal to Middle Eastern society and states for the economic

[60] Rodney Wilson, 'Arab Government Responses to Islamic Finance: the Laws of Egypt and Saudi Arabia', *Mediterranean Politics*, vol. 7, no. 2, 2002.

policies that have been pursued. In terms of causation, *and* responsibility, the Middle Eastern states have been and *are*, autonomous actors – just as Taiwan, Korea, Singapore and others are that have successfully, and with far less capital at their disposal, responded to the modern world economy.

The weaknesses of these three general explanations bring into focus the fourth broad form of explanation, that of historical and social factors, in particular the state.[61] The answer to the flawed explanations mentioned so far lies in approaches within historical sociology. This, as seen earlier, takes historical factors, and international context, into account, and examines the impact of each: this approach is one that, again, examines the role of the state, as the central actor in the economic as in the strategic, military and ideological record of Middle Eastern countries. That the state has played and continues to play a central part in the economic development of all societies is now widely recognised; the myth of a market, or growth, independent of state support, regulation or intervention is no longer persuasive.[62] In the case of the Middle East this centrality of the state is compounded by the three other factors analysed in earlier sections of this book. First, as a result of colonial state formation for most Arab states, of revolutions, in the case of Turkey (1923) and Iran (1979), and, in the case of Saudi Arabia and Yemen, non-colonial origin through tribal conquest, power in these societies is held by unaccountable elites. They acquired and maintain control of the state by undemocratic, authoritarian means and to a large degree continue to do so. In terms of the historical sociology of Charles Tilly or Anthony Giddens, and as in early modern Europe, Middle Eastern states are in essence, whatever pleasant adjustments have been made, based on the use and threat of force. Violence is not far away in time, or in the mind of ruled and ruler alike: these elites were, in historical sociological terms, organised groups of robbers who, for all the symbols of legitimation that they mobilise, rule through outside help and privileged access to rent.[63] Democratisation

---

[61] For the most authoritative statement, a brilliant critique of cultural, historically blind and 'anti-imperialist' accounts alike, see Bromley, *Rethinking Middle East Politics*. Richards and Waterbury, *A Political Economy*, also discusses this argument at greater length.

[62] For one cogent demonstration of the state's role in creating modern market economies see Gautam Sen, *The Military Origins of Industrialization and International Trade Rivalry*, London: Pinter, 1984.

[63] During a visit to one Gulf monarchy in the mid-1990s, the author was met at the airport by his guide, a young army major. They had been together less than half an hour and were indeed just driving out of the airpot, when the major turned to him and said, 'Professor, one thing you should know – all our rulers are thieves.' Apart from the remarkably frank, if accurate, nature of this remark, what was also striking was that, even as it assumed a certain moral code in terms of which the observation itself was made, this code was one of universal, nor regional, religious or particularist, character. This remark would have been as clear to a listener in China, or Peru, as it was in the Gulf.

even of a substandard level *is* far away. One prominent family has even had the temerity to put the sword on its flag, though this proved, in 1990, to be of little use. Secondly, as a result of oil, and other rent payments, economic, and in particular financial, resources are even more concentrated in the hands of the state than is the case in other parts of Asia: the state has the ability to disburse these monies as the political elite chooses. Thirdly, the international dimension, that of inter-state rivalry, has its impact on *internal politics*: it is as a consequence of the incidence of inter-state wars, that the security role of the state, the claim of the military on resources, and the central political and economic role of the armed forces combine to reinforce the state's role. In all Middle Eastern states up to the 1980s, Israel and Turkey included, the state was the decisive factor in the pattern of economic growth as in the disbursal of monies within the economy.[64] The privatisation of the 1980s and 1990s made a small but limited overall impact on this.[65] It is in the enduring character of the state, and the interests of those who control it, that the key to the Middle Eastern economic record lies. This has been, and will long remain, the defining feature of nearly all Middle Eastern economies, and will also, as popular resentment rises, become the ultimate testing ground for the survival of these states themselves. Here, again, the argument returns to the *political* character of the economies of the region.

A new era on the horizon: towards the post-oil epoch

As described above, the earlier economic history of the Middle East in the twentieth century falls into certain clear phases: the disruptions of two world wars were followed, in each case, by more tranquil, cautiously expansive phases. In the 1970s, however, the region had entered, it seemed, upon a period of hitherto unparalleled prosperity. In the oil-producing states and those that benefited indirectly from their riches this led to substantial increases in state revenues, infrastructural and other expenditure, and GNP. Elsewhere, a number of states – notably Israel, Turkey and Tunisia – enjoyed growth through greater exports and participation in the ranks of semi-peripheral economies. This appearance of growth was, however, in several respects deceptive. First, while overall growth in the Middle East and North Africa region in the period

---

[64] Bromley, *Rethinking Middle East Politics*; Ghassan Salamé, ed., *Democracy without Democrats? The Renewal of Politics in the Muslim World*, London: I.B. Tauris, 1994; Nazih Ayubi, *Over-stating the Arab State: Politics and Society in the Middle East*, London: I. B. Tauris, 1995.

[65] Richards and Waterbury, *A Political Economy*, chapter 9, 'The Chequered Course of Economic Reform'; Hakimian and Moshaver, *The State and Global Change*.

1962–75 was 4.91 per cent, that in the period 1975–90 fell at an annual average of –0.75 per cent, and in the period 1990–5 reached –0.3 per cent, in both periods the lowest in the world. The large rises in oil revenues, often in countries with small populations, did not translate into large per capita incomes for the region as a whole. If these absolute figures are corrected for population growth, to produce figures for GNP per capita growth, then we get a figure for the period 1962–90 of, on average, –0.47 per cent.[66]

This comparatively poor record for the region as a whole underlines many of the difficulties which economic development faced, not only in terms of a spread of natural endowments, but also in terms of the impact on economics of the range of political factors characterising the region – wars and arms races, state interventions in and distortions of the economy, the persistent discouragement of both entrepreneurial activity, and general levels of administrative and educational competence, and the lack of a trained, internationally competitive labour force. Yet the availability of large sums of money through oil revenues and foreign investment, however unevenly distributed, and the provision of other forms of rent, for security reasons, did contribute to an element of political and regime stability in many countries. Whole reforms facilitated by oil did much to undermine the regime of the Shah in the 1970s, the availability of oil then served nonetheless as a rent to the newly established Islamic regime: within a short space of time, the Islamic regime, composed of a few thousand clerical and lay personnel, and heavily intermarried, had taken hold of state, army *and* rent, alike. In general terms, the Iranian revolution, for all its populism and redistribution of income, created a new ruling elite, an Islamic clerical *nomenklatura*, of perhaps 5,000 men. Given the close bonds of experience, doctrine *and* intermarriage, it would not be entirely inaccurate to see this as another, extended, ruling family, all descended from a real enough ancestor, Imam Khomeini.

The situation after the 1990s, as the region moved into the third millennium, was, however, one in which this kind of rent and other related forms of stabilisation appeared to be less available. The interlude of rent-facilitated boom was for most countries over. To establish any direct, predictive relation between economic trends and political stability would be simplistic, in the Middle East or anywhere else, all the more so since, as noted earlier, oil itself does *not* correlate directly with inter-state conflict or social revolution. While the Middle East has more than once overturned facile optimism based on projections of economic growth and

[66] Ali R. Abootalebi, 'Middle East Economies: a Survey of Current Problems and Issues', *Middle East Review of International Affairs (MERIA)*, vol. 3 no. 3, September 1999.

prosperity, regimes, and peoples, have ways of surprising the doomsayers by surviving serious economic crises.

Nevertheless, at the end of the 1990s, there were a number of long-term trends that did appear at least pertinent, and possibly threatening, to the overall development of the Middle East.[67] In the first place, as already suggested, there were in the 1990s major shifts in the world economy, and in the political economy of international finance and investment, that had, in the main, negative implications for the region. No one could doubt that, for the foreseeable future, the region would remain vital for the provision of a significant proportion of the world's oil and, to a lesser extent, gas. Above all, the prospect of a replacement for the oil-consuming car engine remained remote. Estimates for the period 2000–25 suggested, indeed, an even greater world reliance on the oil produced by a core of Gulf countries – Iraq, Kuwait, Saudi Arabia, Abu Dhabi – than had hitherto been the case.[68] However, other developments, in train since the 1970s and later subsumed in the catchall term 'globalisation', suggested that the Middle East could, and on current showing would, become even more marginal to the world economy than had hitherto been the case. At the level of intergovernmental and international financial institutional criteria, and despite an unquenchable flow of grovelling and evasive reports on this or that 'transition' by extra-regional consultants, the Middle East failed on many counts to meet the criteria for privatisation, freeing of domestic markets from subsidies, good governance and transparency that were now held to be conditions for sustained support and aid, as well as being preconditions for growth. While Middle Eastern states often took *some* formal steps to meet such criteria, they were caught by a set of political dilemmas to which they sought short-term solutions: in so far as they implemented the conditions of the World Bank and the IMF, or other comparable institutions which followed their criteria, and, for example, cut subsidies, shed workers or, indeed, contemplated introducing *taxes*, they provoked political discontent at home. These conditions entailed that state support for employment, and subsidies for prices or social services, be reduced. In so far as the states resisted, or merely appeared to comply, the support they received was reduced. In effect, the states stalled as they could and used IMF and other financial external support as a form of rent. But, faced with external pressure to change on one side, and rising domestic preoccupation with employment and long-term trends on the other, the regimes' room for manoeuvre was narrowing, a hostage above all to the vagaries of oil prices.

[67] For overviews see Roberts, *Visions*, and Thomas Naff, 'Hazards to Middle East Stability in the 1990s', in Marr and Lewis, *Riding the Tiger*.
[68] Dodge and Higgott, *Globalization and the Middle East*.

It was indeed evident that in much of the Arab world this co-operation with the increasingly exigent criteria of global financial credibility was often half-hearted and inadequate[69]: subsidies were cut and agreements on 'restructuring' were signed, but neither the reduction of the state's role in the economy, nor increased accountability, to any significant degree was a mark of Middle Eastern economies in the 1990s.[70] As for credible, public figures on state finance, there was little hope. In terms of private economic relations, the picture was even less favourable. This was most obviously so in regard to flows of private capital, through private bank credit, foreign direct investment or portfolio investment: as already noted, while the total, global figure for net private flows to developing or emerging countries rose in the mid-1990s to $200 billion, the Middle East, Israel excepted, attracted, as we have seen, only a few billion. This limited FDI reflected the broader marginalisation of the Middle East within the new international economic and financial system: the region did not produce significant amounts of goods for export, nor did it attract investment to produce goods there, as a result of a range of negative factors, from political instability and lack of good governance, to the low level of education of the labour force.

The response of many in the Middle East was, moreover, to compound this by their own actions, in particular by capital flight. It was estimated at the end of the 1990s that over $1,500 billion, perhaps over $4,000 billion in regional private capital was invested outside the region (US GDP was, for comparison, $10,000 billion); this, a reverse flow of capital, was the main form of regional participation in global financial markets.[71] As noted above during an investment conference in Bahrain in the mid-1990s local businessmen appealed to the American ambassador to encourage US investment in the region. His reply was blunt: he would promote US investment in Bahrain when they would promote Arab investment there. Here Israel was not entirely an exception: in the early 1990s there were estimated to be around $50 billion of Israeli private money outside the country, marked by the unknown tens of thousands of Israelis, known as *yordim*, 'those who descend', who worked abroad. The largely unseen impact of the second Palestinian *intifadha* was felt here, in investment and longer-term business sense.

The deficiencies of the region, and in particular the lack of competitiveness vis-à-vis other areas, particularly East Asia and Latin America,

---

[69] Richards and Waterbury, *A Political Economy*, chapters 8 and 9.

[70] The story was told of one adviser to the Egyptian government who remarked in the mid-1990s, 'Yes, they agreed to privatise 40 per cent of the state sector – so they privatised 40 per cent of each state company.'

[71] *Middle East Economic Digest*, 11 January 2002.

were borne out by assessments of what would be needed.[72] Speaking at a conference at Georgetown University in September 1996 on the 'Gulf Economies in the Twenty-first Century', Nemir Kirdar, the Iraqi-born financier and chief of Investcorps, a major financial advisory firm, made three suggestions as to how the Gulf could take advantage of the new international climate: enhancing human resources, developing inter-regional economic and financial co-operation, and making its business and regulatory systems more transparent.[73] Anyone listening who was familiar with the region and its practices would have agreed but also known how far these sensible, indeed urgent, suggestions were from reality, or any plausible and proximate future conditions.

To these external pressures were added shifts within the political economy and society of the region itself. First, there was the continuing, if somewhat declining, rise in population, and, related to this, a rise in urbanisation. Between 1830 and 1914 the population of the Middle East region and North Africa, including today's Turkey, as a whole doubled from around 34 to 68 million. A further eighty years later, in the mid-1990s, it stood at 300 million – a four-and-a-half fold growth.[74] The population of the region had doubled in the previous twenty-five years and, in a process that could change only slowly, seemed set to do so again: although in some countries, such as Egypt and Iran, population growth had begun to decline, the Middle East had some of the highest birth rates in the world. The result of this was not only that there were more mouths to feed, but that, with a gap of a decade and a half or more, these same citizens would come into the labour market, and the political arena. Unemployment was already rising; the state's ability to provide employment was declining. For such people the legitimacies of earlier times – nationalist and secularist, or Islamist and revolutionary – had less and less claim. This rise in population was associated also with a rise in urbanisation, as more and more left the land, for lack of work or, even where there was work, because of the attractions of the cities.

The implications of this population rise for politics were not reassuring. As the case of India shows, population growth does not necessarily lead to domestic upheaval. However, the assumption that large numbers of urban dwellers, without adequate employment or acceptable social conditions, would contribute to political stability was hard to sustain, especially as there were political forces with an all-encompassing egalitarian

---

[72] For one pessimistic view, see Cassandra, 'The Impending Crisis in Egypt'.

[73] Nemir Kirdar, 'Opening Remarks: Gulf Economies in the Twenty first Century', First Annual Gulf Economic Conference, Georgetown University, 26 September 1996.

[74] Stephen Humphreys, *Between Memory and Desire*, London: University of California Press, 1999, p. 5.

message (somewhat in contrast to the castes and linguistic variety of India and indeed the hierarchies of Christianity) eager to exploit this situation.

Of equal concern for the longer-run development of the region was its overall environmental balance. One of the most evident consequences of rising populations, incomes and expectations was an increased demand for food. Despite large areas of desert and steppe land, the Middle East has substantial arable land, yet over the years the region slid further and further into an agricultural deficit, as demand rose and output either failed to keep pace or, in some cases, stagnated.[75] In 1999 Iran overtook China to become the largest importer of wheat in the world. With the exception of Israel and Turkey, all the countries of the Middle East were net importers of agricultural and other food products, and spent a considerable amount of their revenues in foreign exchange on food imports. In some cases particular national developments promoted this – the spread of urban areas in Egypt, the displacement of food crops by production of the profitable narcotic *qat* in Yemen.

This increasing deficit in food production was related to, and accentuated by, difficulties with the provision of the most basic of all natural commodities in the region, water. The demand for water is a compound of two, very different factors – direct human needs, for drinking and washing, and the use of water for economic activities, industrial and agricultural. Human need may indeed place pressure on existing provision, again as a result of both absolute population increase and changing quality of life. It is, however, economics not human beings directly which account for the overwhelming percentage of water use: agriculture alone accounts for 80 per cent of the region's consumption. This environmental issue has led to speculation about the *political* consequences of water management. Concern about the politics of water shortages takes two forms: one that of agricultural provision, the other about possible interstate conflicts. The former relates to possible alarm about the ability of the region's states to provide sufficient water to its cities, let alone to grow the crops it needs for projected consumption needs. The latter relates to the fact that most – 90 per cent indeed – of the water in the region is 'trans-boundary', that is, originates in one country and is consumed in another. The three largest river systems of the region all exhibit this: the Nile, tying Egypt to Sudan, Ethiopia and other countries; the Tigris and the Euphrates, linking Syria and Iraq to Turkey; the Jordan river linking Jordan, Palestine, Syria and Israel. Considerable anxiety was expressed during the 1990s about the possibility of these waterways becoming, as

[75] Richards and Waterbury, *A Political Economy*, chapter 6, pp. 145–53.

population pressures rose and state diversion and intervention increased, sources of substantial conflict.

However, both anxieties on food provision and water may, on the basis of the available evidence, have been overstated: food may be purchased on the basis of comparative advantage, and, as some judicious experts, notably Tony Allan, have argued, 'water pessimism' can be countered by 'water optimism'.[76] Apart from the option of taxing water use, which would reduce wastage, the issue of water shortages may have a commercial solution. In economic terms it does not make sense to consume large amounts of scarce water on products, such as cereals, that necessitate enormous quantities of the resource. Rather states have the option of procuring 'virtual water', that is to import commodities that themselves consumed large amounts of water in more bountiful climates. One thing, the experts insist, it most certainly does not make sense to do, on a large scale, is to transport water from one country to another as Israel was planning to do from Turkey. As for the dangers of inter-state conflict, much as it may appear plausible that states would fight for this most primeval and deeply symbolic of resources, there is little evidence that in modern times they have yet done so. Whilst states may indeed protest and dispute over water, and whilst it may provoke or feed considerable suspicion in the region, this does not entail that water will in any direct way lead to war. States may, of course, choose to fight over anything, most notoriously slights trivial or imagined, or designs on flags, or strips of useless earth, the latter invested with 'sacred' character for the occasion, but these are not, in analytic terms, plausible *causes*.

The overriding concern about the Middle Eastern economies must, however, be not the tensions which particular commodities – oil, food, water – may create within and between states, so much as the pressure of the three crises which were developing from the 1990s onwards in poten-tial convergent manner: the marginalisation of the region within the new 'globalised' world economy, the long-run fall in state revenues and the inability of labour markets to provide employment. On the evidence avail-able, it appeared that there was little that the majority of Middle Eastern states were willing, or in some cases able, to do to meet these challenges. The integration in, and competitiveness of, the regional economies was less, not more, at the end of the 1990s than it had been three decades before, prior to the start of the oil boom. While the income gap between the Middle East and western Europe widened, the gap in economic per-formance and financial attractiveness between it and other, previously comparable parts of the developing world, notably South-East Asia, was

[76] For the 'water optimist' case see Tony Allan, *The Middle East Water Question*.

greater. At the same time, the fall in real income from oil, as from other forms of rent, and the inability, or refusal, of states to raise revenue from domestic sources, through taxation above all, reflected the weakness, not the strength, of these regimes: quite simply, behind the walls of their palaces and a barrage of joint communiqués, congratulatory telegrams and fantasaical projects, they were afraid. As for employment, changes in the world economy and in technology placed greater emphasis upon skills and upon not only education but continual re-education, to provide a workforce capable of attracting global capital. Yet in the region literacy rates were 50 per cent, as opposed to 90 per cent in South-East Asia. The gap in terms of technologically relevant skills was far higher, and widening by the day.

The consequences of this convergence of negative trends were not only economic but also political. States were unable or unwilling to take unpopular measures because of the difficulties they faced at home. Nor were they able or willing to pursue alternative paths that would have led them into overt conflict with IFIs or multinational corporations. The causes of this impasse lay not in nature, history or holy text but in politics: they lay in the continued desire by state elites, royal families or military castes to control their societies and economies; in expenditure on military purchases; in the pervasive sense, shared by potential investors inside the region and outside, of an unfavourable legal and state culture; in the case of several countries, continued anxieties about war or instability, and in the continued willingness of their foreign, mainly western advisers, official and unofficial alike, to indulge, for reasons of financial greed, the fantasies of the region's elites. In sum, in international as in domestic politics the Middle East exhibited to the highest degree the salience of states and the impact of an unstable and inefficient *political economy*.

Part IV

Conclusion

10   The Middle East in international perspective

Regional concerns, global context: pretexts and potentialities

This book began with the challenge of relating the study of the Middle East to the broader concerns of International Relations. On the one hand, this involved deploying the categories of International Relations theory to *explain* the Middle East, and seeing how far this particular region can be understood in terms of the concepts of International Relations and historical sociology. The argument was made of any theory that, if it could not help to explain the Middle East, it could not fly. Hopefully enough has been said to show that this challenge can be met, at least in so far as IR has a research agenda represented in the chapters of this book, for analysing the region. At the same time, the theoretical approach suggests a historical perspective, seeing the contemporary state as a product of modern forces.

In particular, four broad claims have been made about the applicability of International Relations to this region: that the region has to be seen in terms of the pattern of its historical incorporation into the global political and economic system, 'differential integration', and that it is this which defines the character, and limited powers, of regional states; that the central category for understanding the international relations of the Middle East and its relations with outside powers is the *institutional*, rather than *juridical* concept, of the state, inviting, but leaving open a study of the influence on its decision-making processes and policy-making; that the international politics of the region have to be seen at three distinct levels, in terms of the interaction of global structures of power, of regional states and of non-state or social movements; and that the belief systems, ideologies, norms of the region while they draw selectively on the past are not traditional but modern phenomena that have to be related to the interests of these contemporary states and their apparatus.

So much for the conceptual system as applied to the region. The other side of the challenge was that relating the Middle East as a set of states, upheavals and events, by no means now contained, to International Relations theory itself. Chapter 1 laid out five broad approaches to the international relations of the Middle East. Each can certainly yield a research agenda and a set of detailed explanations; each can, in this sense, demonstrate its relevance, and, as all good paradigms do, explain most things.[1] Yet the argument of this book has been that the Middle East can illustrate the strengths and weaknesses of these broad approaches not only with regard to the Middle East itself but also with regard to the general analysis of international relations. A purely narrative or biographical approach, rich in detail as it may be, may prejudge discussion of the analytic and comparative issues involved. A realist approach, while it can develop arguments about security and the relation of global system to regional actors, deploys too narrow a concept of the state, and ignores both state–society and transnational factors. It may, as the study of revolutions and social movements shows, obscure the underlying dynamic of change. Foreign Policy Analysis takes us inside the society and the decision-making process, but in so doing its loses focus on the state itself. In its conventional Anglo-Saxon form, the emphasis on culture and values, in particular constructivism, recycles some classic insights of sociology but detaches these too far from the modern context and from the interests and reality upon which they rest, and by which they are shaped. The approach based on the institutional concept of the state, broadly derived from historical sociology, offers the most creative analytic framework, not only as to how politics and international relations are conducted but also as to the historic *origins*, and core *activities*, of states, and allows adjudication of some of the general debates pertaining to the study of the region, be they conflict, state–society tensions and particularly state–class, or the formation of ideologies. Historical sociology also offers a history that is discontinuous, and a break from the assumption of continuity, across centuries and of 'culture' that pervades so much analysis and public discussion of the region.

Yet the institutional concept of the state also faces challenges from the politics of the Middle East. In the first place, any contrast of state and society presumes a boundary between the two that is not always evident, especially in the Middle East. Even in Israel and Turkey, and after some privatisation in the 1980s and 1990s, the state's influence, through banking and the arms industry, reaches far into the economy. In oil-producing states rent provides a means by which nearly all businesses, and employment, are tributary of the state. The question is where the state ends,

---

[1] Thomas Kuhn's *Structure of Scientific Revolutions*, London: University of Chicago Press, 1962, illustrates how scientific paradigms can for long periods fend off 'anomalia'. Realism did just that.

not where the private sector begins. In the state-controlled economies of Egypt and Syria a parallel dependency operates. At the same time, it is in some cases difficult to talk in the political sense of any coherent state where multiple factional and elite groups exist: in Saudi Arabia, to take an extreme case, individual members of the elite pursue policies that are largely independent of the rulers, yet in financial and status terms remain part of the Saudi state. All states have factions and, something more, institutional divisions – hence the concept of the 'polymorphous' state developed by Michael Mann. In liberal societies this is, or should be, transparent, but in authoritarian regimes it is obscure. Another challenge for historical sociology is the question of how, given this statist approach, we can explain the relation of the Middle Eastern state to the broader international context. Here it is necessary to see how this external incorporation, from 1600 onwards, and especially from 1918, produced a particular kind of Middle East state system, and accompanying ideological atmosphere; this broad process is what had, in chapter 9, been termed 'differential integration'. By this is meant the process by which the Middle East has been incorporated into the global system, and reshaped by it, but in a way that accentuates not the similarities, but the differences, between it and the developed world. Globalisation, which ties the world more closely together, but in a more unequal, rancorous and potentially conflictual way, is the most recent chapter in this five centuries old process.

The 'differential' pattern affects not just levels of income and other indices of development, the standard fare of north–south comparisons, but also the very character of the state: Middle Eastern states act, as they must, like other states do, and are shaped by the two inexorable forces of international pressure without and state–society relations within. But the working out of these forces in the Middle East from the early twentieth century has taken a different path from that taken by conceptually similar states in Europe from the early sixteenth century. All states compete, plunder, try to manage the tensions with society, and proclaim outrageous forms of self-legitimation, but they do so in different ways – and, let it be not forgotten, the European state system displayed its *greatest* volatility *and* violence four centuries into its modernity, in the years 1914–45. This book has argued *against* prediction as a test or challenge for social science. We cannot anticipate the events of coming years or decades. We can, however, see the modern state system in IR long-term historic context.

In the first place, the Middle East shares with the rest of Asia and Africa, and with Latin America, a past of economic subordination to a capitalist system that has been expanding since around 1500, but which has over the past two centuries in particular effectively incorporated and subordinated the rest of the world. In the case of the Middle East this economic incorporation may have been somewhat later than elsewhere, but, beginning with the transformation of Egyptian agriculture to produce cotton in the 1860s, it has proceeded apace, as much at the physical and coercive as at the economic level. Secondly, as elsewhere, the process of Middle Eastern state formation has reflected this incorporation: even where the very states themselves, their names and territory, were not, as was the case in all of Latin America and Africa, and in much of Asia and the Middle East, the products of colonial control, the formation of the state, through the needs of domestic control and international relations alike, was determined by these global structures. The states of the Middle East reflect, in their use of oil revenues, the workings of civilian and military apparatuses, the tasks they set themselves in this universal context: above all, of course, Middle Eastern states and ruling elites are directed to maintaining their control over society and economy and in enriching those with privileged access to them.

That these are in many ways weak states, unable to permit themselves to allow greater popular participation or open access to information about state or society, is hardly unique to this region: the weakness of states, as instruments of rule, is widespread in the post-colonial world and has, in fact, gone much further elsewhere, in Africa, than it has in the core Middle East. (Contrast the cluster of 'failed states' in Central Africa to the relative order of, even, Lebanon.) A third context of external formation has been that of international politics itself: the modern Middle East has been incorporated and shaped by developments in the global political and strategic context – from the expansion of Habsburg and Romanov power in the seventeenth century and beyond, through overt colonialism before and after World War I, World War II, through to the Cold War and the age of US dominance which succeeded it. Middle Eastern states wish, and try, to escape from this global political system, but in so doing, as is evident in the case of Iraq and Iran, they and their people pay a high price. The most resolute attempts to resist the modern world were those of the Hamid al-Din rulers of Yemen (1918–62), Imams Ahmad and Yahya and Sultan Said bin Taimur of Oman (1933–70). Imam Yahya declared that if he had to choose between wealth and subjugation and poverty and independence, he would choose the latter. In the end, this could not last: modernity took its toll. While *external* forces more or less accepted this withdrawal, *internal* social forces did not and, as in other countries that had pursued pre-modern autarchy (Ethiopia, Afghanistan), erupted, when finally they did, with *greater* force and dislocation. What ensued was revolution in Yemen in 1962, insurrections in Oman that were suppressed but led to major state transformations after 1970. The Imams and Sultans kept gunboats and markets at bay, they could not stop the spread of ideas and of social change.

The outcome of this history of differential integration has been to produce a region that is closely connected with the rest of the world but which is beset by some distinctive problems, and whose states in their practice, composition and very character internalise this inequality. The first supervening characteristic that results from this is the militarised character of relations between states. The Middle East remains one of the most insecure regions of the world; true, there are two other areas – the China–Taiwan and the India–Pakistan conflicts – where similar insecurity and danger persist, but the Middle East itself has two explosive sub-regions, the Arab–Israeli and the Gulf, between the two of which there is a tenuous, but persistent, interconnection. Decades of negotiation, open and covert, of 'processes' and 'initiatives', have made little progress here, nor, in all probability, will much progress be made for a long time to come. The Arab–Israeli dispute is not the sole focus of conflict in the Middle East. However, beyond the failure to meet Palestinian claims for statehood, and the Israeli need for security, it remains a strategic danger, for those directly involved and for all states in the region who are drawn, to varying degrees, into its orbit. Palestine is also a source of ideological and contestatory mobilisation. The resistance of the Palestinians resonates throughout much of the Middle East and, especially in an era of satellite TV, has done much to mobilise anger amongst the populations. At the same time, throughout the 1990s the unresolved crisis in the Gulf, focused on Iraq, already the sources of three inter-state wars, presaged further conflict. Beyond these two most intense conflicts there are others, such as those between Syria and Iraq on the one side and Turkey on the other, where the danger of future conflict exists. Arms expenditures as a percentage of budgets and GDP remain higher than elsewhere, as do arms imports[2]. Proliferation of weapons of mass destruction has already begun in the Middle East, and has been encouraged by the example of India and Pakistan which, in May 1998, exploded nuclear weapons without major retribution from the outside world. In its effects on the Middle East alone, the Indian decision to explode a nuclear weapon in May 1998 must count as the most irresponsible action in international affairs since 1945. The states of the region are interlocked in the Greater West Asian Crisis, but so, more explosively, are the people, their passions fuelled by what appears to be an integrated international conflict.

Secondly, even where there is no actual military conflict, relations between states remain rigid. One broad trend of the latter part of the twentieth century, evident in Europe and the Americas, and to some degree

[2] See Table 5, p. 337.

in East Asia, was towards something loosely called 'interdependence': by this was meant a lowering of barriers, a reduced sense of insecurity and an increase in transactions that did not involve the state, that is, which were transnational rather than international. Much has been made since the early 1990s of 'non-state' activity in the Middle East region, but this is in large measure a facade: free press, free association or political parties are allowed. Most of what are called NGOs are linked to individuals or agencies of the state, not excluding the intelligence services. If there is no real private sector within states, there can be no meaningful liberal interdependence, of trade, investment or anything else between them. There has, in the proper sense of the word, been very little actual interdependence in the Middle East, relations being controlled by states and focusing on the security agenda. In contexts of inter-state confrontation such economic or social relations are virtually non-existent and ineffective; trade and investment did not, in the twenty years after Camp David, lessen Egyptian–Israeli differences, nor do they play any significant role in relations between Iraq and Iran, or Iraq and Kuwait. Turkey's economic relations, in trade and construction, with the Arab world have had no positive enduring political impact on the foreign relations of these states and may well have made them worse.

Here there is a marked contrast with that other area of persistent inter-state rivalry, China and Taiwan: despite the lack of formal diplomatic relations, and the persistent threat of war, trade and investment flow across the Taiwan straits – Taiwanese investment in mainland China running at many billions of dollars. Even between Arab states there is little effective co-operation between states in terms of trade or investment. Again, there is a need to avoid singularity. In what is a broader than normal pattern, overall levels of regional economic integration are low, and it is not surprising that this is so.[3] The Gulf Co-operation Council has announced plans for progressive reduction of trade barriers, but there is little that these states have to trade with each other. Elsewhere earlier projects, such as the Arab Co-operation Council and the Arab Maghrib Union, failed to advance, the former disappearing altogether when one of its members, Iraq, invaded Kuwait. In one domain there is close collaboration:

---

[3] Mohammed Ayyoub wrote: 'the concept of absolute gains fails to capture the reality of inter-state relationships among Third World countries themselves . . . Although there have been some attempts at building institutions to promote security cooperation and increase economic interactions among regional states, e.g. ASEAN, SAARC, ECOWAS, etc., by and large the relationship among contiguous and proximate states has been one of suspicion if not overt conflict. Many regional cooperation arrangements have been bedevilled by the existence of covert if not overt hostility among members of regional institutions.' 'Inequality and Theorizing in International Relations: the Case for Subaltern Realism', paper presented to Annual Convention of ISA, Chicago, February 2001, p. 12.

ministries of security and intelligence may co-operate with each other, but this is not a harbinger of broader liberal integration, and, even here, one may doubt whether there is much trust. In the words of one Egyptian economist: 'Any attempt now to mention, or even to hint at the possibility of an Arab political or economic cooperation, let alone integration, would be taken as a bad joke.'[4]

This persistence of military and economic confrontation and fragmentation is matched at the level of culture and ideology. There is no shortage in the culture of the region of critical, independent and creative voices: the novels, poetry, music, let alone jokes, of the Middle East are testament enough to the originality and critical spirit of its inhabitants.[5] In this literature there is a rich account of the corruption of rulers, the violence and hypocrisy of males, the stupidities of the clergy, the costs of social and inter-ethnic violence, not to mention the variety and arbitrariness of human beings.[6] The Internet and satellite television are in *some* respects providing a greater diversity of information and more critical voices than was previously the case. But the strength of this autonomous cultural space should not be exaggerated. As explored in chapter 8, many of the voices and media which are 'critical' in one direction, al-Jazira TV or the radical dailies in London, al-Quds and al-'Arab, are in fact controlled by other states and interests, which permit no criticism of their own practices and for which there are clear 'red lines' that the papers may not cross (for example, corruption, monarchical succession, Sunni–Shi'a tensions, treatment of migrant workers). Public space within states is circumscribed by a continued concern of authorities to control and manipulate what is written and transmitted, negatively through censorship and positively through propaganda of various kinds, not least pretentious and lavishly funded but vacuous conferences on fashionable topics of the day. Educational systems are controlled by states and a pervasive mediocrity affects what is taught, written and permitted to be said.[7]

[4] Galal Amin in Derek Hopwood, ed., *Arab Nation: Arab Nationalism*, London: Macmillan, 2001, p. 156.
[5] For the classic discussion see Khalid Kishtainy, *Arab Political Humour*, London: Quartet, 1983.
[6] For example, Mai Ghoussoub, *Leaving Beirut: Women and the Wars Within*, London: Saqi, 1998. Khamsin, ed., *Forbidden Agendas: Intolerance and Defiance in the Middle East*, London: Saqi, 1984. The Lebanese film director Randa Chahal Sabbag has portrayed in her film *A Civilised People* (2000) the barbarities committed by all sides in the war, reminding a society that has chosen, collectively, to deny the recent past of the hatred it experienced and is still unresolved ('A Filmmaker Dissects Lebanon's Civil War', *International Herald Tribune*, 15 June 2000).
[7] Kevin Dwyer, *Arab Voices: the Human Rights Debate in the Middle East*, London: Routledge, 1991; Hazim Saghie, ed., *The Predicament of the Individual in the Middle East*, London: Saqi, 2004; Katerina Dalacoura, *Islam, Liberalism and Human Rights*, London: I. B. Tauris, 1998.

The pressure on society from 'above', from states, is compounded by pressure from another quarter from below, that is, from a changing social and ideological context. Much is made of the (traditional) 'Muslim' character of politics and culture in this region. But this impression of deep-rooted, 'authentic' Islamic politics is inaccurate. The Middle East has, even as a wide-ranging discussion has taken place in Islamic terms, in modern times, and well before 1914–18, been influenced by the serial waves of *secular* ideology that have swept the wider world, from liberalism, through nationalism, communism, socialism and fascism. If liberalism declined after World War II and communism and socialism from the 1970s, other ideological forces have, however, retained or, more often, newly asserted their vitality, notably, in varying forms and combinations, nationalism and, only after the 1960s, Islamism. The intellectual tenacity of nationalism and Islamism is a result not of tradition, but of the failure, and in places the bloody repression, of other secular forces: Iran after 1953 was an example. This was never more in evidence than in the post-Cold War period when they provided much of the idiom in terms of which political debate was conducted. In one sense the hold of these nativist ideas, like the power of the authoritarian state, was a relic of the Cold War, an ideological legacy that too many, in power and without, found it convenient to sustain. Ideological concepts of 'imperialism', 'reason', 'liberalism' (as a term of abuse), 'anti-globalisation' know no origin or end-user certification.[8] In the 1990s, in country after country a regressive and confrontational nationalism was evident – from Arab campaigns 'against "normalisation"', *dhud al-tatbia*, with Israel, to chauvinism within Israeli society, and sustained support for nationalist intransigence, towards Arabs and Kurds, in Turkey. Iran was relatively less affected by this, but here too, as the appeal of a transnational Islamic solidarity waned, a commitment to promoting Iran as a strong nation, *mellat-i bozorg-i Iran*, 'The Great Nation of Iran', was evident across the spectrum, espoused as much by the reformist bloc, following Mohammad Khatami, as by the more conservative forces. Iranian attitudes to neighbouring peoples – for example, Turks, Afghans, Pakistanis, Arabs – spontaneously offered and with no hint of reserve, were noticeably lacking in charity.

It is the ongoing, but, in ideological terms, constantly redefined tension between state and society in general and the social context of the late twentieth century that explains the prevalence of Islamism, and Islamic

---

[8] For critics of Middle Eastern 'nativism' see, for the Arab world, Sadeq al-'Azam, 'Orientalism and Orientalism in Reverse', *Khamsin*, no. 8, 1981, 19XX, and Fouad Ajami, *The Dream Palace of the Arabs: a Generation's Odyssey*, New York: Pantheon, 1998; for Iran Darius Shayegan and Mehdi Boroujerdi. For a classic, all-purpose, excoriation see Bill Warren, *Imperialism*, London: Verso, 1981.

discourse, within the discussion of politics after 1970. In Iran, Turkey, Egypt, to take three cases, the rise of Islamism in the 1970s and 1980s was a product of social change, of resentment at the modernising state, but was also, in considerable measure, a product of international factors, of the Cold War. This is reflected in the failure of secular modernisation programmes of left (Arab socialism) and right (the Shah), of direct encouragement by the west of anti-communist forces, as in Afghanistan, or of the tacit overt encouragement of Islamists, as a counter-weight to the left, in a range of other countries, among them Turkey, Israel/Palestine, Yemen and Algeria. Long before 11 September 2001 the secular and left forces in these countries were feeling the brunt of the counter-revolution: in Afghanistan, Iran, Lebanon, Yemen and Algeria Islamists had attacked and killed their secular foes. Islamist opposition was at the same time a product of prevailing political contexts, of resistance to authoritarian modernising regimes which had been formed in the Cold War context, from Algeria to Iran, and of opposition to foreign intervention, be it of Israel in Lebanon or the USSR in Afghanistan. By the 1990s not only the context, but in some measure also the momentum of these radical Islamist movements had declined, even as the state which most epitomised the Islamist upsurge, Iran, entered into a period of internal debate. It was, in this period, legitimate to talk of a 'crisis of political Islam', a lessening of the Islamist dynamic across the Muslim world combined with a degeneration into nihilistic violence and anarchical sloganeering of the programme and practice of Islamist groups. The latter were more and more raw aspirants to power rather than proponents of any clearly imagined alternative social or ethical order.[9]

Any general question, as to the general context and shared radical discourse, may mask the variety of such movements, though the alternatives posed, 'advance' or 'retreat' of Islamists (that is, whether 'Islamism' is on the rise or is waning), may be mistaken. Tempting as it may have been to try to set all the distinct, national Islamist movements within one frame and political context, no such overall assessment was possible, particularly because of the varying responses of states: some, such as in Egypt, sought accommodation with the Muslim Brotherhood, while others, notably Turkey, long resisted the social and political pressure, only to allow an Islamist government in 2002.[10] The Islamist elites in power

[9] Olivier Roy, *The Failure of Political Islam*, London: I. B. Tauris, 1994; Ibrahim al-Karawan, *The Islamic Impasse*, London: IISS, 1997. But this was an *ideological* failure or impasse, *not* a loss of the militaristic *jihadi* dynamic.

[10] Gudrun Kramer, 'The Integration of the Integrists: a Comparative Study of Egypt, Jordan and Tunisia', in Ghassan Salam, ed., *Democracy without Democrats? The Renewal of Politics in the Muslim World*, London: I. B. Tauris, 1994. See also Basma Kodmany-Darwish and May Chartouni-Dubarry, *Les états Arabes face à la contestation islamiste*, Paris: Armand Colin, 1977.

in Iran and Sudan may have faced problems, and growing popular disillusion, but they showed no sign of retreating from power.[11] The Islamist regime in Afghanistan, the Amirate of the Taliban, in power since 1996, fell only when, in October 2001, it faced attack by the USA. Elsewhere, as with Hizbullah in Lebanon, and with the *salafi* movements within the Arab states of the Gulf, Islamists seemed to be gaining ground. The assaults of al-Qa'ida on 11 September 2001 were but the most spectacular in a campaign it had been conducting against western targets since 1993 and against left-wing and secular Middle Eastern foes much earlier. The depth of support among the 'Islamic public' that the attacks on America revealed was to become the popular underpinning of the 'Greater West Asian Crisis'.

What was of immense significance for the conduct of foreign relations by Middle Eastern states was that this combination of nationalism and religious militancy, Islamist or Judaic, often converged in a composite, or overlapping, response to the outside world. In the Arab world Islamists were in general more than willing to espouse the causes that nationalists upheld, be this opposition to 'normalisation' with Israel, a general suspicion of globalisation, as another imperialist conspiracy, or support for the Ba'th leadership in Iraq, as *ramz al-'arab*, the 'model' of the Arabs. For their part, from the early 1980s onwards, nationalists, with former Egyptian socialists in the lead, more and more, and despite their secular antecedents, accepted Islamist demands, on the position of women, censorship of books[12] or the place of religiosity in public life, and particularly shamefully, in campaigns against independent NGOs, universal human rights standards and even the prohibition of cliterodectomy. This was especially evident in Egypt where the impasse of left-wing Nasserism led all too many intellectuals to adopt the language of 'green', i.e. Islamia, militancy. In Israel, a somewhat comparable process was in train, as the power of the orthodox or *haredim* increased, first in regard to such particular issues of religious concern as education and Sabbath observance in Jerusalem, and then across a broader range of national political issues,

---

[11] For contrasting views of the prospects for change in Iran, see, for an excellent sceptical view, Mohammad-Reza Djalili, *Iran: L'illusion réformiste*, Paris: Presses de Sciences Po, 2001; for an analysis of conflicting trends, Farhad Khosrokhavar and Olivier Roy, *Iran: Comment sortir d'une revolution religieuse*, Paris: Editions du Seuil, 1999; for a more sympathetic argument, based on an analysis of conflicting factions *within* the regime, Ali Ansari, *Iran, Islam and Democracy: the Politics of Managing Change*, London: Royal Institute of International Affairs, 2000.

[12] A 2004 list of Arabic language books published by Saqi in Beirut and banned in Arab states includes dozens of works by liberal Arab writers such as Hazim Saghie, Mohammed Arkoun – as well as non-Muslims writing on the region, including the author of this book, Sami Zubaida, Gilles Kepel, etc.

notably the need to retain control of the West Bank, deemed part of
'historic' or 'ancestral' Israel, and the indivisibility of Jerusalem. All of
this was justified by repetition of choice sentences from holy writ, in this
case the Bible, enjoining massacre, expulsion and destruction.

The consequences for foreign relations in the 1980s and 1990s of this
ideological trend within the region were considerable: states and their
opponents alike across the Middle East, and not excluding Turkey and
Israel, too easily saw in confrontation, denunciation, negative stereotyping and the very cultivation of fear the most easily available means of
reinforcing their own positions. Railing against America, and Zionism,
was standard fare. Political culture and discourse are certainly not the
autonomous cause of the enduring inability of the Middle East to resolve
its inter-state and inter-ethnic differences, but discourses, slogans, polemical distortions certainly help: that is all the more so since, in authoritarian
states, public opinion and the realm of permitted intellectual discourse
that relates to international issues are too often restricted. Those who
propose understanding, or reconciliation, let alone self-criticism, are too
easily denounced by their fellow citizens as traitors, a modern term with
its many local, 'communitarian' variants. Moreover, those to whom they
propose understanding are too easily tempted to see such openings as a
sign of weakness and thereby to discredit those who advocate dialogue
with them: Israeli prime minister Begin humiliated President Sadat on his
visit to Jerusalem in 1977; those among the Arabs who proposed reconciliation with Israel, 'normalisation', after the Oslo Accords of 1993, were
increasingly criticised in the Arab world. Rejection of political engagement is too often the easier option.[13] Yet in some cases the alternative to
a refusal to engage may, in domestic politics, be a deceptive accommodation that the state then betrays. In the late 1980s the Iranian government
lured into 'dialogue' exiled opposition politicians (some of them, such as
the Kurdish leader Abd al-Rahman Qassemlu, personally known to the
author), and then murdered them in cold blood, as it did with Qassemlu
in Vienna in 1989. The greatest illusion of all in politics, apart from mis-
taking one's wishes for reality, is that of basing critique on the premise
that there is one ideal, right, course of action.

Contesting 'globalisation'

Nowhere was this antagonistic response, be it nationalist or Islamist, more
evident in the Muslim world than in regard to the debate on 'globalisation'

[13] Hazim Saghie, ed., *The Predicament of the Individual in the Middle East*, London: Saqi,
2001.

that gathered pace in the second half of the 1990s. This debate, as it developed in the post-Cold War Middle East and beyond, encompassed many of the themes, and critiques, found elsewhere in the world. This critique was, whenever in 'green' form, and emphasising themes like Palestine or the defence of the Arabic language, not therefore an insulated or culturally specific discourse, specific to Muslims or inhabitants of the Middle East, but was rather one which engaged with the range of themes involved in globalisation. It responded in terms similar to those critiques of globalisation found elsewhere. This overlap in discourse was particularly evident in comparison with other non-western societies, such as China, India or Latin America, be it in regard to trade liberalisation, WTO membership, the intrusion of US culture, fast food, changes in patterns of information and family structure. As noted, even St Valentine's Day, 14 February, fell under attack as a symbol of western cultural assault. This was reflected in terminology. While the Arab world agreed on the term *awlama* for 'globalisation' (from *alim*, 'world', an equivalent to French *mondialisation*), the Iranians could not at first choose between the positive *jahani-shodan*, 'world becoming', and the pejorative *jahani-giri*, 'world-grabbing'.

Faced with globalisation, there were three identifiable broad responses: participation, accommodation and denunciation.[14] Some Middle Eastern and indeed Islamic voices advocated participation, indeed welcomed globalisation, on the grounds that Islam as a universal religion should, and could, take the opportunity provided by globalisation to spread its message. These included the Islamic thinker Ali Mazrui and, unexpectedly perhaps, Libyan leader Qaddafi. Others advocated a negotiated accommodation. The latter recognised that globalisation provided challenges, as well as opportunities; they argued that Muslim states and the Muslim religion could work to promote a more co-operative, just world order, drawing on the shared values of east and west, and on the widespread international concern with issues of equality and justice. This second response was expressed by Iranian president Khatami in June 2000: 'We cannot afford to remain heedless of the political, economic and cultural origins, impacts and mechanisms of the consequential phenomenon of globalization . . . Instead of looking at globalization from the viewpoint of hegemony and domination, we ought to foster partnership and co-operation, recognizing the essential contribution to be made by every community and region.'[15] This positive response

---

[14] Fred Halliday, 'The Middle East and the Politics of Differential Integration', in Toby Dodge and Richard Higgott, eds., *Globalization and the Middle East: Islam, Economy, Society and Politics*, London: RIIA, 2002.

[15] BBC, *Summary of World Broadcasts*, ME/3864 MED/18, 12 June 2000.

was nonetheless linked to a critique of western, especially US, domination, to calls for a more equitable international security and trading system and for an end to the domination of the world by one hegemonic power.

The most widespread response was, however, one of denunciation. According to the Lebanese writer George Tarabishi, by 2000 globalisation had become the object of widespread denunciation by the Arab intelligentsia, as an attack on the state, language, nation and fatherland of the Arabs.[16] Globalisation was, in this view, an 'imperialist' project, designed to subordinate the political system, economy and culture of the Arab world, a continuation of western imperialism by another name and by other means. Globalisation became, in effect, a demon against which nationalists and Islamists could fulminate. The Moroccan Islamist leader Abdessalam Yassine saw globalisation as part of a general western assault on the region in his 1998 book, *To Islamize Modernity*: 'The menacing character of the new political order and of economic globalisation proclaim the offensive launched in all directions by the great hegemonic power against the underdeveloped countries which suffer from it more than the rich countries. This politico-economic aggression forces us to mobilise our forces to confront it.'[17] In April 2000 the Iranian spiritual leader Ayatollah Khamene'i advanced a similar argument: 'What is globalisation? It means that a group of world powers, a number of countries – mainly those who have influence over the UN and mainly those countries which have been colonialists in the past – want to expand their culture, economy and traditions throughout the world. They want to set up a share-holding company in which they should hold 95% of its shares, while the rest of world countries have 5%. They want to have authority. They want to make decisions. That is what globalisation means'.[18]

Small wonder then if, parallel to a diffuse ideological resistance to globalisation, the majority of Middle Eastern states should also have appeared to be so little integrated into this changing world economy. As discussed at greater length in chapter 9 there were several indices of this. First, in the field of trade the normal exports of most Middle Eastern countries to the developed world were insignificant. Secondly, with the exception

---

[16] François Zabbal, 'Die arabische Intelligenz und das Gespenst der Globalisierung', *Neue Zürcher Zeitung*, 24 January 2001. For one cogent statement of the pan-Islamist argument in favour of a radical globalisation see Naveed S. Sheikh, *The New Politics of Islam: Pan-Islamic Foreign Policy in a World of States*, London: Routledge, 2003. Of course, as seen above, Islam has no problem in adjusting to nationalism and nation-states.

[17] Abdessalam Yassine, *Islamiser la modernité*, n.p: Al Ofok Impressions, 1998, p. 245.

[18] BBC, *Summary of World Broadcasts*, ME/3822 MED/2, 24 April 2000.

of Israel and Turkey, foreign direct investment in the Middle East itself was extremely low – a few billion dollars at most, out of a total of investment flows to developing countries in the late 1990s of $200 billion. Thirdly, nearly all Middle Eastern states retained a strong hold on their economies, through ownership, subsidies, protection and also, of no little significance, through corruption. Indeed, oil apart, one of the most striking features of international discussion of globalisation and changes in the world economy in the 1990s and 2000s was *how little* the Middle East as a whole was normally included.

There was, of course, much debate on why this was so; many in the region put the blame on the regional or global context, on the insecurity bred by confrontation with Israel, or Iraq, or on a more diffuse but effective western desire to prevent the investment of oil revenues in the region, the better to recycle them to the west. Others alluded to the insecurity bred by government, and elite, intervention in the economies, and the corruption which was pervasive in commercial dealings. As analysed in chapter 9, this pattern was not simply a product of a *lack of connection* between the region and the world economy, since those connections were in some respects very strong, and had been so for centuries: the region accounted for a third of the oil and gas traded on the world economy; Middle Eastern states were in receipt of billions of dollars every year, directly to the Gulf states and, through their policies of support to other Arab states and through remittances, to other Middle Eastern states as well; this money was reinvested in the west, to the tune of between $1.5 billion and $4,000 billion. Any explanation of the lack of FDI and of economic integration in the region itself would have therefore to cover not only why external investors, other than the oil and gas industry, did not invest in the region but also why local investors were so reluctant to do so, and why states, through a reluctance to introduce taxation of any kind, other than on imports, failed to encourage this. Somehow, all of this returned to politics, to the state, and to the unease, to say the least, in its relations to society and other states alike.

Middle Eastern states: structural constraints, real options

To argue for the centrality of the state in politics and international relations is, however, in policy terms two-sided, since for all that states have capacities to pursue different policies internally and externally, the state can also act to resist, or prevent, change: this is true of all the areas of state intervention discussed in this book – political system, and the control of democratisation, the economy, law, ideology, community, class and

gender relations and, not least, foreign relations.[19] Such resistance is not
a result of some regional quirk, 'Islam' or the 'Arab' mind, but is, rather,
a consequence of the factors discussed in this book, the international and
internal forces shaping the state. In the Middle East, for these reasons,
the state has thus served not only to preserve security, but also to block
or resist change, from within and without. Whether it be in the control of
domestic politics, or in the intervention of the state in the economy, or in
the sustained, and in some cases (e.g. GCC) enhanced, manipulation of
cultural life and the media, the state has, in most countries, served so far
to contain those pressures for change which society has generated. Where
it failed, it succumbed to one or other of the dual challenges facing every
state – revolt from within (Iran, 1979) or military assault from without
(Iraq 2003).

The counter-arguments to this emphasis on the state, heard in the
Middle East as much as elsewhere, are two: one 'realist', the other
'structural'. First is argued, in tones echoing Hobbes, that the alternatives to the intervention of the state are less desirable – chaos, violence,
insecurity. In particular, it is claimed, first, that the available oppositions
are regressive and themselves even more dictatorial and, secondly, that
the options open to Middle Eastern states are themselves so limited, by
dint of the regional and international structures in which these states are
located, that they have no freedom to pursue policies other than those
they do. That the states and societies of the region are threatened by
a range of challenges, internal and external, is evident. Indisputably in
many cases the programmes of the opposition forces are themselves auto-
cratic. The Islamist opposition movements seen in many countries would
not inspire confidence as to their democratic or administrative abilities,
or as to their treatment of women. The impact of opposition local pressure *from* below over the 1980s and 1990s with regard to, for example,
freedom of expression, alcohol and *hijab* is evidence enough of that. Here
silence or failure to engage may be a rhetorical strength. In the debate
surrounding al-Qa'ida in 2001 few bothered even to ask what economic
and social development programme it offered, not least since it appeared,
implicitly at least, to hold up the desolate and doomed Islamic Amirate
of Afghanistan, the state of the Taliban, as its model; yet this should be
a major test for any aspirant to power anywhere in the world. Indeed the
greatest single failure of the Islamic project is not what it talks about –
gender, state, 'the West' – but what it fails to talk about – economics.

[19] Hassan Hakimian and Ziba Moshaver, eds., *The State and Global Change; the Political
Economy of Transition in the Middle East and North Africa*, London: Curzon Press, 2000;
Clement Henry and Robert Springborg, eds., *Globalization and the Politics of Development
in the Middle East*, Cambridge: Cambridge University Press, 2001.

However, this is not sufficient defence: states cannot simply take the character of their opponents as a given, since opposition in part reflects the character of the state it challenges. As for the negative impact of regional and international insecurity on the possibilities of liberty, this is too often used by states as an alibi to justify the suppression of dissent: the appeal to concerns of 'internal security' legitimates all coercion. The fate of independent voices in Egypt, Syria, Iraq or Saudi Arabia in the 1990s and beyond has less to do with any genuine threat to the country's security, and more to do with the wish of the state to stifle dissent.

The second, broader, argument on the limited powers of states within global structures, derived from theories of imperialism or structural dependency, pervasive as it is, is even less convincing. This is at once the everyday defence of authoritarian or obstructive states and the particular claim of structural theories of dependence. As all IR and historical sociology studies have long shown, that states are *constrained* by their security, economic and ideological contexts is evident; but this does not mean, and never did mean, that states have *no* choices as to what they do. There are four areas in particular in which states, whatever the external, structural constraints on them, retain options: the quality of leadership and government, not least with regard to corruption; the quality of education; the participation of women in public life, political and economic; the openness of media and publishing.[20] Leadership and government pertain to the qualities of the leaders themselves, the example they set and the values they espouse, but also to the character of the state, in terms of effectiveness, training, decision-making processes and, not least, financial transparency or the lack of it. Education is the key to development and participation in the global economy. The participation of women is not only a means of making use of half of society's human resources, but is also the most effective means of reducing population growth. The openness of media and publishing is essential both for education, and the encouragement of free enquiry, and also for a critical assessment of the policies of both states and their opponents.

On all four of these the majority of Middle Eastern states fare badly; indeed the differentials between these states and not only the developed world but also a comparable region, East Asia, are widening. If the trends evident at the onset of the twenty-first century in each area persist, then the gaps will continue to widen further. For this pattern of Middle Eastern state behaviour, structural explanation, involving international or global factors, is not on its own sufficient. Indeed one of the major preconditions

---

[20] The first three of these are from Paul Kennedy, *Preparing for the Twenty-first Century*, London: HarperCollins, 1993, chapter 14.

for an effective state policy on education, as on economic development, namely capital, is present. At the same time the decision to invest the money outside the region, so-called 'recycling', is a choice of the rulers themselves, not a structural necessity, let alone an imperialist order. This margin of freedom applies equally to the predominant role of the state in the economy: this degree of state role, given the options visible in, say, Korea, Singapore or Taiwan, where the state is certainly still important, is not a given of the global structure but a function of the interests of those who control the state, be it in Kuwait, Syria, Egypt or Turkey. These states operate within a world of unequal power, that of long-standing and ever-enhanced western hegemony, and of differential integration. The mechanisms of that difference are as we have seen not only historic, a product of colonialism up to 1945, but replicated in new forms of economic, financial, technological influence, most recently those associated with globalisation. Yet recognition of that unequal relationship should not preclude the margins of freedom, domestically and internationally, that the states of the Middle East retain. Indeed, the maintenance of differential integration, and, in general, of political deference to the 'west', is something to which the states of the region make their own significant contribution. This is, above all, the powerful message of Bromley's *Rethinking Middle Eastern Politics*, a forceful refution of culturalist and structuralist/imperialist explanations alike.

In lieu of conclusion: three valedictory maxims

In sum, the discussion of theoretical approaches in the Introduction and chapter 1, one intended to underlie the more specific analysis of subsequent chapters, has provided, in schematic form, one overview of how the Middle East has been, and may be, approached in the study of International Relations. The claim has been, *in nuce*, to explain; it is for readers to say how far they think this approach has succeeded. By way of conclusion it may be worth summarising what has been implicit in the discussion so far, namely some other, more implicit and less abstract, in the social science sense 'banal', considerations that may in their own way contribute to the analysis of the region and which are pertinent to this study. Beyond theoretical orientations, these are three broad underlying premises, or maxims, that inform the preceding analysis.

First, it is advisable, while recognising that which is specific to the region, and to particular states within the region, to avoid what I have termed *regional narcissism*, meaning the exaggeration of just how unique or different the region is. Here measured, not overstated, recognition of external context, past and contemporary, may lessen the claims of singularity. This is not least because many are the result *not* of something internal, or timelessly causative, to the region at all, but to the impact of external forces – economic, strategic, intellectual – upon the area. These are forces that also affected Latin America, Africa and East Asia, or which, in the case of the relation between state formation, external pressures, economics and violence, were central to the earlier history of modern Europe and North America as well. The Middle East *was indeed* subjugated to decades of formal external rule and manipulation, and to centuries of informal influence from outside. This has, however, been the fate of the non-European world as a whole. Much is made of the impact of oil, on state–society relations and on work ethic; but the problems of oil-dependent or 'rentier' states are to be found in Venezuela and Nigeria, in Indonesia and Brunei, as much as in the Arabian Peninsula. To take another example, the low levels of regional economic integration characteristic of the region are found, equally, in Africa and the Caribbean. Israel is seen, by its opponents and its supporters, as somehow unique; but the creation of a new society through colonial Europe to third world immigration in Israel is but one of dozens of such cases in the modern world.[21] Few of its supposed peculiarities are specific to the region.

The same need for comparative sobriety goes for perceptions. The Middle East is, as critics of 'Orientalism' insist, often treated in terms of certain demeaning, timeless stereotypes by the press and academic analysts outside. Yet comparable stereotypes about the non-European, be they about religion, women or work practices, can be found in regard to Latin America, Africa, India or China. If the west dislikes 'Islam' it dislikes all other third world cultures equally. There is another problem here: such critics of 'Orientalism' are also endemically silent about the prejudice of Middle Eastern peoples towards the 'west', not to mention each other, this last an area of fervid, but formally denied, interaction. The same goes for the prevalence of conspiracy theory: apart from exploring what historic factors have led to the prevalence of conspiracy theories, to detach this issue from cultural essentialism, the prevalence of such collective cultures in other countries, such as the Balkans or China, can serve as a corrective. The best reflex is to ask, of anything that is said to be specific to the Middle East, whether comparable phenomena cannot be observed elsewhere. Sometimes this may be the case, but the onus of the argument should be on those who claim singularity.

---

[21] For a fine comparative study see Ian Lustick, *Unsettled States, Disputed Lands: Britain and Ireland, France and Algeria, Israel and the West Bank–Gaza,* Ithaca: Cornell University Press, 1993.

As for the second part of 'regional narcissism', the belief that the Middle East is in some way the centre, or pivot, of world politics and attention, no serious analysis of world history in the twentieth century could possibly claim this. In the Cold War, and for all the drama of Suez and other Arab–Israeli conflicts, Europe, East Asia and South Africa were of greater drama, cost and consequence. In the post-Cold War epoch, of US unipolar power and globalisation, the question has rather been whether, and, if so, how, the Middle East, oil apart, matters at all. It *does*, but the case has still to be made, and should be.

A second prudential maxim, implicit and banal as it may be, is the need for *a diversity of analytic and strategic focus*. For many, the Middle East is assimilated, more or less, to one particular conflict: an obvious candidate is the Arab–Israeli dispute, but for others it may be that between Iran and Arab states, for others the unresolved Kurdish issue, while within Yemen the question of *wahda*, or Yemeni unity, has for decades been predominant. Such a search for a single source of conflict is a chimera: *there is no single focus* to the international relations of the Middle East. Much as it is tempting, in analysis and polemic, to see all as part of one seamless web, with a single generic crisis at its core, and while indeed there are interconnections, such simplification, reduction to *one* problem or crisis, is unfounded: the Arab–Israeli conflict, flaring since 1948 into inter-state war, involves directly about 12 million of the over 350 million people of the region; it has been far from being the bloodiest of Middle East conflicts. It tells us little, if anything, about, for example, the, by my count, four Gulf Wars, the socio-economic difficulties of oil-producing states and the corruption they contain, or Sunni–Shi'a relations in the Gulf. The rhetoric of high religiosity and ancestral bias claimed by all participants in this conflict should not prevent other, more measured, analysis. Other disputes in the region have their own distinct origins and costs. Rather than being the expression of *one* root conflict, the Middle East, as defined in this book, is, rather, a mosaic of discrete but increasingly intersecting conflicts, and alliances, now the 'Greater West Asian Crisis'. These conflicts and their transnational connections not only tie the region together but have also, since the 1970s, to an increasing degree interlocked with rivalries, geographically, but not strategically or effectively, outside the region: thus the conflict between India and Pakistan to the south-east, and by extension through the Himalayas that between India and China, and the conflicts of the Balkans to the north-east have been reflected in the Middle East. Herein lies the strategic *and* political context of 11 September 2001, a moment when issues with different origins, above all Palestine, Iraq and Afghanistan, fused into one regionally and globally explosive event: its roots lay in the Cold War but its impact will cast a long sombre shadow over the twenty-first century.

Thirdly, it is advisable, although very difficult, to assert *scepticism about the weight of history* in explaining the behaviour of Middle Eastern states. It is common, as we have repeatedly seen, within the region and without, to explain contemporary events in terms of past, historic or atavistic, forces: the conflict of Medes and Persians, or Jews and gentiles, of nomadic and settled, or in terms of mindsets 'Levantine', Arab', 'Islamic' or whatever. Fundamentalists have in recent years, more than hitherto, made much of historic reference points, of the Crusades, not to mention Muawiya and Yazid, the early Sunni tyrants, or the Battle of Khandaq (AD 627, when the Muslims defeated the Meccan Quraiysh) or the Battle of Qadisyah (AD 636, when the Arabs defeated the Persians, near Kut) and other symbols and events from earlier Islamic times. Certainly contemporary events and the states of the region *do* have deep historical roots and these should be studied; to fail to do so means they cannot be explained, let alone the animosities people who invoke this history may feel. Not least among the tasks of historical analysis is that of seeing how the west contributed to, while not being solely responsible for, the character and conflicts of the region (not least Islamist terrorism). However, the past, remote or more recent, cannot on its own explain the present. By dint of biological reading alone, each generation must, consciously, *reproduce and recreate* a sense of community, entitlement and, not least, hatred. *It is contemporary forces which make use of the past*: they select and use those elements of the past, national, regional or religious, which suit their present purposes. The Arab–Israeli conflict, the Turkish–Kurdish conflict, the Iran–Iraq war of 1980–8, the Iraqi invasion of Kuwait in 1990, the assault of 11 September 2001, all have contemporary causes: they were not pre-ordained a century or, let above fourteen centuries ago. They reflect, as much as anything, a modern international context. Indeed, as argued in chapter 7, the ideologies, nationalist or religious, that do most to invoke the past are themselves modern creations, selected, when not invented, fetishes of the age – *shari'ah, Eretz Israel*, 'Islamic government' to name but three. The promotion of the 'Crusades' is one further such modern discursive selection. The past only has effect in so far as those alive today seek to make it so; hence, the challenge is for those who invoke the past to demonstrate why it does have an effect, rather than it being assumed that this is the case.

In conclusion it may be helpful to record the words of one of the wisest, and most committed, of writers on the region, as clear and resolute now, in the early twenty-first century, as they were when written three decades ago:

So, if I may bring to bear upon your problems the opinion of a foreigner – a foreigner who knows your history and the social and cultural structures of your countries well, but a foreigner nonetheless, however sympathetic to your aspirations – I would like to make an appeal.

Firstly, I appeal for lucidity. Myths may be useful for certain mobilizations, but they end up by mystifying, blinding and misleading the very people who manipulate them. To retreat into myths, especially the use of the past to elucidate today's problems, is another sign of weakness. If forceful ideas are needed to guide action, let them be as close to reality as possible.

Secondly, I appeal for open-mindedness. I have already said that societies which turn in on themselves and on their particular problems are dying, static societies. Living, progressive, dynamic societies are not afraid to borrow in order to get down to the task of forging a new synthesis. Indeed the same is true for individuals. The most appealing and most promising trait of the studious Algerian youths I have met is their thirst for knowledge, their desire to drink at every fountain and to assimilate every input.

Finally, and especially, I appeal for an open-mindeness towards a universal vision of the existing problems, the only kind of vision which is genuinely revolutionary.

I hope I will be forgiven for insisting on the point. There are three ways of devoting oneself: to God, to the group and to Man. To devote oneself to God is to have a faith which it is not given to everybody to share, and which in any case does not, in general, exclude the other types of devotion. To devote oneself to the group to which one belongs is necessary, and when that group is humiliated or oppressed, it becomes a primordial human duty. But the group should not be defied, placed above everything else. That would be what classical Muslim theology calls *shirk*, associationism, the act of assimilating some other person with God. The group is not everything. An exclusive aspiration to the greater glory of the group, taken as a supreme value, would lead to an anarchic world of hate-filled nations in perpetual struggle one against the other.

Beyond the group, ethnic or national, there are universal values which stand above it: liberty, equality and fraternity, for all men. Integral and exclusive nationalism logically leads to a barbaric attitude towards all humanity outside the group. Its motto, 'my country right or wrong', translated into German, stood over the gate of the camp at Buchenwald. And in Algeria, one could ask how, if the nation is the supreme value, can one justify the actions of those Frenchmen who defended the cause of Algerian independence? Were they then traitors? If, on the contrary, the value one places above all others, the vision one holds before one's eyes, is a universal value, namely the struggle against all iniquity, this implies a perpetual renewal, for the forms pose problems which are always new, unexpected and unprecedented.

The Kingdom of God is not of this world, there is no end to history, the struggles will not cease, He who struggles for justice, the militant, the radical revolutionary, he who tackles the root of iniquities, as Marx puts it, will never have the right to settle back into the blissful self-satisfaction of the righteous man through whom Heaven has descended to Earth. I am no prophet and do not like the prophetic style. But if one can draw a lesson from past experience and from rational analysis, it is that the future before us is a future of struggle, a future which demands courageous souls, and thus a future worthy of Man.

There is no reason to believe that such struggles will spare the Muslim world. Man is neither beast nor god, said Aristotle, whom the Muslim Middle Ages knew as *al mo'allim al-awwal*, the first master; he is the *zoon politikon*, whose life is civil society, and whose life is thus protest, struggle and conflict. The man whose life in Muslim society is neither the monkey nor the robot pictured by the colonialists; nor is he the angel in direct communication with the heavens imagined by the naïve, by the apologists and the mystics. He has enjoyed no fantastic privilege nor has he been the victim of some terrible curse. History shows him to have engaged in the struggles and tasks which are common to all humanity. He shares the same kind of aspirations, reactions, conceptions and illusions, the same opposite tendencies, the same efforts to defend himself, to free himself and to enslave others, to conserve and to go forwards, which are the common lot of all mankind. There is no *Homo Islamicus*. The history of the Muslim world is specific, it has its own style and colour, it is an incomparable part of human diversity. But it is not exceptional. Men everywhere have faced similar problems, to be resolved by analogous means. There is no reason to believe that this will not always be so.

To face the forthcoming struggles, one must be armed. One must learn to distance oneself from the myths, to assimilate the lessons of human experience, to reject complacency and self-satisfaction which are causes of stagnation; one must always seek to surpass oneself and the existing situation, in the effort to accomplish the great human tasks. (Maxime Rodinson, *Marxism and the Muslim World*, London: Zed Books, 1979, p. 160)

Appendices

Appendix 1

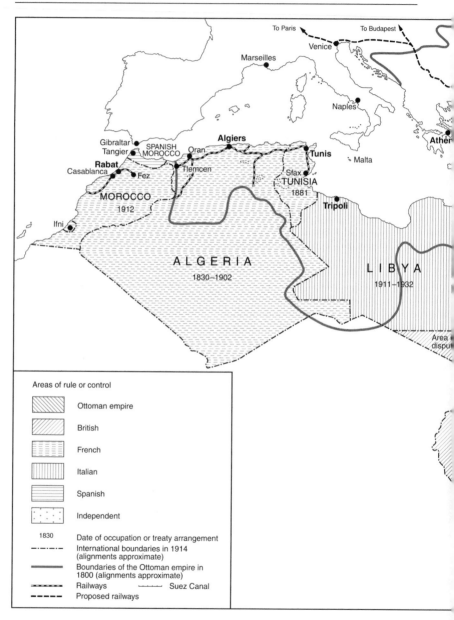

Map 1 Middle East states, 1900

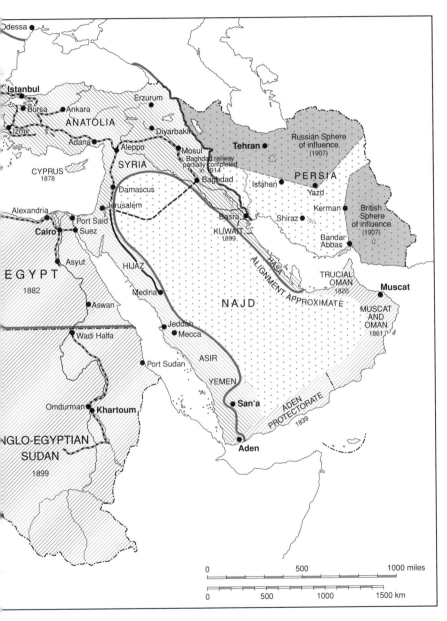

Map 1 (*cont.*)

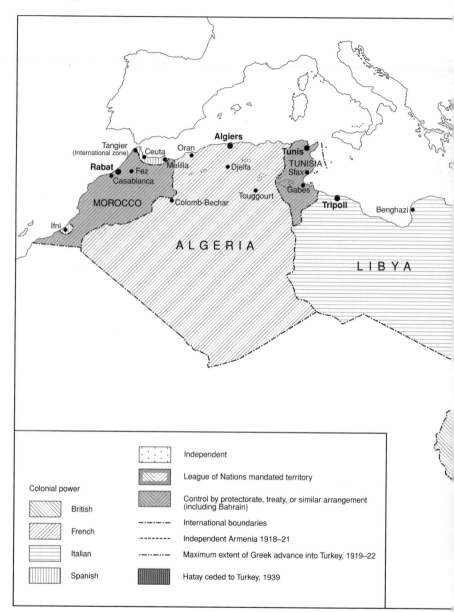

Map 2 Middle East states, 1930

Map 2 (cont.)

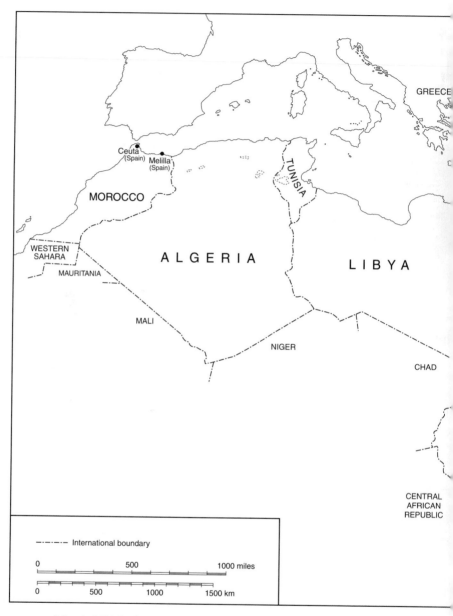

Map 3 Middle East states, 2000

Map 3 (cont.)

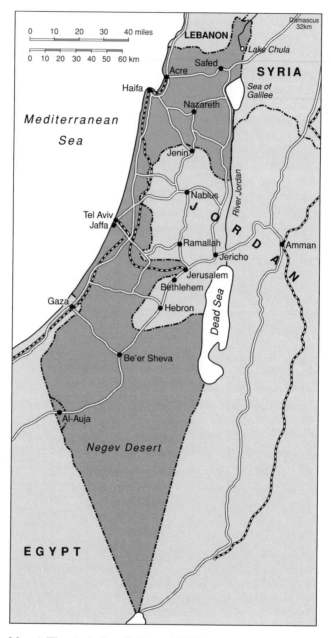

Map 4 The Arab–Israeli dispute, 1949

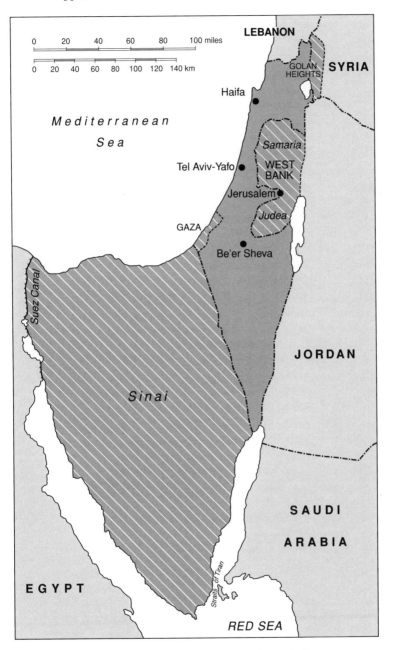

Map 5 The Arab–Israeli dispute, after June 1967

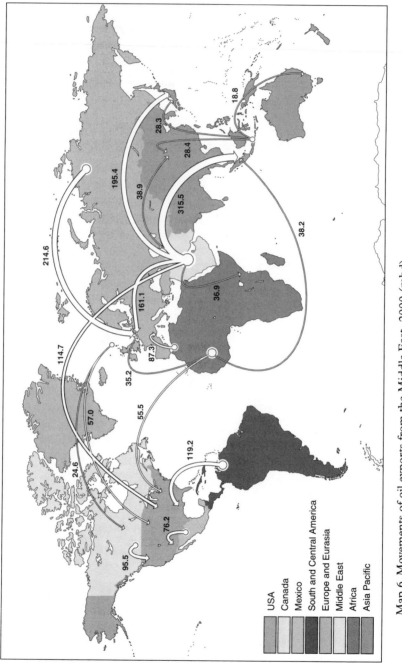

Map 6 Movements of oil exports from the Middle East, 2000 (mbd)
Source: *BP Statistical Review of World Energy 2001*

Table 1. *Middle Eastern states: population growth to 2050*

	Population estimate, mid-1990 (millions)	Population, mid-2001 (millions)	Projected population, 2025 (millions)	Projected population, 2050 (millions)	Projected population, change 2001–2055 (%)	Population of age <15 (%)	Urban dwelling (%)	Rate of natural increase (%)
Bahrain	0.5	0.7	1.7	2.9	300	31	88	1.9
Egypt	55.6	73.4[a]	103.2	127.4	74[a]	36	43	2.0
Iran	18.0	66.1	88.4	100.2	52	36	64	1.2
Iraq		23.6	40.3	53.6	127	42	68	2.7
Israel	4.6	6.4	8.9	10.6	64	29	91	1.6
Jordan	4.1	5.2	8.7	11.8	128	40	79	2.2
Kuwait	2.1	2.3	4.2	6.4	181	26	100	1.8
Lebanon	3.3	4.3	5.4	5.8	35	29	88	1.7
Oman	1.5	2.4	4.9	7.6	218	41	72	3.5
Palestinian Territory	–	3.3	7.4	11.2	239	47	–	3.7
Qatar	0.5	0.6	0.8	0.9	45	27	91	2.7
Saudi Arabia	15.0	21.1	40.9		185	43	83	2.9
Syria	12.6	17.1	27.1	35.2	106	41	50	2.6
Turkey	56.7	66.3	85.2	97.2	47	30	66	1.5
United Arab Emirates	1.6	3.3	4.5	5.1	54	26	84	1.4
Yemen	9.8	18.0	39.6	71.1	295	48	26	3.3

Source: Population Reference Bureau, http://www.prb.org; 1990 data from 1990 World Population Data Sheet produced by Population Concern and PRB

Note: Data for Egypt drawn from 2004 figures

Table 2. *Proven world oil reserves, 2000*

Proven reserves 2000	Barrels (billion)	Reserves/production ratio
North America	64.4	13.8
South and Central America	95.2	39.1
Europe	19.1	7.7
Former Soviet Union	65.3	22.7
Middle East	683.6	83.2
Iran	89.7	65.7
Iraq	112.5	–
Kuwait	96.5	–
Oman	5.5	15.7
Qatar	13.2	47.1
Saudi Arabia	261.7	81.1
Syria	2.5	12.7
UAE	97.8	–
Yemen	41.0	25.2
Other Middle East	0.2	9.0
Africa	74.8	26.8
Asia Pacific	44	15.6
World total	1046.4	39.9

Source: *BP Statistical Review of World Energy 2001*

Table 3. *World oil production by region, 2000*

North America	13.905
South and Central America	6.835
Europe	6.955
Former Soviet Union	8.035
Middle East	22.990
Africa	7.820
Asia Pacific	7.970
World total	74.510

Source: *BP Statistical Review of World Energy 2001*

Table 4. *Middle Eastern oil production, 2000*

	Million barrels per day
Iran	3.770
Iraq	2.625
Kuwait	2.150
Oman	0.960
Qatar	0.795
Saudi Arabia	9.145
Syria	0.540
UAE	2.515
Yemen	0.440
Other Middle East	0.050
Total	22.990

Source: *BP Statistical Review of World Energy 2001*

Table 5. *Military expenditure by region, 1999*

Defence expenditure (US million, 1999 constant prices)		%GDP
NATO	469,176	2.3
Russia	56,800	5.1
Middle East and North Africa	60,023	7.2
Central and South Asia	21,731	5.3
East Asia and Australasia	135,243	3.7
Caribbean, Central and Latin America	35,447	1.8
Sub-Saharan Africa	9,830	4.4

Source: IISS, *The Military Balance 2000–2001*, p. 302

Table 6. *Foreign direct investment by region, 1999*

	FDI ($US billion)
World	865.5
Developed countries	636.5
Developing countries (total)	207.6
Of which:	
South America	72.1
China	40.4
North Africa	3.0
Middle East	6.7
Israel	2.3

Source: UNCTAD, *World Investment Report 2000*

Appendix 2   Chronologies

1911	Italy occupies Libya
1914–18	First World War: Ottoman empire allies with Central Powers, Austria and Germany against Britain, France and Russia
1917	Balfour Declaration, statement committing UK to a 'Jewish national home' in Palestine; British conquer Jerusalem and Damascus
30 October 1918	Mudros armistice: Turkey accepts peace
April 1920	San Remo Conference: major western powers decide allocation of Mandates to UK and France. Treaty of Sèvres: peace imposed on Ottoman empire
March 1921	Cairo Conference settles British plans for administration of Middle East; allocation of Amir Feisal, defeated by French in Syria, to Iraq
1920–2	In former Ottoman Arab areas, delineation of new French and British mandated territories: Syria, Lebanon, Palestine, Jordan, Iraq
1923	Treaty of Lausanne: consolidation of modern Turkey
1932	Independence of Iraq
1936	Independence of Egypt
1941	Britain and Russia occupy Iran
1946	Independence of Syria and Lebanon
1946	Azerbaijan crisis: Russia forced to abandon position in northern Iran in March; Shah's armies reoccupy Azerbaijan and Kurdish, autonomous republics crushed in December
1947	Truman Doctrine proclaims US support for Greece, Turkey and Iran
August 1953	CIA/MI6 coup in Iran
1954	Britain evacuates Canal Zone
1955	Baghdad Pact
1956	Suez crisis: Anglo-French attack on Egypt, in secret agreement with Israel
1957	Eisenhower Doctrine
1958	US and British forces deployed in Lebanon and Jordan after Iraqi revolution
1961	British forces sent to protect newly independent Kuwait
1967	Third Arab–Israeli war; consolidation of US–Israeli relationship

1980	Carter Doctrine designates vital US interest in the Gulf
1983–4	US forces deployed in Lebanon
1987	US and British forces deployed in Gulf to protect Saudi and Kuwaiti shipping
1990–1	Mass deployment of US and allies' forces against Iraq in Operation Desert Storm
1991–2003	Containment of Iraq, through combination of aerial surveillance, sanctions, intrusive inspections and diplomatic pressures
2001	After the attacks of 11 September Washington proclaims 'War against Terrorism'
January 2002	Proclamation by President Bush of 'Axis of Evil' including Iraq and Iran
March–May 2003	US and British forces invade and occupy Iraq

(ii)   Arab nationalism

Third–fourth century AD	Emergence of 'Arabic' language and of poetry known later as that of the *jahiliya* ('period of ignorance')
Early seventh century	Rise of Islam
AD 626	Flight of Prophet Muhammad from Mecca to Medina
AD 632	Death of Prophet, followed by four Caliphs (*khulafa*); division of Islam into majority Sunna and minority Shi'a factions, today roughly 90 per cent and 10 per cent of the total respectively
662–750	Ummayad dynasty, based in Damascus, first of three major Islamic dynasties
750–1258	Abbasid dynasty, based in Baghdad, second Islamic dynasty, mixed Arabic and Persian in culture
1258	Fall of Baghdad to Mongol forces of Hulagu
Fifteenth century	Rise of Ottomans, third Islamic dynasty, Turkish in character
1517	Ottomans occupy Egypt and much of Arab world
1830	French occupy Algeria

1838	Birth of Jamal al-Din al-Asadabadi, known as al-Afghani, prime pan-Islamist and by consequence nationalist militant of nineteenth century (d. 1897), followed by Muhammad Abduh (1849–1905)
1839	Occupation of Aden by British forces, followed by much of coastline of Arabian Peninsula
Late nineteenth century	Rise of cultural movement of revival, or *nahda*, among writers in the Arab east; rise of 'Islamic public' (Reinhardt Schulze) and, concomitantly, of distinct Arab, Persian and Turkish nationalisms; first explicit Arab nationalism in writings of Rashid Rida (1865–1935), with stress on *salafiya*, return to the Islamic doctrines of the *salaf* or 'ancestors', and Abd al-Rahman al-Kawakibi (1849–1902)
1882	Occupation of Egypt by British forces
1914–18	Defeat of Ottomans by British-officered forces, with symbolic participation of small irregular Hashemite units
1915	Secret Anglo-French ('Sykes–Picot') agreement to divide Arab world into British and French zones
1918	Turks leave Yemen: first modern independent Arab state established under rule of Hamid al-Din Imams
1919	Nationalist protest movement in Egypt at British refusal to allow delegation (*wafd*) representing the country to attend Versailles Conference
1920–1	At San Remo and Cairo conferences, post-war partition of Arab world by France and Britain. Modern state system created. Defeat of anti-French and anti-British risings in Syria and Iraq respectively
1922	Treaty of Uqair: defines eastern frontiers of Saudi territory, apportions much of Kuwait to Saudi Arabia
1926	Saudi forces conquer much of central Arabia, establish Kingdom of Najd and Hijaz

1932	Kingdom of Saudi Arabia established. Independence of Iraq
1934	Saudi–Yemeni war, Yemen loses three provinces: Najran, Asir and Jizan
1936	Independence of Egypt. Palestinian guerrilla resistance to Jewish settlement begins
1941	British forces in Iraq crush nationalist uprising of Rashid Ali Gailani
1943	Independence of Syria and Lebanon; founding of Arab Ba'th Socialist Party
1945	Foundation of Arab League
1948–9	Crisis in Arab world as states fail to stop independence and military consolidation of Israel
1949	Successive coups in Syria remove elected system
July 1952	Egyptian revolution, removal of King Farouk, advent of 'Free Officers' to power
July 1956	Nasser, now leader of Egypt, nationalises Suez Canal
October–November 1956	Tripartite attack by UK, France and Israel on Egypt, soon reversed by convergent American and Soviet pressure
July 1958	Revolution in Iraq overthrows Hashemites; Jordanian monarch, supported by UK, survives; formation of United Arab Republic (UAR) with Egypt and Syria; Imam of Yemen joins, then leaves, union with Egypt
1961	Proclamation of socialist measures in Egypt, founding Arab Socialist Union; secession of Syria from UAR
September 1962	Revolution in Yemen; Egyptian forces enter to defend the republic against Saudi-backed royalists
1963	Temporary unity of Egypt, Iraq and Syria ends in rancour; Ba'th take power, enduringly, in Syria, briefly in Iraq
1964	Founding, with Arab state backing, of Palestinian Liberation Organization

June 1967	Defeat of Egypt, Syria and Jordan in war with Israel leads to Israeli occupation of new territories; closure of Suez Canal
November 1967	Withdrawal of Egyptian forces from Yemen; rise of autonomous Palestinian armed units in Jordan
July 1968	Permanent Ba'th seizure of power in Iraq
September 1970	Fighting in Jordan leads to expulsion, over ensuing months, of Palestinian forces. Death of Nasser
1973	Egypt launches October war, followed by negotiations that lead to Israeli withrawal from territories seized in 1967
1975	Following period of increased political and social tension, and armed clashes involving Palestinian forces stationed in the country, civil war breaks out in Lebanon
1976	Syrian forces enter Lebanon on side of Maronites; thousands of Palestinians die in Syrian siege of Tel al-Zaatar camp
1977	President Sadat of Egypt visits Jerusalem; majority of Arab world denounces his decision
1979	Saddam Hussein, now decisively in charge of Iraq, kills dozens of his opponents, proclaims Iraq to be the 'Citadel' of the Arab Revolution, challenges Egypt and Syria for leadership of the Arab world, and is increasingly embroiled on eastern front in conflict with Iran, leading in September 1980 to Iraqi invasion
1980–8	Iran–Iraq war – second longest inter-state war of twentieth century, hundreds of thousands killed; majority of Arab world sides with Iraq, Syria and South Yemen with Iran
1981	Assassination of Sadat; Hosni Mubarak, air force officer, appointed president of Egypt
May 1990	North and South Yemen enter into political union designed, after a transitional period, to lead to full unification of country for first time since early eighteenth century

August 1990	Iraq, frustrated by end of war with Iran, occupies Kuwait
January–February 1991	Iraqi forces expelled from Kuwait; Arab forces fight for first time on side of western powers against another Arab state
April–July 1994	Civil war between northern and southern factions in Yemen leads to victory for North; Yemen effectively unified under President Ali Abdullah Salih
Late 1990s–2003	Arab world increasingly affected by hostility to western sanctions on Iraq and, from September 2000, by start of second Palestinian *intifadha*

(iii)   Iran

1500	Creation of modern Iranian state by Shah Abbas
1736	Nadir Shah invades India
1790s	Emergence of Qajar dynasty in Transcaucasus
1812, 1828	Loss of Georgia, Armenia and Azerbaijan to Russia
1857	Herat crisis. Treaty of Paris gives Iran the right to intervene in Afghanistan to protect its security interests
1891	Tobacco Boycott: first nationwide nationalist mobilisation in modern Middle East
1905–8	Constitutional Revolution, encouraged by Japanese defeat of Russia
1907	As part of broader Anglo-Russian understanding on Asia, including Afghanistan and Tibet, division of Iran into UK, Russian and neutral zones of influence
1908	Discovery of oil at Masjid-I Suleiman
1911	Re-establishment of Qajar autocracy
1914–18	Turkish, British and Russian forces enter Iran
1917–21	Revolutionary guerrilla movement in Gilan Province
1919	Failed British attempt to impose Protectorate on Iran

March 1921	Rez Khan takes power in coup, with British encouragement
1925	Qajar dynasty removed; Reza Khan crowns himself Shah of new, Pahlavi, dynasty
1933	Reza Shah decrees change of name from Persia to Iran; dispute with Anglo-Persian Oil Company (later BP)
1941	Britain and USSR occupy Iran, depose Reza Khan, install his son Mohammad Reza Pahlavi. Founding of Tudeh ('Masses') Party
1945	Proclamation of autonomous republics in Soviet-occupied Azerbaijan and Kurdistan
March 1946	Soviet forces withdraw
December 1946	Shah reoccupies and crushes autonomous republics
1949	Attempt on life of Shah; crackdown on opposition
1951–3	Muhammad Mosadeq, National Front prime minister, nationalises oil; international boycott of Iranian oil imposed; negotiations fail
August 1953	UK–CIA coup deposes Mosadeq and restores Shah; leading clergy support Shah
1957	Founding of SAVAK, Shah's secret police
1961	Shah proclaims 'White Revolution', including land reform and literacy
June 1963	Popular uprising in protest at granting of legal exemption to US personnel serving in Iran; Khomeini emerges as leader
1964	Khomeini exiled to Turkey, then, in 1965, goes to Iraq
1971	Start of Fedayin guerrilla movement, followed by Mujahidin; Shah celebrates 2,500 years of Iranian monarch at Persepolis
1971–3	Oil price rises lead to economic boom and drive for 'Great Civilisation'
1975	Algiers Agreement between Shah and Saddam Hussein ends six years of border clashes and support for opposition groups, delimits Shatt al-Arab and land boundaries

1977	Emergence in public of first critical voices since early 1960s
1978–9	Growing protests, and strikes, weaken and ultimately overthrow Shah's state
January 1979	Shah leaves Iran
February 1979	Khomeini returns to Iran; Bakhtiar transitional government overthrown in armed rising some days later
March 1979	Islamic Republic proclaimed
November 1979	Seizure of US embassy by student group endorsed by Khomeini as part of new radicalisation of regime at home and internationally
1980–8	'The imposed war': Iraq attacks in September 1980; war lasts until August 1988
July 1982	Iran retakes all territory occupied by Iraq in first weeks of war, particularly Fao Peninsula; Khomeini advised to make peace when Iran in strong position, but is persuaded by Guards commander Rafiqdust to pursue victory over Saddam Hussein
1984–8	'Tanker war' in Gulf: Iraq striking Iranian ships, Iran replying by hitting ships of Iraqi allies Kuwait and Saudi Arabia
1987	US forces enter Gulf on Arab side; sink estimated one-third of Iranian navy
1989	Death of Khomeini leads to mass mourning by millions
1997	President Khatami elected on liberal platform; local elections in 2000 confirm popular wish for change
1998	Killing of twelve Iranian diplomats in Mazar-I Sharif, Afghanistan, by Taliban sparks major nationalist upsurge; danger of war narrowly averted by leadership
2004	Reassertion of clerical power by conservative faction; Iran pursues policy of *nami be birun, sakht dar dakhil* ('Gentle to the outside, tough on the inside')

(iv)   Kurdish nationalism

1920	Treaty of Sèvres, Articles 62–4, allows for consultation on Kurdish independence from Turkey
1923	Treaty of Lausanne overrides Sèvres; no mention of Kurdish rights
1919–31	Shaikh Mahmud, '*hukmdar*' of Iraqi Kurdistan, in intermittent revolt
1922–4	Rising of Ismail Agha ('Simko') in Iran
1925	Rising of Shaikh Said in Turkey
January 1946	Proclamation of Mahabad republic, Iran
December 1946	Iranian forces occupy Mahabad; Qazi Muhammad executed
1958	Iraqi revolution; return of Kurdish Democratic Party of Iraq leader Mulla Mustafa Barzani from exile in USSR
1961	Outbreak of fighting between Kurds and Baghdad government
1970	Iraqi–Kurdish agreement on Kurdish autonomous zone; subsequent breakdown of agreement leads to war between Kurds and Baghdad
1975	Shah–Saddam Algiers Agreement: end of Iranian and western support for Iraqi Kurds; mass deportation of Kurds to southern Iraq ensues
1979–81	Democratic upsurge among Kurds of Iran; occupation of cities in western Iran; crushed by Islamic Guards
1984	Start of rising by PKK in Turkey
1988	Iraq launches 'Operation *anfal*' campaign to depopulate Kurdish areas of northern Iraq; poison gas attack on Kurdish city of Halabja in April
1989	Iranian KDP leader Abdul-rahman Qassemlu assassinated in Vienna by Iranian government agents
1991	Following Kuwait war, Kurdish rising in northern Iraq, mass flight of Kurds to Turkey and Iran, and creation of Kurdish safe area, with western protection

1999	Capture of PKK leader Ocalan, followed by PKK ceasefire
June 2004	PKK renews guerrilla war, changes name to 'People's Party'

(v)   Palestine and Israel

Nineteenth Century	Ottoman Palestine is divided into three provinces
1840s	Start of early Zionist movement amongst European Jews, seeking return to ancestral land
1870s	First migration (*aliyah*, or 'ascent') of European Jews to Palestine
1896	Theodor Herzl publishes *The State of the Jews*
1897	Zionist Congress in Basle
1917	Balfour Declaration by British government favours establishment of a Jewish 'national home' in Palestine, provided it does not prejudice rights of existing population
1920s	Consolidation of Jewish community in Palestine
1929	First serious riots between Jews and Arabs over religious sites in Jerusalem
1930	Passfield Report, based on commission set up after 1929 riots, proposes limits on Jewish immigration
1937	Peel Commission recommends three-way partition, into Arab, Jewish and British military areas
1936–9	Palestinian guerrilla movement against Jewish settlement
1939	In shift to a more pro-Arab position, brought on by concerns at imminent world war, British White Paper calls for limit of 75,000 for Jewish immigration, and independence, with Arab majority
1942	Conference of pro-Zionist Jews in New York issues 'Biltmore Declaration', mobilising US support for Zionism

1946	Irregular Jewish forces, Irgun and Lehi, start military action against British forces in Palestine
November 1947	UN General Assembly votes for partition of Palestine into Jewish and Arab states; in December fighting breaks out between Jews and Arabs inside Palestine
May 1948	British unilaterally withdraw from Palestine; independent state of Israel proclaimed in Tel Aviv; war breaks out between Israelis and regular Arab forces
1949	Ceasefire leaves Israel in existence, with rest of Palestine under Jordanian (West Bank) or Egyptian (Gaza) control
Early 1950s	Tentative negotiations between Israel and Egypt fail
October–November 1956	Israel attacks Egypt with British and French support; under US pressure, and Soviet threats, forced to withdraw
1964	Establishment of Palestine Liberation Organization, umbrella group for different Palestinian parties
January 1965	First armed action by al-Fath, reverse acronym for Harakat al-Tahrir Filastin, 'Movement for the Liberation of Palestine', led by Yasser Arafat
1967	Six Day war: Israel occupies West Bank and Gaza, Arab regular armies discredited; rise of militant guerrilla forces in Jordan
September 1970	King Hussein crushes Palestinian forces in Amman, later expelling all fighters to Lebanon
1975	Outbreak of Lebanese civil war in which Palestinians side with Sunni Muslim forces
1976	Syrian forces intervene against Palestinians, leading to deaths of thousands in refugee camp of Tel al-Zaatar
1978–81	Assassination, by Abu Nidal forces on orders of Iraq, of PLO representatives in London and other European cities engaged in negotiations with Israelis

1982	Israel invades Lebanon; fighting in Beirut; Palestinian fighters leave under negotiated settlement, dispersed to Arab states including Yemen, Iraq and Tunis, where the PLO sets up headquarters
1987	First *intifadha*; founding of Hamas, Islamist rival to al-Fath
1988	Palestinian National Council accepts two-state settlement
1991	Beginnings of multilateral negotiations between Arabs and Israel at Madrid
1993	Following secret negotiations mediated by Norway, and with an agreement signed by Arafat and Israeli prime minister Rabin in Washington, peace process with clear goals begins
1995	Assassination of Rabin stalls peace process
1996	Election of Likud government in Israel
August 2000	Failure of negotiations between Arafat and Barak at Camp David
September 2000	Outbreak of second Palestinian uprising or *intifadha*; rising incidence of suicide bombings against Israeli civilian targets
2001	Advent of Sharon as premier in Israel leads to further deterioration of situation
March 2004	Assassination of Hamas leader Sheikh Ahmad Yassin

(vi)   Conflict in the Arabian Peninsula and the Persian Gulf

1899	Anglo-Kuwait Agreement recognises autonomy of Kuwait
1911	Treaty of Da'an: Ottomans recognise autonomy of Imam of Yemen in Zeidi areas
1913	Anglo-Ottoman Agreement delineates boundaries between Yemen and South Arabia
1915	Correspondence between Sharif Hussein of Mecca and British authorities in Egypt on possible alliance against the Ottomans
1916	Rising of Sharif Hussein of Mecca against Ottoman rule

1920–2	Growing assertion of Saudi influence in Arabia
1922	Following Saudi incursion into Kuwait, Treaty of Uqair delineates border between Kuwait and Saudi Arabia
1924	Saudi conquest of Hijaz; Sharif Hussein flees Mecca
1926	Kingdom of Najd and Hijaz; consolidation of Saudi rule
1932	Proclamation of the Kingdom of Saudi Arabia; independence of Iraq
1934	Saudi–Yemeni war; Treaty of Taif allocated three Yemeni provinces to Saudi Arabia
1955–9	War between Sultan of Muscat and Omani Imamate
1956	Demonstrations in Aden and Bahrain against British rule
14 July 1958	Overthrow of Hashemite monarchy in Iraq, start of Iraqi revolution
1961	Independence of Kuwait; Iraqi claim to Kuwait
26 September 1962	Republican revolution in Yemen; start of civil war that lasts until July 1970
1963–7	Nationalist guerrilla movement in South Yemen
1965–75	Guerrilla war in Dhofar, southern province of Oman
30 November 1967	Independence of South Yemen
July 1968	Ba'th Party comes to power in Iraq
1969–75	First Gulf war: protracted border conflict between Iraq and Iran
November 1971	On eve of British departure from the lower Gulf (Bahrain, Qatar, Emirates) Iran seizes islands of Tumbs and Abu Musa from the Emirates
September–October 1972	War between North and South Yemen
1973	Iranian forces despatched to Dhofar
April 1975	Algiers Agreement between Iran and Iraq
November 1975	Defeat of Dhofar movement
February 1979	Triumph of the Iranian revolution; second war between North and South Yemen;

	March proclamation of the Islamic Republic of Iran
September 1980	Second Gulf war: Iraq launches war against Iran; start of Iran–Iraq war
May 1981	Formation of the Gulf Co-operation Council (GCC)
1984	Start of the 'Tanker war', with Iraqi attacks on Iranian tankers and oil installations
1987	US and British naval forces deploy in Gulf to protect Saudi and Kuwaiti shipping from Iranian attacks
July 1987	UN Security Council Resolution 598 calls for ceasefire in Iran–Iraq war
August 1988	Iran accepts Resolution 598
May 1990	Union of North and South Yemen
2 August 1990	Iraq occupies Kuwait
January–February 1991	Third Gulf war: Operation Desert Storm expels Iraq from Kuwait
April 1991	UN Security Council Resolutions 687 and 688 impose military controls and sanctions on Iraq
April–July 1994	Inter-Yemeni civil war; victory of northern forces
December 1998	Operation Desert Fox, US–UK aerial attacks on Iraq following end of UN military inspection visits to Iraq
March–April 2003	Fourth Gulf war: US–UK military assault on, and occupation of, Iraq; removal of Arab Ba'th Socialist Party from power; installation of western military and political administration
June 2004	Installation of new provisional Iraqi government.

(vii)   Islamism

| Eighteenth century | Rise of Wahhabi movement among eastern Arabian tribes, based on strictest of four Sunni schools, Hanbalism, and militantly hostile to Shi'ism; followed teaching of Muhammad ibn Abd al-Wahhab (1703–87) but led by Saudi tribe; captured Karbala |

	1802 and Mecca 1803; pushed back by Egyptian forces, who took Diriyya, Wahhabi capital, 1818
Nineteenth century	Rise of Islamist and nationalist thought among Ottoman subjects, often centred on importance of Islam and need to revive it
1901	Abd al-Aziz al-Saud captures Riyadh, leading to series of advances culminating in establishment of strict Islamic state of Saudi Arabia in 1932
1924	Abolition of Caliphate by Atatürk sparks movement for revival/protection of Islam in Middle East and South Asia
1928	Founding of Muslim Brotherhood in Egypt by Hassan al-Banna
1941	Founding of Jama'ati-i Islami (Islamic Party) by Sayyid Abu al-Ala Mawdudi (1903–79), which was to become major force in Pakistan and influential among South Asian Muslims generally
1949	Execution of Hassan al-Banna
1953	Founding of Hizb al-Tahrir (the Fundamentalist Party of Liberation) in Jordan
1954	Following assassination attempt on his life, Nasser suppresses Muslim Brotherhood
1963–4	Ayatollah Ruhallah Khomeini emerges as popular opposition figure in Iran, in protests against judicial immunity for US servicemen; Khomeini exiled to Turkey, then Iraq
1964	Sayyid Qutb, publishes *Ma'alim fi al-tariq* ('Milestones'), which advocates turning away from the present state, which exists in condition of ignorance, *jahiliya*, to true Islam, and establishing a model Islamic community, or *umma*. This is later a key text for Osama bin Laden
1965	Saudi Arabia, in opposition to secular Arab nationalism of Egypt, establishes World Islamic League, *Rabita al-alim al-Islamiya*
1966	Execution of Sayyid Qutb

1971	Publication of *Hokumat-i islami* ('Islamic Government'), political project based on Khomeini's lectures in Najaf
1974	Militant Islamists seize Military Academy in Cairo as part of attempted coup
1978–9	Mass movement of protest, led and organised by Khomeini's forces, destroys regime of Shah and takes power; proclaims Islamic Republic of Iran, and principle of *velayat-i faqih* (regency of the jurisconsult)
1978–92	Rise of Islamist opposition to communist, later Soviet, forces in Afghanistan; recruiting of support from across Muslim world, particularly Arabs
1979–81	Militant Shi'ite opposition, led by al-Da'wa ('The Call') party, to Sunni-dominated Ba'th regime in Iraq
1979	Seizure of Grand Mosque in Mecca by Saudi fundamentalists
1981	Assassination by Islamist Jihad group of Egyptian President Sadat; violent opposition by radical Islamists of Jihad, in contrast to more moderate forces of Muslim Brotherhood, challenges Egyptian state through 1980s and 1990s
1982	With Israeli invasion of southern Lebanon, rise of militant Shi'ite Hizbullah Party; crushing of uprising by Muslim Brotherhood in Syrian town of Hama
1986	Military coup in Sudan brings Islamist parties into government
1987	Founding of Movement of Islamic Resistance (Harakat al-Muqawama al-Islamiya, or 'Hamas') in Palestine, based on already existing local branch of Muslim Brotherhood
1991	Algerian government, fearing electoral victory of Islamist Islamic Salvation Front (FIS), declares state of emergency, leading to years of civil war
1992	Fall of communist state in Afghanistan; proclamation of Islamic Republic of

	Afghanistan by *mujahidin* groups, who then fall to fighting among themselves
1993	First attack on World Trade Center in New York
1994	Rise in Afghanistan of new, stricter, Islamic movement, Taliban (or 'Islamic Students'), followers of conservative South Asian school of Deoband
1996	Taliban capture Kabul, proclaim Islamic Emirate of Afghanistan, with their leader Mullah Mostafa Omar as their *'amir al-mu'minin*, 'Commander of the Faithful'. Support for radical Muslim groups in Central Asia
1998	First public statements by World Front for Fighting Christians and Jews, generally known as al-Qa'ida; bomb attacks on US embassies in Kenya and Tanzania
11 September 2001	Attacks on World Trade Center towers in New York
October–November 2001	US and allied forces attack Afghanistan, driving Taliban from power
March 2004	Moroccan Islamist group kills nearly two hundred in set of bomb attacks in Madrid

Select bibliography

The leading journals on the Middle East all contain articles of relevance to inter-national relations and the broader political and social context of the countries in question. Of particular relevance are *The British Journal of Middle Eastern Studies, CEMOTI: Cahiers d'Etudes Sur la Mediterranée Orientale et le Monde Turco-Iranien, The International Journal of Middle East Studies, Iranian Studies, Israel Affairs, Maghreb-Mashrek, Mediterraneans-Mediterrannées, The Middle East Journal, Middle East Report, Middle East Studies* and the on-line *Middle East Review of International Affairs* (http://www.meria.biu.ac.il). *Critique: Critical Middle Eastern Studies* provides excellent inter-disciplinary and methodological discussion. There is also a range of journals or publications produced in the region which reflect academic, policy and intellectual concerns, most with some at least semi-formal link to institutions of state. These include *Perceptions: Journal of International Affairs,* Centre for Strategic Research, Ankara; *The Iranian Journal of International Affairs,* Institute for Political and International Studies, Tehran; *Discourse: an Iranian Quarterly,* Center for Scientific Research and Middle East Strategic Studies, Tehran; *Annual Report,* Gulf Research Centre, Dubai; *Middle Eastern Lectures,* The Moshe Dayan Centre for Middle Eastern and African Studies, Tel Aviv University.

1 INTERNATIONAL RELATIONS THEORY AND THE MIDDLE EAST

al-Azmeh, Aziz, *Muslim Kingship: Power and the Sacred in Muslim, Christian and Pagan Politics,* London: I. B. Tauris, 1997

Barnett, Michael, *Dialogues in Arab Politics: Negotiations in Regional Order,* New York: Columbia University Press, 1998

Bill, James, 'The Study of Middle East Politics 1946–1996', *Middle East Journal,* vol. 50, no. 4, 1996

Brown, L. Carl, *International Politics and the Middle East: Old Rules, Dangerous Game,* London: I. B. Tauris, 1984

Gerges, Fawaz, *The Superpowers and the Middle East: Regional and International Politics 1955–1967,* Boulder, CO: Westview Press, 1994

Hinnebusch, Raymond and Ehteshami, Anoushiravan, *The Foreign Policies of Middle Eastern States,* London: Lynne Rienner, 2002

Ismael, Tareq, ed., *The International Relations of the Middle East,* Aldershot: Ashgate, 2000

Jabar, Faleh, *The Shi'ite movement in Iraq*, London: Saqi, 2003

Korany, Bahgat and Dessouki, Ali E. Hillal, eds., *The Foreign Policies of Arab States: the Challenge of Change*, Boulder, CO: Westview Press, 1984

Matthews, Ken, *The Gulf Conflict and International Relations*, London: Routledge, 1993

Tibi, Bassam, *Conflict and War in the Middle East, 1967–91: From Interstate War to New Security*, Second edition, London: Macmillan, 1998

Walt, Stephen, *The Origin of Alliances*, Ithaca, NY: Cornell University Press, 1987.

2 THE MAKING OF FOREIGN POLICY: STATES AND SOCIETIES

Anderson, Lisa, *The State and Social Transformation in Tunisia and Libya 1930–1980*, Princeton: Princeton University Press, 1986

Asad, Talal and Owen, Roger, eds., *Sociology of Developing Societies: the Middle East*, London: Macmillan, 1983

Ayubi, Nazih, *Over-stating the Arab State: Politics and Society in the Middle East*, London: I. B. Tauris, 1995

Ayubi, Shaheen, *Nasser and Sadat: Decision-making and Foreign Policy (1970–1972)*, Lanham: University Press of America, 1994

Barakat, Halim, *The Arab World: Society, Culture and State*, Berkeley: University of California Press, 1993

Bill, James and Leiden, Carl, *The Middle East: Politics and Power*, Boston: Allyn and Bacon, 1974

Bill, James and Springborg, Robert, *Politics in the Middle East*, fourth edition, New York: HarperCollins, 1994

Brecher, Michael, *Decisions in Israel's Foreign Policy*, New Haven: Yale University Press, 1975

Bromley, Simon, *Rethinking Middle East Politics: State Formation and Development*, Cambridge: Polity Press, 1994

Buchta, Wilfried, *Who Rules Iran? The Structure of Power in the Islamic Republic*, Washington, D.C.: Washington Institute for Near East Policy, 2000

Cooper, Mark, *The Transformation of Egypt*, London: Croom Helm, 1983

Gause, Gregory, *Oil Monarchies: Domestic and Security Challenges in the Arab Gulf States*, New York: Council on Foreign Relations, 1994

Hale, William, *Turkish Foreign Policy 1774–2000*, London: Frank Cass, 2000

Halliday, Fred and Alavi, Hamza, eds., *State and Ideology in the Middle East and Pakistan*, London: Macmillan, 1988

Heller, Mark, *Continuity and Change in Israeli Security Policy*, London: International Institute for Strategic Studies (IISS), 2000

Hudson, Michael, *Arab Politics: the Search for Legitimacy*, New Haven: Yale University Press, 1977

Kedourie, Elie, *Politics in the Middle East*, Oxford: Oxford University Press, 1992

al-Khalil, Samir, *The Republic of Fear: the Politics of Modern Iraq*, London: Radius/Hutchinson, 1989

Kienle, Eberhard, *A Grand Delusion: Democracy and Economic Reform in Egypt*, London: I. B. Tauris, 2001

Korany, Baghat and Dessouki, Ali E. Hillal, eds., *The Foreign Policies of Arab States*, Boulder, CO: Westview Press, 1984

Liebman, Charles and Don-Yehiya, Eliezer, *Religion and Politics in Israel*, Bloomington: Indiana University Press, 1984

Lochery, Neil, *The Difficult Road to Peace: Netanyahu, Israel and the Middle East Peace Process*, Reading: Ithaca Press, 1999

Luciani, Giacomo, ed., *The Arab State*, London: Routledge, 1990

Milton-Edwards, Beverly, *Contemporary Politics in the Middle East*, Oxford: Polity Press, 1999

Owen, Roger, *State, Power and Politics in the Making of the Modern Middle East*, second edition, London: Routledge, 2001

Palestinian Society for the Study of International Affairs (PASSIA), *The Foreign Policies of Arab States*, Jerusalem: PASSIA, 1997

Salamé, Ghassan, ed., *Democracy without Democrats? The Renewal of Politics in the Muslim World*, London: I. B. Tauris, 1994

Sharabi, Hisham, *Neo-Patriarchy: a Theory of Distorted Change in Arab Society*, Oxford: Oxford University Press, 1988

Spiegel, Steven, *The Other Arab–Israeli Dispute: Making America's Middle East Policy from Truman to Reagan*, Chicago: University of Chicago Press, 1985

3 THE MODERN MIDDLE EAST: STATE FORMATION AND WORLD WAR

Abrahamian, Ervand, *Iran Between Two Revolutions*, Princeton: Princeton University Press, 1982

Antonius, George, *The Arab Awakening: the Story of the Arab National Movement*, first published 1938; reprinted Capricorn, 1965

Aroian, Lois and Mitchell, R. P., *The Modern Middle East and North Africa*, London: Macmillan, 1984

Berkes, Niyazi, *The Development of Secularism in Turkey*, Toronto: McGill University Press, 1964

Cleveland, William, *A History of the Modern Middle East*, second edition, Boulder, CO: Westview Press, 2000

Cobban, Helena, *The Making of Modern Lebanon*, London: Hutchinson, 1985

Hourani, Albert, *A History of the Arab Peoples*, London: Faber and Faber, 1991

Keddie, Nikki, *Roots of Revolution: an Interpretive History of Modern Iran*, New Haven: Yale University Press, 1981

Kedourie, Elie, *England and the Middle East: the Destruction of the Ottoman Empire, 1914–1921*, London: Bowes and Bowes, 1956

Lenczowski, George, *The Middle East in World Affairs*, fourth edition, Ithaca, NY: Cornell University Press, 1980

Lewis, Bernard, *The Arabs in History*, sixth edition, Oxford: Oxford University Press, 1993

The Emergence of Modern Turkey, Oxford: Oxford University Press, 1961

'The Impact of the French Revolution on Turkey', *Journal of World History*, vol. 1, 1953

The Middle East: 2000 Years of History from the Rise of Christianity to the Present Day, London: Weidenfeld and Nicolson, 1995

Lucas, Noah, *The Modern History of Israel*, London: Weidenfeld and Nicolson, 1974

Lustick, Ian, *Unsettled States, Disputed Lands: Britain and Ireland, France and Algeria, Israel and the West Bank–Gaza*, Ithaca: Cornell University Press, 1993.

al-Naqeeb, Khaldoun, *Society and State in the Arab Gulf and Arabian Peninsula*, London: Routledge, 1990

Ovendale, Ritchie, *The Longman Companion to the Middle East since 1914*, second edition, London: Longman, 1998

Pipes, Daniel, *Greater Syria: the History of an Ambition*, Oxford: Oxford University Press, 1990

Salibi, Kamal, *A House of Many Mansions: the History of Lebanon Reconsidered*, Berkeley: University of California Press, 1989

Schulze, Reinhard, *A Modern History of the Islamic World*, London: I. B. Tauris, 2000

Stein, L., *The Balfour Declaration*, London: Vallentine, Mitchell, 1961

Sykes, Christopher, *Crossroads to Israel*, London: Collins, 1965

Tibi, Bassam, *Arab Nationalism: a Critical Enquiry*, edited and translated by Marion Farouk-Sluglett and Peter Sluglett, London: Macmillan 1990

Die Verschwörung: Das Trauma arabischer Politik, second edition, Frankfurt: DTB Verlag, 1994

Tripp, Charles, *A History of Iraq*, Cambridge: Cambridge University Press, 2000

Charles Tripp and Roger Owen, eds., *Egypt under Mubarak*, London: Routledge, 1989

Vatikiotis, P., *The Modern History of Egypt*, London: Weidenfeld, 1969

Yapp, Malcolm, *The Near East since the First World War*, London: Longman, 1991

4 THE COLD WAR: GLOBAL CONFLICT, REGIONAL UPHEAVALS

Bill, James, *The Eagle and the Lion: the Tragedy of American–Iranian Relations*, London: Yale University Press, 1988

Cottam, Richard, *Iran and the United States: a Cold War Case Study*, Pittsburgh: University of Pittsburgh Press, 1988

Ehteshami, Anoushivaran and Hinnebusch, Raymond, *Syria and Iran*, London: Routledge, 1997

Fisk, Robert, *Pity the Nation: the Abduction of Lebanon*, London: Atheneum, 1990

Gendzier, Irene, *Notes from the Minefield: United States Intervention in Lebanon and the Middle East, 1945–1958*, New York: Columbia University Press, 1997

Goode, James, *The United States and Iran: In the Shadow of Musaddiq*, London: Macmillan, 1997

Heikal, Mohamed, *The Autumn of Fury: the Assassination of Sadat*, London: Deutsch, 1983

The Sphinx and the Commissar: the Rise and Fall of Soviet Influence in the Middle East, London: André Deutsch, 1978

Hirst, David, *Sadat*, London: Faber and Faber, 1983

Keddie, Nikki and Gasiorowski, Mark, eds., *Neither East nor West: Iran, the Soviet Union, and the United States*, London: Yale University Press, 1990

Kerr, Malcolm, *The Arab Cold War*, third edition, Oxford: Oxford University Press, 1971

Kuniholm, Bruce, *The Origins of the Cold War in the Near East*, Princeton: Princeton University Press, 1980

Louis, W. R. and Owen, R. eds., *A Revolutionary Year: the Middle East in 1958*, London: I. B. Tauris, 2002

Quandt, William, *Decade of Decisions: American Policy Toward the Arab–Israeli Conflict, 1967–1976*, Berkeley: University of California Press, 1977

Rathmell, Andrew, *Secret War in the Middle East: the Covert Struggle for Syria, 1949–1961*, London: I. B. Tauris, 1995

Rubin, Barry, *The Great Powers in the Middle East, 1941–1947*, London: Frank Cass, 1981

Paved with Good Intentions: Iran and the American Experience, Oxford: Oxford University Press, 1980

Sayigh, Yezid and Shlaim, Avi, eds., *The Cold War and the Middle East*, Oxford: Clarendon Press, 1997

Schulze, Kirsten, *Israel's Covert Diplomacy in Lebanon*, London: Macmillan, 1998

Seale, Patrick, *The Struggle for Syria*, Oxford: Oxford University Press, 1965

Taylor, Alan, *The Superpowers and the Middle East*, Syracuse, NY: Syracuse University Press, 1991

Wehling, Fred, *Irresolute Princes: Kremlin Decision-making in Middle East Crises, 1967–1973*, New York: St Martin's Press, 1997.

5 AFTER THE COLD WAR: THE MATURING OF THE GREATER WEST ASIAN CRISIS

Cockburn, Andrew and Cockburn, Patrick, *Out of the Ashes: the Resurrection of Saddam Hussein*, London: Verso, 2000

Dalacoura, Katerina, *Engagement or Coercion? Weighing Western Human Rights Policies towards Turkey, Iran and Egypt*, London: Royal Institute of International Affairs, 2004

Dwyer, Kevin, *Arab Voices: the Human Rights Debate in the Middle East*, London: Routledge, 1991

Freedman, Robert, ed., *The Middle East and the Peace Process: the Impact of the Oslo Accords*, Gainesville: University Press of Florida, 1998

Fuller, Graham, *Turkey's New Geopolitics: From the Balkans to Western China*, Boulder, CO: Westview Press, 1993

Graham-Brown, Sarah, *Sanctioning Saddam: the Politics of Intervention in Iraq*, London: I. B. Tauris, 1999

Guazzone, Laura, *The Middle East in Global Change: the Politics and Economics of Interdependence versus Fragmentation*, London: Macmillan, 1997

Hudson, Michael, ed., *Middle East Dilemmas: the Politics and Economics of Arab Integration*, London: I. B. Tauris, 1999

Junemann, Annette, ed., *Euro-Mediterranean Relations after September 11*, London: Frank Cass, 2003

Kepel, Gilles, *Jihad: the Trail of Political Islam*, London: I. B. Tauris, 2002

Litwak, Robert, *Rogue States and US Foreign Policy: Containment after the Cold War*, Washington, DC: Woodrow Wilson Center Press, 2000

Marr, Phoebe and Lewis, William, eds., *Riding the Tiger: the Middle East Challenge after the Cold War*, Boulder, CO: Westview Press, 1993

Mayer, Ann Elizabeth, *Islam and Human Rights: Tradition and Politics*, Boulder, CO: Westview Press, 1999

Niblock, Tim, *'Pariah States' and Sanctions in the Middle East: Iraq, Libya, Sudan*, Boulder, CO: Lynne Reinner, 2001

Nizameddin, Talal, *Russia and the Middle East: Towards a New Foreign Policy*, London: C. J. Hurst, 1999

Roberson, Barbara A., ed., *The Middle East and Europe: the Power Deficit*, London: Routledge, 1998

Ruthven, Malise, *A Fury for God: the Islamist Attack on America*, London: Granta, 2002

Sifry, Micah and Cerf, Christopher, *The Gulf War Reader: History, Documents, Opinions*, New York: Times Books, 1991

6 MILITARY CONFLICT: WAR, REVOLT, STRATEGIC RIVALRY

Abdel-Malek, Anouar, *Egypt: Military Society*, New York: Random House, 1968

Aburish, Saïd K., *Saddam Hussein: the Politics of Revenge*, London: Bloomsbury, 2000

Baram, Amatzia and Rubin, Barry, eds., *Iraq's Road to War*, London: Macmillan, 1994

Barnett, Michael, *Confronting the Costs of War: Military Power, State, and Society in Egypt and Israel*, Princeton: Princeton University Press, 1992

Chubin, Shahram and Tripp, Charles, *Iran and Iraq at War*, London: I. B. Tauris, 1988

Feldman, Shai, *Nuclear Weapons and Arms Control in the Middle East*, London: MIT Press, 1997

Freedman, Lawrence and Karsh, Efraim, *The Gulf Conflict 1990–1991: Diplomacy and War in the New World Order*, London: Faber and Faber, 1993

Heikal, Mohamed, *The Road to Ramadan*, London: Collins, 1975

Karpat, Kemal, *Turkish Foreign Policy: Recent Developments*, Madison: Wisconsin University Press, 1996

Leitenberg, Milton and Sheffer, Gabriel, *Great Power Intervention in the Middle East*, Oxford: Pergamon, 1979

Mohamedou, Mohammad-Mahmoud, *Iraq and the Second Gulf War: State Building and Regime Security*, San Francisco: Austin and Winfield, 1998

Sadowski, Yahya, *Scuds or Butter? The Political Economy of Arms Control in the Middle East*, Washington, DC: Brookings Institution, 1993

Sayigh, Yezid, *Armed Struggle and the Search for a State: the Palestinian National Movement, 1949–1993*, Oxford: Clarendon Press, 1997

Shlaim, Avi, *Collusion across the Jordan: King Abdullah, the Zionist Movement and the Partition of Palestine*, Oxford: Oxford University Press, 1988

7 MODERN IDEOLOGIES: POLITICAL AND RELIGIOUS

Abrahamian, Ervand, *Khomeinism*, London: I. B. Tauris, 1993

Ajami, Fuad, *The Arab Predicament: Arab Political Thought and Practice since 1967*, Cambridge: Cambridge University Press, 1981

The Dream Palace of the Arabs: a Generation's Odyssey, New York: Pantheon, 1998

Akhavi, Shahrough, *Religion and Politics in Iran*, Albany, NY: State University of New York Press, 1981

Avineri, Shlomo, *The Making of Modern Zionism: the Intellectual Origins of the Jewish State*, London: Weidenfeld and Nicolson, 1982

Boroujerdi, Mehrzad, *Iranian Intellectuals and the West: the Tormented Triumph of Nativism*, Syracuse, NY: Syracuse University Press, 1996

Brumberg, Daniel, *Reinventing Khomeini: the Struggle for Reform in Iran*, Chicago: University of Chicago Press, 2001

Christison, Kathleen, *Perceptions of Palestine: Their Influence on US Middle East Policy*, Berkeley: University of California Press, 1999

Cottam, Richard, *Nationalism in Iran*, Pittsburgh: University of Pittsburgh Press, 1964

Cruise O'Brien, Conor, *The Siege: the Saga of Israel and Zionism*, London: Weidenfeld and Nicholson, 1986

Dawisha, Adeed, *Arab Nationalism in the Twentieth Century: From Triumph to Despair*, Princeton: Princeton University Press, 2002

Islam in Foreign Policy, London: Royal Institute of International Affairs and Cambridge University Press, 1983

Elon, Amos, *The Israelis*, Harmondsworth: Pelican, 1981

Gershoni, Israel and Jankowski, James, eds., *Rethinking Nationalism in the Arab Middle East*, New York: Columbia University Press, 1997

Gilsenan, Michael, *Recognizing Islam*, London: Croom Helm, 1982

Haim, Sylvia, ed., *Arab Nationalism: an Anthology*, Berkeley: University of California Press, 1964

Halliday, Fred, *Islam and the Myth of Confrontation*, London: I. B. Tauris, 1996

Nation and Religion in the Middle East, London: Saqi, 2000

Revolution and Foreign Policy: the Case of South Yemen, 1967–1987, Cambridge: Cambridge University Press, 1990

Hourani, Albert, *Arabic Thought in the Liberal Age 1798–1939*, Oxford: Oxford University Press, 1967

Husain, Mir Zohair, *Global Islamic Politics*, New York: HarperCollins, 1995

Jankowski, James and Gershoni, Israel, eds., *Rethinking Nationalism in the Arab Middle East*, New York: Columbia University Press, 1997

Keddie, Nikki, *Iran and the Muslim World: Resistance and Revolution*, London: Macmillan, 1995

Kepel, Gilles, *Muslim Extremism in Egypt: the Prophet and the Pharoah*, London: Zed Books, 1985

The Revenge of God: the Resurgence of Islam, Christianity and Judaism in the Modern World, Cambridge: Polity Press, 1994

Khalidi, Rashid, *Palestinian Identity: the Construction of Modern National Consciousness*, New York: Columbia University Press, 1997

Khalidi, Rashid, Lisa Anderson, Muhammad Muslih and Reeva S. Simon, eds., *The Origins of Arab Nationalism*, New York: Columbia University Press, 1991

Kienle, Eberhard, *Ba'th versus Ba'th: the Conflict between Syria and Iraq, 1958–1989*, London: I. B. Tauris, 1990

Kishtainy, Khalid, *Arab Political Humour*, London: Quartet, 1983

Laqueur, Walter, *A History of Zionism: From the French Revolution to the Establishment of the State of Israel*, London: Weidenfeld and Nicolson, 1972

Levy, Reuben, *The Sociology of Islam*, Cambridge: Cambridge University Press, 1965

Moin, Baqer, *Khomeini, Sign of God*, London: I. B. Tauris, 1993

Mortimer, Edward, *Faith and Power: the Politics of Islam*, London: Faber and Faber, 1982

Piscatori, James, ed., *Islamic Fundamentalism and the Gulf Crisis*, Chicago: The Fundamentalism Project, University of Chicago Press, 1991

Ramazani, R. K., *Revolutionary Iran: Challenge and Response in the Middle East*, second edition, Baltimore: The Johns Hopkins University Press, 1988

Rodinson, Maxime, *Marxism and the Muslim World*, London: Zed Books, 1979

Roy, Olivier, *The Failure of Political Islam*, London: I. B. Tauris, 1994

Ruthven, Malise, *Islam in the World*, second edition, Harmondsworth: Penguin, 2000

Suleiman, Yasir, *The Arabic Language and National Identity*, Edinburgh: Edinburgh University Press, 2003

Tibi, Bassam, *Arab Nationalism: a Critical Enquiry*, third edition, London: Macmillan, 1990

The Challenge of Fundamentalism: Political Islam and the New World Disorder, Berkeley: University of California Press, 1997

Zubaida, Sami, *Islam, the People and the State*, London: Routledge, 1993

8 CHALLENGES TO THE STATE: TRANSNATIONAL MOVEMENTS

Abdelnasser, Walid, *The Islamic Movement in Egypt: Perceptions of International Relations, 1967–1981*, London: Kegan Paul International, 1994

Abdo, Geneive, *No God But God: Egypt and the Triumph of Islam*, Oxford: Oxford University Press, 2000

Abrahamian, Ervand, *The Iranian Mojahidin*, London: I. B. Tauris, 1989

Abu-Amr, Ziad, *Islamic Fundamentalism in the West Bank and Gaza: Muslim Brotherhood and Islamic Jihad*, Bloomington: Indiana University Press, 1994

Ayubi, Nazih, *Political Islam: Religion and Politics in the Arab World*, London: Routledge, 1991

Batatu, Hanna, *The Old Social Classes and the Revolutionary Movements of Iraq*, Princeton: Princeton University Press, 1978

Behrooz, Maziar, *Rebels with a Cause: the Failure of the Left in Iran*, London: I. B. Tauris, 1999

Beinin, Joel, *Was the Red Flag Flying There?: Marxist Politics and the Arab–Israeli Conflict in Egypt and Israel, 1948–1965*, London: I. B. Tauris, 1990

Beinin, Joel and Lockman, Zachary, *Workers on the Nile, 1882–1954*, London: I. B. Tauris, 1988

Chaliand, Gerard, *The Kurdish Tragedy*, London: Zed Books, 1994

Chaliand, Gerard and Ternon, Yves, *The Armenians: From Genocide to Resistance*, London: Zed Books, 1980

Cole, Juan and Keddie, Nikki, eds., *Shi'ism and Social Protest*, New Haven: Yale University Press, 1986

Dalacoura, Katerina, *Islam, Liberalism and Human Rights*, London: I. B. Tauris, 1999

Do leu Pinto, Maria, *Political Islam and the United States*, Reading: Ithaca Press, 1999

Eickleman, Dale and Piscatori, James, *Muslim Politics*, Princeton: Princeton University Press, 1996

Enayat, Hamid, *Modern Islamic Thought*, London: Macmillan, 1982

Esposito, John, ed., *The Iranian Revolution: Its Global Impact*, Miami: Florida International University Press, 1990

Fandy, Mamoun, *Saudi Arabia and the Politics of Dissent*, London: Macmillan, 1999

Fuller, Graham and Francke, Rend, *The Arab Shi'a: the Forgotten Muslims*, London: Macmillan, 2000

Gerges, Fawaz, *America and Political Islam: Clash of Cultures or Clash of Interests?*, Cambridge: Cambridge University Press, 1999

Hafez, Mohammed, *Why Muslims Rebel: Repression and Resistance in the Islamic World*, Boulder, CO: Lynne Reinner, 2003

Halliday, Fred, *Arabia without Sultans*, Harmondsworth: Penguin, 1974; reprinted London: Saqi, 2001

Hourani, Albert, *Arabic Thought in the Liberal Age, 1798–1939*, Oxford: Oxford University Press, 1961

Khamsin, ed., *Forbidden Agendas: Intolerance and Defiance in the Middle East*, London: Saqi, 1984

Laqueur, Walter, *Communism and Nationalism in the Middle East*, London: Routledge and Kegan Paul, 1956

Lockman, Zachary, *Comrades and Enemies: Arab and Jewish Workers in Palestine, 1906–1948*, Berkeley: University of California Press, 1996

Lockman, Zachary and Beinin, Joel, *Intifadha: the Palestinian Uprising against Israeli Occupation*, London: I. B. Tauris, 1990

Lustick, Ian, *For the Land and the Lord: Jewish Fundamentalism in Israel*, New York: Council on Foreign Relations, 1988

Norton, Augustus Richard and Greenberg, Martin, eds., *The International Relations of the Palestine Liberation Organisation*, Carbondale, IL: Southern Illinois University Press, 1989

Rodinson, Maxime, *Cult, Ghetto and State*, London: Zed Books, 1983

Rubin, Barry, *The Transformation of Palestinian Politics: From Revolution to State-Building*, Cambridge, MA: Harvard University Press, 1999

Schulze, Kirsten, Martin Stokes and Colm Campbell, *Nationalism, Minorities and Diasporas: Identities and Rights in the Middle East*, London: I. B. Tauris, 1996

Tawil, Raymonda Hawa, *My Home, My Prison*, London: Zed Books, 1983

Vali, Abbas, *Modernity and the Stateless: the Kurdish Question in Iran*, London: I. B. Tauris, 2000

el-Wazir, Hanan, 'De la révolution à la construction d'un état: le Mouvement de Libération Nationale de la Palestine (le Fatah) et l'Autorité National Palestinienne, Ph.D. thesis, Department of Political Sciences, University of Geneva, 2000

Yamani, Mai, *Changed Identities: the Challenge of the New Generation in Saudi Arabia*, London: Royal Institute of International Affairs, 2000

9 INTERNATIONAL POLITICAL ECONOMY: REGIONAL AND GLOBAL

Allan, Tony, *The Middle East Water Question: Hydropolitics and the Global Economy*, London: I. B. Tauris, 2001

Amin, Galal, *Whatever Happened to the Egyptians? Change in Egyptian Society from 1959 to the Present*, Cairo: American University of Cairo Press, 2000

Amuzegar, Jahangir, *Managing the Oil Wealth: OPEC's Windfalls and Pitfalls*, London: I. B. Tauris, 1999

Ayubi, Nazih, ed., *Distant Neighbours: the Political Economy of Relations between Europe and the Middle East/North Africa*, Reading: Ithaca Press, 1995

Beblawi, Hazem, and Luciani, Giacomo, eds., *The Rentier State*, London: Croom Helm, 1987

Birks, J. S. and Sinclair, C. A., *Arab Manpower: the Crisis of Development*, London: Croom Helm, 1980

Hakimian, Hassan and Moshaver, Ziba, eds., *The State and Global Change: the Political Economy of Transition in the Middle East and North Africa*, London: Curzon Press, 2000

Henry, Clement M. and Springborg, Robert, *Globalization and the Politics of Development in the Middle East*, Cambridge: Cambridge University Press, 2001

Issawi, Charles, *An Economic History of the Middle East and North Africa*, New York: Columbia University Press, 1982

Karl, Terry Lynn, *The Paradox of Plenty: Oil Boom and Petrostates*, Berkeley: University of California Press, 1997

Kerr, Malcolm and el-Yassin, Sayed, eds., *Rich and Poor in the Middle East*, Boulder, CO: Westview Press, 1982

Keyder, Caglar, *State and Class in Turkey: a Study in Capitalist Development*, London: Verso, 1987

Kubursi, Afif, *Oil, Industrialization and Development in the Arab Gulf States*, London: Croom Helm, 1984

Niblock, Tim and Murphy, Emma, eds., *Economic and Political Liberalization in the Middle East*, London: British Academic Press, 1993

Owen, Roger and Pamuk, Sevket, *A History of Middle East Economies in the Twentieth Century*, London: I. B. Tauris, 1998

Richards, Alan and Waterbury, John, *A Political Economy of the Middle East*, second edition, Boulder, CO: Westview Press, 1998

Rodinson, Maxime, *Islam and Capitalism*, London: Allen Lane, 1974

Rumaihi, Muhammad, *Beyond Oil: Unity and Development in the Gulf*. London: Saqi, 1986

Stork, Joe, *Middle East Oil and the Energy Crisis*, New York: Monthly Review, 1975

Vandewalle, Dirk, *Libya since Independence: Oil and State-building* London: I. B. Tauris, 1998

Waterbury, John, *The Egypt of Nasser and Sadat: the Political Economy of Two Regimes*, Princeton: Princeton University Press, 1983

Wilson, Rodney, *Economic Development in the Middle East*, London: Routledge, 1995

10 THE MIDDLE EAST IN INTERNATIONAL PERSPECTIVE

Arab Human Development Report 2002, Geneva and New York: UNDP, 2002, http://www.undp.org/rbas/ahdr

Cammack, Paul, Pool, David and Tordoff, William, *Third World Politics: a Comparative Introduction*, London: Macmillan, 1988

Dodge, Toby and Higgott, Richard, *Globalization and the Middle East: Islam, Economy, Society and Politics*, London: Royal Institute of International Affairs, 2002

Halliday, Fred, *The World at 2000*, London: Palgrave, 2000

Khalidi, Rashid, *Resurrecting Empire. Western Footprints and America's Perilous Path in the Middle East*, London: I. B. Tauris, 2004

Roberts, John, *Visions and Mirages: the Middle East in a New Era*, Edinburgh: Mainstream, 1995

Index